An Evening with Benjamin Franklin and Thomas Jefferson

Dinner Wine and Conversation

James M. Gabler

Bacchus Press
Palm Beach, FL

*Thomas
Jefferson*

*Benjamin
Franklin*

Preface

I am sure that many of us have had secret fantasies about sharing some part of history with the people who were actually there. There is a bit of Walter Mitty in all of us. Over the years my fantasy has been to have dinner with my two favorite Founding Fathers—Benjamin Franklin and Thomas Jefferson, and that is how *An Evening with Benjamin Franklin and Thomas Jefferson: Dinner, Wine and Conversation* evolved. In this fictional but fact-based account, you (the reader) are taken back in time to eighteenth century Paris where you meet Benjamin Franklin and Thomas Jefferson. In the comfort of Jefferson's Paris residence on the Champs-Elysées, you sit down with these two great Americans and, in response to your questions, they tell in *their own words* the most interesting stories of their lives.

The most popular literary methods for traveling into the past include time machines (H.G.Wells), unconsciousness from a blow to the head (*A Connecticut Yankee in King Arthur's Court*), traveling faster than the speed of light (Superman), falling down a rabbit hole (*Alice in Wonderland*), the popular television version of a genie popping from a bottle and granting a wish, and dreams. I decided on a dream sequence because everyone can relate to a dream; dreams are unrestricted in time and space, and allow access to a vast amount of information—everything you have ever heard, read, experienced or imagined.

Your surrogate for this fascinating evening is an American history professor by the name of Jack Osborne. To substitute yourself for Jack at the dinner table you need only imagine yourself there. You may protest that you do not have sufficient knowledge of history or wine to play the part of Jack Osborne. The transition, however, is no more difficult than an actor or actress being given a script and asked to play a totally unfamiliar role. Jack's questions to Dr. Franklin and Mr. Jefferson will serve as your script, and with the slightest bit of imagination you will hear their voices and words, feel their presence, the weight of their knowledge, and the excitement of their stories.

Franklin and Jefferson discuss their early years, their embarrassments, disappointments and intrigues, the women in their lives, the calumny and slander they suffered at the hands of their political enemies, slavery, their religious beliefs, their opinions of George Washington, John Adams, John Paul Jones, Marquis de Lafayette, and others.

Jefferson, when told of the despicable acts of terror involving 9/11, tells how he would have handled our response based on his experience while president in dealing with the Muslim Barbary pirate states who captured our merchant ships, enslaved the crews, and held them for ransom. When informed of the Abu Ghraib torture scandals, they discuss and contrast the treatment of prisoners during the Revolutionary War.

You travel with Franklin to Scotland, Ireland and France and join him for dinner and wine with his friends along the way. You accompany Jefferson and John Adams into the English countryside, sail Lakes George and Champlain with Jefferson and James Madison, and join Jefferson in his carriage as he travels alone through southern France, northern Italy, Germany and Holland. You are with Franklin in London and accompany him on evening visits to his clubs. During Franklin and Jefferson's years in Paris, you will meet John Adams, Marquis de Lafayette, John Paul Jones (accused of attempting to rape the gardener's wife), the charismatic British spy, Edward Bancroft, who served as Franklin's private secretary and close friend, and others.

Franklin and Jefferson's stories are, for the most part, told in their own words, either by way of direct quotes or paraphrases of quotes. There are some instances where their words are those of contemporaries. In those instances the information is based on knowledge with which Franklin or Jefferson would have been familiar, and the source of the information is identified in the Source Notes at the end of the text. I invite your attention to the nearly 900 Source Notes because they provide citations for the factual sources drawn upon, and authority to support Franklin and Jefferson's comments.

Why, you may ask, were Franklin and Jefferson in Paris? Franklin arrived in France in December 1776 to obtain money and arms for the American Revolution and to forge, if possible, an alliance with France. He was successful in achieving these goals, and in so doing, he became the most popular and respected foreigner in Europe. He occupied a portion of a spacious estate known as the Hôtel de Valentinois, which was owned by a wealthy merchant, Le Ray de Chaumont, and his wife, located in Passy, a suburb of Paris. It stood on top of a hill with terraced gardens, a lake, and avenues of clipped lindens leading down to the Seine, and a view looking back to Paris. Franklin enjoyed his eight and a half years in France: the diplomatic mission, the intellectual atmosphere of the salons, the beauty and vivacity of the women, and French wines.

Congress sent Jefferson to Paris in 1784 to serve as a trade commissioner with John Adams and Benjamin Franklin, who was there and serving as the first American minister to France. When Franklin asked Congress to be relieved of his duties so he could return home, Jefferson succeeded him as the American minister. After little more than a year in Paris, Jefferson moved into a new home, the Hôtel de Langeac, in a new but fashionable area located on the ChampsElysées and rue de Barri, and across the street from the Grille de Chaillot. It was a much larger house than the one he had previously occupied with a garden, stables, horses, carriages, cook, and a regular coachman. The Hôtel de Langeac became the scene of many dinners where France's best wines were served to an appreciative coterie of friends, both American and French. Dinner guests could view the Champs-Elysées through three windows draped with blue silk damask. A fifteen-foot dining room table could seat twenty and was ornamented with silverware, biscuit figurines, and a crenellated porcelain bucket used for cooling wine glasses. Wines from Jefferson's cellar made their rounds in beautiful crystal decanters.

Four days after Jefferson's arrival in France he dined with Franklin, and with their dinner they drank wines from Franklin's cellar of more than 1100 bottles. This was the first of many meals that fueled their friendship. Jefferson was impressed with the Bordeaux wines he drank at Franklin's house and four months later, when he made his first contact with John Bondfield, the American consul in Bordeaux, he ordered 144 bottles of "such wine" as he had drunk at "Dr. Franklin's house." Jefferson went on to stock his wine-cellar with many of the world's best wines. Given their mutual love of wine, I thought it appropriate that the dinner be accompanied by Jefferson's favorite French wines, and wine a topic of conversation throughout the evening. The main dinner course is beef á la mode and the recipe is from the new (2005) Jefferson cookbook *Dining at Monticello: In Good taste and Abundance*.

Since the publication of *Passions: The Wines and Travels of Thomas Jefferson* in 1995, I have had the pleasure of talking about Jefferson and wine throughout the United States. The question most frequently asked at these events is whether the bottle of "1787 Lafitte" [sic] engraved with the initials "Th. J.", and sold by Christie's at auction on December 5, 1985 for $156,450 (the world's most expensive bottle of wine), was ever owned by Thomas Jefferson. Jefferson addresses that question in this book.

A more detailed account of why the "1787 Lafitte" bottle (and other bottles bearing the engraved "Th. J." initials) probably lack a Thomas Jefferson provenance is provided in Appendix A at page 313 and titled, "Research Report: Chateau Lafite 1787, with initials 'Th. J'." This previously unpublished essay was written a week after the Christie auction by Lucia Goodwin Stanton, then the director of research at Monticello, and currently the Shannon Senior Research Historian at Monticello.

A great deal time was spent researching and writing *An Evening with Benjamin Franklin and Thomas Jefferson: Dinner, Wine and Conversation*, and I enjoyed every minute of it. It was so enjoyable that when errands or personal matters required me to interrupt my writing schedule, I felt a tinge of annoyance. I hope my enthusiasm comes through in the stories you are about to share with two of the most extraordinary men in history.

I owe Alison Chaplin an incalculable debt of gratitude for her splendid work in copy editing the manuscript, for her ideas on the dream sequence that takes the reader back in time to eighteenth century Paris, and for her many excellent subject transition suggestions. Without her help this book would not exist in its present form. I am indebted to Dr. William Franklin for his careful reading of the manuscript, which saved me from a number of errors, for his suggestions for improvement of some of the dialogue, and for ideas relating to the dream sequence. I thank Hudson Cattell for reading the manuscript and offering suggestions, Walter Isaacson and Robert M. Parker, Jr. for reading the manuscript and commenting for attribution, Lucia Stanton for permission to print her *Research Report: Chateau Lafite 1787, with initials "Th.J"*, the Thomas Jefferson Foundation, Inc. for permission to reproduce the Beef à la Mode recipe, Colleen Ando for the cover design, Kristin Meyer for typesetting, Roy Goodman of the American Philosophical Society for leading me to a cache of Franklin wine information, and my wife, Anita, for her understanding and encouragement.

I am also grateful to the Library of Congress, New York Public Library, American Philosophical Society, Philadelphia, Goucher College, Johns Hopkins University and Loyola College in Baltimore for providing research facilities.

Jim Gabler

I'm sure that if I told my fiancée, my friends, or my academic colleagues about my incredible experience of having dinner last evening with Benjamin Franklin and Thomas Jefferson at Mr. Jefferson's residence in Paris, they would say I dreamed it. But it's hard to believe it was a dream—it felt so real. I can still taste the wines, especially the Chateau d'Yquem, and the delicious French beef; I can still hear my hosts' voices and words, and feel their presence, and the weight of their knowledge, and the excitement of their stories. I learned too much for a dream!

Or did I? Maybe everything they told me was really only what I had read at some time or another in their papers and had forgotten that I knew. After all, my field is American history, and my expertise is in the period from 1735 to 1835, which brackets the period they were talking about. I've heard that the brain never forgets anything you've read, seen or experienced; it's all in there somewhere, a jumble of information far vaster than even the Internet. The problem is accessing it. So, maybe it was a dream, and the dream was some kind of superior access system—Google on steroids. I don't know how it worked; all I know is that it was incredibly real, full of details that I didn't know I knew.

Nothing unusual happened yesterday that led to this fascinating evening; it was a normal day. As I do every morning, I went for a jog along the Santa Barbara coast, a routine worth far more to me than the cardiovascular exercise I get from it. It's a personal catharsis—a wonderful time to be alone and reflect on everything happening in my life.

After I'd showered I went over the lesson plan for my eleven-thirty class on the "Cultural Aspects of the Revolutionary War." I had to be sure I could answer the question that one of the sophomores had asked about how many glasses of wine a day Jefferson drank—like sophomores everywhere, he's more interested in the wine-drinking habits of the eighteenth century than in anything else about its culture.

I skipped lunch and spent the afternoon at the library researching Jefferson's interests in exploration, especially his longing to explore the territory beyond the Mississippi. Not many people know that years before he selected Meriwether Lewis to explore the American West, he had secured commitments for this purpose from two other men, John Ledyard and André Michaux.

Dinner would have been with my fiancée, Terri, but she was away on a marine biology assignment in Mexico, so I went with Hayes McClerkin, a fellow professor, to the Wine Cask and had a couple glasses of a local pinot noir with grilled abalone. Hayes is pretty knowledgeable about my period, and he told me some interesting stuff about how Tobias Smollett crossed the Alps following the same route that Jefferson took when he visited northern Italy. [1]

Before I went to bed I poured a glass of port, sat in my favorite chair facing the ocean, and opened the book I'm reading, *Passions: The Wines and Travels of Thomas Jefferson*. As I read, I imagined myself traveling with Jefferson on his fascinating three-and-a-half-month trip through southern France. Approaching ancient Carcassonne, I could see off to my left the crenellated fortress town high on a hill. Before we set out for Bordeaux, I walked its ramparts and cobblestoned narrow streets with Jefferson. In Bordeaux I imagined walking with Jefferson through the vineyards of Châteux Haut Brion, and wondered if he knew that John Locke, a man he considered 'one of the three greatest men the world had ever produced,' had walked through these same vineyards a hundred years before him. [2]

I next remember placing the book in my lap, and closing my eyes. Suddenly, I felt myself tumbling through black space for what seemed a long time. Then I felt a gentle rocking, and heard the sound of horses' hooves slowly clattering along a cobble-stone street. I was in a horse-drawn carriage that stopped in front of a large iron gate. As I got out I looked down and saw that I was dressed in off-white cotton slacks, a yellow-striped shirt with matching gold tie, a blue blazer, and black loafers without socks.

Beyond the iron gate there was a courtyard and the entrance to a house facing a small street running perpendicular to what I instantly recognized as the Champs-Elysées. I know this part of Paris well, so even though it all looked different from what I remembered, the house looked familiar to me, and I felt certain that the little street had to be the rue de Berri. I glanced to my right and saw on the other side of the Champs-Elysées the Grille de Chaillot, one

Grille De Chaillot

of many tollgates that once circled Paris for levying taxes on all goods coming into the city. It looked like the illustration that I use in my "Cultural Aspects" class when I'm explaining the origins of the word "turnpike." I knew that Jefferson's mansion was located directly across from the Grille de Chaillot, so I was standing in front of the Hôtel de Langeac, Jefferson's Paris residence. I couldn't believe it, and I pinched myself to wake up, but nothing happened. [3]

It was a beautiful autumn evening, cooled by a gentle breeze, and highlighted by a setting orange sun. To the right of the iron gate I noticed a blue sash embroidered with gold grapes. I pulled on it, and I heard the tinkle of bells. A moment later a young man came out of the house and walked toward me. When he reached the gate he said, "Monsieur Jack Osborne?"

"Qui, monsieur," I replied.

"Doctor Franklin and Mr. Jefferson are expecting you," he said, as he opened the gate and led me across the courtyard toward the house. The servants' quarters and the stables were to my left on the other side of the courtyard. We entered a circular room with a skylight. There were three doorways, one leading to the dinning room, another to a petit salon, and a third to a large oval salon with the ceiling decorated with a painting of a rising sun. [4] The servant motioned that I should enter the large salon. I did, and there seated in armchairs by floorto-ceiling French doors that looked out to a garden was Benjamin Franklin and Thomas Jefferson. Jefferson stood and immediately walked toward me. He was tall and erect, and elegantly dressed in a front cutaway tail coat fashioned

3

Plaque where Hôtel de Langeac stood.

from red silk damask, patterned with alternating large and small rosettes, an ivory satin collar and lapels, a ruffled ivory silk cravat, with matching silk breeches, stockings, and buckled shoes. He extended his hand. "Welcome Mr. Osborne. I am Thomas Jefferson."

"It is a pleasure to meet you Mr. Jefferson."

We shook hands. His hand was large and his grip strong. He had thick coppery hair, a sharp chin, turned up nose, and friendly hazel eyes. He was at least six feet two, with a trim, powerful looking physique that came from daily exercise that included power walks through the Bois de Boulogne and around Paris. [5]

Jefferson turned and we faced Benjamin Franklin seated by a table. "And there, Professor Osborne, is Dr. Franklin, 'so long the ornament of our country and I may say of the world,' " Jefferson said with a wave of his hand in the direction of Franklin. [6]

As I approached Dr. Franklin, he stood and extended his hand. He was taller than I had imagined, at least five feet nine or ten inches. He had a round face and thin tight lips, and his high domed forehead featured thinning gray hair. Although he was not fat, he was overweight. [7] Franklin, in his late seventies, looked tired, but there was a twinkle in his eyes and strength in his voice that belied his age. He was wearing glasses and leaning on a

4

crab-tree stick that he was known to carry everywhere. He was far less formally dressed than Mr. Jefferson. An unembroidered brown coat covered simple homespun attire.[8] "It is a pleasure to meet you, Professor Osborne. You have come a long way to have dinner with us," he said.

"Thank you both for honoring me with your presence." I said. "I am a teacher of eighteenth century and early nineteenth century American history, and although I respect and admire all our Founding Fathers, you are my two favorites."

"Well, well," Jefferson said. "Such praise calls for a glass of wine. You are our guest Professor Osborne, so what shall it be?"

"Am I limited to the wines you have purchased to date, or can I select from any of the wines you bought during your five years in France?"

"Your visit with us is special, and you can select any wine that I purchased during my stay in France or at any other time. Do you need help with the wines?"

"The wines you bought while in France are well documented, and I am familiar with most of them."

"That being the case, Thomas, why don't we let the professor pick all the wines we are going to drink with dinner," Franklin said.

"A splendid idea. And professor, I'm not sure that you are aware of this, but the service of wine in France was entirely different from the United States, and tonight we are going to follow the French tradition."

"I'm afraid I don't know the difference."

"In America wine was not served until after the meal, or when the cloth was removed. In France it was served with the meal."[9]

"Today in America, we follow the French tradition and serve wine with the meal; it would be helpful if I knew the menu," I said.

"Yes, of course," said Jefferson. "As a first course we are going to have oysters from Normandy, a

Jefferson and Franklin, from Trumbull's Declaration of Independence

northern region of France. Then macaroni, lightly tossed in olive oil, Parmesan cheese and anchovies. For the third course, beef à la Mode with potatoes and two different kinds of peas from my garden. For dessert, ice cream in a puff pastry. So, professor, what shall we drink now, and with dinner?"

"Gentlemen, please don't call me professor. I much prefer that you call me Jack."

"Then you must call us Thomas and Benjamin," Franklin said.

"Thank you, Dr. Franklin, but I will feel uncomfortable addressing you by your first names. So if you don't mind, I prefer addressing you by your surnames."

"All right Jack, you are our guest, and we will defer to your wishes," Jefferson said.

"Mr. Jefferson, when you traveled to Champagne, you discovered a wine in Ay that you thought superior to the Champagne supplied for the king's table by the Benedictine monks at Hautvillers. I would like to try that Champagne as our aperitif wine."

"I remember it well, but how do you know about it?"

"A book has been written about all the wines you purchased and drank, and about your travels, especially your fascinating three-and-a-half-month trip through southern France." [10]

Jefferson shook his head and smiled. "Yes, I remember that trip. 'I never passed three months and a half more delightfully.' " [11] Jefferson looked to the salon entrance and called, "Petit." The man who had ushered me into the house entered the salon. He was Jefferson's efficient and trusted *maitre d 'hotel*, Adrien Petit. "Petit, please bring us a bottle of Monsieur Dorsey's Champagne, 1783 vintage. And Jack, why don't you tell Petit what other wines you would like served with dinner so that he can decant them and have them ready."

I thought for a moment. "With the oysters I would like to try your favorite Meursault, Goutte d'Or. Montrachet with the spaghetti course, and 1784 Haut Brion and 1784 Château Margaux to accompany the beef."

"And don't forget dessert," Franklin cautioned.

"Ice cream in puff pastry deserves nothing less than 1784 Château d'Yquem," I said.

Franklin smiled. "Our guest has impeccable taste."

CHÂTEAU MARGAUX.

Château Margaux

"Indeed, indeed," Jefferson said. "Jack, I'm curious about something you said. I suggested for a second course macaroni, but you called it spaghetti. What is spaghetti?"

"Wasn't what you called 'macaroni' long, thin strands of pasta?"

"Yes. The best macaroni in Italy was made from a particular sort of flour called semola, from Naples, but in almost every shop a different sort of flour was commonly used, but if the flour was of a good quality, it would always do well."

"The best pasta is still made from semolina flour," I said.

"Some things never change," Franklin said.

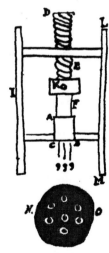

"A paste was made from flour, water and yeast, and when pressed through an iron plate with holes in it by use of a screw, it came out in strands which, when sufficiently long, were cut and spread to dry. The macaroni press that my secretary, William Short, purchased for me in Italy came with a set of plates with holes of different shapes and sizes that could be changed to make different sorts of macaroni."[12]

"Today that style of pasta is called spaghetti or linguine, so your macaroni is our spaghetti," I said.

Macaroni Press

7

Petit returned carrying a silver tray containing three wine glasses and the Champagne in a crystal decanter. He placed the tray on a small table near Jefferson. Jefferson lifted the decanter and poured our glasses. He swirled his wine, smelled the bouquet, and said, "You will note, Jack, that this is a still Champagne. 'Sparkling wines were little drunk in France but were alone known and drunk in foreign countries, and sold for about an eighth more.' " [13]

He took a sip and smiled. "Do you like it?"

"Yes. It tastes like a dry white Burgundy. But today, even the French prefer sparkling Champagne. Still Champagne, though available, is pretty much a drink of the past."

We were standing by the French doors looking out into the garden. I could see corn, and a small trellised vineyard. "Is that corn and grapes?"

"Yes," Jefferson said, "I cultivate in my own garden here Indian corn for the use of my table, to eat green in our manner. I have also planted some Burgundy vines that I obtained in 1787, and some German Rheingau vines that I brought back from a trip to the German wine country the following year." [14]

"Mr. Jefferson and I understand, Jack, that this meeting was arranged so that we can answer your questions, and we are agreeable. But I have 'sometimes almost wished it had been my destiny to be born two or three centuries hence.' [15] I have wished it possible 'to invent a method of embalming drowned persons, in such a manner that they might be recalled to life at any period, however distant; for having a very ardent desire to see and observe the state of America an hundred years hence, I should prefer to any ordinary death, the being immersed with a few friends in a cask of Madeira, until that time, then to be recalled to life by the solar warmth of my dear country.' [16] And now, given that wish, I am curious to know something about the country that we risked our lives and fortunes to establish as a free and democratic nation. How large is it? What is the population? And is it still free and democratic?"

"You would both be very proud of the United States. The population is nearly 300 million, and it is still the world's bastion of freedom and democracy. Forty-eight contiguous states are bordered on the north by Canada, on the south by Mexico, and in the east and west by the Atlantic and Pacific oceans. Mr. Jefferson, it includes all the land that you acquired while president in the Louisiana Purchase, and all the territory that your secretary and friend, Meriwether Lewis, explored. [17] There are two other states, Alaska and Hawaii. Alaska was the forty-ninth state admitted to the union, and it is the largest state in landmass, but the smallest in population. It is located in the northwest of North America. Our fiftieth state is Hawaii and consists of a series of islands in the Central Pacific. To give you an idea of our economic wealth, the United States occupies six percent of the world's land mass, has six percent of its people, but accounts for nearly one-third of the world's gross domestic product." [18]

"You must forgive me, Jack, if I sit down," Franklin said, sitting in the chair he occupied when I entered the room. "I suffer in my old age from gout and a bladder stone, and both ailments affect my ability to stand for long periods." Jefferson indicated with his hand that I too should be seated.

"Well," said Franklin, "we are certainly pleased to learn that the United States has politically and economically endured and prospered for more than 200 years."

"I don't want to leave you gentlemen with the impression that the United States has not had its share of wars and problems. Not long after the Revolutionary War, as Mr. Jefferson knows, we fought Great Britain to a stalemate in the War of 1812, which assured American independence. A dispute with Mexico over the annexation of Texas resulted in a war. This was followed in 1861 by our bloody Civil War, in which more Americans died than in nearly all our other wars combined. The great issue of slavery and the attempt by the southern states to secede from the union were resolved with the surrender of the South in 1865. In 1898 we went to war with Spain after the explosion and sinking of an American warship. The United States was victorious in two world wars, and we fought wars in Korea and Vietnam. Our three most recent wars have been in the Middle East against Iraq twice, and Afghanistan. But the war that we will fight in the years to come is against a more elusive enemy—worldwide terrorists."

"What do you mean by 'worldwide terrorists,'?" Franklin said.

"Islamic fundamentalist groups have carried out hundreds of terrorist acts, usually, but not exclusively, by bombings that have resulted in destruction and death throughout the world. For example, from 1970 until September 10, 2001, a period of only thirty-one years, there have been more than 130 terrorist acts resulting in death or injury to American citizens. [19] Then on September 11, 2001, a great tragedy happened to our country, which has changed the world forever."

"What was it?" both men said in unison.

"First let me tell you something about how we travel today. It is far different from in your day, when horses and carriages were the accepted method of land travel, and sailboats plied the seas. There are motorized carriages now called

9

cars and trucks, and huge engine-driven boats. The fastest method of travel, however, is through the air in flying vehicles we call airplanes. Some commercial airplanes carry nearly 400 passengers and fly at speeds well in excess of 500 miles an hour. Even larger airplanes are scheduled for the future, and many military airplanes travel faster than the speed of sound.

"With that as background, here is what happened: On the morning of September 11, 2001, nineteen Arab men hijacked and took control of four commercial American airplanes by subduing or killing the pilots and the airplanes' other personnel. Two of the airplanes were deliberately crashed into two 110story buildings known as the 'Twin Towers' in New York City. The crashes created huge explosions of fire, causing both buildings to collapse. At about the same time, a third hijacked airplane slammed into the Pentagon in Washington, the nation's largest military building, killing hundreds more. The fourth plane, also heading to Washington with a probable crash destination of the Capitol building or the White House, crashed in barren land eighty miles southeast of Pittsburgh when the passengers attacked the hijackers. As a result of these 'evil, despicable acts of terror,' [20] nearly 4000 innocent people were killed."

"Who was responsible for these terrorist acts?" Jefferson said.

"An international Islamic terrorist network known as Al Qaeda. Its leader is an Arab by the name of Osama bin Laden. At the time of the attacks, Al Qaeda's headquarters were in Afghanistan, with training camps there and in other Arab countries."

"What was the response of our republic's leaders?" Franklin asked.

"President George W. Bush declared war on terrorists throughout the world and launched war in Afghanistan to destroy Al Qaeda bases and to overthrow the Taliban, the country's Muslim fundamentalist rulers, who harbored Al Qaeda."

"Were we successful?" Jefferson asked.

"In Afghanistan, yes. The Taliban was quickly defeated, and a government friendly to the United States is now in power. But Osama bin Laden escaped, and Al Qaeda and other terrorist groups still operate throughout the world, so the global war against terror continues.

"Al Qaeda is just one of many Muslim fundamentalist groups that have the avowed goal of uniting all Muslims in the overthrow of their governments and establishing governments that follow the rule of the caliphs, the successors of the Prophet Muhammad. These groups are vehemently anti-Western, perceiving the

United States as the prime infidel and evil enemy of Islam. They see us as providing support for what they regard as 'heretic' regimes." I took a sip of wine and looked Jefferson in the eye. "Under the circumstances that I have described, Mr. Jefferson, as president of the United States, what would you have done?"

Jefferson bristled, and he pushed his wine glass to the side, his face flushed with anger. "The record is very clear on what my response would have been. It would have been the same as your president's. As you know, soon after the United States gained its independence, pirates from the Barbary States on the coast of North Africa—Algiers, Morocco, Tunis and Tripoli, all Muslim states—constantly raided our merchant ships and not only stole the cargoes, but also enslaved the crews and held them for ransom. In a letter to James Monroe in 1784, I suggested that we send half a dozen frigates under the command of John Paul Jones to the Mediterranean to destroy the pirates and their ships by 'constant cruising and cutting them to pieces.' [21]

"When I visited John Adams in England in the spring of 1786, we attempted to negotiate with Ambassador Abdrahaman of Tripoli. The price he demanded for peace, however, was too high. When Adams and I asked him under what authority his country was carrying out these criminal acts, the ambassador said that it was 'founded on the laws of their prophet, that it was written in their Koran, that all nations who should not have acknowledged

their authority were sinners, that it was their right and duty to make war upon them wherever they could be found, and to make slaves of all they could take as prisoners, and every Muslim who should be slain in battle was sure to go to paradise.' [22]

"I came away convinced that the best solution to the Barbary pirates' menace was war, and I expressed that opinion in a letter to John Adams a few months later. In fact, while in Paris, I tried to form an international concert of nations to war against these pirates states. My efforts failed because most nations, including the United States, found it easier to pay tribute. [23]

11

"When I became president I had a chance to do something about those terrorist acts, and I did. The pasha of Tripoli, Yusuf Karamanli, had issued an edict to the United States, pay tribute to him or he would declare war on us. When we didn't pay tribute, he declared war on the United States. The style of his demand admitted but one answer. Congress was in recess, so I took it on myself to send a squadron of frigates into the Mediterranean under the command of Commodore Edward Preble. Our ships cruised their waters and bombarded their harbors. Karamanli, however, showed his defiance by boarding our disabled frigate *Philadelphia*, capturing and imprisoning Captain William Bainbridge and his crew of more than three hundred men, and demanding a ransom of three million dollars for their release.

"Preble blockaded and bombarded Tripoli. Under orders from Preble, an American force under the command of Lieutenant Stephen Decatur sailed into the port of Tripoli in the dead of night and, in what Lord Nelson called 'the most bold and daring act of the age,' burned the *Philadelphia*. [24] Six months later Decatur and his men returned, boarded the anchored Tripolian fleet, and in hand-to-hand combat defeated them, and captured three enemy gunboats." [25]

"Sounds like an eighteenth century Entebbe," I said.

"What is an Entebbe?" Franklin asked.

"In June 1976, four terrorist hijacked an airplane and diverted it to Entebbe, Uganda, in the heart of Africa. The crew and the passengers were released except for 105 Jewish passengers, whom the terrorists huddled in the airport terminal. The terrorists, later joined by three other terrorists, threatened to execute all the Jewish prisoners unless fifty-three jailed Palestinian terrorists were immediately released. The Jewish state of Israel, founded in 1948, like you, Mr. Jefferson, decided instead to launch a military raid. On July 3, four Israeli C-130 transports landed in the dead of night at the Entebbe airport. Three vehicles moved down the ramp of one of the transports with over one hundred Israeli commandos inside. They raced to the terminal and, in a surprise attack, killed the seven terrorists and freed the Jewish hostages."

"Splendid," Jefferson exclaimed. "But wait, I'm not finished. Some months later Captain William Eaton led a land force of Marines and foreign mercenaries 700 miles across the Libyan Desert and, in a surprise attack on Tripoli's second city, Derna, captured it. These victories, together with our continued assaults on their cities and harbors eventually brought Algiers, Morocco, Tunis and Tripoli to the peace table although we did pay $60,000 for the release of Captain Bainbridge and his crew. I was able to report in my sixth annual message to Congress that

'The states on the coast of Barbary seem generally disposed at present to respect our peace and friendship.'[26] So, yes, my response to the acts of terror of September 11, 2001, would have been the same as President Bush's response. 'The best response to an aggressive act is to punish the first insult because an insult unpunished is the parent of many others.'"[27]

"I never had the privilege to serve as president," Franklin said, "so I can't cite a specific example of my response to a terrorist act such as the horror you describe, but when I returned from England and learned of the barbarous acts of murder being committed by the British army in America, my resolve for independence and for war, if necessary, was total. I wrote a letter to my friend William Strahan in London that sums up how I felt towards England, and how I would have responded to the terrorists. 'You are a member of Parliament and one of the majority that have doomed my country to destruction. You have begun to burn our towns and murder our people. Look upon your hands! They are stained with the blood of your relations. You and I were long friends. You are now my enemy and I yours.'"[28]

"But, Dr. Franklin, it's my understanding that you did not mail that letter," I said.

"That's true, but it shows my rage and

Franklin's terse letter to his friend, William Strahan, breaking off relations.

my clear intentions. Jack, murder in any form is murder, and it must be redressed. So, I too would have taken whatever actions necessary to destroy those persons and institutions connected in any way with the terrorist acts of September 11, 2001." Franklin paused. "Speaking of military airplanes, I assume that some of those airplanes are used to deliver bombs against an enemy."

"Yes," I said.

"The first time I saw humans lifted into the air I thought of its war potential. I witnessed Paris's first balloon ascension on August 27, 1783. It was filled with hydrogen gas, rose rapidly 'till it entered the clouds, when it seemed to me scarce bigger than an orange and soon after became invisible.' Three months later I saw the first balloon ascent of human passengers, and still another balloon flight by Charles and Robert Montgolfier from the Tuileries Gardens. I thought almost immediately that the balloon might become an effective instrument of war and 'possibly give a new turn to human affairs. Convincing sovereigns of the follies of wars may perhaps be one effect of it; since it will be impracticable for the most potent of them to guard his dominions. Five thousand balloons, capable of raising two men each, could not cost more than five ships of the line; and where is the prince who can afford so to cover his country with troops for its defense as that ten thousand men descending from the clouds might not in many places do an infinite deal of mischief before a force could be brought together to repel them?' " [29]

"The events of 9/11 convinced Congress that law enforcement and national security authorities needed new laws to effectively fight terrorism. Accordingly, six weeks after 9/11 the USA Patriot Act, 342 pages of new and amended laws, was passed. The Patriot Act significantly increased the surveillance and investigative powers of law enforcement agencies by allowing broad and easy legal methods for obtaining search warrants and carrying out secret investigative procedures. The law also increased the authority of the attorney general to detain and deport immigrants with little or no judicial review. And without any question, in the attempt to make the country safer, the act eroded certain of our civil liberties. [30] What do you think, Dr. Franklin, of such a law?"

"I don't know enough about this Patriot Act to make a detailed comment, but as a general proposition, 'Those who would give up essential Liberty, to purchase a little temporary safety, deserve neither liberty nor safety.' "

"This Patriot Act reminds me of the Alien and Sedition Acts that the Federalist Congress passed and President John Adams signed in 1798," Jefferson said. "They too claimed that those reprehensible acts were needed as war measures. The Alien Act required immigrants to reside in the U.S. for fourteen years instead of five years before becoming citizens, gave the president the authority for two years to expel any foreigner he considered dangerous, and provided that in time of war aliens might be deported, or imprisoned, as long as the president decreed it. [31]

"The Sedition Act punished 'false, scandalous and malicious writing or writings against the government of the United States, or either house of the Congress of the United States or the President of the United States' with fines or imprisonment. Most of those arrested and convicted under that law were members of my Republican Party. [32]

"One of my first decisions after becoming president was to discharge every person under punishment or prosecution under the sedition law, because 'I considered that law to be a nullity, as absolute and palpable as if Congress had ordered us to fall down and worship a golden image; and that it was as much my duty to arrest its execution in every stage, as it would have been to have rescued from the fiery furnace those who should have been cast into it for refusing to worship the image.' "[33]

"As result of our recent war with Iraq, many Iraqi soldiers and others became prisoners. At a prison in Iraq known as Abu Ghraib, and at other prisons, it has been disclosed, investigated and documented that many of these Iraqi prisoners and detainees were physically and mentally tortured, and some killed, by beatings, removal of clothing and sexual humiliation, terrorization by dogs, threats of imminent death, exposure to extremes of temperatures, prolonged and painful stress positions, and other methods."[34]

"Are there not international accords that make such prisoner treatment illegal?" Franklin said.

"Yes, the Geneva Conventions are such an accord to which the United States is a signatory. Many people believe that no event in recent history has been more damaging to the image of the United States than these prisoner tortures. It may also endanger American soldiers who will be taken prisoner in future wars. Did the torture of prisoners take place during the Revolutionary War?"

Franklin spoke first. "At one point during the war, plans were being made for Captain John Paul Jones and General Lafayette to conduct lightning raids on English coastal towns. Because I wanted Englishmen captured treated with care, I thought it necessary to caution Captain Jones to show humanity toward his prisoners. I instructed him that 'as many of your officers and people have lately escaped from English prisons either in Europe or America, you are to be particularly attentive to their conduct toward the prisoners which the fortune of war may throw in your hands, lest the resentment of the more than barbarous usage by the English in many places towards the Americans should occasion a retaliation, and an imitation of what ought rather to be detested and avoided for the sake of humanity and for the honor of our country.' I also thought that similar sentiments should inform Captain Jones's conduct in other areas, and I pointed out that 'although the English have wantonly burnt many defenseless towns in America, you are not to follow this example, unless where a reasonable ransom is refused, in which case your own generous feelings as well as this instruction will induce you to give timely notice of your intention that sick and ancient persons, women and children may be first re-moved.'[35] Jones assured me that I could count on him in this regard."[36]

"In any war, random violations of human rights will occur," Jefferson said, "but in the American Revolution, our policy was to treat captured prisoners humanely. For example, in January 1779, after the surrender of General John Burgoyne at Saratoga, more than 4,000 British and Hessians captured soldiers were marched from Boston into the Charlottesville area as interned prisoners. The living conditions were bad when they arrived in my neighborhood. The barracks were unfinished, the weather was unbearable, and much of the food provisions spoiled. When I heard the rumors that the prisoners would be moved elsewhere, I took the matter up with Governor Patrick Henry. 'Is an enemy so execrable,' I asked Henry, 'that, though in captivity, his wishes and comforts are to be disregarded and even crossed? I think not. It is for the benefit of mankind to mitigate the horrors of war as much as possible. The practice, therefore, of modern nations, of treating captive enemies with polite-ness and generosity, is not only delightful in contemplation, but really interest-ing to all the world, friends, foes, and neutrals.'[37] Henry was understanding and agreed to keep them in the Charlottesville area and improve their living conditions. The barracks were completed, and they were giving gardens to tend and their own poultry.[38]

"The two highest-ranking officers, other than Burgoyne, became my neigh-bors. Major General William Phillips, second in command to Burgoyne, rent-ed Colonel Carter's place, Blenheim. Philip Mazzei went to Europe as a finan-cial agent for the State of Virginia, but, before leaving, he rented Colle to the ranking Hessian, Major General Baron Frederick Adolphus de Riedesel, who

ENCAMPMENT of the CONVENTION ARMY

Captured British and Hessian troops at Charlottesville.

16

had been captured at the battle of Saratoga and interned along with his troops. His wife, the Baroness Friderike von Riedesel, and their three small daughters, joined General Riedesel. My wife, Martha, and I met the Riedesels at a dinner party given by General Phillips. The baroness was stout and handsome, wore riding boots, and charmed us with her operatic singing. The Riedesels became our friends, but our circle of friends among the prisoners was wider than our two families. War and politics were put aside as music furthered our friendship. I played the violoncello, with a young German captain, Baron de Geismar, on the violin, and the baroness singing Italian arias. Geismar befriended me nine years later when I traveled down the Rhine visiting the German vineyards." [39]

"Was it Burgoyne's surrender at Saratoga that resulted in the Treaty of Alliance and brought France into the war, Dr. Franklin?"

"Yes," Franklin said. "France wanted the alliance, but so long as the war went badly for us, the king's minister of foreign affairs, Comte de Vergennes, would do nothing more than surreptitiously furnish us help in the form of arms and money. Vergennes was fearful we would lose the will to persevere with the war. The summer and fall of 1777 were full of bad news: Washington's evacuation of New York, General William Howe's advance on Philadelphia, and the march of general Burgoyne's army south from Canada. [40] In November, we learned that Philadelphia had fallen to Howe's army. Despite the bleak news, I was convinced that we could successfully maintain the war, and I told Arthur Lee so in a meeting we had on November 27. [41] Just before noon on December 4, we received the news of a staggering American military victory; Burgoyne's entire army had surrendered at Saratoga!"

"Did Saratoga change the diplomatic picture?"

"Completely." A smiling Franklin continued, "Two days after receiving the news of the American victor y at Saratoga, Vergennes's emissary, Conrad-Alexandre Gérard, called to congratulate us and to invite us to renew our proposal for an alliance. I drafted the proposal, and we submitted it. The British also realized that Burgoyne's defeat had changed the complexion of the war and that it had the potential of sparking a French alliance. In an attempt to head it off, the British ministry sent Paul Wentworth to Paris. Wentworth, born an American, and a former member of the New Hampshire council and agent for New Hampshire in London, met twice with Silas Deane. [42] He told Deane that the British ministry had been forced into the war against their will, and now wanted to rectify their mistake. Wentworth requested a meeting with me. The French knew, of course, that Wentworth was in Paris and were suspicious of the purpose of his trip. On January 6, I consented to talk with Wentworth knowing the French would learn of the meeting and that it might goad the French into an alliance." [43]

"Wentworth memorialized his meeting with you in a letter to William Eden who had originally recruited Wentworth as a spy," I said.

"Oh, he did, did he? I would be interested in knowing what he said."

"He reported that he reminded you that you had formerly favored an imperial union rather than American independence, but you said it was too late, and that now nothing less than full independence would satisfy America. Wentworth said that when you recounted your previous negotiations to find a peaceful solution, you worked yourself into a passion and resentment. Wentworth said he suggested that your personal resentments should be put aside in the cause of your country, and that the resolution of peace was too great to mix private quarrels with."

"Yes, I remember," Franklin said. "And I told him that my anger did not come from a feeling of personal injuries, but from the barbarities inflicted on my country, the burning of towns, the neglect and ill-treatment of prisoners."

Signature page of the Treaty of Alliance between France and the United States, February 6, 1778.

"Wentworth reported that he had never known you so eccentric, noting that normally 'nobody says less, generally, and keeps a point more closely in view,' but on this day, you were 'diffuse and unmethodical.'"

Franklin was beaming. "Well, perhaps it never occurred to Mr. Wentworth that I used him as a ploy, for the effect our meeting might have on Vergennes." His smile broadened. "It may have been a coincidence, but the day after my meeting with Wentworth, the king's council, with Louis XVI's consent, voted in favor of a treaty of amity and commerce and a treaty of alliance that was signed on February 6," Franklin said, with a wink. [44]

"What happened to General Burgoyne?"

"Almost nothing. He was paroled and sent back to England upon his promise not to engage in further hostilities. [45] But that's not the end of the Burgoyne story," Franklin said. "Congress revoked Burgoyne's parole, and because he was still technically a prisoner of war, he was required to return to America."

"Did he?" I asked.

"Burgoyne engaged Edmund Burke to represent him. [46] Burke had remained friendly to the American cause and wrote me and asked that I intercede on Burgoyne's behalf. He pointed out that in vigorously prosecuting the war, Burgoyne had been following the king's orders and the soldier's code. He then said, 'If I were not fully persuaded of your liberal and manly way of thinking, I should not presume, in the hostile situation in which I stand, to make an application to you. I apply, not to the Ambassador of America, but to Doctor Franklin the Philosopher; my friend; and the lover of his species.' " [47]

"Did you intercede?"

"It so happened that I had just received authority from Congress to offer Burgoyne's freedom in exchange for that of Henry Laurens who was being held a prisoner in the Tower of London after being captured at sea. [48] I made that offer to Burke, and although the British ministry was not then ready to make the swap, Laurens was eventually set free, and Burgoyne was not required to return to America as a prisoner of war." [49]

"What you have told me are examples of kindness to enemy prisoners in the face of what you call enemy barbarous acts of murder, but what about the Asgill case? Didn't General Washington threaten to hang an innocent captured British officer by the name of Asgill? Doesn't that transcend torture?"

"No," Franklin said. "The circumstances that led to it were so egregious that justice demanded retaliation, and knowledge of the situation will help you understand why. An American artillery captain, Joshua Huddy, was captured at Toms River, New Jersey on March 24, 1782. The British commanding general, Sir Henry Clinton, turned Captain Huddy over to a group of Loyalists ostensibly for an exchange of prisoners. A Loyalist board, under the authority of my son William, issued an order that Huddy be hanged. A British captain by the name of Richard Lippincott carried out that order and left Huddy's body dangling from a tree. [50]

"Local citizens were outraged and petitioned General Washington to retaliate. Washington gathered his officers and asked them for their opinions in writing with respect to the following questions. If the British military should refuse to surrender the murderer, i.e., Captain Lippincott, should we:

1. Resort to retaliation?
2. If so, on whom should the punishment be inflicted?
3. How shall the victim be designated?

"To avoid bias, Washington ordered his officers to write their opinions without discussion and place them in sealed envelopes.

"Washington's officers overwhelmingly voted for retaliation; the victim should be an officer of equal rank, and designated by drawn lot. Thirteen British captains' names were collected. Captain Charles Asgill, a nineteen-year-old soldier from a noble English family, who had been taken prisoner at Yorktown, had the misfortune to have his name drawn. General Washington brought the matter to the attention of Congress. Congress approved the proposed retaliation." [51]

"So we have a situation," I said, "where an innocent young man is going to be executed if the British do not surrender Captain Lippincott."

Franklin nodded in the affirmative. "Lord Shelburne sent a personal appeal to me to intercede on behalf of Asgill. [52] I refused, and told him, 'If the English refuse to deliver up or punish this murderer, it is saying that they prefer to preserve him rather than Captain Asgill. It seems to me therefore that the application should be made to the British ministers.' [53] When a British court-martial acquitted the guilty soldier on the ground that he was following orders, American outrage demanded the arrest of my son, and William promptly fled to England. [54]

"General Washington made it clear that the decision to hang Asgill in retaliation was 'unalterably fixed' unless the British commander in chief, Sir Henry Clinton, surrendered Captain Lippincott, Captain Huddy's murderer. As General Washington put it, 'while my duty calls me to make this decisive determination, humanity dictates a fear for the unfortunate offering, and inclines me to say that I most devoutly wish his life may be saved; this happy event may be attained; but it must be effected by the British commander in chief. He knows the alternative which will accomplish it, and he knows that this alternative will avert the dire extremity from the innocent.' [55]

"Major General William Heath was appointed to meet with a British officer of equal rank. Washington refused General Carleton's request to allow the presence of Frederick Smyth, royal chief justice of New York, at the meeting citing the sole issue to be 'whether the perpetrator of the wanton and cruel murder of Huddy is to be given up, or a British officer to suffer in his place.' General Carleton then called off the meeting with Heath and sent the court-martial proceedings and documents by courier." [56]

"What did the British do?"

"Captain Lippincott's court-martial resulted in his acquittal with the declaration: 'The court having considered the evidence for and against the captain, and it appearing, that, though Joshua Huddy was executed without proper authority, what the prisoner did, was not the effect of malice or ill will, but proceeded from a conviction that it was his duty to obey the board of directors of associated loyalists, and his not doubting their having full authority to give such orders, the court is of the opinion that he is not guilty of the murder laid to his charge, and therefore acquit him.' General Carleton, however, expressed to General Washington his personal abhorrence of the act and court-martial verdict, and gave the strongest assurances that a further inquisition would be made with bringing the guilty to punishment. General Washington, very troubled with ordering the hanging of an innocent man, decided to wait until the results of the inquisition were complete. This was one of three such postponements. [57]

"In the meantime, this young soldier's family, through his mother, Lady Theresa Asgill, expressed their profound grief at the prospect of their innocent son being hanged. Lady Asgill beseeched King George for his compassion and assistance. Hence, the letter I received from Lord Shelburne. Fearful that England's influence was insufficient to save her son, Lady Asgill took the unprecedented action of writing directly to the French foreign minister, Comte de Vergennes, a gentleman and a friend of mine. Her passionate and heart-rending sorrow captured the count's heart, and he took the matter up with King Louis and Queen Marie Antoinette, who expressed their desire that Asgill's life be spared.

"On July 29, Comte de Vergennes wrote to General Washington and requested that Asgill be released. Vergennes pointed out that though Asgill was our prisoner, 'he is among those whom the arms of the king contributed to put into your hands at Yorktown.' In other words, Asgill's capture resulted from a joint American-French military victory. Vergennes made it clear that, 'in seeking to deliver Asgill from the fate that threatens him, I am far from engaging you to seek another victim; the pardon, to be perfectly satisfactory, must be entire.' The count enclosed a copy of Lady Asgill's letter. Washington immediately sent a copy of Vergennes and Lady Asgill's letters to the president of

Congress noting, 'they contain a very pathetic and affectionate interposition in favor of the life of Captain Asgill.'

"Comte de Vergennes's letter was read to Congress, and an Act of Congress was passed on November 7, 1782, ordering Asgill's release. General Washington sent a copy of the order to Asgill with a note that he was personally relieved and pleased by Congress's decision. [58] General Washington wrote to Vergennes and told him that his letter 'had no small degree of weight in procuring that decision in favor of Captain Asgill.'" [59]

All three of us sat in silence for a few moments, thinking of young Asgill's close escape, but then, remembering how short was the time available to me, I turned to another area that had always intrigued me. "Dr. Franklin, to change the subject to something more personal, you retired from active business at the age of forty-two. Why so young?"

"Because, Jack, I had made enough money to live comfortably, and I had a burning desire to finish my electrical experiments, and then spend my remaining years in public service." [60]

"How did you accumulate enough wealth to allow you to retire so early?"

"The chronology or the theory?"

"Both."

"The theory is simple. The way to wealth, if you desire it, is as plain as the way to market. It depends chiefly on two words, *industry* and *frugality*: that is, waste neither *time* nor *money*, but make the best use of both. Without industry and frugality nothing will do, and with them everything. [61] Conversely, as Poor Richard put it:

'Women and wine, game and deceit,

Make the wealth small and the wants great'

"As for the chronology, you may remember that I was born in Boston and started in the printing trade there at the age of twelve, indentured to my brother James. My indenture was supposed to last until I was twenty-one, but our relationship was always stormy and exacerbated by beatings I received from James. At age seventeen I decided to leave my brother, and when James learned of this, he contacted the other Boston printers, who, in turn, refused to employ me. Unable to find work in Boston, I arranged for passage to New York aboard a sloop 'under the notion that I had got a naughty girl with child, whose friends would compel me to marry her, and therefore I could not appear or come away publicly.' I sold some of my books to raise a little money and was taken on board privately. Three days later I arrived in

The house in which Benjamin Franklin was born, Milk Street House, Boston.

New York but the sole printing house there was fully staffed. The owner suggested that work might be available in Philadelphia. [62]

"I left New York, and after an arduous trip, arrived in Philadelphia in my working clothes, dirty, tired, and hungry with only a Dutch dollar and a copper shilling in my pocket. At a local bakery I bought three great puffy rolls, and with a roll under each arm, and eating the other, I walked up Market Street and past the home of Deborah Read, my future wife, who was standing with her father in the doorway. She later told him that I made, as I certainly did, a most awkward, ridiculous appearance.

"I found work at Samuel Keimer's printing house, and eventually took lodging at the Read residence. With clean, pressed clothes, I made a more respectable appearance in the eyes of Miss Read than I had done when she first happened to see me eating my roll in the street.

"Shortly after my arrival in Philadelphia, I met Sir William Keith, the governor of the Pennsylvania province, who took an immediate liking to me. Keith urged me to establish my own printing business, and he promised to send me public business and do me every other service in his power. Keith wrote a letter to my father strongly recommending the project. Encouraged by Keith's promises, I returned to Boston, showed my father Keith's letter, and asked for a business loan. My father thought me too young and inexperienced to start my own business and declined to make the loan.

"Returning to Philadelphia, I stopped in Newport, Rhode Island, to visit my brother John. On leaving Newport, I boarded a sloop for New York along with other passengers including two young women and a matron-like Quaker woman. The Quaker woman, sensing a daily growing familiarity between me and the two young women, took me aside and said, 'those are bad women and I advise thee to have no acquaintance with them.' At first, I protested, but after being told some things the Quaker woman had heard and observed, I promised to follow her advice. When the boat docked in New York the two women gave me their address and invited me to come see them, but I didn't take them up on their offer. The next day the captain discovered several items missing from his cabin. Knowing that these were a couple of strumpets, he got a warrant to search their lodgings, found the stolen goods, and had the thieves punished. Relieved to have escaped the clutches of the two prostitutes, I learned a lesson, but one I didn't always follow.

"Back in Philadelphia, I resumed working for Mr. Keimer, and began to court Deborah Read for whom I had great respect and affection. Governor Keith continued to urge me to start my own printing business and promised to furnish me with letters of recommendation to his friends in London, and a letter of credit that would allow me to buy there the press equipment I needed.

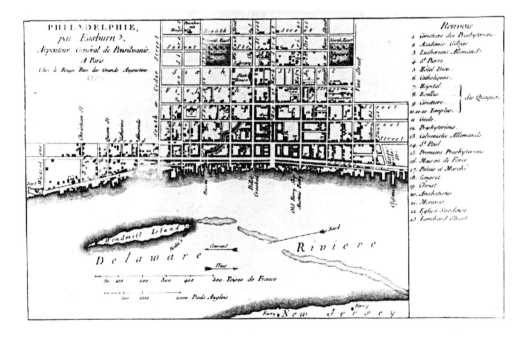

Philadelphia, 1777

"One of my friends during this time was James Ralph, who shared my interest in reading. Ralph was ingenious, genteel in his manner, and extremely eloquent. Ralph worked as a clerk for a merchant but aspired to be a poet. Although Ralph was married and the father of a child, he decided to accompany me to London.

"My decision to go to London convinced Deborah's mother that any thoughts of marriage Deborah and I might have would have to wait until I returned. Perhaps, too, she thought my expectations not so well-founded as I imagined them to be.

"As the London sailing date approached, my repeated requests of Keith for the letters were met with a variety of excuses as to why they were not available. Finally, moments before my ship's departure, I stopped by Keith's office and asked for the letters. Keith's secretary told me that the governor was tied up in 'business of the utmost importance,' but that Keith would send the letters on board. I returned to the ship a little puzzled, but still not doubting. When the ship arrived in London and the captain's mail bag was opened, there were no letters from Keith for me. In explanation of why Keith played such pitiful tricks on a poor ignorant boy, I reasoned that he wished to please everybody; and, having little to give, he gave expectations.

"Stranded in London with little money, Ralph and I took lodgings together and became inseparable companions. To my surprise, Ralph told me that he did not intend to ever return to his family in Philadelphia. I also forgot my engagements to Miss Read, to whom I never wrote more than one letter, and that was to let her know I was not likely soon to return. I immediately got work at a famous printing house, and Ralph, unable to find employment, lived off me.

"Ralph took up with a young woman, a Mrs. T——, who lived in our apartment house. Eventually, Ralph and Mrs. T—— moved out and found lodgings of their own. Ralph soon learned, however, that Mrs. T——'s income as a milliner was insufficient to support him and her child. Ralph moved to the country, adopted my name, took a job teaching children reading and writing, and recommended Mrs. T—— to my care. Ralph continued his pursuit of the muses and sent me almost daily specimens of an epic poem he was then composing. In the meantime, Mrs. T——, having on Ralph's account lost her friends and business, was often in distress, and used to send for me and borrow what I could spare to help her out. I grew fond of her company, and, being at the time under no religious restraint, and presuming of my importance to her, I attempted familiarities (another erratum) which she repulsed with proper resentment, and told Ralph about my behavior. Outraged, Ralph returned to London, severed our friendship, and used the incident as an excuse to cancel his indebtedness to me.

"On the voyage over, I had struck up a friendship with a Quaker merchant by the name of Denman, and we stayed in touch while in London. One day when we were together, Mr. Denman announced that he was about to return to Philadelphia and suggested that I return with him. I was penniless, but Denman offered to loan me the money for my passage home (thrift, a quality I would later apply to my life, had not yet become a tenet), and a position as a clerk in a store that Denman was going to open. I had grown tired of London, and I accepted.

"When our ship docked in Philadelphia in October 1726, I found sundry alterations. Keith was no longer governor, and Deborah Read's friends, despairing of my return after the receipt of my letter, had persuaded her to marry another, one Rogers, a potter, which she did in my absence. 'With him, however, she was never happy, and soon parted from him, refusing to cohabit with him or bear his name, it now being said that he had another wife. He was a worthless fellow, tho' an excellent workman, which was the temptation of her friends. He got into debt, ran away in 1727 or 1728 to the West Indies, and died there.'

"My employment by Mr. Denman ended abruptly six months after we set up shop when Denman became ill and died. Denman, ever the gentleman, forgave my debt to him.

"I did not like or trust Samuel Keimer, but being without any job prospects after Denman's death, I reluctantly accepted Keimer's offer to manage his printing house. Within less than a year, I formed a partnership with a friend and set up my own print shop.

"I lived in Philadelphia four years before I married Deborah Read. During this time I was busy establishing myself in the printing trade, starting a newspaper, trying to marry women with money, and cavorting with prostitutes. [63]

"My idea of the ideal marriage partner was a woman who would bring with her a dowry of money as would pay off my remaining debt for the printing house. Although my first attempt in this regard resulted in failure, it turned my thoughts to marriage. I looked around and made overtures of acquaintances in other places; but soon found that the business of a printer being generally thought a poor one, I was not to expect money with a wife, unless with such a one as I should not otherwise think agreeable. My hopes in this regard were doomed because I had very little to offer a woman of status or money. I had no formal education, no family social status, no money (I was in debt and struggling to establish myself in a poor man's trade), I was not handsome, and I did not bring to my relationships with women the one emotion that can conquer all negatives—love. Falling in love was simply not a part of my emotional makeup at that time in my life. [64]

"While I shopped for a wife, my hard-to-be-governed passions hurried me frequently into intrigues with low women who fell in my way. These experiences were attended with some expense and great inconvenience, and a continual risk to my health by a distemper, which of all things I dreaded, though by great good luck I escaped it. My association with prostitutes began during my eighteen months in London and continued on my return to Philadelphia. [65]

"Given my situation, and my guilty feelings about Deborah's marriage to Roger and the circumstances surrounding it, I renewed my relationship with her, and on September 1, 1730, we entered into a common-law marriage, a marriage without a formal ceremony. We simply declared publicly that we intended to live together as man and wife, an arrangement that was legal in Pennsylvania at the time. Deborah 'proved a good and faithful helpmate. We throve together and mutually endeavored to make each other happy.' [66]

"Shortly after our marriage, I surprised Deborah by bringing home an illegitimate son, William. [67]

"For twenty-four years after my marriage, my life was a whirlwind of events, interests, and accomplishments. I expanded the print shop to include a general store that Deborah operated. [68] In 1729, when I was twenty-three, I started a newspaper, the *Pennsylvania Gazette*, launched *Poor Richard's Almanack*, 'a proper vehicle for conveying instruction among the common people, who bought scarce any other books.' [69]

"Poor Richard was the spokesman of its essays and proverbs. 'It soon came to be in such demand that I reaped considerable profit from it, vending annually near ten thousand.' [70] In 1736, I obtained the job of clerk to the Pennsylvania Assembly, the colony's ruling body, and that gave me a better 'opportunity of keeping up an interest among the members. I was appointed the official printer for the assembly, and this led to the business of the votes, laws, paper money, and other occasional jobs for the public that on the whole were very profitable.' Eventually I became the official printer for Maryland, New Jersey, and Delaware." [71]

Franklin took a sip of wine and licked his lips. "Very nice, Thomas, very nice indeed. Where did you buy this wine?"

THE

Pennſylvania *GAZETTE*.

Numb. XL.

Containing the freſheſt Advices Foreign and Domeſtick

From Thurſday, September 25. to Thurſday, October 2. 1729.

Front page of the first issue of The Pennsylvania Gazette.

"Three years after you left France, I visited Champagne and discovered this wine at the winery of Monsieur Dorsay in Ay. Of all the Champagnes I tasted during that visit, I found Monsieur Dorsay's the best, and I bought his remaining supply of the year 1783, sixty bottles. Later, while serving as secretary of state, I purchased Dorsay's Champagne for President Washington."

Franklin took another sip and continued. "A year later I became the postmaster of Philadelphia, and 'tho the salary was small it facilitated the correspondence that improved my newspaper, increased the number demanded, as well as the advertisements to be inserted, so it came to afford me a very considerable income.' I also came up with the idea of setting up print shops in other colonies in partnership with young printers who needed financial help, some of whom were my own journeymen. I supplied the presses, the type, and other necessaries, and in turn took one-third of the profits for the duration of the contract. Before I retired, I had entered into more than two dozen partnerships or financial arrangements spread throughout the colonies and even in Antigua." [72]

Franklin looked at Jefferson and me. "Am I boring you?"

"No," we said in unison.

"Let me think," Franklin said. "I invented a stove. I formed the Junto, a book club, and along with its members and other friends, I organized the first circulating library in America, the first Philadelphia fire department, and a fire insurance company. [73] I drafted rules and legislation for improving police efficiency and better street lighting, and supported the establishment of a hospital. I was instrumental in founding the Academy of Philadelphia [74] and the American Philosophical Society. In 1751, I was elected to the Pennsylvania Assembly, and two years later I was appointed deputy postmaster-general for the Colonies." [75]

"I understand, Dr. Franklin, that a year before you retired you were instrumental in raising a private army of more than ten thousand armed men for the protection of Pennsylvania."

"That's true, Jack."

"How did that come about?"

"In 1747, French and Spanish privateers entered the Delaware Bay, plundered two plantations just below New Castle, and captured a ship and killed the captain. A few months later, rumors spread that six French privateers, and perhaps others, were going to sack Philadelphia. At the time, Pennsylvania was a propprietary colony, and the Assembly, controlled by pacifist Quakers, refused to provide funds for the defense of the colony. The rich Philadelphia merchants refused to give money to protect Quaker property and their own. The German farming population sided with the Quakers, and the Scotch-Irish, living farther in the interior, did not feel the danger of a seaboard invasion. [76] It was evident to me, however, that something had to be done. I determined to try what might be done by a voluntary association of the people. To promote this I first wrote and published a pamphlet entitled *Plain Truth*, in which I stated our defenseless situation in strong lights, with the necessity of union and discipline for our defense, and promised to propose in a few days an association to be generally signed for that purpose. I pointed out that the danger was not only from the sea. What if the French aroused the Indians to attack the back country? 'Perhaps,' I wrote, 'some in the city, towns, and plantations near the river may say to themselves: "An Indian war on the frontiers will not affect us; the enemy will never come near our habitations; let those concerned take care of themselves." And others, who live in the country, when they are told of the danger the city is in from attempts by sea, may say: "What is that to us? The enemy will be satisfied with the plunder of the town, and never think it worth his while to visit our plantations; let the town take care of itself." Those are not mere suppositions, for I have heard some talk in this strange manner. But are these the sentiments of true Pennsylvanians, or fellow-countrymen, or even of men who have common sense or goodness? Is not the whole province one body?' I calculated that we had at least (exclusive of the Quakers) 60,000 fighting men acquainted with firearms. The pamphlet and the articles that I wrote in the *Gazette* had a sudden and surprising effect. The militia association plan was laid before a large meeting and 1,200 signed up. Word of the association spread through Pennsylvania and over 10,000 joined as volunteer members of the militia." [77]

"Didn't the officers of the Philadelphia companies choose you to lead them?"

"Yes, but I thought myself unfit for that challenge and recommended someone else. I did, however, organize a lottery to finance the building of a fort below the city and to supply it with cannons." Franklin took a sip of wine and his face took on a reflective expression. Looking over to Jefferson, he said, "Drinking this wine reminds me of how wine played a major part in equipping our fort. 'We didn't have any heavy cannons and we bought thirty-nine in Boston, and sent to London for additional cannons, but realizing that they would not arrive until summer, I and three commissioners went to New York to ask Governor George Clinton for an interim loan of some cannons. He at first refused us peremptorily; but at dinner with his council, where there was great drinking of Madeira wine as the custom of that place then was, he softened by degrees, and said he would lend us six. After a few more bumpers he advanced to ten; and at length he very good-naturedly conceded eighteen. They were fine cannon, 18-pounders, with their carriages, which we transported and mounted on our battery by April 1748. The Association kept a nightly guard while the war lasted, and among the rest, I regularly took my turn of duty there as a common soldier.'[78]

"When I reached the age of 42, I retired. My new leisure allowed me to turn my interests to the passionate study of electricity. 'I never was before engaged in any study that so totally engrossed my attention and my time as that did.' I conveyed my electrical observations and findings in letters to Peter Collinson, a London merchant and botanist. Collinson published my letters in a booklet titled *Experiments and Observations in Electricity* (1751), which was translated into French and circulated throughout Europe. My kite experiments, demonstrating

Lightning rod.

that lightning was a form of electricity, followed in 1752, and a year later, I invented the lightning rod." [79]

"Dr. Franklin, you are the embodiment of the American dream."

"And that is?"

"That in America, the land of opportunity, anyone, regardless of birth, race, religion, or social class, can achieve wealth and status through the application of industry, frugality, virtue, and ambition. You made that dream come true, and you have been an example for millions of Americans." [80]

Franklin smiled, looked over at Jefferson and winked.

"You mentioned how you set up print shops in other colonies in partnership with young printers who needed financial help. Today that method of doing business is called franchising," I said.

Franklin sipped his wine and looked out toward the garden. He was smiling. "I don't know what it's called, but it worked for me. Additionally, I established about eighteen paper mills throughout the Colonies, had rental properties in Philadelphia and some coastal towns, loaned substantial amounts of money repayable with interest, and was involved in land speculation ventures." [81]

"You would be known today as an entrepreneur and a capitalist," I said. "But why did you refuse a patent for your popular stove, known then, and still sold today, as the Franklin stove?"

" 'Because we enjoy great advantages from the inventions of others, and we should be glad of an opportunity to serve others by our invention, and this we should do freely and generously.' That same reasoning applied to my other inventions. I never patented the lightning rod or bifocal glasses. [82]

" 'There are three ways for a nation to acquire wealth. The first is by *war*, as the Romans did, in plundering their conquered neighbors. This is *robbery*. The second by *commerce*, which is generally *cheating*. The third by *agriculture*, the only *honest* way, wherein man receives a real increase of the *seed* thrown into the ground, in a kind of continual miracle, wrought by the hand of God.' " [83]

"*The Way to Wealth* stands with your *Autobiography* as your best-known writing. There are estimates that it has been separately published in over 1,300 editions and translated into almost every language. How did writing *The Way to Wealth* come about?"

"On the voyage to England in 1757, I decided that the coming autumn edition would be my last edition of *Poor Richard's Almanack*, and what became known as *The Way To Wealth* emerged from the preface of the 1758 edition. I came up with the idea of creating a new character, Father Abraham, a faithful subscriber to the almanac. When Father Abraham, 'a plain, clean, old man, with white locks,' was asked by a member of a group what he thought of the present economic condition of the country, he responded with a soliloquy of capitalist aphorisms or economic maxims taken from previous editions of *Poor Richard's Almanack.*"[84]

"Help me remember. What are some pearls of advice from *The Way to Wealth*?"

"God helps them who help themselves; sloth, by bringing on diseases, absolutely shortens life; but dost thou love life, then do not squander time, for that is the stuff life is made of; if time be of all things the most precious, wasting time must be the greatest prodigality; lost time is never found again; laziness travels so slowly that poverty soon overtakes him; there are no gains without pains; if we are industrious we shall never starve; at the working man's house hunger looks in, but dares not enter; never leave that till tomorrow, which you can do today; little strokes fell great oaks; leisure is the time for doing something useful; keep thy shop, and thy shop will keep thee; not to oversee workmen is to leave them your purse open; buy what you do not need, and soon you will sell your necessities; a ploughman on his legs is higher than a gentleman on his knees; it is easier to suppress the first desires than to satisfy all that follow it; the second vice is lying, the first is running into debt; if you will not hear reason, she will surely rap your knuckles." Franklin stopped and looked up from what he was reading. "Here, take this and read the rest of it at your leisure," he said, handing to me a little booklet. "This is what was later published under the title *The Way to Wealth*."[85]

I turned to Mr. Jefferson and he immediately said, "I think the word you used to describe Dr. Franklin's business acumen was entrepreneur. I wasn't an entrepreneur like Dr. Franklin. My wealth came by way of inherited privilege. My father died when I was fourteen and land was my primary inheritance, some 3,750 acres, a plantation, twenty-five slaves, the residue of my father's estate, a thorough classical education, and an established position in society. When I turned twenty-one I started buying and selling land. By the beginning of the Revolution in 1775, I owned some 4,874 acres spread across Virginia as far south as the Natural Bridge.[86]

"After I finished the two-year course of study at William & Mary College, George Wythe, who had educated himself in Latin, Greek, mathematics and philosophy, took me into his law office as an apprentice. Part of my legal training included the experience of listening to the 'sublime eloquence' of Patrick

Henry when he spoke in the Virginia House of Burgesses. Wythe and I traveled the revolutionary trail together, both signing the Declaration of Independence. We remained friends until Wythe's death in 1806; he was poisoned by a grandnephew.

"On the social side, I was part of Virginia Royal Governor Francis Fauquier's circle of educated older men who enjoyed music, literature, and knowledge. I also found other entertainment, spending freely at coffeehouses and drinking punch in Raleigh's, Campbell's, Charlton's, Vaughan's, and other taverns, winning and losing at backgammon, buying a horse, seeing a tiger in a traveling curiosity show, and dreaming of spending two or three years traveling through Europe.

"In 1767, I opened my law practice in Williamsburg, and although I continued in it for seven and a half years, the law was never personally satisfying or financially rewarding. Between 1767 and 1770, I was employed in more than 300 cases, but client payments were another matter. In the first five years of my practice I billed 2,119 pounds, collected 797, and 1,322 remained uncollected. [87]

"When I was 28, I married Martha Wayles Skelton at The Forest, the home of her father John Wayles, on New Year's Day 1772. She was twenty-three. Her death at the age of thirty-three was my greatest sadness and disappointment." Franklin cast Jefferson a sympathetic look. " 'That single event wiped away all my plans and left me a blank which I had not the spirit to fill up.' " [88]

"You were married just ten years?"

"Yes, and during that time we had six children, but only two, Martha and Mary, survived the measles, mumps, whooping cough, and scarlet fever of childhood."

"I understand your wife had been married before."

"Yes. She had married Bathurst Skelton when she was eighteen and was widowed with a son by the time she was nineteen. Her son died before we were married."

Martha Jefferson.

"How would you describe your marriage?"

"It was a very happy marriage. I described it in my autobiography as a period of 'uncheckered happiness.' "

"But because you destroyed all your correspondence with Martha, and chose not to talk about her, we know very little about her. Most of your biographers portray her as beautiful but slight, genteel, a gracious hostess, musically gifted on the harpsichord, and a devoted wife and mother."[89]

Jefferson nodded.

"What caused your wife's death?"

"Martha became ill after the birth of our daughter Lucy Elizabeth, and her health continued to deteriorate over four months. I was in constant attendance. As she sank into a coma, I was led from the room almost insensible, and I fainted. Her death on September 6, 1782, sent me into a stupor of mind that rendered me as dead to the world as was she whose loss occasioned it. I kept to my room for three weeks and thereafter rode incessantly for hours on end. It was a month before I could write a letter, and then only to express that 'this miserable kind of existence is really too burdensome to be borne. Were it not for the infidelity of deserting the sacred charge left me, I could not wish its continuance a moment.' "[90]

"And that charge was, Mr. Jefferson, your three daughters?"

"Yes, and I had taken in my sister Martha's family of six children after the death of her husband Dabney Carr."

I wanted to let Jefferson recover so I looked to Dr. Franklin. He had listened intently to Jefferson's remarks. "What was the biggest disappointment in your life, Dr. Franklin?"

"My loyalist son, William. It was well-known that he was a bastard. [91] I took him from his mother, brought him into my home after my marriage to Deborah, gave him my name, provided him with an excellent private education, and lavished love and affection on him. When I was elected to the Pennsylvania Assembly in 1751, I got William appointed to the clerkship I was vacating. When I was appointed deputy postmaster of the Colonies, I made William postmaster of Philadelphia, and a year later named him continental comptroller. [92] In the summer of 1757, I left for London and took William with me. I enrolled him in the Inns of Court, and he became a lawyer. We traveled together on business and vacations to Scotland, Holland, Flanders, and throughout England. My influence was vital in securing his appointment in 1762 as the royal governor of New Jersey. [93] I was proud of him and accompanied William through New Jersey when he took his oath of office as royal governor. But despite all this, when it came time to choose sides in the fight for our independence, William remained loyal to the Crown.[94] He tried to convince me that a continental congress was a bad idea. He argued in favor of Bostonians making restitution for the tea they had destroyed. That letter infuriated me, and I pointed out that England had 'extorted many thousands of pounds from Americans unconstitutionally and that England ought to be the one to make restitution.' And I told him, he was a thorough courtier, and saw everything with government eyes.[95]

"The position as royal governor went to his head. He took on airs and loyalist thinking. At some point, it became clear to me that nothing I could say or do would dissuade him from his betrayal of our cause. He was one of them, not one of us, and we became estranged forever. In a letter to William after the war I summed up my feelings in these words: 'Nothing has ever hurt me so much and affected me with such keen sensations as to find myself deserted in my old age by my only son; and not only deserted, but to find him taking up arms against me, in a cause wherein my good fame, fortune and life were all at stake.' "[96]

"During the war, wasn't William arrested, tried, convicted, and incarcerated?"

"Yes. Here is what happened. William in effect was acting as a spy against us by reporting to the British ministry in London any intelligence he could gather that was damaging to the American cause. The Continental Congress ordered the disarming of all potential threats against our cause. William refused to accept the order, and the leader of the local militia intercepted William's 'Secret and Confidential' mail addressed to Lord Germain, the Secretary of State for the American Colonies, and ruled that the contents betrayed the American cause. William was held in contempt, called an enemy of the liberties of our country, placed under house arrest, and allowed no visitors. At his trial, he was arrogant and defiant, and he was found guilty. He was sent under guard to Governor Jonathan Trumbull in Connecticut, placed under his authority and incarcerated."[97]

"Didn't William's wife, Elizabeth, plead with you to help your son?"

"She did."[98]

"And did you help him?"

"I didn't lift a finger on his behalf. I left him to his fate."[99]

"What eventually happened to William?"

"In an exchange of prisoners, William was released in September 1778, and he immediately took up residency in British-occupied New York, where he served as head of the Board of Associated Loyalists. In this capacity he authorized a series of raids on our forces, one of which resulted in the lynching of Captain Huddy, which led to the Asgill case."[100]

"Was there ever reconciliation between you and William?"

"No. On my return to America from France, we met in Southampton but there was no pleasure in seeing him. It was a business meeting. Out of deference to me, his property in America had not been confiscated. At this meeting, I bought all of his property in America and had much of it deeded to his son Temple. I never exchanged another letter with him. I never forgave him, and I disinherited him in my will."[101]

"What about embarrassments?" I said. "Were you ever publicly embarrassed, Mr. Jefferson?"

"Yes, of course."

"Do you mind telling me about it?"

"Certainly not. I don't know whether to call it an embarrassment or bruised feelings, but about a week after arriving in London in 1786, John Adams took me to the court of St. James's Palace and presented me to King George and Queen Charlotte. 'On my presentation, it was impossible for anything to be more ungracious than their notice of Mr. Adams and myself. I saw at once that the ulcerations in the narrow mind of this mulish being left nothing to be expected on the subject of my attendance.'[102] The king's conduct, of course, was not lost upon the circle of his subjects in attendance, and though I was entertained at dinners by a few Englishmen who were American sympathizers, members of the British ministry ignored me during the remainder of my stay."[103]

"Do you think that King George's ungracious behavior was because he remembered the Declaration of Independence and the litany of crimes of which you accused him?"

A smile crept across Jefferson's face. "Perhaps," he said with shrug.

"Was there ever an occasion when you were publicly embarrassed, Dr. Franklin?"

"Yes, and it was a lot more protracted than our host's kingly slight."

"Also received from the British?"

"Yes, the British ministry, or more particularly the Privy Council, which consisted of the king's top ministers, who acted with his authority and on his behalf. Their roots can be traced to those who counseled William the Conqueror. They were a ver y powerful group.[104] I was called there ostensibly because of a petition the Massachusetts Assembly had filed for the removal of

John Hutchinson as governor. The solicitor general, a nasty prosecutor by the name of Alexander Wedderburn, immediately turned the focus of the hearing on how I had obtained the Hutchinson letters."

"I'm afraid I'm confused," I said. "What are the Hutchinson letters?"

"I'm sorry," Franklin said. "John Hutchinson, a wealthy merchant, was the governor of Massachusetts, and his brother-in-law, Andrew Oliver, was the lieutenant governor. Hutchinson and Oliver, between 1767 and 1769, wrote a series of letters to the British ministry advising that the political problems in Massachusetts were a result of a subversive minority of men, and offered suggestions on how to best subdue that unrest. [105] A member of Parliament, whose name shall remain anonymous, gave me copies of those letters. After reading the letters, it was my opinion that the content of the letters was behind why England had sent troops to Boston and had implemented other offensive measures. I sent them to my friend Thomas Cushing in Boston with the admonition that they not be made public. [106] They were published, however, creating a furor with outspoken patriots such as Samuel Adams and John Hancock and, in turn, the British ministry. What Hutchinson said in those letters led the Massachusetts Assembly to petition for his removal.

"A month before I was summoned before the Privy Council, two men engaged in a duel in Hyde Park because one accused the other of leaking the letters. One of the men was required to retire because of injuries, but when his friends accused the other man of not having fought fairly, a second duel was scheduled. When I learned of the rematch, I wrote to the *London Chronicle* and confessed that I had obtained and transmitted the letters to Boston. So, when Mr. Wedderburn's questions quickly focused on how the letters had been obtained, and not the merits of the petition, I expressed my surprise stating that I thought the meeting was to be political, not legal and personal. Accordingly, I requested the right to be represented by legal counsel. The Lord President agreed to my request, and the hearing was postponed for three weeks to allow me to engage counsel and prepare. In retrospect, the postponement turned out to be a mistake, because in the interim between the first and second hearings, news of the Boston Tea Party reached London. This act of violence roiled the British ministry and made Hutchinson, in their eyes, the defender of liberty and me the enemy." [107]

"I know what the history books say about the events in Boston, but I would very much like to hear your account of it," I said.

"Parliament had given the East India Company special tax advantages on tea it brought into the Colonies. This gave the company a great financial advantage over the American merchants who bought their tea at auction. Urged on by Sam Adams, a group of about fifty Bostonians, disguised as Indians, stormed the East India Company ship *Dartmouth*, dumped some 90,000 pounds of tea into the Boston harbor, and stealthily disappeared into the night. [108]

"The British government considered the destruction of the tea at Boston a lawless outrage that amounted to high treason and sought redress. I too felt that restitution should be made, and in a letter to Samuel Adams, John Hancock, Tom Cushing and William Phillips, I urged reparation for the destroyed tea. [109] Parliament closed the port of Boston until the tea, valued at 15,000 pounds, was paid for. General Thomas Gage, commander-in-chief of the British army in America, was made governor of Massachusetts and the number of soldiers there was substantially increased. The response of the other colonies to Massachusetts' call for aid was prompt and generous, and the Boston Tea Party became a colonial rallying point. [110]

"Lord Chatham proposed a plan in the House of Lords for healing the growing differences and restoring peace. [111] Although several lords spoke in favor of considering Lord Chatham's plan, the majority was clearly opposed, and the plan 'was treated with as much contempt as they could have shown to a ballad offered by a drunken porter.' I left the House of Lords thinking that these lords who claimed sovereignty over three million virtuous and sensible people in America appeared to have scarce discretion enough to govern a herd of swine. [112] At one point in my negotiations, I thought that I had given convincing proof of my sincere desire of promoting peace when, on being informed that all that was wanted for the honor of the government was to obtain payment for the tea, I offered, without any assurance of ever being reimbursed, to pay for it, if the acts against Massachusetts were repealed. [113] My offer was not accepted.

"With the destruction of the tea in Boston as a background, the second Privy Counsel meeting convened on the morning of January 29, 1774, in a room called the Cockpit."

"Why was it called the Cockpit?" I asked.

"During the time of Henry VIII, cockfights were held there, and considering what happened to me that day, it was aptly named." [114]

"What happened?"

"Well, it was a full house, all thirty-six Privy Council chairs were filled, and there was an air of intensity and expectancy in the room. It began with a reading of the Massachusetts petition and the Hutchinson-Oliver letters. My counsel, John Dunning, spoke, and while pointing out that the matter at hand was a petition of grievance from loyal subjects and not a legal proceeding, Mr. Wedderburn interrupted him. For the next hour, Wedderburn excoriated and belittled me. He called me the 'first mover and prime conductor,' the 'secret spring,' the 'inventor and planner' of the unrest in Massachusetts, the main conspirator to dishonor and defame two respected servants of the king. He accused me of obtaining the letters by fraudulent and corrupt means, and for malignant purposes, and by so doing, I had forfeited the respect of society and my peers.

"By not owning up to the theft and publication of the letters, I had, Wedderburn said, almost caused the murder of one man, referring, of course, to the duel, and he characterized my conduct as 'expressive of the coolest and most deliberate malice, without honor. Amidst these tragical events, of one person nearly murdered, of another answerable for the issue, of a worthy governor hurt in his dearest interests, the fate of America in suspense, here is a man who with the utmost insensibility of remorse, stands up and avows himself the author of all. I can compare it only to Zanga in Dr. Young's Revenge:

Know then 'twas—I
I forged the letter, I disposed the picture;
I hated, I despised, and I destroyed.
I ask, my Lords, whether the revengeful temper attributed, by poetic fiction only, to the bloody African, is not surpassed by the coolness and apathy of the wily American.'

"Wedderburn scorned my argument that the letters belonged in the public domain. The letters, he said, were private, 'as sacred and as precious to gentlemen of integrity as their family plate or jewels are.' Wedderburn posed the question: 'What had betrayed a wise man,' meaning me, 'into such conduct?' The answer, he exclaimed, was that I wanted to be governor! He then exhorted the Privy Council not to replace Governor Hutchinson 'in order to make room for Dr. Franklin as a successor.'" [115]

"What did you do while this diatribe was taking place?" I asked.

"I remained silent, and friends told me I stood conspicuously erect, without the smallest movement of my body. I refused to answer his scurrilous remarks." [116]

"What was the decision of the Privy Council?"

"The Massachusetts petition was rejected. And within forty-eight hours of the hearing, I was notified of my dismissal as deputy postmaster general, a position that I had held for twenty-one years." [117]

"How did you feel about this humiliating experience?"

"I was very angry, but also despairing for America, for I now realized our voices were not to be heard by the British ministry. As I told my friend Thomas Cushing, 'When I see that all petitions and complaints of grievances are so odious to government that even the mere pipe which conveys them becomes obnoxious, I am at a loss to know how peace and union is to be maintained or restored between the different parts of the empire. Grievances cannot be redressed unless they are known; and they cannot be known but through complaints and petitions. If these are deemed affronts, and the messengers punished as offenders, who will henceforth send petitions? And who will deliver them? Where complaining is a crime, hope becomes despair.' [118] But a few days later, my anger had turned to pride. To my sister I wrote, 'Intending to disgrace me, they have rather done me honor. No failure of duty in my office is alleged against me; such a fault I should have been ashamed of. But I am too much attached to the interests of America, and an opposer of the measures of administration. The displacing me therefore is a testimony of my being uncorrupted.' [119] My treatment by Wedderburn before the Privy Council, the council's glee in witnessing it, and my dismissal as deputy postmaster general came down to one thing: I was too much of an American." [120]

"Being discharged as the deputy postmaster must have sent a clear message as to where you stood with the ministry," I said.

"It did indeed. At my favorite clubs and coffeehouses, I immediately felt an uncomfortable coolness, and there was a perceptible drift away from me by some friends. The London newspapers joyfully joined in the character assassination calling me an 'old snake,' a 'traitor,' 'old doubleface,' a 'grand incendiary,' and my Craven Street residence became 'Judas's office.' There were rumors that I might be arrested and imprisoned and, of course, my lobbying activities were at an end." [121]

"Did you ever forgive the British government for the humiliation to which it subjected you that morning?"

"No. I marked my resentment in my attire. At the second hearing, I dressed in a dark Manchester velvet suit and a long ornate wig. [122] I wore that same suit on two other important occasions in my life: when I signed the Treaty of

Alliance with France in 1778, and again in1783 when I signed the Treaty of Paris that assured our independence as a free nation. [123]

"I remember another occasion when the Cockpit came to mind. In December 1776, on my way from the coast of France to Paris, I stopped overnight at an inn and learned that the English historian Edward Gibbon was there. The first volume of his great work, *The History of the Decline and Fall of the Roman Empire* had been published. I sent him a note inviting him to dinner, but he refused, saying he would not associate with anyone in revolt against his king. I sent him another note telling him that when he was ready to write the decline and fall of the British Empire, which I expected soon, I would be happy to furnish him with the ample materials in my possession." [124]

"But, Dr. Franklin, you remained in London for fourteen months after that dreadful experience. Under the depressing circumstances you have outlined, how did you spend your time?"

"I became depressed, even tearful at times. There were, however, still some conciliatory voices in England, so I remained hopeful that war could be avoided. I stayed in England thinking that I might in some way contribute to a peace, and an opportunity did present itself."

"How?"

"At a Royal Society meeting in early November, a member by the name of Raper mentioned that a fashionable English widow, Lady Caroline Howe, the sister of Admiral Richard Howe and General William Howe, the commanders of England's naval and land forces at the beginning of the Revolution, desired to play chess with me, fancying she could beat me. 'I told him I had been long out of practice but would call on her, but I put it off. I ran into Raper later that month, and he reminded me that I had not kept my promise to Lady Howe. He offered to take me to her, which he did. I played a few games with her, whom I found of very sensible conversation and pleasing behavior, which induced me to accept her invitation to meet again.'" [125]

"Wasn't this about the same time your wife was dying in Philadelphia?"

"Yes, but I didn't know she was dying. And if you are implying, Jack, that the chess meetings were flirtatious in nature, you are wrong. They were setup by Lady Howe to bring me into secret contact with her brother, Admiral Howe. After our first meeting, I accepted an invitation to play again a few days later. On this occasion, we talked about a variety of things, including her interest in math. And at some point she said, 'What is to be done about this dispute between Great Britain and her colonies?' I said, 'They should kiss and be friends.'

She then suggested that the government should employ me to settle the differences, saying that nobody else could do it better, but I told her the ministers would rather abuse me than employ me. She agreed that I had been treated shamefully. [126]

"Our next meeting was on Christmas day, and as soon as I arrived, she told me that her brother, Admiral Howe, wanted to meet with me and would I consent to such a meeting. I agreed, and shortly the admiral arrived. He too said that I was the man best suited to reconcile our differences, and that if I would offer some suggestions, he would pass them along to the proper ministers. I reminded him that the Continental Congress had made it clear what the Colonies wanted. I agreed, however, to secretly meet with him a week later at Lady Howe's residence. [127]

"At this meeting, Lord Howe asked if I thought it might be helpful if Great Britain sent an envoy to America. I told him that it might be quite helpful if that person was of rank and dignity. Lady Howe, who sat in on our meetings, said, 'I wish, brother, you were to be sent thither on such a service. I should like that much better than General Howe's going to command the army there.' Lord Howe handed me a piece of paper and asked me if I knew anything about it. It was a copy of my 'Hints for a Conversation' in which I had outlined seventeen points towards reconciliation, and I readily admitted that the plan was mine. Howe said he was rather sorry that the propositions were mine because there was no chance they would be accepted by the British authorities. He urged me to rewrite my proposals so that they 'would be acceptable.' To keep my authorship secret, he suggested that Mrs. Howe could recopy my new plan. If I agreed to his proposal, Howe said I could 'expect any reward in the power of the government to bestow.' This was, of course, an implied bribe, but I liked and trusted Howe, and the next day I submitted to Lady Howe a slightly revised plan containing essentially the same set of proposals. Lord Howe and I continued our talks well into February, but nothing positive emerged from them except the stunning realization on my part that Parliament would never accept American rights." [128]

"When did you know for sure that war was inevitable?"

"My realization arose from no one single event. It evolved from a series of events that happened early in 1775. First, on January 19 King George opened Parliament with a speech proclaiming that all the colonies were in criminal resistance. A few weeks later, the House of Commons systematically ignored all colonial petitions. And, finally, Parliament voted to have the king declare Massachusetts in open rebellion. [129]

"In addition, an attitude had developed within the British ministry and gentry of virulence and arrogance toward America epitomized by a comment made by a General Clarke one evening at my friend John Pringle's house. The general had the 'folly to say in my hearing that with a thousand British Grenadiers, he would undertake to go from one end of America to the other, and geld all the males, partly by force and partly by a little coaxing.' I knew then it was time to go home. I didn't hear of the bloody battles in Concord and Lexington until I arrived in Philadelphia on May 5." [130]

"Any other disappointments?" I said, looking from Dr. Franklin to Mr. Jefferson.

"I'm sure there were many," Jefferson said, shaking his head. "My last year as governor of Virginia was certainly a vast personal disappointment to me for a number of reasons."

"Because of Benedict Arnold's raid on Virginia?" I said.

"That certainly played a part."

"I was living comfortably in Paris at the time," Franklin said. "What happened?"

"The Virginia Council was in session in Richmond during the winter of 1780–81. On December 31, an aide to General Thomas Nelson, commander of the Virginia militia, notified me that twenty-seven ships had entered the Chesapeake. It was not known whether they were British or French, and I told General Nelson to do whatever he thought necessary. I did not call out the militia or order a special meeting of the council, but I did alert the coastal militia commanders of a possible emergency. Two days later I was advised that a British fleet had reached Jamestown. I now called up the militia, and gave orders for the removal of official records and military supplies. At 5 A.M. on January 4, I received word that the ships had landed at Westover, only twenty-five miles from Richmond. I also learned that the 'parricide' traitor Benedict Arnold was marching a force of nearly a thousand toward Richmond. With too few militia available to defend the city, the Council and I left. Arnold's 'cowardly plunderers' entered Richmond unmolested and sacked the city." [131]

"And you were blamed for this?" I said

"As governor, I became the scapegoat. I was responsible for the defense of the state, and what Arnold's troops did with impunity showed how ill-prepared Virginia was for war. I was charged with incompetence for not calling up the militia sooner, and for not providing for better defense of the state during my term as governor. I was also accused of cowardliness for failing to lead the militia in resistance. To add to my personal misery, three months after the Arnold raid on Richmond my daughter Lucy Elizabeth died and my wife, who suffered attacks of depression, went into a deep depression, and I did not feel I could leave her. The whole experience embittered me, and caused me to think that 'public service and private misery were inseparably linked together.' When my second term expired on May 31, 1781, I refused reappointment and retired to Monticello." [132]

"Wasn't this about the time you were almost captured by the British?" I said.

"Yes. Four days after my resignation as governor, at sunrise on June 4, a neighbor named Jouett rode up the mountain to warn me and my guests that a British cavalry of 250 men under the command of a Colonel Tarleton was in Louisa, only thirty miles away. Jouett then rode on to Charlottesville to warn the legislature. Tarleton sent a detachment under the command of Major McCleod on to Monticello to capture me. When they arrived, the house was vacant, and they found but one slave, Martin, standing on a plank on the portico under which he had just finished stashing the family silver. McCleod and his troops followed Tarleton's orders not to damage Monticello, but they did help themselves to some of my wines. [133]

"My estate at Elk Ridge that General Charles Cornwallis occupied for ten days did not receive the same gentle treatment. Cornwallis's troops destroyed all the growing crops of corn and tobacco, burned the barns and fences, took all the livestock, and carried off twenty-seven slaves. Had he been to give them freedom, he would have done right; but it was to consign them to inevitable death from small-pox and putrid fever, then raging in his camp." [134]

"What was your opinion of Benedict Arnold?"

"He was the greatest of all traitors and one of only two men I hated." [135]

"Who was the other?"

"The 'scalp-buyer' Henry Hamilton, the British lieutenant-governor of Detroit, who encouraged the Indians to commit atrocities against children, women, and men in Virginia's western frontiers." [136]

A moment of silence followed. My choice of subject was not a happy one, but my hosts did not shirk it.

"I recall another time in my life when I felt a keen sense of disappointment," Franklin said. "It happened after I had been in France about four years. Our war effort was desperate for money. General Washington wrote to me saying that 'Our present situation makes one of two things essential to us: a peace, or the most vigorous aid of our allies, particularly in the article of money.' I learned that Congress was sending John Laurens, as a special commissioner, and other advisors to France, to secure an emergency loan, a loan that I had secured in the amount of six million livres before Laurens arrived. In addition, Congress appointed John Adams to negotiate peace. By those two acts, it seemed clear that Congress had lost confidence in me. I thought it better to resign than run the risk of being dismissed, and I sent Congress my resignation." [137]

"Why do you think this came about?"

"Two reasons. At this time, the war was going badly for us, and Congress was desperate for money to carry on the war effort. Additionally, Ralph Izard and Arthur Lee and his brothers, powerful voices within Congress, continued to spread false and libelous accusations against me."

"Lee libeled you on many occasions, even asserting that 'Congress had the fullest evidence and conviction that Dr. Franklin was both a dishonest and incapable man,' " I said. [138]

"Fortunately," Jefferson said, "Congress had the good judgment to refuse Dr. Franklin's resignation, and to appoint him along with Adams and John Jay, commissioners to negotiate the peace with Great Britain." [139]

"And I esteemed it an honor," Franklin said.

"As I recall," I said, "Congress instructed you, and when I say, you, I mean, of course, Adams and Jay as well, that the two nonnegotiable items were America's independence and the continuation of the treaty with France."

"That's correct."

"But despite Congress's mandate, you agreed with your fellow commissioners to negotiate the peace with Britain without including or telling the French." Franklin's eyes were downcast. "Why did you let that happen when you were of the belief that 'the true political interest of America consists in observing and fulfilling, with the greatest exactitude, the engagements of our alliance with France?' " [140]

Franklin looked up and stared at me. "The two British peace emissaries, Richard Oswald and Thomas Grenville, tried to divide me from France during negotiations before the arrival of Adams and Jay, but at that time I held fast to our alliance. There was no doubt that a separate peace with us was a top British priority, and I made Comte de Vergennes aware of it." [141]

"Why did England send two peace emissaries?" I asked.

"That's an interesting question that requires a complicated answer. Shortly before the Boston Massacre, Lord Frederick North became England's prime minister. Aside from the fact that he personally disliked me, [142] Lord North, along with the king, was the architect of Britain's uncompromising stance against America's grievances and the aggression England pursued in conducting the war. [143] Upon Lord North's resignation shortly after Cornwallis' surrender at Yorktown, a new ministry was appointed. Lord Rockingham became prime minister. Lord Shelburne, a friend of mine who had shown consideration towards the colonies, was appointed secretary of state for colonial affairs, and Charles James Fox, also a moderate toward America, was appointed secretary of state for foreign affairs. This meant that peace negotiations with the United States came under Shelburne's aegis, but with France, Spain and Holland under Fox's. Jealous and bitter rivals, the two secretaries each sent a peace emissary to France to talk with me.[144]

"Shelburne sent Oswald, 'a gentleman of the strictest candor and integrity,' and a man more my age. After our first meeting we 'parted exceedingly good friends.' [145] Fox sent as his agent young Thomas Grenville, the son of my former nemeses, George Grenville. After meetings with both men, I favored to treat with Oswald, but it became moot when Rockingham died, and Shelburne succeeded him. This led to Fox's resignation and Grenville's replacement to the Paris negotiations. [146]

"Jay on his arrival in Paris made it clear that he did not trust the French to protect our interests. In a letter to Robert Livingston, then president of Congress, he wrote, 'This court chooses to postpone an acknowledgment of our independence by Britain, to the conclusion of a general peace in order to keep us under their direction until not only their and our objects are attained, but also until Spain shall be gratified in her demands.' When Adams, who distrusted the French as much as he distrusted me, arrived in Paris, he made it clear in a conversation with me that he sided with Jay. I went along with the strategy of my fellow commissioners because I too had come to believe that a separate negotiating channel with Britain was in our best interests. A month later we reached a preliminary settlement with the British." [147]

"How did the French react when they found out?"

"Vergennes expressed his disappointment, even his outrage, but he seemed placated when I pointed out that nothing had been agreed to in the preliminaries contrary to the interests of France, and no peace was to take place between us and England until France had concluded its settlement."[148]

I turned to Jefferson. "It is well known, Mr. Jefferson, that you were no admirer of monarchs and monarchies."

"I told George Washington 'I was much an enemy to monarchies before I came to Europe. I am ten thousand times more so, since I have seen what they are. There is scarcely an evil known in these countries which may not be traced to their king, as its source, nor a good, which is not derived from the small fibers of republicanism existing among them. I can further say, with safety, there is not a crowned head in Europe, whose talents or merits would entitle him to be elected a vestryman by the people of any parish in America.' "[149]

"Have you any personal opinions of specific monarchs you would care to share?"

"While in Europe, I often amused myself with contemplating the characters of the then reigning sovereigns of Europe: Louis XVI was a fool, of my own knowledge, and in despite of the answers made for him at his trial. The king of Spain was a fool, and of Naples the same. They passed their lives in hunting, and dispatched two couriers a week, one thousand miles, to let each other know what game they had killed the preceding days. The king of Sardinia was a fool. All these were Bourbons. The Queen of Portugal, a Braganza, was an idiot by nature. And so was the king of Denmark. Their sons, as regents, exercised the powers of government. The king of Prussia, successor to the great Frederick, was a mere hog in body as well as in mind. Gustavus of Sweden and Joseph of Austria were really crazy, and George of England, you know, was in a strait waistcoat There remained, then, none but old Catherine, who had been too lately picked up to have lost her common sense. In this state Bonaparte found Europe; and it was this state of its rulers which lost it with scarce a struggle. These animals had become without mind and powerless; and so will every hereditary monarch be after a few generations. Alexander, the grandson of Catherine, is as yet an exception. He is able to hold his own. But he is only of the third generation. His race is not yet worn out. And so ended the book of kings, from all of whom the Lord delivers us."[150]

"Having gotten that off your chest, Mr. Jefferson, what was your opinion of George Washington?"

"I knew General Washington intimately and thoroughly, and I would describe his character in terms like these: His mind was great and powerful, without being of the very first order; his penetration strong, though not so acute as that of a Newton, Bacon, or Locke; and as far as he saw, no judgment was ever sounder. It was slow in operation, being little aided by invention or imagination, but sure in conclusion. Hence the common remark of his officers, of the advantage he derived from councils of war, where, hearing all suggestions, he selected whatever was best; and certainly no general ever planned his battles more judiciously. But if deranged during the course of the action, if any member of his plan was dislocated by sudden circumstances, he was slow in a readjustment. The consequence was that he often failed in the field, and rarely against an enemy in station, as at Boston and York.

"He was incapable of fear, meeting personal dangers with the calmest unconcern. Perhaps the strongest feature in his character was prudence, never acting until every circumstance, every consideration, was maturely weighed; refraining if he saw a doubt, but, when once decided, going through with his purpose, whatever obstacles opposed. His integrity was most pure, his justice the most inflexible I have ever known, no motives of interest or consanguinity, of friendship or hatred, being able to bias his decision. He was, indeed, in every sense of the words, a wise, a good, and a great man. His temper was naturally irritable and high-toned; but reflection and resolution had obtained a firm and habitual ascendancy over it. If ever, however, it broke its bonds, he was most tremendous in his wrath. In his expenses he was honorable, but exact; liberal in contributions to whatever promised utility; but frowning and unyielding on all visionary projects, and all unworthy calls on his charity.

"His heart was not warm in its effecting, but he exactly calculated every man's value, and gave him a solid esteem proportioned to it. His person, you know, was fine, his stature exactly what one would wish, his deportment easy, erect and noble; the best horseman of his age, and the most graceful figure that could be seen on horseback. Although, in the circle of his friends, where he might be unreserved with safety, he took a free share in conversation, his colloquial talents were not above mediocrity, possessing neither copiousness of ideas, nor fluency of words. In public, when called on for a sudden opinion, he was unready, short, and embarrassed. Yet he wrote readily, rather diffusely, in an easy and correct style. This he had acquired by conversation with the world, for his education was merely reading, writing, and common arithmetic, to which he added surveying at a later day. His time was employed in action chiefly, reading little, and that only in agriculture and English history. His correspondence became necessarily extensive, and, with journalizing his agricultural proceedings, occupied most of his leisure hours within doors.

"On the whole, his character was, in its mass, perfect, in nothing bad, in few points indifferent; and it may truly be said, that never did nature and fortune combine more perfectly to make a great man, and to place him in the same constellation with whatever worthies have merited from man an everlasting remembrance. For his was the singular destiny and merit, of leading the armies of his country successfully through an arduous war, for the establishment of its independence; of conducting its councils through the birth of a government, new in its forms and principles, until it had settled down into a quiet and orderly train; and of scrupulously obeying the laws through the whole of his career, civil and military, of which the history of the world furnishes no other example.

"How, then, can it be perilous for you to take such a man on your shoulders? I am satisfied the great body of republicans think of him as I do. We were, indeed, dissatisfied with him on his ratification of the British treaty. But this was short-lived. We knew his honesty, the wiles with which he was encompassed, and that age had already begun to relax the firmness of his purposes; and I am convinced he is more deeply seated in the love and gratitude of the

George Washington

republicans than in the pharisaical homage of the federal monarchists. For he was no monarchist from preference of his judgment. The soundness of that gave him correct views of the rights of man, and his severe justice devoted him to them.

"He had often declared to me that he considered our new constitution as an experiment on the practicability of republican government, and with what dose of liberty man could be trusted for his own good; that he was determined the experiment should have a fair trial, and would lose the last drop of his blood in support of it. And these declarations he repeated to me the oftener and more pointedly, because he knew my suspicions of Colonel Hamilton's views, and probably had heard from him the same declarations that I had, to wit, 'that the British constitution, with its unequal representation, corruption, and other existing abuses, was the most perfect government which had ever been established on earth, and that a reformation of those abuses would make it an impracticable government.' I do believe that General Washington had not a firm confidence in the durability of our government. He was naturally distrustful of men, and inclined to gloomy apprehensions; and I was ever persuaded that a belief that we must at length end in something like a British constitution had some weight in his adoption of the ceremonies of levees, birthdays, pompous meetings with Congress, and other forms of the same character, calculated to prepare us gradually for a change which he believed possible, and to let it come on with as little shock as might be to the public mind.

"These are my opinions of General Washington, which I would vouch for at the judgment seat of God, having been formed on an acquaintance of thirty years. I served with him in the Virginia Legislature from 1769 to the Revolutionary War, and again, a short time in Congress, until he left to take command of the army. During the war and after it, we corresponded occasionally, and in the four years of my continuance in the office of secretary of state, our intercourse was daily, confidential, and cordial. After I retired from that office, great and malignant pains were taken by our federal monarchists, and not entirely without effect, to make him view me as a theorist, holding French principles of government, which would lead infallibly to licentiousness and anarchy. And to this he listened the more easily, from my known disapprobation of the British treaty. I never saw him afterward, or these malignant insinuations should have been dissipated before his just judgment, as mists before the sun. I felt on his death, with my countrymen, that 'verily a great man hath fallen this day in Israel.' [151]

"I should add that George Washington and Dr. Franklin were men of few words. I served with General Washington in the legislature of Virginia before the Revolution, and during it with Dr. Franklin in Congress. I never heard either of them speak ten minutes at a time, nor to any but the main point, which was to decide the question. They laid their shoulders to the great points, knowing that the little ones would follow of themselves."

"And," said Franklin, "Mr. Jefferson was himself a silent man except for when it was important to be heard."

"Speaking of George Washington," I said, "I recall that you were a member of Congress and in attendance in Annapolis when he resigned his commission as commander-in-chief."

Jefferson nodded. "Yes, I was a member of the committee charged with making arrangements for his stay in Annapolis when he arrived late in December 1783. The day before the resignation ceremony Congress hosted a dinner in Washington's honor at Mann's tavern for over two hundred 'distinguished guests.' After dinner glasses were raised in thirteen toasts beginning with 'to the United States,' and ending with 'to the long health and happiness of our illustrious general.'[152]

"The next morning the small gallery of the State House was jammed with people anxious to witness this historic event. As the clock struck twelve, Thomas Mifflin, President of the Continental Congress, called upon Washington to speak. Washington's hand shook as he read. Washington's address was worthy of him, and it was an 'affecting scene.'[153] When he finished reading, he reached into his pocket for the commission and handed it to President Mifflin. An historic era had ended."[154]

"Dr. Franklin, what was your opinion of George Washington?"

"I thought him a great man, and said so in a letter I sent him from France. Remembering that he too had been attacked by rivals, I told him that 'Should peace arrive after another campaign or two, and afford us a little leisure, I should be happy to see Your Excellency in Europe and to accompany you, if my age and strength would permit, in visiting some of its ancient and most famous king-

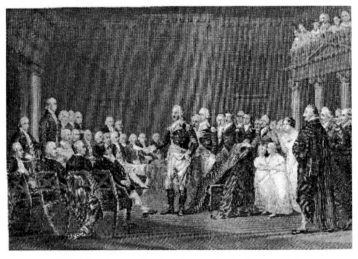

Washington resigning his commission, 1783.

doms. You would, at this side of the sea, enjoy the great reputation you have acquired, pure and free from those little shades that the jealousy and envy of a man's countrymen and contemporaries are ever endeavoring to cast upon living merit. Here you would know and enjoy what posterity will say of Washington. For a thousand leagues have nearly the same effect with a thousand years. The feeble voice of those groveling passions cannot extend so far either in time or distance. At present I enjoy that pleasure for you, as I frequently hear the old generals of this martial country (who study the maps of America and mark upon them all your operations) speak with sincere approbation and great applause of your conduct; and join in giving you the character of one of the greatest captains of the age. I must soon quit the scene, but you may live to see our country flourish, as it will amazingly and rapidly after the war is over.' [155]

"And I treasured a farewell letter I received from President Washington in September 1789. 'Would to God, my dear sir,' declared Washington, 'that I could congratulate you upon the removal of that excruciating pain under which you labor, and that your existence might close with as much ease to yourself as its continuance has been to our country and useful to mankind. If to be venerated for benevolence, if to be admired for talents, if to be esteemed for patriotism, if to be beloved for philanthropy, can gratify the human mind, you must have the pleasing consolation to know that you have not lived in vain. And I flatter myself that it will not be ranked among the least grateful occurrences of your life to be assured that, so long as I retain my memory, you will be recollected with respect, veneration, and affection by your sincere friend, George Washington.'" [156]

"What about Alexander Hamilton, Mr. Jefferson. What did you think of him?"

"Mr. Hamilton and I were at opposite ends of the political spectrum, and we were not friends. A conversation that John Adams and I had with Hamilton one evening at my house in Philadelphia highlights our differences. While John Adams was vice-president, and I secretary of state, I received a letter from President Washington, then at Mount Vernon, desiring me to call together the heads of departments, and to invite Mr. Adams to join us (which, by-the-by, was the only instance of that being done) in order to determine on some measure which required dispatch; and he desired me to act on it, as decided, without again referring to him. I invited them to dine with me, and after dinner, sitting at our wine, having settled our question, other conversation came on, in which a collision of opinion arose between Mr. Adams and Colonel Hamilton, on the merits of the British constitution, Mr. Adams giving it as his opinion, that, if some of its defects and abuses were corrected, it would be the most perfect constitution of government ever devised by man. Hamilton, on the contrary, asserted, that with its existing vices, it was the most perfect model of government that could be formed; and that the correction of its vices would render it an impracticable government. And this you may be assured was the real line of difference between the political principles of these two gentlemen. [157]

"I certainly had Colonel Hamilton in mind when I wrote to Thomas Paine that 'It is but too true that we have a sect preaching up and pouting after an English

Alexander Hamilton

constitution of king, lords and commons, and whose heads are itching for crowns, coronets and miters.' [158]

"Another incident took place on the same evening, which will further show Mr. Hamilton's political principles. The room was hung around with a collection of the portraits of remarkable men, among them were those of Bacon, Newton and Locke. Hamilton asked me who they were. I told him they were my trinity of the three greatest men the world had ever produced, naming them. He paused for some time: 'The greatest man,' said he, 'that ever lived, was Julius Caesar.' 'Mr. Adams was honest as a politician, as well as a man; Hamilton honest as a man, but, as a politician, believing in the necessity of either force or corruption to govern men.' " [159]

"On reading John Adams's diary and letters it is clear that he was not only jealous of you, Dr. Franklin, but he also didn't like you, and summed up, I suppose, in what he wrote to Benjamin Rush following your death." [160]

Franklin's eyebrows arched. He leaned forward as if in anticipation and said, "If you have it available Jack, I would like to hear what he wrote to Dr. Rush."

I removed a paper and read, "The history of our Revolution will be one continued lie from one end to the other. The essence of the whole will be *that Dr.*

Franklin's electrical rod smote the earth and out sprang General Washington. That Franklin electrified him with his rod, and thence forward these two conducted all the policy, negotiation, legislation and war.' "[161]

Grinning, Franklin looked at Jefferson. Jefferson was smiling. "Thomas, he left you out."

"How did Adams handle it when word reached Paris that Congress had dispensed with the three-man commission and elected you sole minister plenipotentiary?"

"Adams took it well. In fact, he said it was what he had recommended. Arthur Lee, however, was embittered and refused to hand over his papers to me."

"There is a sequel to Adams's gracious exit," I said. Franklin stared at me and waited. "Adams left Paris for Nantes where he was waiting to set sail for America. The ship scheduled to take him home, the *Alliance*, was reassigned to the command of John Paul Jones. As he waited for another ship, Adams convinced himself that you and Jones had conspired to delay his trip home."[162]

"Surely you are not serious," Franklin said. "I sent him a letter with a copy of Sartine's letter requesting on behalf of the king that the *Alliance* be ordered to Lorient to be joined with John Paul Jones' squadron. [163] What possible motive could I have had in keeping Adams in France?"[164]

John Paul Jones, 1781

"Here is what he confided to his diary. You be the judge. 'I am jealous that my disappointment is owing to an intrigue of Jones's. Jones, Chaumont, Franklin concerted the scheme. Chaumont applied to Mr. de Sartine for the letter. [165] If this suspicion is well founded I am to be made the sport of Jones's ambition to be made a commodore. Is it possible that I should bear this? Another suspicion is that this device was hit upon by Franklin and Chaumont to prevent me from going home, lest I should tell some dangerous truths. Perhaps, Jones's commodoreship, and my detention might both concur. Can I bear either? It is hard, very hard but I must bear everything. I may as well make virtue of necessity, for I cannot help myself.

" 'Does the old conjurer dread my voice in Congress? He has some reason for he has often heard it there, a terror to evil doers. I may be mistaken in these conjectures, they may be injurious to Jones and Franklin and therefore I shall not talk about them, but I am determined to put down my thoughts and see which turns out.

" 'It is decreed that I shall endure all sorts of mortifications. There is so much insolence, and contempt, in the appearance of this. Do I see that these people despise me, or do I see that they dread me? Can I bear contempt—to know that I am despised? It is my duty to bear everything—that I cannot help.' " [166]

John Adams. Copy of painting by or after John Singleton Copely, circa 1783.

Franklin looked at Jefferson and shook his head. I continued, "During the peace talks Adams was distrustful of both you and France. He told his diary that 'Franklin's cunning will be to divide us. To this end he will provoke, he will insinuate, he will intrigue, he will maneuver.' [167] But despite his many abrasive comments about you, Adams had some kind words too," I said.

"Such as?"

"He wrote that your 'reputation was more universal than that of Leibnitz or Newton, Frederick or Voltaire; and his character more beloved and esteemed than any or all of them. His name was familiar to government and people, to kings, courtiers, nobility, clergy, and philosophers, as well as plebeians, to such a degree that there was scarcely a peasant or a citizen, a *valet de chambre*, coachman or footman, a lady's chambermaid or a scullion in a kitchen who was not familiar with it and who did not consider him a friend to humankind. When they spoke of him they seemed to think he was to restore the golden age. His plans and his example were to abolish monarchy, aristocracy, and hierarchy throughout the world.' " [168]

"It's interesting to know that Adams had moments when he held me in such high regard," Franklin said, "but there was another side of Adams that resented my many friends, and what he called my too many frivolous pleasures. I am told that he also said: 'He loves his ease, hates to offend, and seldom gives any opinion till obliged to do it. Although he has as determined a soul as any man, yet it is his constant policy never to say yes or no decidedly but when he cannot avoid it. His rigorous taciturnity was very favorable to this singular felicity. He conversed only with individuals, and freely only with confidential friends. In company he was totally silent.'"[169]

"And from reading some of your comments about John Adams, I take it that you were not particularly fond of him," I said.

"I won't argue with you, Jack, but out of curiosity, give me a couple of examples."

"To Robert Morris you wrote, 'I hope the ravings of a certain mischievous madman here against France and its ministers, which I hear every day, will not be regarded in America.'"[170] Franklin smiled. "When you wrote Henry Laurens saying you wished he would come to Paris, you added, 'Mr. Jay will probably be gone, and I shall be left alone, or with Mr. A., and I can have no favorable opinion of what may be the offspring of a coalition between my ignorance and his positiveness.'[171]

"I know, Mr. Jefferson, that your relationship with John Adams ranged from best of friends to political enemies, but over all, what did you think of him as a man and politician?"

"He was 'vain, irritable, and a bad calculator of the force and probable effect of the motives which govern men. This is all the ill which can possibly be said of him. He was as disinterested as the being which made him. He was profound in his views and accurate in his judgment, except where knowledge of the world was necessary to form a judgment.' I told James Madison that 'he is so amiable that I pronounce you will love him, if ever you become acquainted with him. He would be, as he was, a great man in Congress.'[172] 'I can say with truth that one act of Mr. Adams's life, and only one ever gave me a moment's personal displeasure. I did consider his last appointments to office' just before I became president 'as personally unkind.'"[173]

"There was one judgment in which Adams was profoundly wrong, and we can all thank God that he was wrong," I said.

"What was that?" Franklin asked.

"About a year before the fighting started, but when it was clear to most

Americans that a break with England was going to occur, Mr. Adams entered in his diary: 'I wander alone and ponder. I muse, I mope, I ruminate. We have not men, fit for the times. We are deficient in genius, in education, in gravel, in fortune—in everything. I feel unutterable anxiety. God grant us wisdom, and fortitude.' " [174]

"Mr. Adams's anxieties were understandable in those dark times, but he had the strength to carry on as did the rest of us. And Jack, you have brought us the splendid news that our American successors in life have been able to take very good care of our country and themselves" Franklin said.

I nodded, and then said to Mr. Jefferson, "Is it true the Aaron Burr was indicted for the murder of Alexander Hamilton while still serving as vice president and president of the Senate?"

"Yes. The Grand Jury in Bergen County, New Jersey, indicted Burr for the murder of Hamilton, but that did not stop Burr from taking his seat as president of the Senate." [175]

"I realize that Aaron Burr became your vice-president by virtue of having received the second most votes for the presidency. I also understand that the two of you were never friends. But after the murder of Alexander Hamilton and your dropping him in favor of George Clinton as your second-term vice-president, he seems to have gone off the deep end. What happened?"

"I had heard rumors for some time about Burr's conspiratorial Western activities, but I needed hard evidence before moving to suppress him. In October 1806, I received a letter from General James Wilkinson, then the governor of the Louisiana Territory, setting out the details of a conspiracy that included an invasion of Mexico. [176] I convened my cabinet and advised them that the former vice president was in the West pursuing acts of a 'Catilinarian character'. His scheme was to split the nation in half by separating the Western states from the Atlantic states, and form the Western states into an independent confederacy led by him. We sent letters to the necessary authorities warning of the plot, and gunboats were sent to stop by force, if necessary, suspicious persons going down the Mississippi. A month later I issued a presidential proclamation ordering the arrest of Burr and his conspirators. [177] Burr and his brigands made it to New Orleans, but his conspiracy collapsed under the sheer weight of his lies and delusions. Crooked gun that he was, Burr ran off into the woods disguised as a riverboat captain. He was arrested near Mobile and brought to Richmond for trial." [178]

"How did you understand the Burr conspiracy to come about?"

"Burr and I were never close. Long before he murdered Hamilton, I had lost faith and respect for him. In fact, I distrusted him. [179] He knew he was not going to be my running mate when I stood for reelection in 1805. So, he ran for governor of New York with the support of some Federalists, but lost. This election defeat further embittered him toward Hamilton, and their mutual animosity led to the duel that resulted in Hamilton's death. [180] While still vice president, and under indictment for the murder of Hamilton, Burr approached Anthony Merry, the British minister at Washington, and offered to 'lend his assistance to his Majesty's government in any manner in which they may think fit to employ him.' In particular, Merry reported to his superiors that Burr had in mind a plan 'to effect a separation of the western part of the United States from that which lies between the Atlantic and the mountains, in its whole extent.'" [181]

Young Aaron Burr

"What did Burr want in return?" Franklin said.

"Money and ships to carry out his plan."

"Did the British ministry cooperate?"

"No, but Burr continued to tell anyone who would listen that the British government stood ready to back him with money and ships. I later learned that when he was told by Merry that the British government would not get involved in his harebrained scheme, he toyed with the lunacy of sneaking armed desperadoes into Washington, seizing me, plundering the treasury, stealing ships from the naval yard, and sailing off to New Orleans." [182]

"What happened to Burr after his arrest?"

"He was taken to Richmond, arraigned before Chief Justice John Marshall, and indicted for treason. General Wilkinson, the government's chief witness, was nearly indicted himself. [183] Marshall's construction of the law and instructions to the jury made conviction impossible. [184] I lost track of Burr after that, although I heard that he spent time in Europe, and it was reported that in Paris when he attempted to contact Talleyrand, Talleyrand left word that Alexander Hamilton's portrait hung over his fireplace." [185]

Petit entered the room, whispered something to Jefferson, and left. "Gentlemen," Jefferson said, "I'm advised that dinner is served."

Jefferson led the way into the dining room, a large rectangular room with three windows that looked out onto the Champs-Elysées. The windows were hung with large blue silk damask draperies. On the far wall was a fireplace, a marble mantel decorated with a series of biscuit figurines, and on each side of the fireplace a marble-topped table, one supported by a tripod with snake feet, the other by two pairs of snake feet. [186]

I was struck by a fifteen-foot dining-room table lined with fifteen chairs covered in blue silk, seven on each side of the table, and one at the far end head of the table. There were, however, only three place settings, one at the head of the table and one on each side. The table was ornamented with three lighted pairs of silver candelabra placed on flat plaques of glass with silver balustrades, and a crenellated porcelain bucket (*seau crénelé*) used for cooling wine glasses. [187]

Mr. Jefferson walked me to the head of the table. "Jack, you are our guest, so please sit here between us. Benjamin, please take the seat with a view of the Champs-Elysées." Before sitting down Jefferson slipped off his coat and handed it to Petit. A few moments later Petit returned and placed a crystal decanter containing a white wine on the table in front of Jefferson. [188] "Before the oysters are served, I thought we could continue our discussion and enjoy a dry white wine that was a favorite of mine during my years in France."

As Jefferson poured our glasses, Franklin said, "What is it?"

"What Jack requested. It is a white Burgundy from Meursault called Goutte d'Or, or drop of gold. The vineyard, only thirteen acres, was owned and operated by a family with Burgundian roots to the sixteenth century." [189]

"You'll be interested to know Mr. Jefferson that the Goutte d'Or vineyards still exist, and today Goutte d'Or has several owners, with the main exporters to the United States being Domaine des Comtes Lafon, Domaine Francois Gaunoux, Louis Latour, Louis Jadot, and Domaine Rene Manuel. Other Meursaults of equal reputation at the time you visited Burgundy were Les Perrières, Les Combettes, Les Charmes and Les Genevrières. [190] These five vineyards continue to make outstanding dry white Burgundies, and together with ten other Meursault vineyards, they enjoy *Premiers Crus* classification." [191]

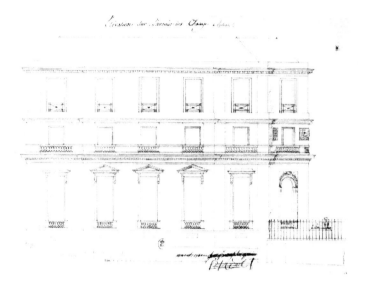

Hôtel de Langeac, south side along the Champs-Elysées.

"What does *Premiers Crus* status mean?" Franklin said.

"Perhaps it will help if I explain how Burgundy wines are classified. At the top of the heap, the most expensive and presumably the finest wines are the *Grands Crus* or 'Great Growths'. There are only thirty *Grands Crus* vineyards in the entire Côte d'Or. [192] The next category of importance is vineyards classified *Premiers Crus* or First Growths and account for about 11 percent of Burgundy's production." [193]

"Have you had a modern day Goutte d'Or, Jack? If so, how does it compare with what we are drinking?" Jefferson said.

"I have, and there is a remarkable similarity of bouquet and taste. And why not? They come from the same grape, same soil, same exposure, same climate, and essentially the same method of winemaking."

"And to ensure their authenticity," Jefferson said, "I went to the added expense of having my Burgundy wines purchased at the vineyard and bottled by Etienne Parent."

"How much extra did it cost to have the wines bottled?" I asked. "Here is an invoice from Parent for a *feuillette* of Montrachet."

"Excuse me for interrupting Mr. Jefferson, but who was Parent, and what is a *feuillette*?"

"Parent was a wine merchant and cooper who became my burgundian wine counselor and friend. He introduced me to Montrachet and Goutte d'Or. I ordered all my Burgundy wines through Parent. He would purchase the wines of the best vintages and bottle them for me. A *feuillette* was a Burgundian barrel that held about 125 bottles or 114 liters of wine." [194]

"How much more expensive was Montrachet than Goutte d'Or?"

"A *feuillette* of Montrachet generally cost about 300 livres, and a *feuillette* of Goutte d'Or 100 livres, so Montrachet was three times as expensive."

"Today," I said, "the price difference has significantly widened." Looking down the length of the table, I said, "This is one of the largest dining tables I've seen."

"When fully set, it can accommodate twenty guests at dinner," Jefferson said. "Jack, you mentioned that many of the wines that Dr. Franklin and I enjoyed are still available in 2005, more than two hundred years after we both left France and returned to America. We would be interested to know what wines have proved their worth over two centuries, and are available in the United States."

"Virtually all the wines you favored are available in the United States. Let's start with the first vineyards you visited in Burgundy on your trip through southern France. You rated Chambertin, Clos de Vougeot, and Vosne the best red Burgundies. They are still wines of great distinction. With respect to VosneRomanée, you did not designate the order of rank, but one did exist: Romanée-Conti, La Tâche, Richebourg, and Romanée-St-Vivant, in that order."

"I considered Volnay the equal in flavor to Chambertin but relegated it to fourth place because it was lighter in body, lacked longevity, and did not bear transportation as well. I noted, however, that it had two distinct advantages over the wines of Chambertin and Clos de Vougeot; it cost only one-quarter as much, and it was ready to drink after one year."

"Unfortunately," I said "you never identified a particular vineyard from which you purchased your Volnay wines, but vineyards of special recognition then and now are Cailleret and Champans, with most of the Volnay vineyards still producing quality wines. Parent once sent you a Pommard instead of Volnay, from the vineyard of Clos de la Commeraine. All of these vineyards still exist and produce quality wines.

"You called Montrachet the best white wine of Burgundy, and your favorite table dry white of Burgundy was from the little village of Meursault, Goutte d'Or. As we discussed earlier, both Montrachet and Goutte d'Or still produce outstanding wines.

"From Burgundy you traveled through the Rhône Valley, and your first visit was to the vineyards of Côte Rôtie. You recognized the red wines of Côte Rôtie for their color, strength, bouquet, taste, and ability to age, but made the comment that they were not yet of such high estimation as to be found commonly at the good tables of Paris. Well, that has changed. The wines of Côte Rôtie are available throughout the United States and are of consistent high quality. The wines of producers such as Guigal and Jasmin receive not only the recognition and respect that has been traditionally reserved for the *Grands Crus* Burgundies and Bordeaux, but also the prices that go with greatness. [195]

"You called Château Grillet the best white wine of the northern Rhône. Grillet still exists and has the distinction of being the smallest vineyard in France with its own Appellation Contrôlée, consisting of about eight and a half acres."

"Does it still produce good-quality wines?" Jefferson asked.

"Yes, but some wine connoisseurs say it has slipped from the pinnacle of 'best' white wine of the northern Rhône. Although you did not single out the red wines of Hermitage for special praise, you did acknowledge their high quality. You listed the owners of the best vineyards, and the great red Hemitages of today come from those same vineyards. Like Côte Rôties, red Hermitages are very fashionable today and, I might add, very expensive. You so esteemed the silky white Hermitage marked with a touch of sweetness, you called it the 'first wine in the world without exception.' " [196]

"My white Hermitage came from the House of Jourdan," Jefferson said. "But by the term 'silky' I did not mean 'sweet,' but 'sweetness in the smallest degree only.' " [197]

"The Jourdan vineyards are still with us but not under the name of Jourdan. They were inherited by the Monier family, who, because of their ancestry, revived the name Chastaing de la Sizeranne. The Jourdan vineyards now belong to the house of M. Chapoutier, who calls his red Hermitage La Sizeranne. Chapoutier's popular white Hermitage is Chante-Alouette (Lark's Song). Chapoutier also produces a superb white Hermitage called 'Ermitage De L'Orée,' limited to 300 or 400 cases per year. It is one of the best dry white wines I've ever drunk, and worthy of the high esteem you accorded white Hermitage." [198]

Petit was standing inconspicuously at the end of the room behind me, and moved forward when Jefferson beckoned him with the wave of his hand. "Petit, please bring us a bottle of Monsieur Jourdan's white Hermitage."

"Since both of you were Bordeaux wine drinkers, you will be interested to know that 68 years after your visit there, Mr. Jefferson, the wines of Médoc were classified according to quality as First, Second, Third, Fourth and Fifth Growths. The same four vineyards that you named the 'best' were the only wines designated First Growths in that classification and retain that distinction today. The other twelve wines you named for special distinction were all included in the classification."

"How did this classification come about?" Franklin asked.

"In 1855 the Exposition Universelle was held in Paris, and at the request of the French authorities, a group of Bordeaux wine merchants prepared and submitted a list of the leading wines of Bordeaux. Of the more than one thousand vineyards considered, all 61 of the red wines listed, except for Château Haut Brion from Graves, were from the Médoc, and all of the 23 white wines listed were sweet and from Sauternes and its surrounding communes. This classification or ranking was based primarily on the prices the wines had sold at over many years.

"The 61 red wines were divided into five groups: First Growths (four châteaux); Second Growths (15 châteaux); Third Growths (14 châteaux); Fourth Growths (10 châteaux); and Fifth Growths (18 châteaux). Sauternes and its surrounding communes were classified in three categories. Château d'Yquem, your favorite Sauternes, Mr. Jefferson, was classified a Great First Growth to distinguish it from its competitors. Thereafter, 11 châteaux were ranked as First Growths, and 12 châteaux as Second Growths."

"What about the sweet white wines of Frontignan, and the sweet white wines of Muscat de Rivesaltes? Are they still produced and available?" Jefferson asked.

"Wines from Frontignan are not popular today, and probably not as good as they were when you drank them at dinner at Monsieur Lambert's house. [199] The same can be said for Muscat de Rivesaltes. Both wine varieties can be found in limited quantities in major American markets."

"I became acquainted with the wines of Limoux when I traveled through Languedoc along the Canal-du-Midi, and I imported them during my retirement years. The Limoux vineyards produced sweet and sparkling wines. The best known wine was Blanquette de Limoux. Its name came from the grape from which it was made. It was a pale, sweet, white sparkling wine that lost its sweetness with age. Not an enthusiast of sparkling wines, I ordered my Limoux *non-mousseaux*."

"Blanquette de Limoux is still produced from vineyards around the town of Limoux near Carcassonne," I said. "The best wines of Limoux are white, a still wine and two sparkling wines, Blanquette de Limoux and Vin de Blanquette.

"During your visit to Bordeaux you became acquainted with a dry white Graves called Château Carbonnieux; it is still popular. The story is told of a Turkish sultan who, because of his religion, did not drink alcoholic beverages, but imported Carbonnieux, thinking it spring water. After consuming a bottle, he remarked, 'French water is so delicious, why do the French bother to make wine?'"

Franklin and Jefferson laughed.

"In your travels through the German vineyards you singled out for praise Mosel wines from the vineyards of Brauneberg, Wehlen, Grach, Piesport, Zelting and Bernkastel. These vineyards still produce outstanding wines. The same is true for the Rheingau wines you especially enjoyed from Schloss Johannisberg, Rüdesheim and Hochheim."

"I was quite fond of a red wine from the hills around Nice. It was made by a vintner named Sasserno," Jefferson said. "Is Sasserno's wine available in the United States?"

"Sasserno's red wine came from the vineyards of Bellet near Nice, and to-day red, white, and rosé wines are made from those vineyards and exported to the United States. They aren't easy to find, but they can be found in a few top-end wine shops in New York and Washington, and other major cities.

"When you visited Turin you tasted a wine that you called 'Nebiule.' It was the precursor of today's Nebbiolo grape that makes some of Italy's best wines: Barolo, Barbaresco, Gattinara and Ghemme. You found the 'Nebiule' wine singular, melding three contradictory characteristics."

Turin

"As I recall," Jefferson said, "it was 'about as sweet as the silky Madeira, as astringent on the palate as Bordeaux, and as brisk as Champagne.' And I thought it a pleasing wine."

"It has undergone a complete transformation, producing today big, fullbodied, dry, mouth-puckering red wines."

"What has caused the difference in taste?" Franklin asked.

"The method of making these red wines has changed radically. Throughout the eighteenth century, and well into the nineteenth century, fermentation was never allowed to finish, leaving the wine sweet and often unstable. It was not until the 1840s that the big, dry wines we know today as Barolos and Barbarescos emerged. The incomplete fermentation left them slightly fizzy which probably explains Mr. Jefferson's 'brisk as Champagne' comment. [200]

"From Tuscany you imported Montepulciano, Chianti, Carmignano, Artimino and Pomino. All of these vineyard areas still produce wines, many of which are outstanding.

"At one time during your presidency you became enamored with dry pale sherry saying 'that if I should fail in the means of getting it, it will be a privation which I shall feel sensibly once a day.' Dry pale sherry is a popular wine today, along with a variety of other sherries that cover the taste spectrum from bonedry to very sweet.

"Your choice in Madeira was 'of the nut quality and of the very best.' Madeira

Artimino

is still with us, but its quality is not what it used to be, and its production has skidded dramatically."

"The great vineyards of our time seem to have survived very well," Franklin said.

"Very well indeed," I said, "but many new great wine regions have developed since your time. One could say that we are living in the golden age of wine-making,"

"Where are these new wine regions?" Franklin asked.

"In the United States, California, on the West Coast, is the leading producer of wine, and many of its wines have gained world recognition. In fact, an English wine merchant living in Paris was the catalyst behind the wine explosion of California wines onto the world wine scene."

"How did it happen?" Franklin said.

"The merchant operated a wine shop and wine school in Paris. After a trip to the California wine country, he organized a blind tasting of French and California wines, and invited nine French wine experts to serve as the judges. Six California Chardonnays were pitted against four white Burgundies, and six California Cabernet Sauvignons against four classified red Bordeaux. When the identity of the wines was revealed, the French experts learned to their consternation that the wine they thought the best red was a 1973 Stags Leap Wine Cellars from Napa Valley. They had preferred it over such Bordeaux icons as 1970 Mouton Rothschild and 1970 Haut Brion. [201]

"The experts' preference in white wines also was strongly California. Here, not only was first place awarded to 1973 Château Montelena, but the judges' third and fourth place selections were also California Chardonnays. *Time* magazine's Paris correspondent attended the tasting and posted the results in an article titled 'Judgment of Paris.' The tasting results astonished the world and transformed the California wine industry." [202]

"A marvelous story," Franklin said, striking his fist on the table.

"And you, Mr. Jefferson, predicted that result over two hundred years ago," I said.

"I did? Refresh my recollection, Jack."

"You said, 'We could in the United States make as great a variety of wines as are made in Europe, not exactly the same kinds, but doubtless as good.'

"High-quality wines are produced in the states of Oregon and Washington, both located on the west coast north of California. You will recall, Mr. Jefferson, that in the spring of 1791 you and James Madison took a vacation trip to up-state New York and parts of New England."

"I remember it well."

"On your return you left Guilford, Connecticut, and sailed the Sound for Long Island. You landed in the morning on the northeastern tip of Long Island at Oyster Pond Point, now Orient Point. Your journey from Greenport to Palmer, a distance of about twenty miles, took you through a countryside that today is planted in vines and produces many excellent wines. [203]

"All fifty states in the union now produce wine, and many fine wines are made throughout the United States. Outside the United States many great wines are produced in what is referred to as New World countries such as Australia, South Africa, New Zealand, and in Chile and Argentina in South America."

"Very interesting," Jefferson said. The conversation ceased as we savored our wines.

James Madison

I motioned to the figurines lining the mantel. "Those figurines all seem to feature Cupid, and I think I can identify two of them."

Franklin turned so he could see them. "Which two?"

"The one on the left appears to be Diana with Cupid, and next to it, Venus with Cupid."

"That's correct," Jefferson said. "The other two are Apollo with Cupid and Hope with Cupid. Often the figurines decorate the dining table, but when ladies dine, I never allow Venus to be placed on the table in competition with the lady guests." [204]

Petit entered carrying three glass platters, each containing a dozen oysters on the half shell. He placed them in front of us. I lifted an oyster with the small fork that had been provided. It was crisp and meaty with a sweet taste and slightly nutty aftertaste. "They're delicious," I said.

"Thank you," Jefferson said. "They are from Normandy, a region of France that I feel has the best oysters. I love oysters, and when accompanied by a fine dry Burgundy such as this Goutte d'Or, they are the perfect first course to an elegant dinner." [205]

Franklin twirled the wine glass beneath his nose. "The wine has a lovely bouquet—scents of oatmeal and pears."

"And tastes even richer with the oysters," I said.

Petit returned with a decanter of wine and three wine glasses. Jefferson poured the new wine and handed a glass each to Dr. Franklin and me. "This is the Jourdan white Hermitage. Let's compare the two wines."

I swirled the Hermitage and smelled the bouquet, the scent of apricots, I thought. I took a sip, and let the wine cover my palate before swallowing. I looked up at Jefferson, and he said, "What do you think, Jack? Do you like it?"

"I like it very much. On the nose it has the suggestion of apricots. It is full-bodied, with an almost exotic taste, rich and nutty with a subtle apricot edge, and though not sweet, with a touch or hint of sweetness. It is remarkably similar in taste and style to the Chapoutier Ermitage De L'Orée that I mentioned earlier."

Franklin tasted both wines. "I agree with Jack's description of the Hermitage with one addition: I get a wisp of lemon on the bouquet."

"In your opinion, Jack, which wine goes best with the oysters?" Jefferson asked.

I ate another oyster and sipped both wines. "The Meursault, because it is drier, a bit more acidic, and has a mineral quality on the taste that marries especially well with the salty-earthy taste of the oysters."

"But as good as the wines and oysters are, don't let them stand in the way of your questions Jack, and we won't let them get in the way of our answers," Franklin said.

"By all means, let the conversation continue," Jefferson said, as he lifted an oyster into his mouth.

"Did you ever envision that wines of the quality of this Goutte d'Or could be made in America, Mr. Jefferson?"

"I envisioned the production of high-quality wine in America, especially in Virginia, and I thought Philip Mazzei, who showed up at Monticello in November 1773, the embodiment of that vision."

"Wait a minute," Franklin interjected. "I remember Mazzei. I first met him when he called on me in London. He introduced himself, told me that the grand duke of Tuscany had ordered two of my stoves, but he didn't know where to buy them. I didn't either, but he persuaded me to help him find them. We were not successful, but we did locate some similar stoves, and I instructed the workmen on how to make two stoves according to my design. It was through me that Mazzei met Thomas Adams, a Virginia merchant living in London. As I recall, a Mrs. Norton gave an annual Christmas dinner for Virginians living in London, and Adams introduced Mazzei to his circle of friends. [206] It was through the urgings of Adams and me that Mazzei eventually decided to come to America."

"Mazzei devised an elaborate plan," Jefferson said, "to produce wine, oil and silk in Virginia, but he had trouble getting financial backing in London. Thomas Adams became Mazzei's advisor and arranged a grant for him of some five thousand acres from the Virginia Assembly. [207] But when Mazzei arrived in Virginia, he found the land offer unacceptable because it was divided into many parcels and separated by great distances. Adams, who was building a home in Augusta County, about 160 miles northwest of Williamsburg, offered to sell Mazzei land adjoining his estate, and Mazzei set out with Adams to examine the property. Monticello being on their way, they stopped to visit me, arriving late at night. Early the next morning Mazzei and I went for a walk, and Mazzei found the vineyard land he had been looking for, a four hundred acre tract adjoining Monticello to the east. He named it 'Colle.' The land had a 'southeast aspect and an abundance of lean and meager spots of stony and red soil, without sand, resembling extremely the Côte of Burgundy from Chambertin to Montrachet where the famous wines of Burgundy are made.' [208] I thought that Mazzei was right in preferring the southeastern face of this ridge of mountains. Our morning stroll along Monticello's hillsides sparked a lifetime friendship between us and caused me to become a partner in Mazzei's vineyard project."

"Yes," I said, "I remember reading in Mazzei's autobiography that, by the time the two of you returned to Monticello, everyone was up. Adams looked at you and said: 'I see by your expression that you've taken him away from me. I knew you would do that.' You smiled, and without looking at him, said, 'Let's have breakfast first and then we'll see what we can do.'" [209]

"I don't recall whether it was on that morning walk or later that I learned that Mazzei had grown up in a mountain village in Tuscany. As a young man he studied medicine at the Santa Maria Nuova Hospital in Florence, but was dismissed for drinking wine before taking communion on Holy Thursday.

Undeterred, he went to Leghorn and established a successful medical practice. But ever restless, Mazzei left Italy for Smyrna, Turkey, where he continued the practice of medicine for two and a half years. Bored with life in Smyrna, and armed with a supply of Turkish opium and a few other local products, Mazzei sailed for England in December 1755. In London he sold his Turkish goods for a sizable profit, rejected offers to resume his medical practice, and made a living giving Italian language lessons to the British gentry. The profits from the sale of the Turkish goods gave him the idea of opening a shop specializing in wines, silks, olive oil, anchovies, Parmesan cheese, and other Italian products that were virtually impossible to buy in London.

"Mazzei told me that his Virginia vineyard plans called for planting ten thousand vines from France, Italy, Sicily, Spain, and Portugal, planting about four thousand olive trees from places where the best oil was made, and a sufficient quantity of silk worm eggs from Italy and Sicily to make silk. So far as I know, Mazzei's experiment was the first commercial venture to grow grapes and make wine in America, and I was enthusiastic about it. I envisioned for the first time the production of high-quality wine in America, especially in Virginia. But Mazzei needed more than land; he needed money, and a partnership evolved." [210]

"Who became partners, and what did it cost?" I asked.

The Port of Leghorn

70

"A share was set at fifty pounds sterling, and Mazzei's viticulture experiment captured the imagination of such prominent Virginians as George Washington, George Mason, Governor Earl Dunmore, Thomas Randolph, Thomas Adams, Washington's stepson John Park Custis, and me. I later acquired a second share by buying the interest of Thomas Randolph. Mazzei was given four shares and the right to use for his household such necessaries as he raised."

"Was Mazzei's venture successful?"

"No. Unfortunately, the war intervened, and Mazzei's vineyard was disbanded when he went to Europe as a financial agent for Virginia. Before leaving he rented Colle to the German general. Riedesel's horses destroyed in one week the whole labor of three or four years." [211]

"I have heard another explanation for why Mazzei's experiment failed," I said.

"What is that?"

"An Englishman by the name of Isaac Weld visited Colle after it was disbanded and said that the experiment failed because 'the vines which the Italians found growing there were different, as well as the soil, from what they had been in the habit of cultivating, and they were not much more successful in the business than the people of the country.' [212] Weld went on to predict that 'We must not, however, from hence conclude that good wine can never be manufactured upon these mountains. It is well known that the vines, and the mode of cultivating them, vary as much in different parts of Europe as the soil in one country differs from that in another. It will require some time, therefore, and different experiments, to ascertain the particular kind of vine, and the mode of cultivating it, best adapted to the soil of these mountains.' And today, Mr. Jefferson, winemaking in Virginia flourishes with nearly one hundred wineries producing quality wines made from *Vitis vinifera* grapes, Cabernet Sauvignon, Merlot, Chardonnay, Sauvignon Blanc, Riesling, and others. You would be proud of the support your native state has given to these modern-day Philip Mazzeis. If you were to set out today from Monticello to Washington, you could drink along the way a variety of fine Virginia wines at wineries, restaurants, hotels, and inns."

"I am delighted to hear that, but it doesn't surprise me. I recall that about two years after I left the presidency, a young man by the name of John Dorti visited me a Monticello and said he was interested in starting a vineyard. He wanted to know what I thought were the prospects for growing grapes and making good wine in Virginia. I told him that it was desirable that wine

71

should be made in Virginia, because we had every soil, aspect and climate of the best wine countries, and I myself had drunk wines made in Virginia and Maryland of the quality of the best Burgundy." [213]

"What is the situation with wine production in my state, Pennsylvania, today?" Franklin asked.

"You would be proud of Pennsylvania's wine progress, Dr. Franklin. There are nearly ninety wineries spread across the state producing a wide variety of wines from *Vitis vinifera*, hybrid, and American grapes.

"You mentioned, Dr. Franklin, that shortly after your secret meetings with Lord Howe in London you realized that it was time to go home. When did you leave, and how were you greeted on your return?"

"I left London in March and arrived in America in early May, unaware of the fighting that had occurred at Lexington and Concord. I was greeted warmly by my fellow Philadelphians, and the next morning I was chosen by the Assembly to be one of Pennsylvania's delegates to the Second Continental Congress, which was to meet in Philadelphia in four days. I soon met with my son, William, the royal governor of New Jersey, and my friend Joseph Galloway. We talked and drank till late. I told them I was for independence, and tried to persuade William to resign as governor, and Galloway to sit in the Continental Congress to which he had been nominated. Both refused. Their refusal to join in the fight for independence was a bitter personal disappointment." [214]

"What congressional duties were you assigned?" I said.

"Oh, let me think," Franklin said, putting his right hand on his forehead. "I was made chairman of a committee to establish a postal system and made postmaster general. I was also assigned to committees to promote the manufacture of saltpeter for gunpowder, to arrange the printing of paper money, and to write the declaration by Washington on taking command. [215] The Pennsylvania Assembly appointed me president of the Committee of Safety. I was never so busy. From six to nine in the morning, I was at the Committee of Safety and thereafter in Congress till after four in the afternoon. Soon I was appointed to a congressional committee to devise ways and means to protect colonial trade, and to a committee on Indian affairs. Perhaps the most important committee on which I served was the Committee of Secret Correspondence, the first on foreign affairs with the purpose of seeking foreign support for the war." [216]

"The precursor of what became known as the Department of State," I said.

"Yes, and Jefferson was our first secretary of state," Franklin said with a flourish, holding his glass out in the gesture of a toast.

Franklin returns home.

Then Franklin continued to describe his congressional duties. "The most laborious and debilitating committee on which I served was my appointment, along with three men from Maryland: Samuel Chase, Charles Carroll of Carrollton, and John Carroll, a Jesuit priest, to go to Canada to win Canadian support for the Colonies. Before we reached Canada, I was exhausted. We were detained by the condition of the lakes in which the unthawed ice obstructed navigation, and I developed a fatigue that I thought at my time of life might prove too much for me. At one point, we covered only seven miles in four hours of rowing up the Hudson. When we arrived in Canada, I was suffering from boils and a swelling of my legs that I thought was dropsy. The general attitude toward our mission was hostile, and with news of the arrival of British reinforcements by sea at Quebec, it was clear that we could expect no Canadian help, and John Carroll and I left for home. The journey wore me out. Back in Philadelphia, I slowly recovered, but a recurrence of the gout kept me from Congress for some weeks, and I wrote to General Washington that I knew little of what had passed in Congress since he had left us except that a declaration of independence was being prepared." [217]

"Why did the Second Continental Congress appoint the two of you and John Adams, Roger Sherman and Robert Livingston to draft the Declaration of Independence?"

"Jefferson and I were on so many committees it is impossible to know the criteria for our appointments," Franklin said.

"One of Mr. Jefferson's biographers has him serving on thirty-four during the 1775–1776 sessions," I said. [218]

"I knew it was a great many, but I didn't know it was that many." Franklin continued, "So I don't know the precise thinking of Congress on our selection as the committee members for the drafting the Declaration of Independence. Perhaps Congress thought that between the five of us we had enough literary background to get the job done. But it didn't take five. We met and assigned the task to Thomas, and he got it done in about seventeen days."

"Were there any doubts among your committee members about declaring independence?" I asked.

"No! John Adams supported the Declaration of Independence with zeal and ability, fighting fearlessly for every word of it. No man's confident and fervent addresses more than Mr. Adams's encouraged and supported us through the difficulties we faced." Jefferson said.

"What difficulties?" I asked.

"There were many excellent persons who opposed it on doubts of whether we were provided sufficiently with the means of supporting it, and whether the minds of our constituents were yet prepared to receive it, but who, after it was decided, united zealously behind it." [219]

"According to John Adams's recollection," I said, "when you learned that you were to write it, you asked Adams to write it. He declined. When you asked him why, he said simply, 'Reasons enough.' And you said, 'What can be your reasons?'

"Adams claims he replied, 'Reason 1st. You are a Virginian, and a Virginian should appear at the head of this business. Reason 2nd. I am obnoxious, suspected, and unpopular. You are very much otherwise. Reason 3rd. You can write ten times better than I can.'" [220]

"I have no recollection of that conversation. When asked to write it, I wrote it. [221] When I finished the first draft, and made some changes suggested by John Adams, I sent it to Dr. Franklin with a note. 'Will Dr. Franklin be so good as to peruse it, and suggest alterations as his more enlarged view on the subject will dictate?'"

"I made a few minor changes," Franklin said.

"Small but resounding," Jefferson said. "He crossed out the last three words of the phrase 'We hold these truths to be sacred and undeniable' and added,

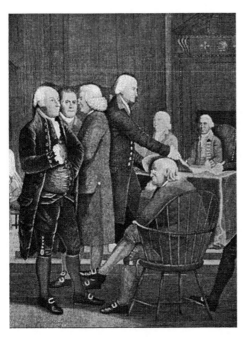

Jefferson submitting draft to Continental Congress. Edward Savage's engraving based on Robert Edge Pine's painting.

'We hold these truths to be self-evident.' [222]

"On July 2, 1776, Congress voted for independence, and then spent the next two days going over my draft line by line. Dr. Franklin perceived that I was not insensible to their mutilations, and to relieve my concerns he told a story of a friend who put a sign outside his shop: 'JOHN THOMPSON, HATTER, MAKES AND SELLS HATS FOR READY MONEY' with a picture of a hat subjoined. Thompson showed the sign to some friends and asked for their suggestions. The first he showed it to thought the word 'Hatter' unnecessary because the words 'makes hats' showed he was a hatter. It was struck out. The next friend observed that the word 'makes' should be omitted because customers would not care who made the hats. He struck it out. Another said the words 'for ready money' were useless, for how else would he sell them, and they were dropped. The inscription now stood, 'John Thompson sells hats.' 'Sells hats!' said another friend; why, nobody will expect you to give them away. What then is the use of the word 'sells'? It was stricken, and 'hats' too was dropped because there was one painted on the board. So the inscription was reduced to 'John Thompson,' with the picture of a hat." [223]

"I know you were angered by the 'mutilations' to your draft, but historians seem generally in agreement that Congress's emendations improved the document," I said. [224]

"I wonder," Jefferson said, "if these same scholars discuss that a major deletion was my indictment of the king for his refusal to end the slave trade?"

"It is generally noted that this passage was cut at the insistence of Georgia and South Carolina." [225]

"Yes, and our northern brethren also, I believe, felt a little tender under these censures; for though their people had very few slaves themselves, yet they had been pretty considerable carriers of them to others." [226]

"The Declaration of Independence was approved by Congress on July 4, 1776, and publicly read on July 8," I said. [227]

"I remember the official signing of the parchment copy on August 2," Franklin said. "John Hancock, then the president of the Congress, after writing his name in large letters said, 'There must be no pulling different ways. We must all hang together.' And I replied, 'Yes, we must, indeed, all hang together, or most assuredly we shall all hang separately.' " [228]

"The Preamble is the section of the Declaration of Independence best remembered today," I said.

"What I tried to do in the Preamble was to sum up the philosophy behind the American Revolution—the vindication of the rights of man, and the need for a new political system. The opening words 'When in the course of human events' places it in a universal historical perspective for humanity everywhere and in every era. It places our new and independent nation 'among the powers of the earth.' Its principles or 'self-evident truths' are:

That all men are created equal;

That they are endowed with unalienable rights;

That these rights include life, liberty, and the pursuit of happiness;

That it is to secure these rights that government is instituted among men;

That governments so instituted derive their powers from the consent of the governed;

That when a government becomes destructive of these ends, men may alter or abolish it; and

That men have the right, then, to institute new governments designed to effect their safety and happiness." [229]

"When you set out the 'self-evident truths' the first was 'That all men are created equal.' What did you mean by 'created equal'?"

"I meant it in the literal sense that a child is born equal in the eyes of nature and God. All subsequent inequalities of color, religion, creed, race, sex, class, wealth, and opportunity derive from society, government or law. Nature did not decree inequality between whites and blacks." [230]

"Something else happened on July 4, 1776. It didn't have any immediate public impact but it was interesting. Do you remember, Thomas?" Franklin said.

"I do. John Adams, you, and I were appointed as a committee to devise a seal of the United States. We recommended a design by Pierre Eugene du Simitière, a Swiss artist then living in Philadelphia. And I loved your motto:

'Rebellion to tyrants is obedience to God.'"[231]

"Declaring independence when you did was a gutsy move," I said. "From my reading of history, the war did not go well for us in the beginning. Washington was defeated on Long Island and only with luck got his army back to Manhattan."

"You are quite right," Franklin said. "The Howes, instead of attacking, made a conciliatory gesture by sending word that Lord Richard Howe would like to meet privately with some members of Congress to see if a settlement could be worked out. Congress appointed John Adams, Edward Rutledge and me to meet with Howe. Since I knew Lord Howe, I wrote him to advise that our committee would meet with him. He chose to meet with us on Staten Island, and offered to send a boat to ferry us over under a flag of truce.

"On the way from Philadelphia, we stopped in New Brunswick for the night. The inn was so crowded that Adams and I had to share a bed in a small room with one window. The window was open and Adams, afraid of the night air, shut it. 'Oh,' I said, 'don't shut the window. We will be suffocated.' Adams said he was afraid of the evening air. I said, 'The air within the chamber will soon be, and indeed is now, worse than the outside air. Come, open the window and come to bed, and I will convince you. I believe you are not acquainted with my theory of colds.' Adams, curious about my theory, which he thought a paradox, opened the window and risked the cold. But he fell asleep while I was explaining it."[232]

"Did you meet with Admiral Howe?" I said.

"Yes. The admiral's barge met us along with an officer who was sent as a hostage to guarantee our safe return. We thought this a childish gesture and took the officer back with us. Pleased to see the return of his officer, Lord Howe greeted me cordially, and I introduced Adams and Rutledge. Inside the house, in a room Adams thought 'not only wholesome but romantically elegant,' we dined on cold ham, tongue, mutton, bread, and good claret. Our meeting with Howe, including dinner, lasted three hours. Howe's secretary, Henry Strachey, took notes.

"Howe was a gentleman and a friend of mine, and he explained to Adams and Rutledge, as he had to me in England, his great affection for America. He said he felt for America as a brother, and if America should fall, he would lament it like the loss of a brother."

"Dr. Franklin," I said, interrupting, "would you like to hear how John Adams recorded your reply to Lord Howe's comment?"

Franklin's features formed a quizzical look that was immediately replaced with a soft smile. "Yes, I would very much like to hear what Adams said."

Meeting between Lord Howe and committee of Congress.

"Dr. Franklin with an easy air and a collected countenance, a bow, a smile and all that naiveté which sometimes appeared in his conversation and is often observed in his writings, replied, 'My Lord, we will do our utmost endeavors to save Your Lordship that mortification.'"

Pleased with Adams's comment, Franklin continued, "The long and short of our meeting was that Howe could talk to us only as individuals and not as members of Congress, because the king did not recognize the legitimacy of Congress. I told him that it was not necessary to distinguish between Congress and individuals, and that our conversation should be held as among friends. Howe explained that the king's 'most earnest desire was to make his American subjects happy, to cause a reform in whatever affected the freedom of their legislation, and to concur with his Parliament in the redress of any real grievances.'

"Adams told Howe that Congress had declared for independence at the instruction of all the colonies, and that we had no power to treat with him except as a Congress. Rutledge made it equally clear that our independence was not a negotiable issue stating that South Carolina would not become a colony again even if Congress desired it.

"Howe repeated that he had no authority whatever, nor did he expect that he would ever have, to treat with the colonies as independent states. Clear that the issue of independence could not be resolved, Lord Howe said he was sorry that we had had the trouble of coming so far for so little purpose. Our meeting adjourned with both sides knowing there was nothing to do but resume hostilities."

"Didn't the meeting with Lord Howe whet your appetite for peace negotiations with England?" I said to Franklin.

"In what way?"

"Shortly after your meeting with Lord Howe, didn't you outline plans for peace that might be negotiated with England and suggest that such negotiations would 'furnish a presence for BF's going to England where he has many friends and acquaintances, particularly among the best writers and ablest speakers in both Houses of Parliament?' And if the negotiations failed, you would still be influential enough 'to work up such a division of sentiments in the nation as greatly to weaken its exertions against the United States and lessen its credit in foreign countries.' "[233]

"That's true. But the cornerstone of my plan remained unconditional independence, and the reason I thought the timing right was that it might force France into signing an alliance with us. As it turned out, my plan became moot when in October Congress appointed Silas Deane, Arthur Lee, and me commissioners to France to obtain money, arms and an alliance."[234]

I turned to Jefferson. "Didn't Congress also appoint you to that commission?"

"Yes. I received notice from John Hancock that I had been appointed a commissioner to France to serve with Dr. Franklin and Silas Deane. I had told Dr. Franklin that I would like to go with him, but circumstances of my wife's health caused me to decline.[235]

"I remained proud of every member of Congress who signed the Declaration of Independence. I remember at the age of 73, after the death of Benjamin Rush, reminiscing to John Adams about those of us who still remained. 'Another of our friends of Seventy-Six is gone, my dear sir, another of the co-signers of the Independence of our country. And a better man than Dr. Benjamin Rush could not have left us, more benevolent, more learned, of finer genius, or more honest. We too must go; and that ere long. I believe we are under half a dozen at present; I mean the signers of the Declaration. Yourself, Gerry, Carroll, and myself, are all I know to be living. I am the only one south of the Potomac. Is Robert Treat Paine, or Floyd living? It is long since I heard of them, and yet I do not recollect to have heard of their deaths.' "[236]

As if he had been dropped on a string, Petit appeared with three wine glasses and a decanter of white wine that he placed in front of Jefferson. Jefferson looked up at Petit and said, "Le Montrachet?" Petit nodded, turned and left.

Jefferson handed us each a glass and poured the wine. Dutifully we swirled our glasses and took in the wine's bouquet. We then sipped the wine and allowed it to pour over our palates before swallowing. "Like the Goutte d'Or, this is also of the 1784 vintage, a particularly great vintage throughout France." Jefferson took another sip and said, "Well, Jack, as our twenty-first-century wine connoisseur, what is your opinion of this wine?"

"As fine a wine as the Goutte d'Or was, I like this wine even better."

"Why?" Franklin asked.

"It has an exotic, forthcoming bouquet of hazelnuts. On the palate it is fullbodied with balanced acidity, and a rich taste of spicy fruit that carries through on the aftertaste. It has a distinction that words can't do justice to."

"I agree," Franklin said. "It is a wine of breed and quality that has to be experienced to be fully appreciated. Thank you, Thomas, for sharing this wine with us."

Petit served the spaghetti course. Franklin was the first to comment. "This macaroni dish complements the Montrachet."

"They are perfect together" I added. Watching Dr. Franklin enjoy his wine prompted my next question. "I suppose, Dr. Franklin, that your enjoyment of wine developed during your eight and a half years in France."

"French wines, yes, but I had been a wine enthusiast long before my years in France. When I lived in Philadelphia my drinking was confined pretty much to rum punch and Madeira. [237] During my adult years in England, the range was a bit wider. At club gatherings wine, often claret, punch, porter and beer were usually available. Some of the best claret I drank was during my visits to Scotland at friends' dinner parties. In London I bought wine from a local wine merchant, and from a Burgundian winemaker with the unlikely name of Thomas O'Gorman. O'Gorman sent me a hogshead of wine of what he called 'the right sort for you.' [238] I even received wine from home. A Pennsylvania vintner by the name of Thomas Livezey sent me wine made from 'some small wild grapes.' [239] I told Livezey that his wine was excellent and that I was applying the wine 'towards winning the hearts of the friends of our country.' My wine merchant was very desirous of knowing what quantity of it might be had and at what price. [240]

"During my years in France, I purchased most of my Bordeaux wines through John Bondfield, the American Consul in Bordeaux, and from V. & P. French & Nephew. Most of my Burgundies came from Saussett and Masson, and Thomas O'Gorman. On one occasion, O'Gorman sent me seven *feuillettes* of his wine, six red and one white, of the 1775 vintage. [241] I recall Bondfield shipping me two hogsheads of Médoc wines for inspection with the promise of two more if the wine met my approval. [242] From V. & P. French & Nephew in Bordeaux, Temple ordered for my account four hundred and eighty bottles of the best claret fit for immediate consumption. This wine was represented to be better than any claret they had previously sent me." [243]

"If I remember correctly, a *feuillette* contained 125 bottles," I said.

"That's correct," Franklin said.

"Mr. Jefferson said that your wine cellar contained more than 1100 bottles."

"That's a fair estimate," Franklin said. "Here is a copy of my wine cellar inventory of February 1779." [244]

I studied it. "If my arithmetic is correct it totals 1132 bottles of Champagne, Burgundy, Bordeaux and sherry wines, plus one piece of red Bordeaux and two pieces of *vin ordinaire*. What was…"

"A piece was a wooden barrel that held the equivalent of 250 bottles," Franklin said. [245] Franklin took a sip of wine, extended his arms with the palms up, looked from Jefferson to me, and said, "Gentlemen, I have a confession to make."

Jefferson said, through a wry smile, "And that is?"

"As good as the French wines were, I retained my love for Madeira." He reached in his jacket, removed a sheet of paper and handed it to me. "Here is an inventory of my cellar on September 1, 1782. What do you notice about it, Jack?"

I made a quick calculation. Of the 1188 bottles of wine listed, 216 bottles were Madeira. "You had a large supply of Madeira, and an even larger supply of Champagne. And like the Champagne Mr. Jefferson served us, all but twentyfour bottles were of the non-sparkling variety." [246]

"Yes, and all of my Madeira had that true nut flavor." [247]

"In fact, you were so fond of Madeira that you sometimes used it as a metaphor," I said.

Franklin looked at me quizzically. "I'm afraid I don't remember."

"In a letter to your friend Strahan you said, 'You may say my *advice* smells of Madeira. You are right. This foolish letter is mere chit-chat *between ourselves*, over a *second* bottle." [248]

"Are you aware, Jack, that I used to write wine-drinking songs?"

"Yes, but I can't remember them," I said.

"Then let me sing you one that I wrote some 30 years ago." Franklin began singing:

'The antediluvians were all very sober
For they had no wine, and they brewed no October;
All wicked, bad livers, on mischief still thinking,
For there can't be good living where there is not good drinking.
Derry down

'It was honest old Noah first planted the vine,
And mended his morals by drinking its wine;
He justly the drinking of water decried;
For he knew that all mankind, by drinking it, died.
Derry down

'From this piece of history plainly we find
That water's good neither for body or mind;
That virtue and safety in wine-bibbing's found
While all that drink water deserve to be drowned.
Derry down

'So for safety and honesty put the glass round.' [249]

"Here is another drinking song that I wrote at an earlier date. I sent it to a French friend, Abbé de la Roche. It is about a singer who exhorts his companions to seek happiness in love, in riches, and in power. In the chorus they reply, singing together, that happiness is not to be found in any of those things, but is only to be found in friends and wine. It begins:

Singer

'Fair Venus calls; her voice obey,
In beauty's arms spend night and day.
The joys of love, all joys excel,
And loving's certainly doing well.

Chorus

Oh! No!
Not So!
For honest souls know,
Friends and a bottle still bear the bell. [250]

Singer

'Then let us get money, like bees lay up honey;
We'll build us new hives, and store each cell.
The sight of our treasure shall yield us great pleasure;
We'll count it, and clink it, and jingle it well.

Chorus

Oh! No!
Not So!
For honest souls know,
Friends and a bottle still bear the bell.

Singer

'If this does not fit ye, let's govern the city,
In power is pleasure, no tongue can tell;
By crowds though you're teased, your pride shall be pleased.
And this can make Lucifer happy in hell!

Chorus

Oh! No!
Not So!
For honest souls know,
Friends and a bottle still bear the bell.

Singer

'Then toss off your glasses, and scorn the dull asses,
Who, missing the kernel, still gnaw the shell;
What's love, rule, or riches? Wise Solomon teaches,
They're vanity, vanity, vanity still.

Chorus

That's true;
He knew;
He'd tried them all through;
Friends and a bottle still bore the bell.'

"I wrote several verses to help celebrate Polly Stevenson's birthday. Here is the third verse:

*Three Positions of the Elbow,
illustration to Franklin's
letter in praise of wine,
drawn by Temple. His
arguement that the human
elbow was "providentially
devised to make drinking
more natural and easy."*

'No hospitable man, possessed of generous wines,
While they are in his vaults, repines
That age impairs the casks; for well he knows
The heavenly juice
More fit for use
Becomes, and still the older better grows;
He only keeps it there 'till it refines.
Then, when the cooper can no longer
Hold the moulding wood together,
(Though he pretends with hoops to make it stronger)
Bring, says the Master, bottles hither:
Time hurts not glass: the wine must be preserved
And at my table served:
There thro' the chrystal vase it shines;
The *chosen guests* enjoy it and extol it;
The happy company are happier made;
This! This is Wine indeed! Pray what d'ye call it?
O! 'tis my *Anno Domini!* he said.
Then round and round the cheerful board it flies,
And turns to wit that never dies.'[251]

"Wasn't one of your French drinking friends an abbé by the name of André Morellet?"

"Yes. I met Abbé Morellet in England in the spring of 1772. We immediately found that we had a variety of common interests, which included a taste for wine and singing. Morellet, a liberal French intellectual, lived at the home of my lady friend Madame Helvétius, and we became close friends during my last five years in France. Morellet composed a drinking song that suggested that the real reason for the American Revolution was my wish to rid myself of drab English beer and drink good French wines. I responded with this letter on wine. 'You have often enlivened me, my dear friend, by your excellent drinkingsongs; in return, I beg to edify you by some Christian, moral, and philosophical reflections upon the same subject. *In vino veritas*, says the wise man, Truth is in wine. Before the days of Noah, then, men, having nothing but water to drink, could not discover the truth. We hear of the conversion of water into wine at the marriage of Cana as a miracle. But this conversion is, through the goodness of God, made every day before our eyes. Behold the rain that descends from heaven upon our vineyards; there it enters the roots of the vines, to be changed into wine; a constant proof that God loves us, and loves to see us happy.'"

I looked at Jefferson and he was smiling broadly. "Dr. Franklin, what were your favorite French wines?"

Franklin took a reflective sip of his wine as he ran a lifetime of wines through his head. "Champagne, claret and Burgundy, and, Jack, some of the best clarets I ever drank were in Scotland at the tables of David Hume and Lord Kames."[252]

"Scotland? How can that be?"

"It's interesting how it evolve," Franklin said. "Although Scotland and England were a united kingdom after 1603, by the turn of the eighteenth century all the political power was in the English-dominated Parliament in London. This was a period of strained relations between England and France, so much so that French wine was prohibited in the United Kingdom from 1679 to 1685 and again from 1690 to 1696.[253] And when the French wine prohibition was lifted, the Methuen Treaty of 1703 between England and Portugal raised the duties on French wine by fifty percent more than Iberian wine duties.[254] What had once been a flow of French claret to England became a trickle. The Bordeaux winemakers, fearful of losing the English market, responded by improving the quality of their wines."[255]

"Which in turn increased the price of claret even more, and made it so expensive that it was available only to the wealthy," I said.

"That was the situation in England, but not in Scotland," Franklin said. "Scotland had a tradition of importing and drinking French claret that went back to the thirteenth century, when Scots merchants sailed directly to Bordeaux, then the capital of the English province of Gascony. [256] The Scots jealously guarded their wine-trading rights with France, and paid little attention to Parliament's restrictive wine laws. Throughout the eighteenth century vast amounts of claret were smuggled into Scotland, especially through the port of Leith. The common method of announcing its arrival was to send a hogshead of claret through the town on a cart, and anyone who wanted to sample it had only to go to the cart with a jug. All sections of society indulged in drinking the smuggled wine." [257]

"How did the smugglers avoid getting caught by English custom ships?" I asked.

"That, of course, was the smuggler's risk, but the coastline of Scotland is daunting, so catching the smuggler was no easy task. Also, contraband wine was usually not shipped direct from Bordeaux to Leith or Inverness but re-routed via Dutch ports and ships: Bordeaux to Holland to Scotland. So you see, Jack, while England suffered through the eighteenth century with strong port and little claret, Scotland was knee-deep in good claret." [258]

"Mr. Jefferson, you are universally acknowledged to be America's first wine connoisseur, and by many, the most knowledgeable wine expert of the eighteenth century. We now know of Dr. Franklin's great love of wine, but what other Founding Fathers enjoyed the cup?"

"John Adams was an enthusiastic wine drinker and at one point had a substantial collection of wines. At a dinner party with John Paul Jones and the officers of the *Poor Richard*, Adams made the comment that they 'practiced the old American custom of drinking to each other which is always agreeable to me.' [259] Dinner at the Adamses was always accompanied or followed by wine. John Adams acquired an early taste of French hospitality and French wines when he arrived in Bordeaux in 1778 and was invited aboard a French vessel to have dinner with the captain where he said he enjoyed 'excellent claret' with dinner.

"The next day Adams received a lesson on the Bordeaux wine hierarchy from a negociant from Blaye who rated Châteaux Margaux, Haut Brion, Lafite and Latour the best wines of Bordeaux and referred to them as 'First Growths.' That afternoon, Adams again dined 'in the fashion of the country, fish, beans and salad, and claret, Champagne and mountain wine.' [260]

"During his stays at The Hague and Paris, Adams had accumulated a large supply of wines. In fact, just before receiving word that he had been appointed

America's first minister to England, he had ordered 500 bottles of French wine. When he arrived in London in May 1785, he was told to his dismay that diplomatic immunity could not save him from paying the English duty of six to eight shillings on every bottle of wine brought into the country. In a state of shock, he frantically wrote me asking me to stop the shipment of all his wines except one case of Madeira and Frontignan, adding, 'I am sorry to give you this trouble but I beg you to take the wine, at any price you please. Let your *maitre d 'hotel* judge, or accept it as a present, or sell it at *vendue* that is, let Petit dispose of it as he will.'[261]

John Paul Jones

"In a follow-up letter he pleaded, 'For mercy sake stop all of my wine but the Bordeaux and Madeira and Frontenac. And stop my order to Rouen for the 500 additional bottles I recently ordered. I shall be ruined, for each minister is not permitted to import more than 500 or 600 bottles which will not more than cover what I have at The Hague which is very rich wine and my Madeira, Frontenac and Bordeaux at Auteuil.'[262]

"The day before receiving Adams's first urgent message, I had arranged for the shipment of his wines. On receiving his message, I immediately sent my *maitre d 'hotel*, Petit, to stop the boat leaving Paris for Rouen, but Petit was not in time. The boat had just departed.[263]

"I also reported to Adams the arrival of a sixty gallon cask of wine that held 215 bottles of red wine from Gaillac, probably Cahusac, which I could not taste and determine its quality because it was in a cask within a cask, a security measure. Adams advised that this cask of wine was not paid for but he had sampled it, and it was a good wine 'and very, extremely cheap.' He asked me to take it for myself, which I did—cheerfully.[264]

"Finally, Adams notified me that he had written to the U.S. consul in Rouen, Anthony Garvey, to forward all of his wine as he believed he would easily obtain an order to receive the wines without paying duties." [265]

"What about your best friends, James Madison and James Monroe? Did they enjoy wine?"

"Very much so. Mr. Madison served as my secretary of state, and he and his charming wife, Dolly, joined me many evenings for dinner and wine. When Mr. Monroe was elected to the 'splendid misery' of the presidency in 1817, I spent all but five lines of my letter of congratulations discussing the wines I recommended for his presidential wine cellar. Here is a copy of that letter," Jefferson said, handing me a letter.

As I glanced at it, Dr. Franklin said, "Read it aloud, Jack."

> I shall not waste your time in idle congratulations. You know my joy on the commitment of the helm of our government to your hands. I promised you, when I should have received and tried the wines that I ordered from France and Italy to give you a note of the kinds which I should think worthy of your procurement; and this being the season for ordering them, so that they may come in the mild temperature of autumn, I now fulfill my promise. They are the following:

> Vin Blanc, Liqoureux d'Hermitage de M. Jourdan à Tains. This costs about 82 1/2cents a bottle put on shipboard. Vin de Ledanon (in Languedoc) something of the port character but higher flavored, more delicate, less rough. I do not know its price, but probably about 25 cents a bottle. Vin de Roussillon. The best is that of Perpignan or Rivesalte of the crop of M. Durand. It costs 72 cents a gallon, bears bringing in the cask. If put into bottles then it costs 11 cents a bottle more than if bottled here by an inexplicable and pernicious arrangement of our tariff.

> Vin de Nice. The crop called Bellet, of M. Sasserno, is the best. This is the most elegant everyday wine in the world and costs 31 cents the bottle. Not much being made it is little known at the general markets.

> Mr. Cathalan of Marseilles is the best channel for getting the first three of these wines and a good one for the Nice, being in their neighborhood and knowing well who makes the crops of best quality. The Nice being a wine foreign to France occasion some troublesome forms. If you could get that direct from Sasserno himself at Nice, it would be better. And by the bye, he is very anxious for the appointment of consul for the United States at that place. I knew his father well, one of the most respectable merchants and

men of the place. I hear a good character of the son, who has succeeded to his business. He understands English well, having passed some time in a counting house in London for improvement. I believe we have not many vessels going to that port annually and yet as the appointment brings no expense to the United States, and is sometimes salutary to our merchantsand seamen, I see no objection to naming one there. There is still another wine to be named to you, which is the wine of Florence called Montepulciano, with which Appleton can best furnish you. [266] There is a particular very best crop of it known to him and which he has usually sent to me. This cost 25 cents per bottle. He knows too from experience how to have it so bottled and packed as to ensure it bearing the passage which in the ordinary way it does not. I have imported it through him annually 10 or 12 years and do not think I have lost one bottle in 100. I salute you with all my wishes for a prosperous and splendid voyage over the ocean on which you are embarked, and with sincere prayers for the continuance of your life and health. [267]

"Did George Washington enjoy wine?"

"Yes. Washington was a lifelong enthusiast of good Madeira, and when I served as his secretary of state, I purchased for him Champagne, Yquem, Frontignan and Lafite." [268]

"Madeira was much more popular in your time than it is today," I said.

"Why do you think that is?" Franklin asked.

"There are several reasons. The invasion of two deadly vine diseases, odium and phylloxera, devastated the Madeira vineyards and caused a dramatic cutback in its production. Also, lifestyles have changed, and with it a taste for 'lighter' wines. Madeira is perceived as heavy and sweet. But I suspect that the demise of Madeira as a popular wine probably has more to do with its decline in quality than with changing lifestyles or production. Douglas H. Thomas, a Baltimore banker, and an acknowledged Madeira expert in the early 1900s, wrote to a friend in 1909: 'There is very little really good Madeira in existence. I meet with "Old Madeira" sometimes at dinners, but almost invariably it turns out to be strong, "roachy" stuff which politeness requires me to drink and smack my lips over.'" [269]

Both Franklin and Jefferson shook their heads sadly, and I decided to change the subject. "You would have been proud of the accomplishments of our athletes at last year's 2004 Olympics in Athens, Greece. They won more gold medals and more total medals than any other nation, but despite these athletic achievements, we are a nation that is rapidly becoming overweight and obese. Two out of every three adult Americans are categorized as overweight or obese, conditions that increase the risks of heart disease, high blood pressure, diabetes, stroke, gallbladder disease, and colon, breast, and prostate cancer."

Jefferson and Franklin looked at one another in stunned silence. Finally, Franklin spoke. "You know, of course, that the answer to this problem lies in exercise and diet. What has happened to the American tradition of vigorous physical activity and exercise?"

"There are many Americans," I said, "who stay fit by their work activities or through daily regimes of exercise and balanced diets, but the trend is clearly moving in the other direction. You said, Dr. Franklin, that exercise is an important answer to America's overweight and obesity problems. What did you do for exercise?"

"I was an early and enthusiastic believer in daily exercise. While growing up in Boston, I did a great deal of swimming. [270] I made it a habit to swim in the river for two or three hours, even in cold weather. [271] One day when I was about nineteen and living in London, I was returning by boat from Chelsea and some friends urged me to show how good a swimmer I was. I dove into the water and swam at the same speed of the boat for over three miles. This feat established my reputation among my young English friends as a powerful swimmer. [272]

"I also got considerable exercise while working as a pressman in London. The job required the carrying of heavy lead type. But rather than carry one set of type at a time like the other pressmen, I added to my physical activities by carrying two sets of type, one in each hand while running up and down the stairs. [273]

"My son William became ill when he was the royal governor of New Jersey, and I emphasized in a letter to him that exercise is of the greatest importance to avoid diseases. I told him that in considering the different kinds of exercise, I thought that the quantum of each should be judged not by time or distance, but by the degree of warmth produced in the body. There is more exercise in *one* mile's riding on horseback, than in *five* in a coach; and more in *one* mile's walking on foot, than in *five* on horseback; to which I added, that there is more in walking *one* mile up and down stairs, than *five* on a level floor. I found the dumbbell another exercise of the latter compendious kind; by the use of it I had in forty swings quickened my pulse from 60 to 100 beats in a minute, counted by a second watch. [274]

"But as you can see, Jack, as I've grew older I did not follow my own advice on the benefits of proper diet and exercise. As a result I've grown fat and afflicted with the gout. Here's something you should read later. It would take too much time to read now," Franklin said, handing me a sheath of papers. "It's a bagatelle that I wrote to Madam Brillon, a young French woman I seriously pursued during my early years in France. It's the story of how overeating and lack of exercise caused me to become fat and develop the gout. It's called 'Dialogue between Franklin and the Gout.'"

"Like Dr. Franklin, I too have been a lifelong advocate of daily vigorous exercise," Jefferson said. "Shortly after arriving in Paris, I acquired a pedometer and made calculations of the length of my stride in both winter and summer, and I recorded how many double steps it took to walk to certain designated places in Paris from my home here. I walked at a fast pace, in excess of four miles an hour. [275] In a letter to my future son-in-law, I set out my thoughts on exercise. 'If the body is feeble, the mind will not be strong. The sovereign invigorator of the body is exercise, and of all the exercises walking is best. A horse gives but a kind of half exercise, and a carriage is no better than a cradle. No one knows, till he tries, how easily a habit of walking is acquired. A person who never walked three miles will in the course of a month become able to walk fifteen or twenty without fatigue. I have known great walkers and had particular accounts of many more; and I never knew or heard of one who was not healthy and long-lived. Not less than two hours a day should be devoted to exercise and the weather should be little regarded. A person not sick will not be injured getting wet.' [276] I remained physically fit well into my old age, and walking was the main form of my exercise. While here in Paris I established the routine of leaving work at noon for a two hour walk through the Bois de Boulogne." [277]

"Daily exercise obviously kept your body in superb condition," I said. "Your overseer, Edmund Bacon, who didn't meet you until you were sixty-three, describes you as being 'six feet two and half inches high, well proportioned, and as straight as a gun-barrel. He was like a fine horse—he had no surplus flesh.' Bacon also spoke of how strong you were, saying that you out performed your son-in-law, who was known for his strength, on your strength-measuring machine." [278]

Jefferson smiled. "Another bit of advice I gave on the value of exercise was to my nephew Peter Carr. I told him to 'give two hours every day to exercise, for health must not be sacrificed to learning. A strong body makes the mind

91

strong. Walking very far is the best possible exercise. A little walk of half an hour in the morning, when you first rise, is advisable also. It shakes off sleep. Rise at a fixed an early hour, and go to bed at a fixed an early hour. Sitting up late at night is injurious to the health, and not useful to the mind.' "[279]

"In the past thirty or so years in the United States there has been a strong movement by women to be recognized and treated by men as equals—economically, politically, and socially. The movement is known as feminism."

"Have American women achieved those goals?" Franklin asked.

"No, not completely, but enormous strides have been made."

"Although I'm the author of the Polly Baker story, which gained worldwide sympathy for the poor and downtrodden women of the world, I'm afraid that my treatment of women falls far short of the equality aspirations of the American woman of your time."[280]

"What was the Polly Baker story about, and how did it help women's rights?" I asked.

"It is about Polly Baker, a young unmarried woman, who was being prosecuted for the fifth time for having a bastard child. She spoke in her own defense before a court of judicature in Connecticut, and she argued her case so well that the judges acquitted her, and the next day one of the judges married her. It was first published in London on April 15, 1747, and reprinted in England and America, without anyone knowing that it was a satire that I had written attacking hypocrisy and discrimination toward women and sex."[281]

"Will you read it?" I said.

Franklin reached into a leather case, removed some papers, and began to read:

> May it please the Honorable Bench to indulge me a few words: I am a poor unhappy woman; who have no money to fee lawyers to plead for me, being hard put to it to get a tolerable living. I shall not trouble your Honors with long speeches; for I have not the presumption to expect, that you may, by any means, be prevailed on to deviate in your sentence from the law, in my favor. All I humbly hope is that Your Honors would charitably move the governor's goodness on my behalf, and my fine may be remitted.
>
> This is the fifth time, gentlemen, that I have been dragged before your courts on the same account; twice I have paid heavy fines, and twice have been brought to public punishment, for want of money to pay those fines. This may have been agreeable to the laws; I do not dispute it. But since laws are

sometimes unreasonable in themselves, and therefore repealed; and others bear too hard on the subject in particular circumstances; and therefore there is left a power somewhere to dispense with the execution of them; I take the liberty to say, that I think this law, by which I am punished, is both unreasonable in itself, and particularly severe with regard to me, who have always lived an inoffensive life in the neighborhood where I was born, and defy my enemies (if I have any) to say I ever wronged man, woman, or child.

Abstracted from the law, I cannot conceive (may it please Your Honors) what the nature of my offence is. I have brought five fine children into the world, at the risk of my life: I have maintained them well by my own industry, without burdening the township, and could have done it better, if it had not been for the heavy charges and fines I have paid. Can it be a crime (in the nature of things I mean) to add to the number of the king's subjects, in a new country that really wants people? I own I should think it rather a praiseworthy, than a punishable action. I have debauched no other woman's husband, nor enticed any innocent youth: These things I never was charged with; nor has any one the least cause of complaint against me, unless, perhaps the minister, or the justice, because I have had children without being married, by which they have missed a wedding fee. But, can even this be a fault of mine? I appeal to Your Honors. You are pleased to allow I don't want sense; but I must be stupid to the last degree, not to prefer the honorable state of wedlock, to the condition I have lived in. I always was, and still am, willing to enter into it; I doubt not my behaving well in it, having all the industry, frugality, fertility, and skill in economy, appertaining to a good wife's character. I defy any person to say I ever refused an offer of that sort: On the contrary, I readily consented to the only proposal of marriage that ever was made me, which was when I was a virgin; but too easily confiding in the person's sincerity that made it, I unhappily lost my own honor, by trusting to his; for he got me with child, and then forsook me: That very person you all know; he is now become a magistrate of this county; and I had hopes he would have appeared this day on the bench, and have endeavored to moderate the court in my favor; then I should have scorned to have mentioned it; but I must complain of it as unjust and unequal, that my betrayer and under, the first cause of all my faults and miscarriages (if they must be deemed such) should be advanced to honor and power, in the same government that punishes my misfortunes with stripes and infamy.

I shall be told, 'tis like, that were there no act of assembly in the case, the precepts of religion are violated by my transgressions. If mine, then, is a religious offence, leave it, gentlemen, to religious punishments. You have already excluded me from all the comforts of your church communion: Is not that sufficient? You believe I have offended Heaven, and must suffer eternal fire: will not that be sufficient? What need is there, then, of your additional fines and whippings? I own, I do not think as you do; for, if I thought, what you call a sin, was really such, I would not presumptuously commit it. But how can it be believed, that Heaven is angry at my having children, when, to the little done by me towards it, God has been pleased to add his divine skill and admirable workmanship in the formation of their bodies, and crowned it by furnishing them with rational and immortal souls?

Forgive me gentlemen, if I talk a little extravagantly on these matters; I am no divine: But if you, great men, [turning to some gentlemen of the Assembly, then in Court] must be making laws, do not turn natural and useful actions into crimes, by your prohibitions. Reflect a little on the horrid consequences of this law in particular: What numbers of procured abortions! and how many distressed mothers have been driven, by the terror of punishment and public shame, to imbrue, contrary to nature, their own trembling hands in the blood of their helpless offspring! Nature would have induced them to nurse it up with a parent's fondness. 'Tis the law therefore, 'tis the law itself that is guilty of all these barbarities and murders. Repeal it then, gentlemen; let it be expunged forever from your books: And on the other hand, take into your wise consideration, the great and growing number of bachelors in the country, many of whom, from the mean fear of the expense of a family, have never sincerely and honorably courted a woman in their lives; and by their manner of living, leave unproduced (which I think is little better than murder) hundreds of their posterity to the thousandth generation. Is not theirs a greater offence against the public good, than mine? Compel them then, by a law, either to marry, or pay double the fine of fornication every year. What must poor young women do, whom custom has forbid to solicit the men, and who cannot force themselves upon husbands, when the laws take no care to provide them any, and yet severely punish if they do their duty without them? Yes, gentlemen, I venture to call it a duty; 'tis the duty of the first and great command of nature, and of nature's God, increase and multiply: a duty, from the steady performance of which nothing has ever been able to deter me; but for its sake, I have hazarded the loss of the public esteem, and frequently incurred public disgrace and punishment; and therefore ought, in my humble opinion, instead of a whipping, to have a statue erected to my memory. [282]

I laughed, and Jefferson smiled and said, "There were two marvelous stories that Dr. Franklin told me that I loved telling my friends, and one of them related to Polly Baker."

I looked at Dr. Franklin and he was, as usual, smiling. "Tell me," I said to Jefferson.

"Abbé Reynal, a French friend of ours, had put in his *Histoire des deux indes* Polly Baker's speech. One evening Reynal visited Dr. Franklin, and Silas Deane was there. Deane told the abbé, in Dr. Franklin's presence, that the story could not be true because there was no law against bastardy in Connecticut. When Reynal insisted that he had documentary proof of its authority, Dr Franklin began to shake with laughter."

We looked at Franklin, and he was already shaking with laughter. Jefferson waved his hand toward him and said, "Dr. Franklin, you tell Jack the rest of the story."

Franklin took a moment to regain his composure before speaking. "I said, 'M. l'Abbé, I am going to set you straight. When I was young and printed a newspaper, it sometimes happened that I was short of material, and to amuse my customers I used to fill up the vacant space with anecdotes and fables of my own making. Polly Baker is one of those stories.'

"The abbé without a moment's hesitation exclaimed with a laugh, 'Oh, very well, Doctor, I had rather relate your stories than other men's truths.'" [283]

I turned to Jefferson, "What was the other Franklin story that you enjoyed telling?"

"Abbé Reynal had a party to dine with him one evening at his home in Passy. Half the party was Frenchmen and the other half Americans. During dinner Reynal got on his favorite topic, his theory that American animals and American men were smaller than European animals and men because of an inherent degeneracy. Dr. Franklin, noticing the position of the guests, stood and said, 'Come, M. l'Abbé, let us try this question by the fact before us. We are here one half Americans and one half French, and it happens that the Americans have placed themselves on one side of the table and our French friends on the other. Let both parties rise and we will see on which side nature has degenerated.' The Americans were tall and large and the French small and diminutive, especially Abbé Reynal."

95

"In my time, with the exception of aristocratic French women, women did not expect to share equally with men," Franklin said. "It is not that I mistreated them, but men, including me, thought a woman's place was in the home. Having said that, I should add that my wife worked in our print-shop store and kept the books."

"Speaking of your wife Deborah, Dr. Franklin, would you characterize your relationship with her as one of 'uncheckered happiness?' " I said.

Franklin's stare was so intense and melancholy that I was sorry that I had asked the question. "I mentioned earlier how I met my wife and the circumstances that led to our common-law marriage," he said.

"Yes," I said, "it assuaged your guilt and erased your 'great erratum.' "

"I would say that the first twenty or so years of our marriage served both of us well. She was a good helpmate, raised my son William and our daughter Sally, and kept the household in 'peace and good order.' In addition to cooking, cleaning, and the care of the children, Deborah ran the stationary shop and helped in my printing business and in the management of the Philadelphia post office. When I retired in 1748, our relationship changed. My time and attention were consumed by my passions for my electrical experiments and public affairs—passions that caused me to virtually abandon my wife psychologically and eventually physically." [284]

Franklin, discussing at dinner in France the Abbé Raynal's theory of degenerate Americans, and finding that he is taller than most men present.

"Would you say that Deborah became widowed, so to speak, when you left for London in the spring of 1757?" I said.

"What do you mean by 'widowed'?"

"Well, you were gone for five years, returning only briefly before heading back to London where you stayed until after your wife's death. So for all practical purposes, Deborah lived the last 18 years of her life without you."

"I was home two of those years."

"Yes, but away on business much of that time."

"We corresponded, exchanged gifts, and I provided for her comfort and security." Franklin paused. "But it is true that in my absence, Deborah assumed responsibility for the family affairs."

"She became the father and mother to your daughter Sally," I said. "And when rioters threatened to destroy your new house on Market Street, Deborah 'maid one room into a magazin' and took up arms to defend the house from attack."

Deborah Franklin

"Yes, and I was quite proud of her actions."

"Why did rioters threaten to destroy your Philadelphia house?"

"Because passage of the Stamp Act brought on a firestorm of mob protest throughout the Colonies, and the people of Pennsylvania not only thought that I was in favor of it, but that I had actually brought it about."[285]

"What was the Stamp Act and why was it so unpopular?"

"Great Britain emerged from the Seven Years War with a large national debt and virtual control of northeastern North America. But its new land acquisitions had to be policed. Where was the money to come from? George Grenville, then prime minister, and Parliament came up with the idea of raising the necessary funds by laying a stamp tax on nearly every form of paper used in the Colonies: newspapers, legal documents, almanacs, playing cards, etc."[286]

"And you were in favor of such a tax?"

"No. I and others appeared before Grenville and protested. When Grenville said he might listen to an alternative plan, I proposed one in the form of paper currency at interest. The idea here was that the people most likely to use paper money, merchants and the wealthy, would pay most of the taxes. Grenville, however, was 'besotted with his stamp scheme' and went ahead with it, and I acquiesced to its passage never thinking that it would be so violently opposed.

In fact, Grenville granted me the right to name the stamp commissioner for Pennsylvania, and I named my friend John Hughes, who was immediately approved." [287]

"What happened?"

"As I mentioned, the reaction to the Stamp Act in America was violent, especially in Boston, New York and Philadelphia. John Hughes reported that he was told that his house would 'be pulled down and the stamps burnt.' To which he replied, 'I will defend my house at the risk of my life.' Fortunately, our friends rallied around both my wife and Hughes, and the threatened violence did not take place." [288]

"What became of the Stamp Act?"

"I continued to speak against it in Parliament and to the Earl of Dartmouth, head of the Board of Trade. I warned against sending troops to enforce it, and recommended suspending it. The Grenville ministry was replaced by one led by Lord Rockingham, and a more conciliatory approach was followed that resulted in its repeal." [289]

"Getting back to your wife, would it be unfair, Dr. Franklin, to say that what your wife wanted most was for you to come home?"

Franklin's face showed the strain of the conversation, and he remained quiet for a long moment before answering. "When I returned to England in 1764, and I didn't come home in a year or two, Deborah did become discouraged over my absence, and I told her that I would soon return. When I did not return after three years, Deborah admitted that she was 'in the darke and my life of old age is one contineuwd state of suspens.'" [290] Franklin looked down at his dinner and then back at me. "The next year she suffered a stroke. She blamed the stroke on distress from my 'staying so much longer' than she expected."

"Yet you lingered in London for another seven years. You had lived, you said, 'so great a part of my life in Britain,' and had 'formed so many friendships in it,' that you could not help loving the mother country." [291]

"My life in London was completely different from anything my wife had ever experienced. I don't deny that I enjoyed London, going to my clubs, and meeting important and intellectually stimulating people, even royalty. I admit that I was flattered when the king of Denmark, Christian VII, asked to meet me, and when he invited me to dine with him. [292] There was nothing in Philadelphia to match those experiences and pleasures."

Franklin shot a look at Jefferson and quickly turned back to me. "But that is not an excuse for my conduct. There can be no doubt that my treatment of my wife during the last seventeen years of her life was, at best, benign neglect, and certainly not one of the highlights of my career." [293]

I felt very uneasy with the conversation and decided to turn to another subject. "Slavery no longer exists in the United States but it took four bloody years of civil war between the South and the North to free the slaves, and another 100 years of segregation before African-Americans were given equal rights. I know that Mr. Jefferson owned slaves, but what about you Dr. Franklin? Did you ever own slaves?"

"I owned slaves for more than thirty years and ran advertisements in my newspaper for slaves. [294] As a young man, I equated the loss of a slave's life with the loss of property."

"In what way?" I asked.

"For example, in 1731, when I was twenty-five years old, I wrote in my newspaper, *The Pennsylvania Gazette*: 'The smallpox has now quite left the city. The number of those who died here is exactly 288 … 64 of the number were Negroes; if these be valued at £30 per head, the loss to the city is near £2,000.'

"I bought my first slave Peter, and his wife, Jemima, when I was forty-two years old. Later I bought a ten-year-old boy named Othello for my wife, and I accepted a slave named George as partial payment for a debt. [295] I arrived in London in late July 1757 with my son William and two slaves, Peter and King. [296]

"My early objections to slavery were not on moral grounds, but based on the fact that it encouraged indolence among whites. [297] The first enlargement of my understanding occurred one day in Philadelphia in 1763. I visited a black school run by Reverend William Sturgeon. There I saw firsthand the natural capacities of the Negro race. The students appeared all to have made considerable progress in reading for the time they had been in the school, and most of them answered readily and well the questions of the catechism. I was much pleased, and from what I then saw gave me a higher opinion of the natural capacities of the Negro race than I had ever before entertained. That visit dispelled any thoughts that I might have entertained that Negroes were intellectually inferior to whites. [298]

"By the late 1760s, I had freed my slaves. And by 1772, I had formed some fierce antislavery opinions. In an article printed in the *London Chronicle*, I lashed out against the slave trade. 'Can sweetening our tea with sugar be a reason for such cruelty? Can the petty pleasure of taste compensate for so much misery produced among our fellow man by this pestilential, detestable traffic in bodies and souls?' A year later I had come to see slavery as a practice that had long disgraced our nation. [299]

"I endorsed the section in Thomas's draft of the Declaration of Independence that condemned the slave trade and Britain's refusal to allow the American colonies to restrict it, but the southern colonies insisted on deleting that section. It is true that I acquiesced in the compromises on slavery at the Constitutional Convention, believing, as I said in my closing speech that the bargain struck was the best that could be achieved at that time and place. By the mid-1780s, I was convinced slavery must be eradicated."

"What brought you to that conviction?"

"When I returned from France in 1785, I joined the first abolitionist group, called the Society for Promoting the Abolition of Slavery and the Relief of Negroes Unlawfully Held in Bondage. It had been founded ten years earlier by a group of Philadelphia Quakers who believed freedom was a gift from God that everyone was entitled to. Two years later I accepted the society's presidency, and as president I wrote a plan whose aim was to restore to the Negro race the rightful enjoyment of their civil liberties. The antiabolitionist argument was that the emancipated slave would become a burden to society for lacking power of choice in his life, he had never learned to choose; lacking responsibility, he had become irresponsible, a problem that concerned all of us. We realized that slavery was such an atrocious debasement of human nature that its very extirpation, if not performed with solicitous care, could become a source of serious evils. So we published a plan for the education of former slaves, and I solicited public support. The plan was 'to instruct, to advise, to qualify those who have been restored to freedom, for the exercise and enjoyment of civil liberty; to promote in them habits of industry, to furnish them with employment suited to their age, sex, talents, and other circumstances; and to procure their children an education calculated for their future situation in life; these are the great outlines of the annexed plan which we have adopted, and which we conceived would essentially promote the public good, and the happiness of these our hitherto much neglected fellow-creatures.' [300]

"In my last years I became a ferocious advocate against slavery, convinced that it was an atrocious debasement of human nature. In February 1790, I forwarded an antislavery petition to Congress. It read in part, 'Mankind are all formed by the same Almighty Being, alike objects of his care, and equally designed for the enjoyment of happiness.' I argued in the petition that our revolution was about asserting as a birthright that 'all men are created equal' and that laws ought to be 'administered without distinction of color to all descriptions of people.' To tolerate less would contradict the meaning of the revolution, and it was the duty of Congress to restore liberty to those unhappy men who alone in this land of freedom were degraded into perpetual bondage, and who amidst the general joy of surrounding freemen, groan in servile subjection."

"What happened to your petition?"

"My petition prompted Congressman James Jackson from Georgia to invoke the Bible in defense of slavery. The Bible endorsed slavery, he said, because it brought barbarians to the Gospel. And besides, he asked, who would work the fields of the South? In response I wrote to the *Federal Gazette* that the congressman's speech put me in mind of a similar one made about 100 years before by Sidi Mehemet Ibrahim, a member of the divan of Algiers. I included in Ibrahim's speech denunciations of attempts to outlaw Barbary piracy and free the enslaved Christians sailors: 'If we cease our cruises against the Christians, how shall we be furnished with the commodities their countries produce, and which are so necessary for us? If we forbear to make slaves of their people, who in this hot climate are to cultivate our lands?' To free the Christian slaves would deprive them of exposure to the Muslim faith, 'sending them out of light in darkness.' Ibrahim's speech was a hoax that I had made up, but it used the power of analogy and satire to show the stupidity of Jackson's argument in favor of slavery." [301]

I turned to Jefferson. "I must tell you, Mr. Jefferson, that the biggest knock against you is that despite being the author of the noblest words ever written about equality and liberty, you believed in slavery, were a slave owner, and, except for a few slaves, did not emancipate them at the time of your death. How do you explain this striking contradiction?"

"First and foremost, I did not believe in slavery. I was born into the culture of slavery and its concomitant racial bias. As I pointed out in *Notes on the State of Virginia*, the culture of slavery was a vicious cycle with 'commerce between master and slave a perpetual exercise of the most unremitting despotism on the one part, and degrading submissions on the other. Our children see this, and learn to imitate it; for man is an imitative animal. The parent storms, the child looks on, catches the lineaments of wrath, puts on the same airs in the circle of smaller slaves, gives a loose to his worst of passions, and thus nursed, educated, and daily exercised in tyranny, cannot but be stamped by it with odious peculiarities.' [302]

"Convinced that agriculture was the best occupation, I gave up the law, became a plantation owner, and grew large crops of tobacco and wheat, which required field hands and muscle power, so the economics of operating a plantation dictated the use of slave labor. My slaves were generally well cared for and fairly treated. I always thought that slavery was 'a great political and moral evil,' and should be done away with, but I thought the system of slavery would have to endure until a plan of education, emancipation, and deportation could be worked out. [303]

"In my *Notes on the State of Virginia* I proposed a plan of gradual emancipation. All slaves born after the passage of the act would be educated at public expense in a useful trade. At the age of maturity they would be set free and expatriated to some place such as Santo Domingo. [304]

"I was in favor of the discontinuance of the slave trade before the Revolution, and proposed it in my draft of the Declaration of Independence. I opposed slavery on moral grounds because it undermined the morals and industry of the owners and degraded the victims. [305] In my *Autobiography* I wrote, 'Nothing is more certainly written in the book of fate than that these people are to be free.'"

"Some of today's politicians, who would like to write you out of history, claim that you were all rhetoric and no action," I said.

"What do you mean by that, Jack?"

"That your actions belie your words: you didn't do anything to abolish slavery."

"If that is the accusation against me, it is false and misleading. In 1769, while a member of the House of Burgesses, I helped draft a bill to allow 'manumission by deed,' a procedure whereby a slave-owner could transfer by deed his 'property interest' in a slave back to the slave, thereby setting the slave free. A year later, in the case of *Howell v. Netherland*, I argued on behalf of a third-generation mulatto slave client that 'we are all born free,' that slavery was contrary to natural law, and he should be free." [306]

"Were you successful?" I asked.

"No, but my efforts to abolish slavery didn't end there. In 1776 and in 1783, in two drafts of a constitution for the State of Virginia I inserted clauses prohibiting the importation of slaves into Virginia. The 1783 draft went further and stated: 'The General Assembly shall not have power to permit the introduction of any more slaves to reside in this state, or the continuance of slavery beyond the generation which shall be living on the 31st day of December 1800; all persons born after that day being hereby declared free.' [307]

"In the 1783–84 session of Congress, I drafted and submitted, and Congress enacted into law as the Ordinance of 1784, the 'Report on the Government of the Western Territories.' That report provided that 'after the year 1800 of the Christian era, there shall be neither slavery nor involuntary servitude ... otherwise than in punishment of crimes' in any part of the United States outside of the original thirteen colonies. This prohibition against slavery was deleted from the bill by a single vote. [308]

"As for my book *Notes on the State of Virginia*, I was reluctant to publish it for 'fear that the terms in which I speak of slavery may produce an irritation which will revolt the minds of our countrymen against reformation, and indispose the people towards the great object I have in view—that is, the emancipation of their slaves—and thus do more harm than good.' Only when reassured by my two most trusted friends, James Madison and James Monroe, did I consent to its publication." [309]

"It is true," I said, "that Abraham Lincoln, president during our bloody Civil War, which was fought primarily over the issue of slavery, and the person who issued the Emancipation Proclamation freeing all slaves, said, 'The principles of Jefferson are the definitions and axioms of free society ... All honor to Jefferson—to the man who, in the concrete pressure of a struggle for national independence by a single people, had the coolness, forecast, and capacity to introduce into a merely revolutionary document, an abstract truth, applicable to all men and all time, and so to embalm it there, that today, and in all coming days, it shall be a rebuke and a stumbling-block to the very harbingers of reappearing tyranny and oppression.' [310]

"The Preamble of the Declaration of Independence has served for more than two centuries to 'fill men's heads with dreams of freedom' and equality, which today have become a force that is starting to sweep the world," I said. "Seeing you as the spokesman for this enlightenment, many people hold that 'few people in human history did more, in the sum total of their lifetimes, to dismantle the institution of slavery than Jefferson.' " [311]

"That is good to hear Jack, and confirms my belief that 'my character is not within the power of my political enemies. It is in the hands of my fellow citizens at large, and will be consigned to honor or infamy by the verdict of the republican mass of our country, according to what they themselves will have seen, not what their enemies and mine shall have said.' " [312]

"I think the Montrachet goes well with the macaroni dish. When you mentioned that the sauce contained anchovies, I was concerned that they might overpower the Montrachet, but their delicate touch to the sauce seems to enhance the wine's taste. On a lighter note, Mr. Jefferson, did you ever drink a wine you didn't like?"

Jefferson thought for a moment. "Very few, but on reflection there is a wine that I remember in particular that was disappointing enough to provoke a definition of my tastes in wine. On my visit to Nice in May 1787, I met a local wine merchant, André Sasserno, of whom I have spoken. At Sasserno's house, I sampled the wines of Bellet—white, red, and rosé—that came from vineyards in the hill country a few mile northeast of Nice. I found the wines good, 'though not of the first quality.' My opinion regarding these wines later changed from good to 'remarkably good.' I felt differently when, in retirement, I tasted one of 300 bottles of this wine I had ordered from Sasserno's son: 'My taste for the wines of Nice, and for the particular quality of it which I drank at your father's house in Nice, and which M. Spreafico sent me in 1816, will, I fear, become a troublesome circumstance to you; and chiefly perhaps because the expressions characterizing subjects of taste and flavor in one language have not always terms synonymous in another. To remove this difficulty, I will explain to you the particular terms we use to designate particularly different flavor or characters of wine. These are 1. sweet wines, such as Frontignan and Lunel of France, Pacharetti *doux* of Spain, Calcavallo of Portugal, vin du Cap, etc. 2. acid wines, such as the vins de Grave, du Rhin, de Hochheim, etc. 3. dry wines, which have not the least either of sweetness or acidity as Madere sec, Pacharetti sec, vin d'Oporto, etc. 4. silky wines, which are in truth a compound in their taste of the dry dashed with a little sweetishness, barely sensible to the palate. The silky Madeira we sometimes get in this country is made so by putting a small quantity of Malmsey into the dry Madeira. There is another quality which is often found in the dry and the silky wines, which quality we call rough or astringent, and the French also, I believe, call it astringent. There is something of this in all the wines of Nice which I have seen, and so much of it in those of Oporto as to approach to bitterness while it is also dry. Our vocabulary of wines being thus explained, I will observe that the wine of Bellet sent to me by Mr. Spreafico in 1816 was silky and a little astringent, and was the most delicious wine I ever tasted, and the most esteemed here generally. That of 1817 was dry, a little astringent, and an excellent wine. That of 1818, last received, has its usual astringency indeed, but is a little acid; so much so as to destroy its usual good flavor. Had it come in the summer, I should have suspected its having acquired its acidity by fretting in the hold of the ship, or in our hot warehouses, on a summer passage. But it was shipped at Marseilles in October, the true time for shipping delicate wines for this country. With these explanations of the meaning of our terms, I will now pray you, Sir, to send me through Mr. Cathalan, 150 bottles of the wine of Bellet of the silky quality sent me in 1816 by Mr. Spreafico, if to be had; and if that was of an accidental *recolte* [vintage] not always to be had, then send it of the dry quality, such as was sent me in 1817.'"[313]

"What would you say, Mr. Jefferson, was your daily consumption of wine?"

"My measure was a perfectly sober one of three or four glasses at dinner, and not a drop at any other time. But of these three or four glasses, *Je suis bien friand*, I am very fond."[314]

"In the last election campaign for the presidency, our current president, George W. Bush, and his opponent, Senator John Kerry, and their constituents hurled some nasty political rhetoric at one another. For example, the Kerry team accused Bush of 'using the war on terror as a political tool and a political weapon in seeking to silence dissent.' Bush responded by accusing Kerry of 'Playing politics with terror in his attacks on Mr. Bush's Iraq policy.'"[315]

"What you've just related is fluff compared to what went on in our time," Franklin said. "Let me give you some necessary information. In November 1762, I returned to Philadelphia after five years in London. At the time Pennsylvania was, in effect, owned by the Penn family under a proprietary charter

Two Jefferson wine glasses 1790–1810.

granted by Charles II to William Penn. The governing body was the Pennsylvania Assembly, of which I had been a member since 1751. For a number of reasons, I was opposed to Pennsylvania's proprietary form of government, and I led a cabal within the assembly to petition the Crown to turn Pennsylvania into a royal colony. My actions were opposed by the Penn family and their supporters, and when I ran for reelection to the Pennsylvania Assembly in 1764, those powerful interests saw to it that I was vilified. I was accused in the press of lechery (fathering an illegitimate son by a 'kitchen wench' named Barbara), of starving and dumping the child's mother's body in an unmarked grave, of making a deal with the Crown in exchange for the governorship of Pennsylvania, of stealing my ideas of electricity, of buying my honorary doctorate degrees from Oxford and St. Andrews, and of embezzling colony funds. Also, a comment I made earlier about German immigrants being Palatine boors was translated to read Palatine hogs and that cost me dearly within the German communities. And these scurrilous attacks on my character worked! I lost the election. But the Penn family victory was only temporary, because the assembly voted to send me back to England to work toward ending proprietary rule in Pennsylvania." [316]

"Many Americans today would find that hard to believe," I said.

"Hard to believe?" Jefferson said. "Let me give you some examples of dirty infighting that went on during the presidential campaign between John Adams and me. To the standard charges against Adams of being a monarchist and warmonger, we can add statements in the press that he was a 'repulsive pedant,' a 'gross hypocrite,' and 'in his private life, one of the most egregious fools upon the continent.' Adams was 'that strange compound of ignorance and ferocity, of deceit and weakness,' a 'hideous hermaphroditical character which has neither the force nor firmness of a man, nor the gentleness and sensibility of a woman.'

"Adams's accuser was James Callender, the same man who would later slander me. 'The reign of Mr. Adams,' said Callender, 'has hitherto been one continued tempest of malignant passions.' Once, according to Callender, Adams had become so enraged that he tore his wig off, threw it to the floor, and stamped on it. By what 'species of madness' had America submitted to accept such a man as president? 'The historian will search for those occult causes that induced her to exalt an individual who has neither the innocence of sensibility which incites it to love, nor that omnipotence of intellect which commands us to admire. He will ask why the United States degrades themselves to the choice of a wretch whose soul came blasted from the hand of nature, of a wretch that has neither the science of a magistrate, the politeness of a courtier, nor the courage of a man?' Adams's sole objective was to make war on France, Callender said. The choice was clear—Adams and war, or Jefferson and peace."[317]

"I must tell you, Mr. Jefferson, that there are those who believe that you not only encouraged Callender's attacks on Adams's public acts, but that you also did nothing to dissuade Callender's personal attacks. [318] Many believe that to encourage him, you sent him support money in the guise of payments for copies of his book, *The Prospect before Us*. Abigail Adams, outraged by what she called your dealings with Callender and the fact that you released him from prison, flat-out told you that Callender was the reason the Adamses severed their friendship with you, or as she put it, 'This was the sword that cut asunder the Gordian knot.' "[319]

"I know of her charge, and that the Adamses were alienated from me by belief in the lying suggestions, contrived for electioneering purposes, that I mixed in the activity and intrigues of Callender. My most intimate friends can testify that I was perfectly passive. They would sometimes, indeed, tell me what was going on; but no man ever heard me take part in such conversations; and none ever misrepresented Mr. Adams in my presence, without my asserting his just character. With very confidential persons I have doubtless disapproved of the principles and practices of his administration—this was unavoidable—but never with those with whom it could do him any injury. Decency would have required this conduct from me, if disposition had not; and I am satisfied that Mr. Adams's conduct was equally honorable towards me. But I think it part of his character to suspect foul play in those of whom he is jealous, and not easily to relinquish his suspicions. [320]

"But Callender was no respecter of persons. Shortly thereafter, he turned on me, saying that it would have been advantageous to my reputation if my head had been cut off five minutes before I began my inaugural speech. This sort of venom was followed with attacks on my moral character, including the Sally Hemings story, and the Walker story. His accusations were widely disseminated by the Federalist press. These charges were, of course, renewed when I stood for reelection in 1805, together with charges that I showed cowardice when I was governor, and that I hired Callender to write scurrilous lies about Washington, Adams and other Federalists.

"Callender aside, I became a constant butt for every shaft of calumny that malice and falsehood could form, from the presses, public speakers, or private letters. One newspaper warned that my election would lead to civil war, and hordes of Frenchmen and Irishmen would come to America and destroy everything we held dear. I was accused of cheating my clients as a lawyer. The old claim that I was anti-religious was revised, and people were told that if I were elected president they would have to hide the family Bibles. [321] A Reverend Cotton Mather Smith slandered me with the accusations that I had obtained my property by fraud and robbery, and that in one instance I had defrauded and robbed a widow and fatherless children of an estate to which I was executor, both absolute falsehoods." [322]

"Since Callender was the malignancy that caused the break in the friendship between John Adams and you, how did it come about that you reconciled and carried on a rich and intimate correspondence for the rest your lives?"

"This is how it came about. Edward Coles, Madison's personal secretary, paid Mr. Adams a visit in Quincy and during their conversation Coles assured Mr. Adams of my continued affection. On hearing that Adams exclaimed: 'I always loved Jefferson, and still love him.'

"When Coles reported that to me, I wrote to Benjamin Rush and said, 'That is good enough for me.' Indeed, I thought our not writing to each other disgraceful to us both, as indicating minds not sufficiently elevated to prevent a public competition from affecting our personal friendship. I had the same good opinion of Mr. Adams I always had. I knew him to be an honest man, an able one with his pen, and he was a powerful advocate on the floor of Congress. Rush wrote to Adams and reported that I had extended the olive branch, which I had. [323] On Christmas day, Adams wrote to Rush and said, 'You exhort me to forgiveness and love of enemies, as if I considered, or had ever considered Jefferson as my enemy. This is not so; I have always loved him as a friend ... Of what use can it be for Jefferson and me to exchange letters?' [324] Fortunately, Adams changed his mind and a week later wrote me a letter that initiated the renewal of our friendship. [325]

"I returned his letter, commenting on how he and I have been 'wonderfully spared, and myself with remarkable health, and a considerable activity of body and mind. I am on horseback three or four hours of every day; visit three or four times a year a possession I have ninety miles distant, performing the winter journey on horseback. I walk little, however, a single mile being too much for me, and I live in the midst of my grandchildren, one of whom has lately promoted me to be a great-grandfather. I have heard with pleasure that you also retain good health, and a greater power of exercise in walking than I do.

But I would rather have heard this from yourself, and that, writing a letter like mine, full of egotisms, and of details of your health, your habits, occupations and enjoyments, I should have the pleasure of knowing that in the race of life, you do not keep, in its physical decline, the same distance ahead of me which you have done in political honors and achievements. No circumstances have lessened the interest I feel in these particulars respecting yourself; none have suspended for one moment my sincere esteem for you.'[326]

"Adams and I had acted in perfect harmony, through a long and perilous contest for our liberty and independence. A constitution has been acquired, which, neither of us thinks perfect, yet both consider as competent to render our fellow citizens the happiest and the securest on whom the sun has ever shone. If we do not think exactly alike as to its imperfections, it matters little to our country, which, after devoting to it long lives of disinterested labor, we have delivered over to our successors in life, who will be able to take care of it and of themselves."[327]

"Since you obviously feel, Mr. Jefferson, that over the years the press has been guilty 'for every shaft of calumny which malice and falsehood could form' against you, what do you believe is the proper way to operate a newspaper?"

"'By restraining it to true facts and sound principles only. Yet I fear such a paper would find few subscribers. It is a melancholy truth that a suppression of the press could not more completely deprive the nation of its benefits than is done by its abandoned prostitution to falsehood. Nothing seen in a newspaper can now be believed. Truth itself becomes suspicious by being put into that polluted vehicle. The real extent of this state of misinformation is known only to those who are in situations to confront the lies of the day with facts within their knowledge. I really look with commiseration over the great body of my fellow citizens, who, reading newspapers, live and die in the belief that they have known something of what has been passing in the world in their time; whereas the accounts they have read in newspapers are just as true a history of any other period of the world as of the present, except that the real names of the day are affixed to their fables. General facts may indeed be collected from them, such as that Europe is now at war, that Bonaparte has been a successful warrior that he has subjected a great portion of Europe to his will, but no details can be relied on. I will add that the man who never looks into a newspaper is better informed than he who reads them, inasmuch as he who knows nothing is nearer to truth than he whose mind is filled with falsehoods and errors. He who reads nothing will still learn the great facts, and the details are all false.

" 'Perhaps an editor might begin a reformation in some such way as this. Divide his paper into four chapters, heading the first as truths, the second as probabilities, the third as possibilities, and the fourth as lies. The first chapter would be very short, as it would contain little more than authentic papers and information from such sources as the editor would be willing to risk his own reputation for their truth. The second would contain what, from a mature consideration of all circumstances, his judgment should conclude to be probably true. This, however, should contain rather too little than too much. The third and fourth should be professedly for those readers who would rather have lies for their money than the blank paper they would occupy.

" 'Such an editor, too, would have to set his face against the demoralizing practice of feeding the public mind habitually on slander, and the depravity of taste which this nauseous ailment induces. Defamation is becoming a necessity of life; so much so that a dish of tea in the morning or evening cannot be digested without this stimulant.'

"Having freely expressed my opinion about the press, and 'despite the calumny and slander leveled against me and many others by newspapers, let me affirm that I am for freedom of the press, and against all violations of the Constitution to silence by force and not by reason the complaints or criticisms, just or unjust, of our citizens against the conduct of their agents.' [328]

"Our first object should therefore be to leave open all the avenues to truth. The most effectual is freedom of the press. It is, therefore, the first shut up by those who fear the investigation of their actions. The firmness with which the people withstood the abuses of the press in my time, the discernment they manifested between truth and falsehood, show that they may safely be trusted to hear everything true and false, and to form a correct judgment between them. It results from the use of reason and common sense." [329]

"Wasn't Callender arrested for what he wrote about President Adams?" I said.

"Callender was promptly arrested and prosecuted under the Sedition Act for inciting the American people against their president. In May he went on trial in a federal court in Richmond. When Governor Monroe asked me about Callender's defense, I said that I thought it essentially just and necessary that he be substantially defended. But Samuel Chase, the presiding federal judge, conducted a biased court and, of course, Callender was found guilty and sentenced to nine months in jail and fined two hundred dollars. When I became president, I pardoned Callender. [330]

"Upon his release from prison, Callender asked to be postmaster general in Richmond. I decided against it, and this rebuke, coupled with the delay in reimbursing him the $200 fine he had been assessed at the time of his trial, set him off. He charged me with breach of promise and complete indifference toward him."

"In the Sally Hemings story, what did Callender accuse you of?"

"That one of my slaves, Sally Hemings, became my mistress after the death of my wife, and was the mother of several of my children."

"Is it true that your wife Martha's father, John Wayles, was Sally's father?"

"I personally don't know that to be a fact, but the oral tradition as handed down by certain slaves was that John Wayles was the father of the six youngest children Sally's mother, Betty Hemings, brought to Monticello after Wayles's death. Sally was the youngest." [331]

"If that tradition is correct, Sally was your wife's half sister."

"Yes," Jefferson said, nodding his assent.

"I felt constrained to ask the hard question. I had requested that our meeting be a no-holds-barred discussion, and I decided to go ahead and ask it. "Mr. Jefferson, is there any truth to Callender's accusations?"

"I will answer that question the same way I did when it was raised two hundred years ago. With regard to all the charges leveled against me, I said in a letter to my secretary of the navy, Robert Smith: 'The enclosed copy of a letter to Mr. [Levi] Lincoln will so fully explain its own object, that I need say nothing in that way. I communicate it to particular friends because I wish to stand with them on the ground of truth, neither better nor worse than that makes me. You will perceive that I plead guilty to one of their charges, that when young and single I offered love to a handsome lady. I acknowledge its incorrectness. It is the only one founded on truth among all their allegations against me.'"

"And that handsome lady was?"

"Betsy Walker, the wife of my friend John Walker. John and I had grown up together and were classmates at William & Mary. When John married Betsy in June 1764, I was one of the bridesmen. In the summer of 1768, John went off to upstate New York to help negotiate a treaty with the Indians. He asked me to look after his wife and child while he was away. He was gone four months, and during that time, I offered love to Betsy."

"And?"

"She properly refused me. Betsy let nearly twenty years elapse before she told John, and another ten years went by before he made an issue of the incident, goaded by my political enemies, who let the story leak."[332]

"What was the outcome?"

"I apologized to John and he accepted my apology."[333]

"Would you like to know where history now stands on the Sally Hemings matter?"

Jefferson stared at his wine glass but said nothing. "Oh, come, Thomas," Franklin said, "let's not just give information; let's find out what we can when we can."

Jefferson nodded. "All right, where does history stand on the subject, Jack?"

"Your statement to Robert Smith proved sufficient to convince most historians through the ages that there was no truth to Callender's allegations and similar rumors that circulated from time to time. In 1971, however, an historian by the name of Fawn Brodie broke ranks with the 'Jefferson is innocent of sex with Sally' mold. Her remarks created quite a stir at the time, but within a few years it faded and subsequent biographers dismissed Professor Brodie's assertions that you had engaged in sex with a slave. Then something happened that may have changed forever the thinking about your relationship with Sally Hemings."

"What was that?" Franklin asked.

"DNA testing."

Franklin said, "What is DNA?"

"DNA is the abbreviation for deoxyribonucleic acid, a chromosome molecule that carries genetic coding unique to each person. Through laboratory tests, DNA can be extracted from body tissue such as blood, semen, and hair and matched against another person's DNA to determine paternity and much more. DNA is found in all people; it is self-replicating, and it is responsible for passing along hereditary characteristics from one generation to the next."

"What happened?" Jefferson said.

"Eugene Foster, an American pathologist came up with the idea of matching your descendants' DNA with the descendants of Sally's children by using the Y chromosome found in DNA. As Dr. Foster explained, the Y chromosomal DNA was used because it is passed unchanged from generation to generation and from father to son only. Because you did not have male children, Dr. Foster obtained a blood sample from a male descendant of your paternal uncle, Field Jefferson, and from a male descendant of Sally's youngest son, Eston.

"Callender had specifically accused you of fathering Sally's first child,

Thomas Woodson, while you and Sally were in Paris. For more than two hundred years, the Woodson family has claimed to be your descendants. Therefore, Dr Foster took blood samples of five male descendants of Thomas Woodson.

"Because several of your grandchildren claimed that your nephews, Peter and Samuel Carr, had fathered Sally's children, blood samples of descendants of their paternal grandfather were taken. All the blood samples were then hand-carried by Dr. Foster to a scientific laboratory in England where the DNA tests were performed." I paused and took a sip of wine. Franklin and Jefferson were staring at me with great intensity, but both patiently waited for me to continue.

"In October 1998, *Nature*, a respected English scientific journal, published an article written by Dr. Foster titled, 'Jefferson fathered slave's last child.' The test results showed no match between the DNA of the descendants of you and Woodson, which means that Callender's accusations that you fathered Thomas Woodson were false. There was no match between the DNA of the descendants of Woodson, Hemings and Carr, which means that neither Peter nor Samuel Carr fathered Thomas Woodson or Eston Hemings. There was, however, a DNA match between the descendants of your uncle Field Jefferson and the descendants of Eston Hemings, Sally's youngest son. This finding does not necessarily mean that you are the biological father of Eston as the title of Dr. Foster's article states. The Y chromosomal DNA match means that you or any one of about twenty-five Field Jefferson descendants living at the time could be Eston's father.

"Shortly after Dr. Foster's DNA results were made public, The Thomas Jefferson Foundation formed a committee to investigate Eston Hemings' paternity. The committee concluded that Dr. Foster's DNA study was conducted in a manner that meets the standards of the scientific community, and its scientific results are valid, and that the weight of all known evidence from the DNA study, original documents, written and oral historical accounts, and statistical data indicates a high probability that you fathered Eston Hemings.

"Interestingly, a committee of thirteen scholars commissioned by the Thomas Jefferson Heritage Society examined essentially the same material and unanimously concluded that allegations that you fathered any of Sally Hemings's children is by no means proven. With the exception of only one member, their individual conclusions ranged 'f rom serious skepticism about the charge to a conviction that it is almost certainly untrue.'"[334]

Jefferson remained silent and I quickly changed the subject. "What type of education did you provide your daughters, Mr. Jefferson?"

"Remember, Jack, at the time women were not allowed admittance to American colleges and universities. But I was concerned for my daughters' educations. When Martha was thirteen I laid out the following study program for her. 'From eight to ten, practice music. From ten to one, dance one day and draw another. From one to two, draw on the day you dance, and write a letter the next day. From three to four, read French. From four to five, exercise in music. From five till bedtime, read English, write.' I also expected her to write to me by every post, informing me what books she had read and what tunes she learned, and enclosing her best copy of every lesson in drawing. I also suggested that she write one other letter every week, and take care not to misspell a word. In addition, when Martha accompanied me to France, I arranged for her admission to a fashionable school in Paris, the Convent of Panthemont." [335]

"Dr. Franklin, a number of your biographers have said you neglected your daughter Sally, that you did not take the time to understand her, to get to know her, or to provide for her the education and the privileges she deserved." [336]

"I think that is an unfair assessment of the education I provided my daughter. Although as a young man I had argued in favor of providing girls with educations equal to those of boys, I must admit that I did not provide my daughter with an education equal to that of my son. I saw to it, however, that she learned reading, writing, and arithmetic, and when she expressed an interest in French, I got her French lessons. I also insisted that she learn accounting, a more practical tool in case of widowhood than either dancing or music. For the most part I urged Sally to perfect her domestic skills. [337]

"Also, I was thirty-seven when Sally was born, and I was working as hard as or harder than I had ever worked. When I retired five years later, my time was devoted to my electrical experiments. When Sally reached adolescence, I left for England, where I spent the next five years." [338]

"You took your son William with you to London, but not Sally."

"Sally was fourteen and needed her mother's care, and her mother would not come to England because of a mortal fear of the ocean."

"I'm not trying to be confrontational. I'm just pointing out what some historians of my time have said, and that is, when you got to London, you found time to lavish attention and affection on your landlady's young daughter, Polly Stevenson." [339]

"When I arrived in London in 1757, I took quarters at 7 Craven Street, the home of Margaret Stevenson, a widow. Polly was living there at the time with her mother. She later went to live outside London with an elderly aunt. She was eighteen, pretty, vivacious, educated, and intelligent, with a mind thirsty for knowledge. Shortly after we met, Polly proposed a correspondence on matters of moral and natural philosophy. I was pleased to oblige, and I became her teacher. [340] She was inquisitive and an apt student. Some of the topics we discussed were about barometers, insects, rising tides in rivers, why water becomes warmer after being pumped, waterspouts, bubbles in teacups, fire, distillation of seawater, electrical storms, why rain is not salty, why wet clothes do not cause a cold, and many other subjects. I instructed her on morals, science, and education." [341]

"You wrote her more often than you did your own family: poems, notes of tenderness and warm affection, and on one occasion told her that 'not a day passes that I do not think of you.' "[342]

"There is no doubt that Polly and I had a very close relationship that lasted thirty years. [343] But when she told me that she might 'live single' the rest of her life and devote herself to learning, I lectured her on the values of marriage, being a good wife, and raising a family.

"In the summer of 1769, I visited Paris, and on my return, Polly could hardly wait to tell me about a young doctor by the name of William Hewson whom she had met. Polly was thirty at the time, and within a year, they were married. I gave her away in marriage." [344]

"And you and Polly remained close friends?" I asked.

"Oh, yes. One of Polly's best friends, Dorothea Blount, felt neglected by Polly's marriage and complained to me. I teased Polly, telling her that 'your old Dolly and I have agreed to love each other better than we ever did to make up as much as we can our supposed loss of you.' [345]

"In September, Polly and Dr. Hewson moved in with us at Craven Street. On the twenty-second, Polly's mother left on a trip to Rochester, and I decided to publish the *Craven Street Gazette*, a newspaper devoted exclusively to the events of our household."

"I would love to hear some of the stories you covered," Jefferson said.

Franklin's eyes twinkled with satisfaction and nostalgia. "One story went something like this: 'This morning Queen Margaret, accompanied by her first maid of honor, set out for Rochester. It is whispered that the new family administration, which took place on her Majesty's departure, promises, like all other new administrations, to govern much better than the old one.

" 'We have good authority to assure our readers that a cabinet council was held this afternoon at tea; the subject of which was a proposal for the reformation of manners and a more strict observation of the Lord's day. The result was a unanimous resolution that no meat should be dressed tomorrow; whereby the cook and the first minister (Polly and her husband) will both be at liberty to go to church, the one having nothing to do and the other no roast to rule. It seems the cold shoulder of mutton and the apple pie were thought sufficient for Sunday's dinner. All pious people applauded this measure, and it is thought the new ministry will soon become popular.

" 'It is now found by sad experience that good resolutions are easier made than executed. Notwithstanding yesterday's solemn order of council, nobody went to church today. It seems the Great Person's broad-built bulk lay so long abed that the breakfast was not over till it was too late to dress. At least that is the excuse.

" 'This evening there was high play at Craven Street House. The Great Person lost money. It is supposed that the ministers, as is usually supposed of all ministers, shared the emoluments among them.

" 'This morning Lord Hutton called at Craven Street House. He imparted to the Big Man a piece of intelligence important to them both, viz, that the amiable and delectable Miss Dorothea Blount has made a vow to marry absolutely him of the two whose wife should first depart this life. It is impossible to express the various agitations of mind appearing in both their faces on this occasion. Vanity at the preference given them over the rest of mankind, affection to their present wives, fear of losing them, hope, if they must lose them, to obtain the proposed comfort, jealousy of each other in case both wives should die together, etc., etc., etc., all working at the same time jumbled their features into inexplicable confusion. They parted at length with professions of outward appearances indeed of ever-enduring friendship, but it was shrewdly suspected that each of them sincerely wished health and long life to the other's wife; and that, however long either of these friends might like to live himself, the other would be well pleased to survive him.' " [346]

Franklin looked up, and Jefferson and I howled with laughter.

"Was Polly's marriage a happy one?" I asked.

"Polly had a very happy marriage, but, unfortunately, it didn't last long. Just before the birth of her third child, Dr. Hewson cut himself during an autopsy, developed septicemia, and died. She never remarried." [347]

"After you left England, did you ever see Polly again?"

116

"Yes. In the winter of 1784–85, she joined me in Paris with her three children. A year later she and her children followed me to Philadelphia and she was with me to the end."

"Were women included in your plans for the Pennsylvania Academy?"

"No. With respect to the education of women, I was not in the forefront. I told Polly Stevenson when I learned that she was thinking of renouncing marriage and devoting herself to the study of philosophy that there is no rank in natural knowledge of equal dignity and importance with that of being a good wife." [348]

"What about you, Mr. Jefferson. Did you provide your daughters with fatherly advice?"

"Yes. One day my daughter Martha asked if it was true that the world was coming to an end. I told her 'I hope you will have good sense enough to disregard those foolish predictions that the world is to be at an end soon. The Almighty has never made known to anybody at what time he created it; nor will he tell anybody when he will put an end to it, if he ever means to do it. As to preparations for that event, the best way is for you to be always prepared for it. The only way to be so is, never to say or do a bad thing. If ever you are about to say anything amiss, or to do anything wrong, consider beforehand. You will feel something within you which will tell you it is wrong, and ought not to be said or done. This is your conscience, and be sure to obey it. Our Maker has given us all this faithful internal monitor; and if you always obey it, you will always be prepared for the end of the world; or for a much more certain event, which is death. This must happen to all: it puts an end to the world as to us; and the way to be ready for it is never to do a wrong act.' " [349]

"While we are on the subject of education, did either of you believe that a young man could get a better education in England than here at home?"

"Why send an American youth to Europe for education?" Jefferson asked. "What are the objects of an useful American education? Classical knowledge; modern languages, chiefly French, Spanish, and Italian; mathematics; natural philosophy; natural history; civil history; and ethics. In natural philosophy, I mean to include chemistry and agriculture, and in natural history, to include botany as well as the other branches of those departments. It is true that the habit of speaking the modern languages cannot be so well acquired in America, but every other article can be as well acquired at William & Mary College as at any place in Europe. When college education is done with, and a young man is to prepare himself for public life, he must cast his eyes (for America) either on law or physics. For the former, where can he apply so advantageously as to Mr. Wythe? For the latter, he must come to Europe: the medical class of students, therefore, is the only one which need come to Europe.

"If he goes to England, he learns drinking, horse racing, and boxing. These are the peculiarities of an English education. It appears to me, then, that an American, coming to Europe for education, loses in his knowledge, in his morals, in his health, in his habits, and in his happiness. I had entertained only doubts on this head before I came to Europe; what I saw and heard, since I came here, proves more than I had even suspected. Cast your eye over America: who are the men of most learning, of most eloquence, most beloved by their countrymen, and most trusted and promoted by them? They are those who have been educated among them, and whose manners, morals, and habits are perfectly homogeneous with those of the country.[350]

"But despite my emphasis on a classical education, what I valued more than all things was good humor. For thus I estimate the qualities of the mind: First, good humor; second, integrity; third, industry; fourth, science. The preference of the first to the second quality may not at first be acquiesced in, but certainly we had all rather associate with a good-humored, light-principled man than with an ill-tempered rigorist in morality."[351]

Franklin and I smiled over Jefferson's dislike for the morality rigorist, and I thought of several in modern political life who fit the description. Then I asked Jefferson, "Did you give your daughters much specific advice?"

"Here is a litany of specific things I advised my daughters about: At all times let their clothes be clean, whole, and properly put on from the moment they rise till they go to bed, as nothing is so disgusting to our sex as a want of cleanliness and delicacy;[352] to always be truthful because no vice is so mean as the want of truth and at the same time so useless; to never be angry, since anger only serves to torment ourselves, to divert others, and alienate their esteem; to be industrious and apply themselves to useful pursuits;[353] to buy anything that they had not money in their pockets to pay for, because it gives much more pain to the mind to be in debt than to do without any article; and to stay on good terms with their neighbors. It is almost the most important circumstance in life, since nothing is so corroding as frequently to meet persons with whom one has any difference. The ill-will of a single neighbor is an immense drawback to the happiness of life, and therefore their good-will cannot be bought too dear.[354] I emphasized that harmony in the marriage state is the first object to be aimed Nothing can preserve affections uninterrupted but a firm resolution never to differ in will and a determination in each to consider the love of each other of more value than any other object whatever." [355]

"That is sound advice not just for a daughter but for all of us," I said.

"I remember how concerned I was for the emotional and physical safety of my grandson, Thomas Jefferson Randolph, when he went off alone to school in Philadelphia at the age of fifteen. I took the time from my presidential duties to write him a lengthy letter of advice. I pointed out that, thrown on a wide world, among entire strangers, without a friend or guardian to advise him, and with so little experience of mankind, his dangers were great, and still safety rested with himself. A determination never to do what is wrong, prudence, and good humor would go far towards securing him the estimation of the world. I reminded him that I was in a similar situation at fourteen, when my father died, and I remembered the various sorts of bad company with which I associated from time to time. The only reason I did not become as worthless to society as some of them did was because I had the good fortune to become acquainted very early with some characters of very high standing, and to feel the incessant wish that I could become what they were. Under temptations and difficulties, I would ask myself, What would Dr. Small, Mr. Wythe, Peyton Randolph do in this situation? What course in it will ensure me their approbation? I am certain that this mode of deciding on my conduct tended more to correctness than any reasoning powers I possessed. Knowing the even and dignified line they pursued, I could never doubt for a moment which of two courses would be in character for them. Whereas, seeking the same object through a process of moral reasoning, and with the jaundiced eye of youth, I should often have erred. From the circumstances of my position, I was often thrown into the society of horse racers, card players, fox hunters, scientific and professional men, and of dignified men; and many a time I asked myself, in the enthusiastic moment of the death of a fox, the victory of a favorite horse, the issue of a question eloquently argued at the bar, or in the great council of the nation, well, which of these kinds of reputation should I prefer? That of a horse jockey, a fox hunter, an orator, or the honest advocate of my country's rights? I assured, my grandson that this self-catechizing habit led to the prudent selection and steady pursuit of what is right.

"I mentioned good humor as one of the preservatives of our peace and tranquility and when imitated and aided artificially by politeness, it becomes an acquisition of first-rate value. Politeness is the practice of sacrificing to those whom we meet in society all the little conveniences and preferences that will gratify them and deprive us of nothing worth a moment's consideration; it is the giving a pleasing and flattering turn to our expressions that will conciliate others and make them pleased with us as well as themselves. How cheap a price for the good will of another!

"But in stating prudential social rules I did not omit the important one of never entering into dispute or argument with another. I never saw an instance of one of two disputants convincing the other by argument. I have seen many, on their getting warm, becoming rude and shooting one another. Conviction is the effect of our own dispassionate reasoning, either in solitude, or in weighing within ourselves, dispassionately, what we hear from others, while standing uncommitted in argument ourselves. I used you, Benjamin, as the classic example. I told my grandson that one of the rules that above all others, made Doctor Franklin the most amiable of men in society was 'never to contradict anybody.' If Benjamin Franklin was urged to announce an opinion, he did it rather by asking questions, as if for information, or by suggesting doubts. When I hear another express an opinion that is not mine, I say to myself, he has a right to his opinion, as I to mine; why should I question it?

"Be a listener only, keep within yourself, and endeavor to establish with yourself the habit of silence, especially on politics. In the fevered state of our country, no good can ever result from any attempt to set one of these fiery zealots to rights, in either fact or principle. They are determined as to the facts they will believe and the opinions on which they will act. Get by them, therefore, as you would by an angry bull; it is not for a man of sense to dispute the road with such an animal. I reminded my grandson to look steadily to the pursuits which had carried him to Philadelphia, to be very select in social companions, and to avoid taverns, drinkers, smokers, idlers, and dissipated persons generally, for it is with such that broils and contentions arise."[356]

"Dr. Franklin, you once gave some advice to a young man in the form of a letter titled 'Old Mistresses Apologue.' It certainly is different advice from that offered by Mr. Jefferson to his grandson."

Franklin, with a sheepish grin said, "Keep in mind, Jack, the young man to whom I wrote my letter of advice was a bit older than Mr. Jefferson's grandson."

"Historians and public officials considered your letter of advice so salacious, so indecent, and so potentially embarrassing to your historical reputation that they refused to publish it! It was hidden from the public's view for 181 years

120

and not published in full until 1926, when it appeared in Frank Russell's biography, *Benjamin Franklin: The First Civilized American.*" [357]

"What in the world did they find salacious or indecent about it? As I recall, I counseled marriage as the proper remedy for sex, but advised my friend that, should he not marry, then in all his amours he should prefer old women to young ones." Franklin opened his leather case, removed some papers, and handed them to me, "Here is a copy of the letter. Read it aloud, Jack, so that Mr. Jefferson can decide whether it's good advice:

My Dear Friend:

I know of no medicine fit to diminish the violent natural inclinations you mention, and if I did, I think I should not communicate it to you. Marriage is the proper remedy. It is the most natural state of man, and therefore the state in which you are most likely to find solid happiness. Your reasons against entering into it at present appear to me not wellfounded. The circumstantial advantages you have in view by postponing it are not only uncertain, but they are small in comparison with that of the thing itself, the being married and settled. It is the man and woman united that make the compleat human being. Separate, she wants his force of body and strength of reason; he, her softness, sensibility and acute discernment. Together they are more likely to succeed in the world. A single man has not nearly the value he would have in that state of union. He is an incomplete animal. He resembles the odd half of a pair of scissors. If you get a prudent healthy wife, your industry in your profession, with her good economy, will be a fortune sufficient.

But if you will not take this counsel, and persist in thinking commerce with the sex inevitable, then I repeat my former advice, that in all your amours you *should prefer old women to young ones*. You call this a paradox, and demand my reasons. They are these.

1. Because as they have more knowledge of the world and their minds are better stored with observations, their conversation is more improving and more lastingly agreeable.

2. Because when women cease to be handsome, they study to be good. To maintain their influence over men, they supply the diminution of beauty by an augmentation of utility. They learn to do 1000 services small and great, and are the most tender and useful of all friends when you are sick. Thus

they continue amiable. And hence there is hardly such a thing to be found as an old woman who is not a good woman.

3. Because there is no hazard of children, which irregularly produced may be attended with much inconvenience.

4. Because through more experience, they are more prudent and discreet in conducting an intrigue to prevent suspicion. The commerce with them is therefore safer with regard to your reputation. And with regard to theirs, if the affair should happen to be known, considerate people might be rather in-clined to excuse an old woman who would kindly take care of a young man, form his manners by her good counsels, and prevent his ruining his health and fortune among mercenary prostitutes.

5. Because in every animal that walks upright, the deficiency of the fluids that fill the muscles appears first in the highest part. The face grows lank and wrinkled, then the neck, then the breast and arms, the lower parts continuing to the last as plump as ever. So that covering all above with a basket, and re-garding only what is below the girdle, it is impossible of two women to know an old from a young one. And as in the dark all cats are grey, the pleasure of corporal enjoyment with an old woman is at least equal, and frequently supe-rior, every knack being by practice capable of improvement.

6. Because the sin is less. The debauching a virgin may be her ruin, and make her for life unhappy.

7. Because the compunction is less. The having made a young girl miserable may give you frequent bitter reflections, none of which can attend making an old woman happy.

8thly and lastly. They are *so grateful*!!

This much for my paradox. But still I advise you to marry directly; being sin-cerely your affectionate friend." [358]

I looked at Jefferson who was smiling broadly, and remarked, "After Dr. Franklin's advice to his young friend, any question I ask is going to be an anti-climactic."

"Indeed," Jefferson said, his smile broadening.

"Her goes," I said. "Currently the United States has a tremendous national debt. As we talk it is in excess of more than eight trillion dollars, and increasing at a rate of over one and three quarter billion dollars per day. I'm sure it won't come as a surprise to learn that this astronomical debt has a lot of fiscally conservative people very concerned. How do you gentlemen feel about national debt?" [359]

"Two years before I became president, I wrote to Elbridge Gerry, 'I am for a government rigorously frugal and simple, applying all the possible savings of the public revenue to the discharge of the national debt.' So that is where I stand," Jefferson said. [360]

"Earlier, Mr. Jefferson, we were speaking of personal disappointments. Wasn't the financial indebtedness you incurred, especially in your retirement years, a personal disappointment?"

Jefferson's brow furrowed. "Yes, a profound disappointment and a 'deadly embarrassment during my remaining years.' One night I was 'lying awake from painful thoughts when an idea came to me like an inspiration from the realms of bliss.'"

"What was it?" I asked.

"To dispose of my property by lottery. The legislature had to authorize all lotteries, and I let it be known that their approval was to me almost a matter of life and death. The legislature voted their approval unanimously. Friends told me that I turned white when I learned that Monticello had to be included in the plan, although with the proviso that I could remain there for life. I died before the plan went into effect." [361]

"You left debts of more than $100,000, but in the end it worked out." I said.

"What do you mean 'it worked out'?" Jefferson said.

"It took some fifty years, but your debts were ultimately paid off." [362]

"I was not president of the United States, or secretary of the treasury like Alexander Hamilton, so I was never confronted with the problem," Franklin said. "Throughout my life, however, I had been an advocate of frugality. On the other hand, frugality is not always the answer. Benjamin Vaughan, my English editor, had inquired if I knew a remedy for the American penchant for luxury, on which Vaughan had heard travelers remark disapprovingly. I replied that I knew of no such remedy, and added that the problem was much exaggerated, and in any event, it might not be a problem at all. 'Is not the hope of being one day able to purchase and enjoy luxuries a great spur to labor and industry? May not luxury, therefore, produce more than it consumes?'" [363]

Petit entered with a large tray holding six wine glasses and two crystal decanters of red wine. He placed the two decanters in front of Jefferson and positioned two glasses to the right of each of us. "Monsieur Jefferson, le Château Haut Brion est à votre gauche; est à droite le Château Margaux."

"Thank you, Petit." Jefferson stood, and with the Haut Brion decanter in his left hand and the Margaux decanter in his right he poured our glasses.

As he poured his own wine, I said, "Speaking of luxury, we are about to drink two of the world's most expensive wines. Mr. Jefferson, you drank the four first growths, Lafite, Latour, Margaux, and Haut Brion, and I'm interested to know how you compared them in taste."[364]

"You are about to experience two of the wines yourself. But generally speaking, Lafite was known for its silky softness on the palate and its charming perfume. Latour had a fuller body, and, at the same time, a considerable aroma that lacked the softness of Lafite. Château Margaux, on the other hand, was lighter, and possessed all the delicate qualities of Lafite except that it had not quite so high a flavor. Haut Brion had more spirit and body than any of the preceding, but was rough when new and required being kept longer in the wood, while the others benefited from bottling in much less time."[365]

"Your description, Mr. Jefferson, is a remarkably accurate comparison of their styles today," I said.

The three of us swirled the Haut Brion, inhaled the bouquet, and then sipped the wine. We followed the same procedure with the Château Margaux. Finally, Jefferson looked up and said, "Well, Jack, what's your verdict?"

"They are both fabulous wines. The Margaux has a silky softness, a forthcoming bouquet, and is lighter in body. The Haut Brion bouquet is still a bit closed and has a spine of tannin that needs a few more years of bottle age to reach its maximum potential. But when it is fully mature, its underlying richness of fruit will keep it in peak drinking condition for many years to come."

"I'm afraid, Jack, that I'm not familiar with the term 'tannin'," Franklin said.

"Nor I," said Jefferson.

"Tannins," I said, "are a group of chemicals that occur in grapes and impart bitterness or astringency to the taste of wine. Tannins are important in the aging of wines, particularly red wines."[366]

"I think," Franklin said, "both wines are magnificent and will be even better with the beef, and I'm ready to move in that direction."

As if on cue, Petit entered carrying a large beef à la mode on a silver platter.

"These two great wines," I said, "remind me of an auction that occurred twenty-five years ago that resulted in the highest price ever paid for a single bottle of wine. And, Mr. Jefferson, that bottle of wine involves you."

Jefferson's eyebrows arched. "Me?" he said, pointing his right index finger toward his chest. "How can that be?"

While I spoke, Petit carved the beef with surgical precision and placed heaping portions on our plates with an assortment of roasted vegetables.

"It involves a cache of eighteenth century Bordeaux wine bottles allegedly found 'behind a cellar wall in an old house in Paris,' and engraved with the initials 'Th.J.' The owner of the bottles brought them to the attention of Michael Broadbent, then the wine director of Christie's auction house in London, and one of the bottles engraved '1787 Lafitte Th.J.' was consigned to Christie's for auction. The Christie's auction catalog captioned the bottle: 'The 1787 Th.J. Lafitte. The Property of Mr. Hardy Rodenstock. Château Lafite—Vintage 1787 Pauillac. Pre-1855 classification. Almost certainly bottled at the château.' The catalog gives a description of the bottle, the level of its contents, and states, 'Th.J. are the initials of Thomas Jefferson.' It goes on to detail your purchases of Bordeaux wines.

"The '1787 Lafitte Th.J.' was auctioned at Christie's in London on December 5, 1985. After the auction *The New York Times* reported: 'A nearly two-century-old bottle of Lafite, believed to have been part of an order set aside for Thomas Jefferson, commanded $156,450 today at an auction here.' The winning bid, by Christopher Forbes on behalf of *Forbes* magazine, was by far the highest price ever paid for a single bottle of wine. Here," I said, "is a photograph of the Forbes 1787 Lafitte bottle." After looking at it, Jefferson passed the photograph to Franklin.

"According to the Christie's auction catalog, the cache of bottles included 'a bottle of 1787 Château d'Yquem … From the same bricked up Paris cellar Mr. Rodenstock also acquired three bottles of 1787 Branne Mouton, (now Mouton Rothschild), Chateau Margau [*sic*], the Lafite and another bottle of Yquem.' [367]

"Whether this bottle was ever owned or possessed by you, Mr. Jefferson, has evoked much comment. To clear up any ambiguity about its Jefferson provenance, did you ever own or possess this '1787 Lafitte Th.J.' bottle?"

Jefferson turned and looked at Franklin and back to me. His lips were curved in a slight smile. "Jack, I never owned or possessed that bottle, and there are a number of very good reasons that should refute any claim that I did. All the bottles you mentioned, except for the 1784 Yquem, are of the 1787 vintage. A careful examination of my records will show that I never ordered or owned any Bordeaux wines of the 1787 vintage. I don't recall ever mentioning in a letter, or otherwise, a desire for Bordeaux wines of the 1787 vintage. My

1787 Lafitte Th. J.

records show that when I was in Bordeaux, I purchased 180 bottles of 1784 Château Margaux for myself and sent 72 bottles of the same vintage to my brother-in-law, Francis Eppes. The cost at Bordeaux was 'three livres per bottle, ready bottled and packed' —the going price for a bottle of the four First Growth wines. [368]

"I made copies of all the letters I wrote and saved those written to me. In addition, I maintained a log of the letters I wrote and received. I kept as well whole parcels of miscellaneous accounts, including the internal customs documents accompanying my wine shipments from Bordeaux to Paris. And, most importantly, I kept daily financial memorandum books recording all my receipts and expenditures. I put so much faith in my memorandum books that I said I would vouch for their accuracy and completeness 'on the bed of death.' " [368a]

"You were meticulous in your record-keeping Mr. Jefferson," I said, "and your records for this period have survived virtually intact, and Lafite 1787 does not appear in a single document, nor does any other Bordeaux wine of the 1787 vintage."

"Also, there are no references in my records of me having purchased Bordeaux wines engraved with my initials. Since the Rodenstock bottles are of the 1784 and 1787 vintages, let me give you a recapitulation of my Bordeaux purchases beginning with my visit to Bordeaux in May 1787. In 1787 I toured for three and a half months through southern France and northern Italy. During the four days I was in Bordeaux, I spent a great deal of time inspecting the vineyards, talking to the owners, the winemakers, and the wine merchants. As a result of those inquiries, I learned that only by purchasing directly from the vineyard owners could I avoid the deception of blending-in of other wines, and that is how I subsequently ordered my wines."

"By ordering direct from the winemaker, Mr. Jefferson, you, in effect, received your wines château bottled, a bottling method that did not become standard practice in Bordeaux until 150 years later, when in 1924 Mouton Rothschild initiated the idea of bottling all its wine at the château. This move revolutionized the distribution of the great Bordeaux wines, because châteaux Lafite, Latour, Margaux and Haut Brion promptly followed Mouton's example. Until 1924, the First Growth estates had traditionally château bottled some of each vintage, but most of their wines were sold in barrels to wine merchants, who bottled, labeled, and sold it. Only the wine merchant knew if the buyer got the wine that he paid for," I said.

"If that's so, then I'm convinced that for 150 years many wine drinkers were getting wines that were something other than what they paid for. To clear up any ambiguity, I will review each of my Bordeaux wine purchases. One of the first things I did upon arrival in Bordeaux was to visit Château Haut Brion and walk through its vineyards. After that visit, I had shipped to my brother-in-law, Francis Eppes, in Virginia, a parcel of 1784 Haut Brion wine, one of the four established as the very best, and the only very fine vintage since 1779. [369] While in Bordeaux, I visited the wine merchant house of Ferger, Gramont & Cie, and ordered 252 bottles of 1784 Château Margaux, fifteen dozen for myself and six dozen for Francis Eppes. I received this order, as did Mr. Eppes. [370]

"Later that year, I wrote from Paris directly to Monsieur Yquem, with a companion letter to John Bondfield, ordering 250 bottles of the 1784 vintage. Within a month, Bondfield advised me that 250 bottles of Yquem were on their way by water carriage, which was equally expeditious, less subject to breakage, and considerable less expensive. Bondfield enclosed a letter from Comte de Lur Saluce, M. d'Yquem's son-in-law, advising that he was now the owner of the estate and that he had drawn and bottled the wine with the greatest care. I received that Yquem order. But you will not find in my letters to M. d'Yquem, or Bondfield, or from Lur Saluce, any mention of having the bottles engraved with my initials. [371]

"Before I left for Amsterdam in March 1788, where I met John Adams and helped negotiate financial arrangements between Holland and the United States, I wrote to M. Pichard, the owner of Château Lafite. I reminded him that we had met when I passed through Bordeaux in May, and said that I would be grateful if he could accommodate me with 250 bottles of the 1784 vintage. I added that if possible to have them bottled at the château, a guarantee that the wine was natural and well drawn. My trip to Amsterdam, and to Germany to visit its vineyards, kept me away from Paris for nearly two months. [372]

"On my return to Paris there was a letter from Bondfield explaining that Lafite's owner, Pichard, had sold his entire 1784 vintage, and though some 1786 Lafite was available, it was not ready to drink. Bondfield suggested that a few hogsheads of 1784 Haut Brion, the next best red wine of that vintage, were still available. [373] I promptly notified Bondfield to send 125 bottles of the 1784 Haut Brion and acknowledged the safe receipt of the 250 bottles of Yquem. [374] Bondfield purchased the Haut Brion and advised that it had been sent by ship. After more than five months of constant expectation of hearing that the Haut Brion was on its way, I wrote him and said, 'If the wine has been forwarded, I will thank you for information of the conveyance by which it came. The Sauterne sent me by the Marquis de Saluce turns out very fine. I shall be glad to receive your draught for both these objects.' [375] Bondfield wrote and explained that his coopers had misdirected the wine. [376] I was disappointed, but expecting to return to America in a few months, and, not knowing when the wine might reach me, I advised Bondfield that if he had not already received the Haut Brion, or engaged to replace it, I could do without it. [377] I ordered no further Bordeaux wines while in France."

"So far as I know, Harvey Rodenstock has never publicly said that his 'Th.J' bottles were owned by you," I said, "but Michael Broadbent, a respected member of the wine trade for fifty years, and the head of Christie's Wine Department for some thirty years, in his latest book states his belief in their Thomas Jefferson authenticity. He writes that 'Jefferson did not trust wine merchants, insisting on the wines being bottled at the chateau, arranging for his agent in Bordeaux to supply bottles engraved (*etiquette* was his instruction) for identification, with the vintage, name of chateau and his initials—more ordinary wines just had the initial scratched—he called this *diamante*—on each bottle, for example, "F" for Frontignan.' " [378]

"Mr. Broadbent is correct that I did not trust wine merchants, but he is mistaken in stating that I ever arranged or instructed my agents in Bordeaux (or anyone else) to supply Bordeaux wine bottles engraved with the vintage, name of the chateau and my initials. And no support for such a contension can be found in my order from Philadelphia in September 1790. I wrote Joseph Fenwick, who was my agent in Bordeaux at that time, 'I trouble you with a commission to receive and forward to me some wines for the President and myself. They are written for in the enclosed letters to the respective owners of the vineyards, and are as follows.

M. le Comte de Lur-Saluce	30. doz. Sauterne for the President
	10. doz. do. for myself
M. de Mirosmenil	20. doz. vin de Segur [379] for the President
Madame de Rozan	10. doz. vin de Rozan for Myself
Monsieur Lambert at	10. doz Frontignan for the President
Frontignan	5. doz. do. for myself' [380]

"In this letter, I said nothing about the bottles being engraved, but I did instruct how the wine packages were to be marked. 'I have directed those for the President to be packed separately and marked G.W. and mine T.I. [381] You will receive them ready packed.'

"In my letter to Lur-Saluce, I wrote, 'He [382] has requested 30 dozen and I would like 10 dozen for myself … Be so kind as to bottle and pack them separately, labeling the 30 dozen G.W. and the ten dozen T.I. in order to prepare for the misfortunes that might occur during shipping.' [383] To Lambert I wrote, 'Be so kind as to send ten dozen bottles for our President, George Washington, and five dozen for me, both white and red, with a greater portion of the latter. The ten dozen should be separately packed and marked G.W. and the five dozen T.I.' [384] The reply letters from Lambert and Mrs. Lur Saluce (her husband had died) made it clear that they understood my instructions were to label the packages containing the wines. Lambert wrote me on February 10, 1791, 'La Caisse de 60. B[outei]lles pour vous est marquée T.J.N.1.et les deux

Châteu Yquem

129

qui sont pour votre illustre General sont sous la marque de G.W. N. 2. et 3. The case of 60 bottles for you is marked T.J.N.1. and the two for your illustrious General are marked G.W. N.2. et 3.'

"In my letter to the owner of Château Latour, M. de Mirosmenil, I ordered 20 dozen for George Washington to be bottled, packed and marked G.W. at the vineyard. [385] Joseph Fenwick's office advised me on February 10, 1791 that the Latour order could not be executed because there was no wine available that would do 'justice' to the estate, and a substitute wine would be secured. The substituted wine was 1786 Château Lafite, so any Lafite connected with my 1790 order would have been marked 'G.W.' not 'Th. J', and of the 1786 vintage not the 1787 vintage.

"My letter to Fenwick advises that he would receive the wines 'ready packed.' For Fenwick to have engraved the bottles would have required the removal of the bottles from their cases so each bottle could be engraved, an expensive undertaking not accounted for in my Memorandum Books."

"The fact that Mr. Rodenstock has refused to tell where he obtained the bottles, beyond saying they were found in a 'bricked-up Paris cellar,' has always bothered me," I said. "Mr. Broadbent admits that Mr. Rodenstock 'is reticent about the provenance.' [386] The provenance of everything is vital to its authenticity. If we knew where Mr. Rodenstock had obtained the bottles, their identity could probably be established, and any possible connection to you, Mr. Jefferson, traced. Rodenstock's refusal to reveal how and where he obtained the bottles obscures that simple solution. But it's moot now."

"What happened?" Jefferson asks.

English wine bottle,
Burgundy wine bottle,
Bordeaux wine bottle

"An American by the name of William Koch bought four of Rodenstock's so-called Jefferson bottles paying nearly a half million dollars for them. When he offered to exhibit the bottles at the Boston Museum of Fine Arts, he was asked about their provenance. Being unsure he checked with the Thomas Jefferson Foundation at Monticello. When the authorities at Monticello expressed doubts that the bottles had ever been owned or in the possession of Mr. Jefferson, Koch, suspicious that he had been scammed, instituted an investigation into the provenance of the bottles.

"The investigation turned up evidence that indicated the bottles had never been owned or possessed by you, Mr. Jefferson. The most telling finding was that the engravings on the bottles, names, dates and the initials "ThJ", had been made by a drill that was not invented until some forty years after your death and..."

"Well, well," Jefferson says, addressing his remarks to Franklin. "Being dead forty years before the bottles were engraved with my initials convinces me that I never owned them." He stares at Jack. "Well, what happened?"

"Koch sued Rodenstock, and after a series legal maneuvers by both sides, Rodenstock threw in the towel."

"What does 'threw in the towel' mean?" Franklin asks.

"Oh, it's an expression that means to surrender or give up. In this case Rodenstock discharged his lawyers and told the judge he was no longer going to participate in the case.

Franklin says, "Can you do that?"

"You can," I said, "but the consequences are disastrous. The judge entered a default judgment in favor of Koch against Rodenstock."

"Koch's outrage didn't end there. He had his wine cellar of over 40,000 bottles examined by experts to determine whether he had been sold other fraudulent wines."

"And?" Franklin asks, his wire rimmed glasses perched at the end of his nose.

"He learned that his cellar was riddled with fake bottles from sources other than Rodenstock, and he vowed to sue everyone who had knowingly sold a fake bottle of wine that ended up in his cellar."

"Isn't that an expensive proposition?" Franklin asks.

"Yes, but in Koch's case the expense is irrelevant. He has lots of money and he's willing to spend whatever it takes to bring the wine fakers to justice."

"Well, I wish him luck but he is facing a long road ahead. Adulterated and fraudulent wines have been a scourge to the public for centuries," Jefferson says. "On my trip through southern France visiting the vineyards I learned that only by buying

131

from the vineyard owner could I get unadulterated wine. Once a wine has been into a merchant's hands, it never comes out unmixed. This being the basis of their trade, no degree of honesty, of personal friendship or of kindred prevents it."[386a]

"So where does Mr. Koch's campaign against the fraudsters stand?" Franklin asks.

"So far only one case has resulted in a jury verdict, but it was a sweet victory. In addition to awarding Koch $380,000 compensatory damages for the 24 bottles he alleged were fakes, the jury awarded him $12,000,000 punitive damages."

"Wow! What was the basis of the punitive award?" Jefferson asks.

"One of the jurors was asked that question and said, 'If someone is planning on selling fake wines, *don't do that.*' "[386b]

"As a matter of curiosity," Franklin said, "did the folks at Forbes ever drink the bottle engraved '1787 Lafitte'?"

"No. The bottle was displayed in a glass case in the lobby of the Forbes Building in New York, but due to the heat from a spotlight, the cork fell in, and the contents ran out."[387]

"The only way the contents are going to run out on these two fabulous wines," I said, waving my hand in the direction of the Margaux and Haut Brion decanters "is when we have drunk the last drops." Pausing to savor the wines, I changed the subject. "If you don't mind, I'd like to talk about your religious beliefs."

Both Jefferson and Franklin nodded their assent

"What religious belief were you, Dr. Franklin?"

"I was not a member of any specific religious denomination. For my parents, devout Calvinists, faith was everything. The only issue was, do you believe? Good works, good deeds meant nothing and will avail you nothing at the final judgment. But for me, virtue and morality reflected in good works were more important than faith, and that was my life long guiding religious tenet. And the Scripture assured me that at the last day, we shall not be examined about what we thought, but what we did; and our recommendation will not be that we said Lord, Lord, but that we did GOOD to our fellow creatures.[388]

"As a young man I determined that without virtue men could have no happiness. I wanted to achieve 'moral perfection' and I made a list of twelve virtues to guide me."

"What were they?" I said.

    1. Temperance: Eat not to dullness; drink not to elevation.

    2. Silence: Speak not but what may benefit others or yourself; avoid trifling conversation.

3. Order: Let all your things have their places; let each part of your business have its time.

4. Resolution: Resolve to perform what you ought; perform without fail what you resolve.

5. Frugality: Make no expense but to do good to others or yourself; i.e., waste nothing.

6. Industry: Lose no time; be always employed in something useful; cut off all unnecessary actions.

7. Sincerity: Use no hurtful deceit; think innocently and justly, and, if you speak, speak accordingly.

8. Justice: Wrong none by doing injuries, or omitting the benefits that are your duty.

9. Moderation: Avoid extremes; forbear resenting injuries so much as you think they deserve.

10. Cleanliness: Tolerate no uncleanliness in body, clothes, or habitation.

11. Tranquillity: Be not disturbed at trifles, or at accidents common or unavoidable.

12. Chastity: Rarely use venery but for health or offspring, never to dullness, weakness, or the injury of your own or another's peace or reputation.

"A Quaker friend saw the list and kindly informed me that at times I could be 'overbearing and insolent.' I accepted his advice and added a thirteenth virtue of 'Humility: Imitate Jesus and Socrates.'[389]

"I soon found that mastering all of these thirteen virtues at once was 'a task of more difficulty than I had imagined,' so I worked on them one at a time.

"Ezra Stiles, president of Yale University, asked me if I would be so kind as to enlighten him on 'my religious sentiments.'[390] I answered him, and this was my final comment on my creed. 'I believe in one God, creator of the universe. That he governs it by his providence. That he ought to be worshiped. That the most acceptable service we render to him is doing good to his other children. That the soul of man is immortal, and will be treated with justice in another life respecting its conduct in this. These I take to be the fundamental principles of all sound religion, and I regard them as you do in whatever sect I meet with them.

"As to Jesus of Nazareth, my opinion of whom you particularly desire, I think the system of morals and his religion, as he left them to us, the best the world ever saw or is likely to see; but I apprehend it has received various corrupting changes, and I have, with most of the present dissenters in England, some doubts as to his divinity; though it is a question I do not dogmatize upon, having never studied it, and think it needless to busy myself with it now; when I expect soon an opportunity of knowing the truth with less trouble. I see no harm, however, in its being believed, if that belief has the good consequence, as it probably has, of making his doctrines more respected and better observed, especially as I do not perceive that the Supreme takes it amiss, by distinguishing the unbelievers in his government of the world with any peculiar marks of his displeasure.

" 'I shall only add, respecting myself, that, having experienced the goodness of that Being in conducting me prosperously through a long life, I have no doubt of its continuance in the next, though without the smallest conceit of meriting such goodness.'

"I added a postscript requesting Stiles not to publish the letter because I have ever let others enjoy their religious sentiments, without reflecting on them for those that appeared to me unsupportable and even absurd. All sects here, and we have a great variety, have experienced my good will in assisting them with subscriptions for building their new places of worship; and as I have never opposed any of their doctrines, I hope to go out of the world in peace with them all." [391]

I turned to Jefferson. "I suppose that most Americans know of your unrelenting fight for the separation of church and state, and I would like to hear how you went about it."

"In the spring of 1779, I proposed the Statute of Virginia for Religious Freedom, a bill to protect citizens in their civil rights against religious intolerance and persecution, which held:

> We the General Assembly of Virginia do enact that no man shall be compelled to frequent or support any religious worship, place, or ministry whatsoever, nor shall be enforced, restrained, molested, or burdened in his body or goods, nor shall otherwise suffer, on account of his religious opinions or beliefs; but that all men shall be free to profess, and by argument maintain, their opinions in matters of religion, and that the same shall in no wise diminish, enlarge, or affect their civil capacities.

"My successful battle for the separation of church and state and for complete religious freedom was a six-year struggle, and it was the bitterest fight I ever fought. [392] In fact, my championing religious freedom brought the everlasting enmity of the clergy then, and it lasted until the end of my life. I was denounced from the pulpit by political preachers as an enemy of Christianity. [393]

"What these so-called men of the cloth soon forgot was the egregious religious intolerance that existed in Virginia before the Statute for Religious Freedom became the law. For over a century the Church of Virginia, under the direction of the Bishop of London, was ruled by small groups of Anglicans who commingled church and government policies, resulting in a combination of church and state. The established church did not tolerate other forms of worship. In 1642, the Puritans and all others who professed a religious faith contrary to the Church of England were driven from Virginia. Later the Quakers were expelled. [394]

"The statute met stiff opposition from religious groups throughout the state and it never reached a third reading. Emboldened by their success, the opposition introduced a bill declaring 'the Christian Religion shall in all times coming be deemed and held to be the established religion of the commonwealth.' Fortunately, this state religion bill was defeated, and, in fact, George Mason introduced a bill that ended the payment of clergymen's salaries out of state funds. [395]

"I consider the government of the United States as interdicted by the Constitution from intermeddling with religious institutions, their doctrines, disciplines, or exercises. This results not only from the provision that no law shall be made respecting the establishment or free exercise of religion, but from that also which reserves to the states the powers not delegated to the United States. [396]

"I am for freedom of religion, and against all maneuvers to bring about a legal ascendancy of one sect over another. [397]

"I was an early and confirmed believer that the state has no business meddling with religion. The state is a society of men constituted for protecting the civil interests of life, health, liberty, and property. The state derives its power from the people, and the people have not entrusted the state with the 'care of souls.' The care of one's soul belongs to the individual, and no man has the power to let another prescribe his faith. [398] I considered religion a private matter, and I looked with tolerance on all forms of religion. [399] I have sworn on the altar of God eternal hostility against every form of tyranny over the mind of man." [400]

"Your fight for religious freedom, Mr. Jefferson, fits squarely the conventional image of you today as the apostle of freedom, an image through actions and words that, in my opinion, you justly deserve. Yet, you wrote and advocated something that is in such striking departure from due process of law, I find it difficult to reconcile with your professed ideals."

"What is that, Jack?"

"The bill of attainder and outlawry you wrote in 1778 against Josiah Phillips and the unnamed members of his group."

Jefferson's face flushed. "They were traitors and murderers. In the words of Patrick Henry, with which I agreed, they were warring against the human race."

"Phillips and his unnamed associates were reputed or alleged traitors and murderers. Your bill of attainder stripped them of the safeguards of a trial by jury for their accused crimes. By legislative edict your bill declared them guilty and allowed anyone to kill them with impunity on the mere supposition that they were associated with Phillips—a total deprivation of due process of law."

"Your comment is lifted out of context. My bill of attainder allowed for a thirty-day grace period whereby Phillips and his gang could surrender to the authorities and receive the benefits of due process. In fact, when they were captured, they were tried and found guilty by regular legal process. So in the end their legal rights were not abrogated."

"That's not the point," I said. "Your bill, when passed by the Virginia legislature, found them guilty and condemned them to death without due process. Edmund Randolph and others connected with the bill of attainder later expressed regret and horror at what they had done, but you steadfastly defended your bill and insisted that an outlaw had no right to the benefits of citizenship and the legal process."[401]

"I make no apologies for the Phillips bill of attainder. You will recall that many years later when discussing my actions in this case I wrote, 'I was then thoroughly persuaded of the correctness of the proceeding, and am more and more convinced by reflection. If I am in error, it is an error of principle.'"

"Your insistence on the correctness of your conduct in the Phillips matter is inconsistent with the principle you proposed five years later when you prepared a new draft constitution for Virginia that denied the legislature any power to 'pass any bill of attainder (or other law declaring any person guilty) of treason or felony.'"[402]

"I agree, Jack, that 'a strict observance of the written laws is doubtless one of the high duties of a good citizen, but it is not the highest. The laws of necessity, of self-preservation, of saving our country when in danger, are of higher obligation. When the army was before York, the governor of Virginia took horses, carriages, provisions and even men by force, to enable that army to stay together till it could master the public enemy; and he was justified.' I felt at the time that the eradication or capture of Phillips and his gang of murderers was of paramount importance for public safety, and I repeat, if I was in error, it was an error of principle."[403]

"Returning to the subject of religion, Mr. Jefferson, do you believe in God?"

"If you are asking me if I believe that God has a direct involvement in our individual lives and intervenes based on prayer, the answer is no. I believe in God the Creator of the Universe as seen in the wonders of nature. I believe that our particular principles of religion are a subject of accountability to our God alone.[404]

136

"An eloquent preacher of a Quaker religious society, Richard Motte, in a discourse of much emotion and pathos, is said to have exclaimed aloud to his congregation, that he did not believe there was a Quaker, Presbyterian, Methodist or Baptist in heaven, then pausing to give his hearers time to stare and to wonder, he added that in heaven, God knew no distinctions, but considered all good men as his children and as brethren of the same family. I believe, with the Quaker preacher, that he who steadily observes those moral precepts in which all religions concur, will never be questioned at the gates of heaven. Of all the systems of morality, ancient or modern, that have come under my observation, none appear to me so pure as that of Jesus. He who follows this steadily need not, I think, be uneasy." [405]

"I can assure you, Mr. Jefferson, that the principle of separation of church and state has been maintained in the United States, and the care of one's soul remains that of the individual."

"I am delighted to know that."

"As I mentioned earlier, the path of our country to greatness has not always been easy. In the 1930s we suffered through a great economic depression, the likes of which Americans had never before experienced. Millions became unemployed, homeless, and destitute. The federal government instituted a number of reform programs. One such program, started in 1935, was a welfare system that guaranteed cash and other benefits to needy families. Over time, many able-bodied people abused the system by taking the benefits and not work. In 1996 Congress passed and the president signed into law the Welfare Reform Act, which was successful in getting many such recipients back into the work force. The poor are now required to work, and when they do, they receive a supplement to their wages, known as the earned income tax credit."

"I was always wary of handouts," Franklin said. "I expressed my thoughts in a letter to my English friend Peter Collinson when I raised the issue 'whether the laws peculiar to England that compel the rich to maintain the poor have not given the latter a dependence that very much lessens the care of providing against the wants of old age. It is godlike to relieve the misfortunes of fellow creatures, but might it not provide encouragements for laziness and supports for folly, may it not be found fighting against the order of God and Nature, which perhaps has appointed want and misery as the proper punishments for, and cautions against as well as necessary consequences of idleness and extravagancy.' I fear the giving mankind a dependence on anything for support in age or sickness, besides industry and frugality during youth and health, tends to flatter our natural indolence, to encourage idleness and prodigality, and thereby to promote and increase poverty, the very evil it was intended to cure. The tax money of the wealthy and well-to-do would be better spent in the creation of civic institutions that promote the success of others."[406]

I took a sip of wine and reflected for a moment on how fortunate I was to be living in the country my two dinner companions help create.

"The nation's capital moved to Washington, D.C. in 1800 and is still there. I'm curious to know what Washington was like when you moved there as the third president of the United States?" I asked Jefferson.

"The roads leading to the new capital, known then as the Federal City, were dirt when I became president in March 1801. When it rained the dirt became rivulets, melding into the mud-colored landscape. There were no hotels, restaurants or coffee-houses, only a few taverns with wretched accommodations. No sidewalks or lamps interrupted the darkness along its few roads. The Federal City, a noble concept on paper, was in reality a cluster of about fifteen boarding houses grouped around the still-unfinished Capitol building and encircled by a forest. The boarding houses had as their residents a transient society, for virtually none of the members of Congress had built houses in Washington or brought their wives with them. They spent only the months there when Congress was in session. Houses were so isolated that numbers were not necessary; instead, they were identified as 'near the president's house, west of the War Office, opposite the Treasury or whatever.'

"For public entertainment, one had the choice of a race track or a theater that was astonishingly dirty and void of decoration. As one resident remarked, 'One must love the drama very much to consent to pass three hours amidst tobacco smoke, whiskey breaths and other stenches mixed up with effluvia of stables, and miasmas of the canal, which the theater is exactly placed and constructed to receive.' Gouverneur Morris, who succeeded me as minister to France and was in the Federal City as a senator, probably described it best when he wrote, 'All we lack here are good houses, wine cellars, decent food, learned men, attractive women, and other such trifles to make our city perfect. It is the best city to live in—in the future.'"[407]

"President Adams and his wife, Abigail, lived in the President's House, now called the White House, for eight months before you moved in, and I remember reading somewhere about Mrs. Adams complaining about 'bells wanting, fires wanting, not a single apartment finished. The half-finished audience room was used as a drying room in which to hang up clothes.' How did you find it when you moved in?"

The Capitol when first occupied by Congress, 1800.

"Abigail did not exaggerate. Although more than $300,000 had been spent on the President's House, the structure was unfinished not only in frame but also in furnishings. The workmen had left out the upper story and had not built cellars, and a great many of my wines were lost because of the scorching summer heat. So in order to keep my wines, I was obliged to add a wine cellar at a depth of sixteen feet underground. The wine cellar was located in the west wing basement and helped form an underground corridor to the icehouse situated on the west lawn. [408]

"I moved into the unfurnished presidential mansion on March 19 and quickly assembled a staff consisting of a chef, steward, coachman, valet-porter, housekeeper, stable boy, washer woman, apprentice cooks, and later a footman. All were paid for out of my $25,000 a year salary.

"In this bleak social environment I readily accepted my role of social leadership, turning my home into the most interesting social center in the city. With the help of Philipe Letombe, the French envoy in Philadelphia, I filled the two most important slots on my staff with two Frenchmen. To administer the White House, I hired Étienne Lemaire, and as my chef, 42-year-old Honoré Julien. The pomp that had been associated with the levees of Presidents Washington and Adams ended. I did away with them."

"It might interest you to know," I said, interrupting, "that John Adams said he held levees once a week so that all of his time might not be wasted on idle visits, but that your 'whole eight years was a levee.' Adams also said that he 'dined a large company once or twice a week, but Jefferson dined a dozen every day.'" [409]

139

The President's House

Jefferson looked at me and smiled. "I'm sure I did have more dinner parties than Adams, and far less formal. In describing an evening at my table one senator said, 'You drink as you please, and converse at your ease.' Or as I put it, 'The principle with us, as well as our political constitution, is the equal rights of all, and if there be an occasion where this equality ought to prevail preeminently, it is in social circles collected for conviviality. Nobody shall be above you, nor you above anybody, pell-mell is our law.' My hospitality encompassed political friend and enemy. The two political parties were never mixed but entertained separately. [410]

"The Georgetown market stalls, with produce picked only hours before, were shopped daily by Lemaire for meats, eggs and vegetables including lettuce, asparagus, peas, tomatoes, squash, eggplant, shad, sturgeon, rockfish, oysters, wild game, venison, duck, pigeon, squirrel, poultry, and a variety of fruits, including local currants, strawberries and watermelons. [411] When Edmund Bacon, my overseer at Monticello, visited the President's House, he shopped with Lemaire and reported:

> Mr. Jefferson often told me that the office of vice-president was far preferable
> to that of president. He was perfectly tired out with company. He had a very
> long dining room, and his table was chock-full every one of the sixteen days I
> was there. There were congressmen, foreigners, and all sorts of people, to dine
> with him. He dined at four o'clock, and they generally sat and talked until
> night. It used to worry me to sit so long; and I finally quit when I got through
> eating, and went off and left them. The first thing in the morning there was
> to go to market. Mr. Jefferson's steward was a very smart man, well educated,
> and as much of a gentleman in his appearance as any man. His carriage-
> driver would get out the wagon early in the morning, and Lemaire would go
> with him to Georgetown to market. [412]

"By the time the members of the Seventh Congress arrived in Washington, personal invitations for dinner were waiting. When Federalist Senator William Plumer received his first dinner invitation, he was struck by the fact that 'his favor' was 'requested' by Thomas Jefferson and not the president of the United States. 'Having a curiosity to know what induced me to adopt such a form,' Plumer asked my friend Senator Giles the reason. The ever-blunt Giles told him 'the president meant it should be considered more as the invitation of a private gentleman, than that of the president. For if he invited as president he must take the list and invite all the members of the houses of Congress. But his present mode will not oblige him, either to invite gentleman of different politics at the same table; or to invite at any time those members who for the hour together abuse him in speeches in Congress, as some gentlemen do.' [413]

"Dinners were lavish, and chef Julien prepared them on a large coal-burning stove in the basement below the north entrance hall. [414] My dinner menus included rice, soup, round of beef, turkey, mutton, ham, loin of veal, cutlets of mutton, fried eggs, fried beef, a pie called macaroni with a rich brown crust, a great variety of fruit, and plenty of good wines. [415]

"I had two dining rooms, one large and one smaller. The formal dining room on the northwest corner was used sparingly for more elaborate functions and when ladies were in attendance. It had a dumbwaiter built into the doorway that rotated into a service area near the basement stairs where the food was brought up. I had a similar arrangement for food service at Monticello. [416]

"My favorite place for dining was the smaller room. Dinners here were usually all men, and to eliminate any perception of rank, I used an oval dining table that seated twelve. Dinner began at four, and in the colonial tradition, beer, porter, or cider were served during the meal. I had the dining room equipped with a number of tiered dumbwaiters shaped like vertical lazy Susans from which guests could serve themselves when not actually served by me. This arrangement ensured privacy. 'You see we are alone,' I would say, 'and our walls have no ears.' Wine was not served until after dinner, when the cloth was removed. This was the American tradition, and dried fruits, nuts, and confections accompanied this part of the meal." [417]

"Someone has calculated that during your eight years as president you purchased more than 20,000 bottles of wine from European countries. What were some of the wines that were served at presidential dinners?" [418]

"From Bordeaux I served Rausan Margaux, Yquem and Filhot for Sauternes, Chambertin from Burgundy, white Hermitage and Champagne. At about this time I had developed a strong preference for old dry, pale sherry, but not exclusively. My taste in Spanish wines ran from Malaga and Pedro Ximenes, both sweet, to pale dry sherries, and dry and sweet Paxarete. I also tried a red sweet wine called Tinto di Rota, which was known in England as Tent.

"Dinner conversations usually centered on my passions: gardening, architecture, books, [419] music, [420] wine, [421] and I enjoyed reminiscing about my five years in France and the men and women who had affected historical events. I was fond of telling about the contrasting personalities of Jacques Necker and Comte de Mirabeau, two of the most important personalities in France. Necker started the evening in high spirits but faded after nine o'clock. Mirabeau, however, started out brooding, but then the wine 'warmed him into life.' For an hour or two, he became the life of the party, pouring out gossip, poetry, and anecdotes. As the night passed on and the wine 'heated him,' his eyes became dilated, his voice choked, with his black hair shaking wildly about his face, he would burst into political prophecies. In a more sober moment, Mirabeau suggested to me that if France were destined to become another America, France would need another Washington, to which I replied: 'Pardon me, Count, but I consider such is the striking originality of your character, you would disdain to imitate any man.' [422]

"I enjoyed telling the story of Marie Antoinette's wondering how it was possible for the people of America to be happy without a court. 'Surely,' she said to me, 'your great deliverer,' meaning, of course, George Washington, 'intends to create nobility?' To which I remember saying, 'Your Majesty, the influence of your own is so powerful that it is the general impression that we can do without them.' [423]

"I also used to tell how the famous Marseilles wine merchant Bergasse could so perfectly imitate the taste of any kind of wine by blending a variety of wines of Languedoc that even the most experienced wine connoisseur could not tell the difference. And his wines did not contain a 'drop of anything but the pure juice of the grape.' [424] Years later I would learn from Stephen Cathalan that Bergasse's wine prices in combination with the high price of bread, beef, and mutton, caused the populace of Marseilles to riot on April 23, 1789, and threaten to destroy his wine cellars. Cathalan called this riot 'the first spark which set on fire the revolution all over France.' Bergasse was so unnerved by the mob's violence that he sold his thriving wine business to other local wine merchants and moved to his native city of Lyon. His son later revived the Bergasse wine business in Marseilles." [425]

"According to John Quincy Adams," I said, "you held forth one evening on the necessity of French and Spanish being a requisite in every young man's education, telling your dinner guests that Spanish was so easy that you had learned it with the help of a 'Don Quixote' and a grammar in the course of a nineteenday passage to Europe." [426]

"Well, I don't remember that conversation, but if John Quincy Adams reported that, it must be true."

"Do you know what he added to his diary entry after making that comment?"

"No."

"'But Mr. Jefferson tells large stories.'"

Franklin burst out laughing, and split second later, so did Jefferson.

"You had committed to serving but two terms as President. Were you ever sorry that you made that commitment?"

"Absolutely not. One of my major objections to the Constitution was that it allowed for the perpetual reeligibility of the president. Here is what I said a few days before leaving the presidency. 'I retire to my family, my books and farms; and having gained the harbor myself, I shall look on my friends still buffeting the storm with anxiety indeed, but not with envy. Never did a prisoner, released from his chains, feel such relief as I shall on shaking off the shackles of power. Nature intended me for the tranquil pursuits of science, by rendering them my supreme delight. But the enormities of the times in which I have lived, have forced me to take a part in resisting them, and to commit myself on the boisterous ocean of political passions. I thank God for the opportunity of retiring from them without censure, and carrying with me the most consoling proofs of public approbation.' [427]

"Six months later I wrote Benjamin Rush, 'I never had a cordial relish for politics, and abhorred the contentions and strife they generated. The times forced me from my first love, the natural sciences. The interest I took in the success of the experiment, whether a government could be contrived to secure man his rightful liberties and acquirements, engaged a longer portion of my life than I had ever proposed. Certainly the experiment could never have fallen into more inauspicious times, when nations openly renounced all obligations of morality, and shamelessly assumed the character of robbers and pirates. In any other time, our experiment would have been easier; and if it can pass safely through the ordeal of the present trial, we may hope we have set an example, which will not be without consequences favorable to human happiness.' [428]

"Yes, but fourteen months before you spoke of being released from the chains of power, you counseled a young Virginia lawyer to make politics an important part of his life."

"I did express contrary thoughts on the subject in a letter to a young Virginia lawyer who was considering leaving the law to go into the army. I counseled him 'to come into Congress. That is the great commanding theatre of this nation,' I told him, 'and the threshold to whatever department of office a man is qualified to enter.' I pointed out that after a little time he could look, at his will, into the military, the judiciary, diplomatic, or other civil departments, with a certainty of being in whatever pleased him. And in the present state of what may be called the eminent talents of our country, he would be assured of being engaged through life in the most honorable employments. I will not say that public life is the line for making a fortune. But it furnishes a decent and honorable support, and places one's children on good grounds for public favor. It proceeds from an ardent zeal to see this government (the idol of my soul) continue in good hands."[429]

"What do you consider the major accomplishments of your life, Mr. Jefferson?"

"If my request was honored, they are inscribed on my tombstone: author of the Declaration of Independence, author of the Virginia Statute for Religious Freedom, and founder of the University of Virginia."

"Your request was honored. We have talked about the first two. Tell me about founding the University of Virginia," I said.

"The founding of the University of Virginia was my last project. I started it at the age of 75, and five and a half years into the project, I remember writing to John Adams that 'I am fortunately mounted on a hobby, which indeed I should have better managed some 30 or 40 years ago, but whose easy amble is still sufficient to give exercise and amusement to an Octogenary rider. This is the establishment of the University, on a scale more comprehensive, and in a country more healthy and central than our old William & Mary.'[430]

"It isn't generally known, but the first official event at the university was a dinner in honor of the Marquis de Lafayette. Lafayette arrived in the United States in the late summer of 1824 at the invitation of Congress and President Monroe. He spent more than a year touring all of the states, and his presence was celebrated wherever he went. I would like to think, however, that the highlight of his trip was his eleven-day stay at Monticello. It had been 35 years since we had seen one another. I held a grand dinner for him at the university, at which all the local dignitaries attended including Madison. Except for one other visit to the university, we spent our time together at Monticello. Between us and our dinner companions, so much red wine was drunk that when Lafayette and his party left on November 15, my wine stock was almost depleted. Although I was expecting any day the arrival of my annual wine supply from southern France, I was afraid of running out and placed an emergency order, explaining, 'In the meantime I must buy from hand to mouth in the country, and for the present must pray you to send me a box of claret of about two dozen by the first wagon. I would refer for its quality to your own taste rather than price, which is no test at all, and generally a mere imposition.' " [431]

LAFAYETTE

Né a Chavagnac 1757

mort à Paris 1834

"I know you are too modest to admit it, but you breathed life into every detail of the university's planning, architecture, construction and organization, and you lived to see that dream come true. And you will be proud to know that the University of Virginia is today one of the great institutions of learning in America."

Franklin raised his glass. "To Thomas Jefferson and the University of Virginia!"

"Mr. Jefferson, we should toast Dr. Franklin too. The Pennsylvania Academy that he founded is known today as the University of Pennsylvania, a great institution of learning."

"To Dr. Franklin and the University of Pennsylvania," Jefferson said, raising his glass.

"I will drink to that," I said. The three of us hoisted our glasses. "How did you go about founding the University of Pennsylvania?" I asked.

"I had long nurtured the dream of starting a college. I had discussed it at Junto meetings as early as 1743. Six years later I wrote 'Proposals Relating to the Education of Youth in Pennsylvania,' a pamphlet that described the need for an academy, what should be taught, and how to raise the necessary money. Two years later we opened the first nonsectarian academy in America with a curriculum geared to practical instruction, and from the beginning it flourished 'beyond expectation.' I was elected president of the board and remained a trustee for the rest of my life. I consider the University of Pennsylvania one of my proudest achievements." [432]

"The University of Pennsylvania proudly claims you as its founder and in 1976 posthumously awarded you an honorary doctor degree," I said.

I waited while Jefferson refreshed Franklin's glass. "I'm curious about something, Mr. Jefferson."

"What is that, Jack?"

"In listing your major lifetime accomplishments, why didn't you include the Louisiana Purchase? Here is an accomplishment that without firing one shot doubled the size of the United States. Your Philadelphia scientist friend, Casper Wistar, called the purchase 'the most important and beneficial transaction which has occurred since the Declaration of Independence, and next to it, most likely to influence or regulate the destinies of our country.' "[433]

Jefferson thought for a moment. "When I heard that James Monroe and Robert Livingston had signed the treaty with Napoleon's representative purchasing 'all Louisiana,' I told my son-in-law that the acquisition 'removes from us the greatest source of danger to our peace.' [434] In fairness, however, much of the credit be-

James Monroe 1755–1828 by Gilbert Stuart NARA.

longs to Livingston and Monroe. After conferring with my cabinet, I sent Monroe to Paris with instructions to purchase the territory east of the Mississippi known as the island of New Orleans and the provinces of East and West Florida. We had not included 'the purchase of the country beyond the Mississippi' in our official instructions to Livingston and Monroe because it 'was not deemed at the time within the pale of probability.' "[435]

"Is it true then that Livingston and Monroe, in purchasing all of the Louisiana territory, exceeded their authority?"

"Yes, but Madison and I, and the rest of my cabinet, immediately realized that they had struck an incredible deal, and any doubts I harbored on constitutionality I quickly forgot when advised by Livingston to act quickly 'without altering a syllable of the terms' because France was 'sick of the bargain' and 'that the slightest pretence will lose you the treaty.' I acted quickly, and Congress ratified the treaty." [436]

"Why do you think that Napoleon insisted on selling all Louisiana for $15,000,000?"

"I think he knew that he was about to go to war with Great Britain, and that once the war began, it would be impossible for France to defend the territory. By selling it to us, he kept it out of the hands and influence of Great

Britain, insured our neutrality in the war, and it brought in much needed money with which to wage his war."[437]

"You had good luck with the French," I said.

Jefferson thought for a moment. "Yes, good luck and many friendships." "Were there any special evenings that you remember more than others?" I asked. Franklin waved his hand in deference to Jefferson.

"An evening I remember well occurred in the spring of 1782. It was on my thirty-ninth birthday, and the Marquis de Chastellux, a major general in the French Expeditionary Forces, paid a visit to Monticello, and he told me that he had had no difficulty recognizing my house on one of the summits as he rode up the mountain."

"In fact," I said, "he recorded the following impression. 'This house, of which Mr. Jefferson was the architect, and often the builder, is constructed in an Italian style, and is quite tasteful, although not however without some faults; it consists of a large square pavilion, into which one enters through two porticoes ornamented with columns. The ground floor consists chiefly of a large and lofty salon, or drawing room, which is to be decorated entirely in the antique style; above the salon is a library of the same form; two small wings, with only a ground floor and attic, are joined to this pavilion, and are intended to communicate with the kitchen, offices, etc. which will form on either side a kind of basement topped by a terrace. Mr. Jefferson is the first American who has consulted the fine arts to know how he should shelter himself from the weather.' "[438]

Chevalier de Chastellux

"Chastellux, at forty-eight, had already gained a reputation throughout France as the author of the two-volume work *Public Happiness*, and as a philosopher, scientist, and soldier," Jefferson said. "Chastellux's intellectual interests were so similar to mine that our feelings and opinions were, as he said, 'in agreement.' He also said that we understood 'each other at the first hint—all these made my four days spent at Monticello seem like four minutes.'"

"Chastellux described you" I said, "as 'a man, not yet forty, tall, and with a mild and pleasing countenance, but his mind and attainments could ser ve in lieu of all outward graces; an American, who without ever having quitted his own country, is musician, draftsman, surveyor, astronomer, natural philosopher, jurist, and statesman; a senator of America, who sat for two years in that famous Congress which brought about the Revolution and which is never spoken of here without respect. A governor of Virginia, who filled his difficult station during the invasions of Arnold, Phillips, and Cornwallis; and finally a philosopher, retired from the world and public business. A gentle and amiable wife, charming children whose education is his special care, a house to embellish, extensive estates to improve, the arts and sciences to cultivate—these are what remain to Mr. Jefferson, after having played a distinguished role on the stage of the new world, and what he has preferred to the honorable commission of Minister Plenipotentiary in Europe.' " [439]

"I remember that Chastellux accompanied me through a park that adjoined Monticello and watched while I fed the deer Indian corn that they ate out of my hand. On another evening, Chastellux and I were conversing over a bowl of punch after Mrs. Jefferson had retired. Our conversation turned to the poems of Ossian. The book was sent for and placed near the bowl, where by our mutual aid the night far advanced imperceptibly upon us. [440]

"Speaking of Monticello," Jefferson said, "what has become of my beloved home?"

"It was a long struggle, but it still stands in all of its glory on top of your mountain. In fact, it is in better shape today than when you lived there."

"How is that possible?" Jefferson said.

"Monticello and much of its grounds survive today because of the vision and generosity of two men, Uriah Phillips Levy and his nephew, Jefferson Monroe Levy. After you died, your estate was in debt, and there was no money to operate Monticello. In 1831, a Charlottesville druggist purchased Monticello and through a combination of deliberate acts, neglect, and stupidity, he nearly destroyed it. Uriah Levy, a naval officer who considered you one of the greatest men in history, visited Monticello in 1836. Despite the wretched condition in which he found the estate, he bought it. Over the next twenty-six years, he spent large sums of money restoring Monticello. Uriah died in 1862 and Monticello remained neglected and its ownership in legal limbo for 17 years while his will was contested.

Monticello

Finally, Uriah's nephew, Jefferson Monroe Levy, purchased Monticello from his uncle's estate in 1879 and set about restoring it. It remained in Jefferson Monroe's hands until purchased by the Thomas Jefferson Foundation on April 13, 1923. Monticello is still owned and operated by the foundation whose mission is to preserve it and to educate the public about your life and achievements."[441]

"Hear! Hear!" Franklin exclaimed.

"And I should add, Mr. Jefferson, that your beloved Monticello is the only home in America to be named a World Heritage Site by the United Nations, which places it in the company of the Great Wall of China and the Pyramids of Egypt. Over 600,000 people visit Monticello each year. But I digress."

"Thank you for telling me that, Jack," Jefferson said with a smile.

I turned to Dr. Franklin and said, "Can you recall any evenings that meant as much to you as Mr. Jefferson's with the Marquis de Chastellux?"

"There were so many extraordinary evenings that it is difficult to pick one over the other." Suddenly his eyes took on a faraway wistful gleam. "There is one I vividly remember. It occurred at a dinner party at my place when my lady friend, the famous Madame Helvétius, shocked the Adams family by her appearance and behavior. And, as I recall, Thomas, you were there. Abigail later said that Madame Helvétius entered the room 'with a careless, jaunty air. Upon seeing ladies who were strange to her she bawled out, 'ah, Mon Dieux! Where is Franklin? Why did you not tell me there were ladies here? How I

149

look!' Her hair was frizzled, over it she had a small straw hat with a dirty gauze half-handkerchief tied over it. She carried on the chief of conversation at dinner, frequently locking her hand into the doctor's and sometimes spreading her arms upon the backs of both my husband and Dr. Franklin. Then throwing her arm carelessly about the doctor's neck. I should have been greatly astonished if the doctor had not told me that in this lady I would see a genuine French woman and one of the best women in the world. For this I must take the Doctor's word, but I should have set her down as a very bad one, although sixty years of age and a widow. After dinner she threw herself on a settee 'where she showed more than her feet,' to which Abigail's daughter Nabby added, 'odious indeed do our sex appear when divested of those ornaments, with which modesty and delicacy adorn them.' " [442]

"I know that the Adamses did not take to the French as easily as Dr. Franklin," I said. "In May 1784, Congress appointed you a commissioner to France along with Dr. Franklin and John Adams to negotiate treaties of commerce with European countries. What was your reception like when you arrived in Paris?"

"Four days after my arrival in Paris, I dined with Dr. Franklin, who lived in the suburb of Passy, a neat village about two miles from Paris. As I'm sure you know, Dr. Franklin had come to France in late 1776 to obtain money and arms for the American Revolution and to forge, if possible, an alliance with France. He was successful in achieving all of these goals, and in so doing, he had become the most popular and respected foreigner in Europe."

"I occupied a portion of a spacious estate known as the Hôtel de Valentinois, which was owned by a wealthy merchant, Le Ray de Chaumont, and his wife," Franklin said. "The mansion stood on the top of a hill with terraced gardens, a lake, and avenues of clipped lindens leading down to the Seine, and a view looking back to Paris. I enjoyed my eight and a half years in France: my diplomatic mission, the intellectual atmosphere of the salons, the beauty and vivacity of the women, and French wines. [443]

"And I'm delighted to say that this was the first of many visits for Thomas, who frequently dined with me. My waistline, unfortunately, became as ample as my bounty as a host. I had contracted with my maître d'hôtel to furnish for each of my dinners a joint of beef, veal or mutton, fowl, or game; two vegetables with hors d'oeuvres of butter, pickles, and relishes; and for desserts—fruits, fruit preserves, cheeses, biscuits, bonbons and ice cream. We drank wines that evening from my wine cellar of over 1100 bottles that included red Bordeaux, Burgundies, sparkling Champagnes and sherries." [444]

Jefferson nodded enthusiastically. "I was so impressed with the Bordeaux wines I drank at Dr. Franklin's house that four months later, when I made my first contact with John Bondfield, the American consul in Bordeaux, I ordered 144 bottles of 'such wine' as I had drunk at Dr. Franklin's house. Bondfield acknowledged the order and sent me four cases containing 36 bottles each of what he called 'our First Growth,' and I had him send a similar shipment to my brother-in-law in Virginia. I immediately drank some of the wine, and when I acknowledged receipt of it, I noted the 'wine good.' [445] Bondfield didn't identify the wine beyond stating that it was a First Growth. Something occurred later, however, that made me suspicious of its First Growth provenance. Shortly after my return from Bordeaux in June 1787, I offered to procure for my merchant friend in Richmond, Alexander Donald, any wines of France he desired, advising him that I had visited all the most celebrated wine cantons, and informed myself with the best *vignobles*. [446]

"Donald accepted my offer and asked me to purchase for him a gross of the best French claret. As a guideline to what he expected, Donald added: 'I tasted some that you sent Mr. Eppes. It was good, but I have drunk better.' [447] My response was to immediately send Donald 124 bottles of 1784 Château Margaux from my own cellar with the explanation: 'You say you have tasted at Mr. Eppes's some wine I had sent him, which was good, but not equal to what you have seen. I have sent him twice, and what you say would correspond with

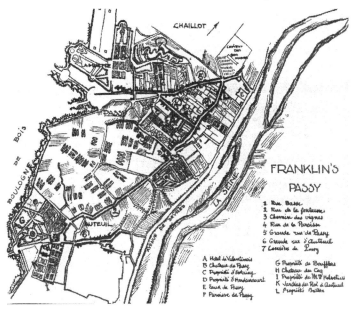

A sketch of Passy and Auteuil in Franklin's time.

151

the first batch. The second was of Château Margaux of the year 1784 bought by myself on the spot, and a part of the very purchase that I now send you. It is the best vintage which has happened in nine years, and is one of the four vineyards which are admitted to possess exclusively the first reputation. I may safely assure you therefore that according to the taste of this country and of England there cannot be a bottle of better Bordeaux produced in France. Its cost to me at Bordeaux three livres a bottle, ready-bottled and packed.'

"The first batch of wines I sent Eppes consisted of 144 bottles ordered through Bondfield in December 1784. My reaction to Donald's criticism of the Eppes claret is proof that my palate had sent me a similar signal, that is, Bondfield's unidentified 'First Growth' did not measure up in quality to the first growth wines I had drunk during my visit to the Bordeaux wine country. I returned from this trip convinced that only by buying directly from the vineyard owner could I get unadulterated wine. The vigneron never adulterates his wine, but on the contrary gives it the most perfect and pure possible. But when once a wine has been into a merchant's hands, it never comes out unmixed. This being the basis of their trade, no degree of honesty, of personal friendship, or of kindred prevents it.'" [448]

After a moment's silence, Franklin resumed his account of his activities in Paris in 1784. "Thomas's visit with me that evening in August coincided with John Adams's arrival in France from London with his wife Abigail, his nineteen-year-old daughter, Abigail, and his seventeen-year-old son, John Quincy. After a temporary residence of four days in Paris at the Hôtel d'York, Adams moved his family into a mansion in the village of Auteuil, about a mile from my residence in Passy, which bordered the Bois de Boulogne and 'far distant from the putrid streets of Paris.' Like me, Adams found the pure air of the country and the silence of Auteuil far more enjoyable than the constant roar of carriages that resounded through the streets of Paris. [449]

"A few days later the Adams family, Thomas and his lovely daughter Martha, and I were guests of Thomas Barclay, [450] and dinner was served in the French style. I remember Abigail Adams saying that she found dinner in the French style, a 'very curious' custom. 'When company are invited to dine, gentlemen meet, they seldom or never sit down, but are standing or walking from one part of the room to the other, with their swords on, and their chapeau de Bras, which is a very small silk hat, always worn under the arm. These they lay aside while they dine, but resume them immediately after. At dinner the ladies and gentlemen are mixed, and you converse with him who sits next to you, rarely speaking to persons across the table, unless to ask if they will be served with anything from your side. Conversation is never general as with us or when company quit the table, they fall into tete-a-tete of two, when the conversation is in a low voice, and a stranger, unacquainted with the customs of the country, would think that everybody had private business to transact. And on with the conversation very pleasantly, with scarcely a word from any other person, till we had finished our ice cream. When the wine began to pass round the table a little more freely, all their tongues began to be in motion.' "[451]

"You were living in a hotel at this time, Mr. Jefferson, so I suppose that you were not able to do much entertaining," I said.

"That's right, Jack, but after two months I moved to a handsome house in the cul-de-sac Taitbout. [452] The house came unfurnished, and I bought furniture, dishes, carpets, etc. My friend Thomas Barclay helped stock my wine cellar with two casks of very good two-year-old brandy, each cask containing fortytwo gallons. [453] I hired a household staff consisting of Marc, the maître d' hôtel, Legrand, *valet de chambre*, and Saget, the *frotteur*, whose sole job was to keep the red tile or parquet floors clean by whirling around the rooms with brushes strapped to his feet. 'Dancing' as Abigail Adams said, 'here and there like a Merry-Andrew.' During the year that I resided at the cul-de-sac Taitbout, all my meals were catered, and my slave-servant James Hemings was apprenticed to several caterers to learn the skills of French cooking. James learned well, and he later became a cook at my place on the Champs-Elysées. [454]

"With a house of my own, I offered free room and board to thirty-one-yearold David Humphreys who had been appointed by Congress to the post of secretary to the American legation. During the war, Humphreys had been an aide-de-camp to General Washington, and on hearing of Humphreys' appointment as secretary, George Washington wrote me, 'In him you will find a good scholar, natural and acquired abilities, great integrity, and more than a share of prudence.' [455]

"Another house guest was William Short, a native of Virginia and a graduate of William & Mary College. I had been one of William's examiners when he was admitted to the Virginia Bar, and when he learned that I had been appointed a commissioner to Paris, he offered to come abroad and serve as my private secretary. Although no such position existed at the time of his arrival in November, he became a permanent member of my household and eventually my secretary." [456]

"Did you and Short remain friends after you left France?"

"Yes. William remained in France as the American chargé d'affaires. He wanted to succeed me as minister, but President Washington gave the appointment to

Gouverneur Morris. Short returned to America in 1802 and set up residence in Philadelphia and became wealthy as a land speculator. He visited me frequently at Monticello. When I was president, I invited him to Washington to acquire firsthand 'an intimate knowledge of our political machine' and to the President's House to 'take your soup with us every day, when you are not otherwise engaged.'[457]

"Another young protégé was John Quincy Adams. Our relationship was so close that John Adams later said, 'I call him our John because, when you were at the cul-de-sac at Paris, he appeared to me to be almost as much your boy as mine.'"[458]

"Aside from General Washington, whom I'm sure you both would agree was the bravest man you ever met, whom else would you place in the 'bravest' category?" I asked.

Franklin spoke first. "Keep in mind, Jack, that all of our colleagues in our fight for independence were very brave men. There was not a coward among them, just the traitor Benedict Arnold. We all risked our lives and fortunes. But for actual individual performances, two immediately come to mind—the Marquis de Lafayette and John Paul Jones."

"I agree with Dr. Franklin's choices of Lafayette and Jones, and would add a third whose bravery did not relate to war, a fellow American whose past achievements and ambitions fascinated me."

"Who was that?" I asked.

"John Ledyard, an American navigator, explorer and soldier of fortune. Ledyard had sailed with Captain Cook on his third voyage in search of the Northwest Passage and witnessed Cook's murder in February 1779. Ledyard later wrote the only personal account of the voyage, *A Journal of Captain Cook's Last Voyage to the Pacific Ocean and in Quest of a North-West Passage*. I met him in Paris in the summer of 1786, shortly before I met Maria Cosway. Without money and living in St. Germain-en-Laye, Ledyard was 'a man of genius, of some science, and of fearless courage and enterprise' and a prodigious walker.

'Ledyard had come to Paris in the hope of forming a company to engage in the fur trade of the western coast of America. He was disappointed in this.'[459] He frequently walked to Paris, a distance of about twelve miles, to visit Lafayette, with whom he became very friendly, or me. He was a frequent dinner guest at my table."

"Ledyard noted in his accounts making 'these trips to Paris often,'" I said, 'sometimes to dine with this amiable Frenchman, and sometimes with our minister, who is a brother to me. I find at our minister's table between fifteen and twenty Americans, inclusive of two or three ladies. It is very remarkable that we are neither despised nor envied for our love of liberty, but very often caressed.' " [460]

"That is so," Jefferson said, and continued his comments on Ledyard. "He greatly admired Lafayette, telling me that 'If I find in my travels a mountain as much above the mountains as he is above ordinary men, I will name it Lafayette.' One evening at dinner, I suggested to Ledyard the 'enterprise of exploring the western part of our continent, by passing through St. Petersburg to Kamchatka, and procuring a passage thence in some of the Russian vessels to Nootka Sound, whence he might make his way across the continent to the United States.' " [461]

"In other words" I said, "Ledyard planned to walk around the world."

"Yes. 'I undertook to have the permission of the empress of Russia solicited. He eagerly embraced the proposition, and M. de Semoulin, the Russian Ambassador, and more particularly Baron Grimm, the special correspondent of the Empress, solicited her permission for him to pass through her dominions to the western coast of America.' To ensure that Ledyard would be able to record significant geographical data such as the height of mountains, I suggested that he tattoo two marks on his arm exactly a foot apart. In this way he could break off a stick of that length and estimate heights by measuring shadows." [462]

"Did Empress Catherine grant Ledyard a passport to walk across Russia?"

"No, she refused permission at once, 'considering the enterprise as entirely chimerical. But Ledyard would not relinquish it.' Undeterred, he set out by way of Copenhagen and Stockholm to St. Petersburg. In March 1787 from St. Petersburg, I heard from him. He said, 'I cannot tell you by what means I came to Petersburg, and hardly know by what means I shall quit it in the further prosecution of my tour round the world by land: if I have any merit in the affair it is perseverance, for the most severely have I been buffeted and yet still am I even more obstinate than before—and fate as obstinate continues her assaults.' [463]

"Ledyard's comment about perseverance was an extraordinary understatement. At Stockholm he learned that the Gulf of Bothnia was not frozen solid enough to walk across as he had planned. So, he headed in the direction of the Artic Circle and circumambulated the gulf, a distance of 1200 miles rather than the 120 miles directly across the gulf. [464]

"After many thousands of miles and within 500 miles of Okhotsk, where he could take a ship to Kamchatka Peninsula and then across to North America, he was stopped. On his arrival at Irkutsk, his Siberian journey ended with his arrest and deportation to Poland." [465]

"I remember reading that he ended up in Africa. How on earth did he get there if his intensions were to explore the North American continent?" I asked.

"When Ledyard was expelled from Russia, he returned to London [466] and went to see Sir Joseph Banks, president of the Royal Society. Banks and some friends had formed the Association for Promoting the Discovery of the Interior Parts of Africa. Banks and his associates were aware of Ledyard's great exploratory ambitions and skills, and commissioned him to proceed to Cairo with the mission of transversing 'the continent of Africa, as nearly as possible in the direction of the Niger, and with the towns and countries on its borders, he shall endeavor to make himself acquainted, and that he shall return to Britain by way of any of the European settlements on the western coast.' [467]

"Ledyard arrived in Cairo in July 1788, and made preparations for a trip across Africa. When I last heard from him he was about 'to plunge into the terrae incognitae of Africa, perhaps never to be heard from again.' [468] I later learned that while waiting for a caravan to take him into the interior, he contacted dysentery. The acid of vitriol he took to remedy it caused a burning pain. A strong dose of tartar emetic used to counter the pain brought on violent bleeding, and on January 10, 1789, at the age of thirty-nine, Ledyard died. Ledyard did not cross Asia, he did not cross North America, and he did not cross Africa, but in the end his consolation was, in his own words, in trying. 'I have known what it is to have food given to me as charity to a madman; and I have at times been obliged to shelter myself under the miseries of that character to avoid a heavier calamity. My distresses have been greater than I have ever owned, or ever *will* own to any man. Such evils are terrible to bear; but they never yet had power to turn me from my purpose. If I live, I will faithfully perform, in its utmost extent, my engagement to the society; and if I perish in the attempt. my *honor* will be safe, for death cancels all bonds.' " [469]

"What a miserable end to a life of extraordinary courage," I said. "I doubt that many people know that years before you selected Meriwether Lewis to explore the American West, you had discussed and encouraged John Ledyard in that pursuit."

"Actually, Jack, I had long had an interest in exploring the West, and shortly after the Revolutionary War, I asked General George Rogers Clark whether he would lead a party in exploring the territory between the Mississippi River and the Pacific Ocean. [470] General Clark declined, so my interest in exploring this vast, unknown territory was renewed when I met Ledyard. Three years after I returned from France, and while serving as secretary of state, I got the American Philosophical Society interested, and we undertook a subscription to engage the famous French botanist and explorer André Michaux to lead an expedition of the Pacific, and we were successful in raising the money to finance Michaux's expedition. [471] My instructions to Michaux included that he 'take notice of the country you go through, its general face, soil, river, mountains, it's productions animal, vegetable, and mineral so far as they may be new to us and may also be useful; the latitude of places; … the names, numbers, and dwellings of the inhabitants, and such particulars as you can learn of them.' " [472]

"What happened to the Michaux expedition?" I said.

"Michaux got started in June 1793, but the expedition was aborted when it was learned that Michaux was a French secret agent whose chief goal was to liberate Louisiana from Spanish rule by a joint attack by a French naval force and American volunteers he was to raise in Kentucky. [473] It took another ten years before I found the man who could pull it off—my personal secretary and friend, Meriwether Lewis, who was also one on the bravest men I ever knew."

"How did that come about?" I ask.

"Shortly after the balloting confirmed that I was the third president of United States, I sent a letter to Captain Meriwether Lewis asking that he become my personal secretary." Jefferson takes a sip of wine, glances at Franklin and then back to Jack. "I wanted Captain Lewis as my secretary for two reasons. He was a neighbor and a friend, and he was a captain in the army who knew which officers were competent and incompetent and which might support my administration." Jefferson lifts the decanter and replenishes Franklin's wine. His smile broadens. "I promised him he would get to "know and be known to characters of influence in the affairs of our country, and give him the advantage of their wisdom."

"Did he accept your invitation?" Franklin asks.

"He did and for the next 27 months, with the exception of a few servants, he and I were the sole occupants of the White House. We dined together every evening that we were in Washington.

"Our dinner conversations ranged from the exquisite taste of his mother's smoked hams to paleontology, math, anatomy, physics, mechanics, astronomy, meteorology, architecture, botany, gardening and, of course, wine. But our conversations never strayed far from one overriding subject–the exploration of our western country.

"From the beginning Captain Lewis was an enthusiastic recruit. With his knowledge of the West and Indian dialects, his innate intelligence, and courage undaunted, he was the perfect candidate to lead the expedition. Yet he accepted on condition that his friend William Clark be elevated to the rank of captain and given co-equal authority. I, of course, acceded to that wish. And that is how the great western exploration was born."

I nod, "And the rest is history."

"Glorious history. The same day I announced the Lewis-Clark expedition I made another announcement."

Jack hesitates, "The Louisiana Purchase?"

"Yes, our country's purchase of the Louisiana territory from France for $15,000,000."

I make a quick calculation. "That's roughly three cents an acre."

Franklin's face shows his astonishment. "Wonderful!" he says, taking a sip of wine.

"All will agree that Meriwether Lewis was a brave man," I said. "Dr. Franklin, you mentioned that John Paul Jones was one of the bravest men you ever knew. Tell me about him."

"Not just brave but also interesting. I became somewhat of a father confessor to John Paul Jones. When he was in Paris he usually stayed with me at my place in Passy. One day after Jones left Passy in March 1779, a local clergyman advised my landlord's wife, Mme de Chaumont, and me of what he called a scandal. Captain Jones, we were told, had tried to rape the wife of the gardener of our estate at about seven o'clock on the evening before he left. I wrote to Jones that the wife had related to us all the circumstances, some of which were not fit for me to write. The serious part of it was that three of her sons were determined to kill Jones if he had not left when he did. The rest occasioned some laughing; for the 'old woman was one of the grossest, coarsest, dirtiest, and ugliest that we may find in a thousand. Mme de Chaumont said it gave her a high idea of the strength of appetite and courage of the Americans.' [474] Mme de Chaumont and I had another chuckle when my investigation revealed that the old woman's assailant was a chambermaid who had stolen one of Captain Jones's uniforms. It was the last night of the carnival before Lent. As a practical joke, the chambermaid, dressed as Jones, and on meeting the old woman in the darkened garden, took it into her head to test the old woman's chastity, which the old woman passed by pushing her attacker away and running to her husband. As for Jones's confession about killing a mutinous mate in Tobago in 1773, fleeing 'incog.' to America and changing his surname to Jones, I told him that assuming he was telling the truth, he had done nothing wrong." [475]

"I seem to recall reading somewhere that Lafayette and John Paul Jones made plans to raid English coastal cities during the war. Whatever came of those plans?"

"After France signed the Treaty of Alliance with the United States in February 1778, Lafayette returned to France with the intention of returning to America with a French army. His expedition in this regard, however, was delayed. Ever impatient, Lafayette came up with a daring plan to launch surprise attacks on English coastal cities, in particular Bath, because 'the best of London society comes together in Bath this time of year.' He thought that the terror that we could have spread would have been felt much more intensely, and that Bath would have furnished some well-qualified hostages. [476]

"The king's tentative approval of the plan sent Lafayette's blood boiling. He wrote Admiral d'Estaing, 'If you undertake an attack on England and land troops and I am not there with you, I shall hang myself!' [477]

"I was told of the plans," Franklin said, "and I endorsed the expedition with enthusiasm. I told Lafayette that I admired the activity of his genius, and the strong desire he had for being continually employed against the common enemy. I too was certain that the coasts of England and Scotland were open and defenseless. And I wrote Lafayette, 'There are also many rich towns near the sea, which 4000 or 5000 men, landing unexpectedly, might easily surprise and destroy, or exact from them a heavy contribution, taking a part in ready money and hostages for the rest. It would spread terror to greater distances, and the whole would occasion movements and marches of troops that would put the enemy to prodigious expense and harass them exceedingly. In war, attempts thought to be impossible do often for that very reason become possible and practicable, because nobody expects them and no precautions are taken to guard against them. Those are the kind of undertakings of which the success affords the most glory.' [478] In that same letter I noted that 'much will depend on a

John Paul Jones, United States Naval Academy Museum.

prudent and brave sea commander who knows the coasts.' I had, of course, John Paul Jones in mind.

"Captain Jones was sent for and arrived at Passy in early April. He and Lafayette spent long hours planning the operation. [479] Because I knew nothing about naval maneuvers, I relied on Antoine de Sartine, the French naval minister, who prepared the plans for the incursions into England after conferring with Lafayette and Jones. But since I was the ranking American representative in France, Captain Jones was my charge. I knew Jones was brave and daring, but also impetuous and touchy on matters of rank, and I was very concerned that a conflict might develop between him and General Lafayette, who would ultimately be in command. Therefore, I cautioned Jones. 'It has been observed that joint expeditions of land and sea forces often miscarry, through jealousies and misunderstanding between the officers of the different corps. This must happen when there are little minds actuated more by personal views of profit or honour to themselves than by the warm and sincere desire of good to their country. Knowing you both as I do, and your just manner of thinking on these occasions, I am confident nothing of the kind can happen between you, and that it is unnecessary for me to recommend to either of you that condescension, mutual goodwill and harmony, which contribute so much to success in such undertakings.' [480] Jones and Lafayette got my message, and they exchanged letters. Jones told Lafayette, 'Where men of fine feeling are concerned there is very seldom any misunderstanding. Without any apology I shall expect you to point out my errors, when we are together alone, with perfect freedom.' [481] And always the gentleman, Lafayette responded, 'I'll be happy to divide with you whatever share of glory may expect us.' [482]

"I reminded Captain Jones that General Lafayette outranked him and would command the ground forces, 'but the command of the ships will be entirely in you, in which I am persuaded that whatever authority his rank might in strictness give him, he will not have the least desire to interfere with you.' Because the operation joined not simply land and sea forces but also Americans and French, 'a cool prudent conduct in the chiefs is therefore the more necessary.' But I told Jones, he need not fear. 'There is honor enough to be got for both of you if the expedition is conducted with a prudent unanimity.'

"I followed this exhortation with formal instructions to Jones. Captain Jones was to accept the French forces Lafayette brought him and conduct them wherever the Marquis requested. Once the troops were landed, Jones was to assist them by all means in his power. He must stay close. I specifically told him, 'You are during the expedition never to depart from the troops so as not to be able to protect them or to secure their retreat in case of a repulse.' [483] Jones said that I could count on him." [484]

"So, what happened?" I said.

"T he king changed his mind. He decided against a hit-and-run operation and decided on a full-scale invasion of Great Britain involving of more than 40,000 troops, but that too fizzled out." [485]

"What did Jones do?"

"Jones took the ship the French provided him, the *Duras*, refitted it, and christened it the *Bonhomme Richard*. And it was in the *Bonhomme Richard* that Jones made himself immortal. With the invasion of England called off, Jones put out to sea. In September 1779, he met off the coast of England the *Serapis*, a larger, more heavily armed vessel. The two ships sailed toward one another with cannons blasting away. Two of Jones's 18-pound cannons exploded in the faces of their gunners, ripping away a chunk of the starboard side. According to Jones, 'The battle thus begun continued with unremitting fury.' [486] The destruction to and carnage aboard the *Bonhomme Richard* was incredible, and Jones soon realized that he could not win a cannon duel with the better-equipped *Serapis*. Jones maneuvered the *Bonhomme Richard* so that it collided with the *Serapis*, and Jones and the sailing master bound the two ships together by lashing a rope around the *Serapis's* jib boom and the *Bonhomme Richard 's* mizzenmast.

Action between the Bonhomme Richard & Serapis.

161

"The battle now raged above deck with Jones's sharpshooters in control, but below deck the heavy cannons of the *Serapis* were taking their toll on the *Bonhomme Richard*. Both ships were on fire and their decks covered with blood and dead bodies. [487] As the *Bonhomme Richard* began to sink, the captain of the *Serapis* convinced that he had won, called out, 'Have you struck? Do you call for quarter?' And Jones, his ship sinking beneath him, and some of his crew wanting him to surrender, defiantly replied, 'I have not yet begun to fight.' [488]

"With the raging battle entering its fourth hour and Jones's men in control of the upper decks, a sailor named William Hamilton climbed the rigging that extended over the deck of the *Serapis*. He carried a bucket of grenades and a lighted slow match. Hamilton lit several grenades and lobbed them toward an open hatch below. One of the bombs rolled into the hatch and exploded, setting off a chain reaction of explosions among the loose powder cartridges in the gun deck. Fire spread like lightning, and the men and cannons of the *Serapis* were decimated. [489]

"Jones told me, 'A person must have been an eyewitness to form a just idea of the scenes of carnage, wreck and ruin which everywhere appeared. Humanity cannot but recoil and lament that war should be capable of producing such fatal consequences.' " [490]

Suddenly, Franklin fell silent. After waiting a few moments, I said, "Surely, Dr. Franklin, you are not going to stop there. What happened next?"

There was a twinkle in the old man's eye. "The *Serapis*'s captain, I think his name was Pearson, climbed to the quarterdeck and struck his colors. Jones issued the order to 'cease firing,' and he accepted Pearson's sword at the surrender ritual aboard the *Bonhomme Richard*. Attempts to save his ship were futile, so Captain Jones and his crew went aboard the *Serapis* and watched from there as the *Bonhomme Richard* sank to a watery grave." [491]

"I knew Jones well, having met him at dinner parties at your place and the Adamses," Jefferson said, "and although I never had the close contact that you had with him, I agree with your assessment of his bravery. John and Abigail Adams made two interesting and astute assessments of Jones. Adams, after dining and drinking with Jones and the officers of the *Bonhomme Richard*, wrote later that Jones 'is the most ambitious and intriguing officer in the American Navy. Jones has art, and secrecy, and aspires very high. You see the character of the man in his uniform, and that of his officers and marines, variant from the uniforms established by Congress. Golden button holes, for himself, two epaulets, marines in red and white instead of green. Eccentricities, and irregularities are to be expected from him—they are in his character; they are visible in his eyes. His voice is soft and still and small, his eye has keenness, and wildness and softness in it.' [492]

"Mrs. Adams formed her assessment after meeting Jones at dinner parties in Paris and through conversation with others. 'From the intrepid character he justly supported in the American Navy, I expected to have seen a rough, stout, warlike Roman—instead of that I should sooner think of wrapping him up in cotton wool, and putting him into my pocket, than sending him to contend with cannon-balls. He is small in stature, well proportioned, soft in his speech, easy in his address, polite in his manners, vastly civil, understands all the etiquette of a lady's toilet as perfectly as he does the masts, sails and rigging of his ship. Under all this appearance of softness he is bold, enterprising, ambitious and active. He is said to be a man of gallantry and a favorite amongst the French ladies; he knows how often the ladies use the baths, what color best suits a lady's complexion, what cosmetics are most favorable to the skin.' " [493]

"Of course, everyone knows about the heroic exploits of the Marquis de Lafayette," Franklin said.

"I'm not sure that I do," I said. "I wasn't aware, for example, that he was involved in a plan to raid English coastal cities."

"Lafayette was fearless in every sense of the word. At sixteen he inherited his title and a vast fortune. Although just a junior officer in the French army, at age nineteen he persuaded Silas Deane to commission him a major general in the Continental Army. France was not at war with Great Britain, and when word leaked that he planned on coming to America to fight on our side, the king issued orders forbidding him to leave France. Lafayette defied the king's orders, purchased a ship, and sailed to America. He was assigned to General Washington's headquarters. Washington and Lafayette took an immediate liking to one another. He was wounded at the battle of Brandywine, was with Washington at Valley Forge, and fought with distinction at the battle of Monmouth. Congress acknowledged his extraordinary battlefield accomplishments and bravery and awarded him a special sword.

"France's entrance into the war after the Treaty of Alliance was for Lafayette a dream come true. In early 1779, he left for France, hoping to return with a French army. Because he had defied the king, he was placed in a sort of political quarantine for a short period, after which he found a favorable climate for his plans to raid the coast of England, foster a revolution in Ireland, and send French troops, ships, and supplies to America. I spoke earlier about plans for raiding the English coast and for an invasion of England itself. When these two operations did not

163

work out, Lafayette returned to America in April 1780 ahead of the French expeditionary force under the command of Rochambeau." [494]

Marquis de Lafayette

"My students, accustomed to seeing the Revolution from the American viewpoint, are often surprised to learn that the American war was just one more chapter in the continuing struggle between England and France for preeminence. So they don't quite understand why France, a monarchy, was willing to side with us against another monarchy."

"Great Britain was the most powerful nation on earth, and France's crafty foreign minister, Vergennes, reasoned that if Great Britain won the war in America, its political and economic strength would allow it to dominate all of Europe," Franklin said. "If Britain lost in America, its hold in that part of the world, and on the Continent, would be weakened. [495]

"On Lafayette's return to America, Washington placed him in command of our troops in Virginia. His skill at harassing and out-maneuvering Lord Cornwallis's larger army proved decisive when Cornwallis withdrew to Yorktown for reinforcements. And as you know, Jack, the rest is history." Franklin took a sip of his wine. The smile on his face clearly showed that he was relishing not just the taste of the wine but also that glorious moment in history when he first learned of Cornwallis's surrender at Yorktown.

I looked at Jefferson, and he too was smiling broadly. I acknowledged their thoughts by saying, "It was a great moment in history then, and remains a great moment in history for all Americans.

"Great moments are usually created by interesting people. What about the most interesting person you ever met," I said, looking from Franklin to Jefferson and back again to Franklin. "Does anyone immediately come to mind?"

"Yes," Franklin said, "Edward Bancroft,"

"Who was he?"

"Edward was a young man of many talents, interests, and identities including physician, scientist, novelist, stock speculator, and my secretary in Paris. He was nearly forty years my junior, but it was always a pleasure to be in his company." Franklin turned to Jefferson. "Surely, Thomas, you remember Bancroft. As I recall, you first met him at my place in Passy."

"I remember being in the company of Bancroft many times at your house, but I actually first met him in Philadelphia in the spring of 1784, shortly before I left for France. As I recall, he had come to America on various business ventures, and he spent about a year there. After you left France, he and I became close friends, and I agree that he was a very interesting man. In fact, I proposed sending Bancroft or John Paul Jones as an emissary to negotiate a Treaty of Amity and Commerce with the Barbary States. [496] He was a frequent dinner guest at my house here, and I engaged him to help me with a number of personal matters in London. Bancroft was also a friend of Lafayette and John Paul Jones. [497] I engaged Bancroft to find out the cost of engraving a map for my book, *Notes on the State of Virginia*, and to arrange the printing of 1800 copies. [498] He was also a great help to me in untangling the convoluted financial and marital problems of the Paradises." [499]

Franklin said, "I first met Edward Bancroft a year or so after I returned to England in 1767. [500] He was only twenty-five and had already lived an exciting life. He was born and raised in Massachusetts of poor parents, his father died when he was two, and his mother married a bartender. As a youngster he studied briefly under Silas Deane after Deane graduated from Yale, but he was mostly self-taught. He soon discovered that he had a natural aptitude for science. When about fifteen he was apprenticed to a physician, but became discontented and did what I had wanted to do, run off to sea. He spent several years practicing medicine on plantations in Surinam, South America. Before coming to London in about 1767, he spent a year traveling between North and South America. He intended to study for his medical degree at the University of Edinburgh, but he abandoned that idea and studied at Aberdeen instead. About the time I met him, he had written and published a book titled *Natural History of Guiana*. He later wrote a novel, a biography of Sir Charles Wentworth, and was a book reviewer for the London *Monthly Review*. We took an immediate liking to one another. I took him under my wing, introduced him to Pringle, Priestly, and other friends, and because of his many achievements including experiments with vegetable dyes, I sponsored his election into the Royal Society.

"Edward was present at my inquisition in the Cockpit, and was one of the few people who publicly defended me in the newspapers afterward." [501]

"Regarding Bancroft," I said, "John Adams confided to his diary a number of things about him, not all of which were complimentary."

Franklin's eyebrows arched. "Such as?"

"Adams said he had written a 'novel which no doubt was recommended to many readers, and procured a considerable better sale, by the plentiful abuse and vilification of Christianity which he had taken care to insert in it.' Adams reported that Bancroft was also a notorious speculator in London stocks. On that count, Adams made the following diary entry: 'Bancroft was a meddler in stocks as well as reviews, and frequently went into the alley, and into the deepest and darkest retirements and recesses of brokers and jobbers, Jews as well as Christians, and found amusement as well perhaps as profit by listening to all the news and anecdotes true or false that were whispered or more boldly pronounced. This information I had from his own mouth.' Adams further noted that 'After the peace he obtained a patent in France for the exclusive importation of the bark of yellow oak for dyers and then he went to England and procured a similar patent there, by both which together he is said to have realized an income of eight hundred a year.' [502]

"Adams also reported that the enormous quantities of cayenne pepper with which he seasoned his food, assisted by generous amounts of Burgundy, would 'set his tongue a running at a most licentious rate both at the table and after dinner,' and Adams said that it gave him a 'great pain.' [503]

"I understand that Bancroft was a frequent dinner guest at your residence at the Hotel Valentinois."

"Yes. And unlike Adams, I found Edward a very interesting conversationalist, and a scintillating dinner companion."

"It would appear, however, that his dinner conversations were 'a great pain' to John Adams," I said.

"Why do you say that, Jack?" Franklin said, turning to Jefferson and rolling his eyes.

"Would you care to hear other Adams observations of Bancroft?"

Franklin smiled and said, "If I must."

"He said that the Bible and the Christian religion were Bancroft's most frequent subjects of invective and ridicule, but that he sometimes fell upon politics and political characters, and 'seldom expressed sentiments of the royal family and the court of France, particularly the queen,' which Adams thought very improper for him to utter or for others to hear. The 'queen's intrigues with the Duchess de

Polinac, her constant dissipation, her habits of expense and profusion, her giddy thoughtless conduct were almost constant topics of his Tittle Tattle.'" [504]

Franklin looked at Jefferson and slowly shook his head.

"And wasn't it under your auspices that Bancroft was first engaged as a spy on behalf of the Colonies?" I said.

"Yes. When the Committee of Secret Correspondence appointed Silas Deane our agent in Europe, I immediately thought that Bancroft could be the perfect source for informing Deane on the political climate in England. So I wrote to Deane and suggested that he make contact by writing to him, under cover, to Mr. Griffiths, at Turnham Green, near London, and to ask Bancroft to meet him in either France or Holland, on the score of old acquaintance. I told Deane that from Bancroft he could obtain a good deal of information of what was then going forward in England, and settle on a mode of continuing correspondence. I suggested that Deane send a small bill to defray his travel expenses, and avoid all political matters in his letter." [505]

"What happened?"

"When Deane arrived in Paris, he sent Bancroft a letter requesting that he come to Paris. Deane enclosed thirty pounds to def ray Bancroft's travel expenses. A month later they met in Paris. Deane was so impressed with Bancroft, and so eager for his help that he told him the real purpose of his mission—to establish a secret relationship with the French and obtain military aid for the Colonies." [506]

"Didn't Bancroft become your secretary when Congress sent you and Arthur Lee to France as commissioners to join Silas Deane in the mission of obtaining France's military and economic aid for the colonies?"

"Yes, and except for his trips back to England from time to time, we were in daily contact. Edward was a friend with whom I spent many enjoyable times." [507]

"But an unreliable friend," I said.

"What do you mean by that?" Franklin countered.

"While employed by you as secretary of the commission and as an informer, Bancroft was also a British spy. If he had an allegiance to anyone other than himself, it was more to the British government than to America. He spied on you, and that is why I say he was an unreliable friend." As I looked at my two hosts, I could see both doubt and consternation on their faces.

"I think, Jack, you had better explain yourself," Franklin said, with more than a touch of annoyance in his voice.

"In 1821, Bancroft died a respected scientist. His treachery as a British spy was not discovered until seventy years later, when it was revealed by the British government. Let me read you a postwar memorandum Bancroft wrote to the British government:"

> I went to Paris, and during the first year, resided in the same house with Dr. Franklin, Mr. Deane, etc., and regularly informed this Government of every transaction of the American commissioners; of every step and vessel taken to supply the revolted colonies with artillery, arms, etc.; of every part of their intercourse with the French and other European courts; of the powers of instruction given by Congress to the commissioners; and of their correspondence with the Secret Committees, etc. [508]

When I looked up, both men were staring at me. Franklin's face was ablaze with anger, his eyes dark and cold. Jefferson's face expressed an array of emotions, chief among them disgust. Franklin spoke first.

"I was warned that there were spies around me, but I never once suspected Edward."

"Nor did I," Jefferson said.

"Nor did John Adams, Silas Deane, Comte de Vergennes, or anyone else except possibly Arthur Lee," I said. [509] "Bancroft was, in the words of a noted historian, 'destined to become one of the most remarkable spies of all time, achieving the astonishing feat of serving simultaneously as an intelligence agent for two nations at war while serving himself first of all, and mastering the art of duplicity so consummately as to conceal his treasons from some of the most astute men of his time and from historians for six decades after his death.' [510] His work as a spy was seen by the British Secret Service as 'a valuable treasure to government.' " [511]

"Why would he have done this?" Jefferson asked Franklin.

Franklin, obviously shaken, shook his head from side to side.

"I can tell you what Bancroft said of his decision to become a British spy," I said.

"I'd like to hear his explanation," Franklin said.

"This is what he wrote a friend:"

> I had then resided near ten years, and expected to reside the rest of my life in England; and all my views, interests and inclinations were adverse to the independency of the Colonies, though I had advocated some of their claims, from a persuasion of their being founded in justice. I therefore wished, that the government of this country might be informed, of the danger of French interference, though I could not resolve to become the informant. But Mr.

Paul Wentworth, having gained some general knowledge of my journey to France, and my intercourse with Mr. Deane, and having induced me to believe that the British Ministry was likewise informed on this subject, I at length consented to meet the then secretaries of state, Lords Weymouth and Suffolk, and gave them all the information in my power, which I did with the most disinterested views. [512]

"How did he communicate his perfidy?" Franklin asked.

"As you know, he frequently went to London, sometimes on missions for you and the Commission. While there, he would stop by the Office of William Eden, the head of British intelligence, and make verbal reports, and sometimes turn over copies of documents. In Paris he used a more clandestine and ingenious method of supplying information to the British. He wrote his reports in invisible ink and placed them in a sealed bottle in the hollow of a plane tree located on the south terrace of the Tuileries Gardens. A messenger picked up his messages at half-past nine every Tuesday evening and left in another bottle any messages to him from Wentworth." [513]

Franklin pushed his wine glass to the side. "Three weeks after my arrival in France," he said, "I received a letter from a woman warning me that I was surrounded by spies. And in view of what you tell me about Bancroft, she was right—I was indeed surrounded by spies. My response to her was the advice I followed in my daily conduct, and I believe it worked. Despite British agents inside our Commission, they were not able to destroy, or even impede the friendship and support that lead to the American-French alliance and ultimately our winning the war."

"What did you do when told by this woman that you were surrounded by spies?"

" 'It is impossible to discover in every case the falsity of pretended friends who would know our affairs; and more so to prevent being watched by spies when interested people may think proper to place them for that purpose. I have long observed one rule, which prevents any inconvenience from such practices. It is simply this: to be concerned in no affairs that I should blush to have made public, and to do nothing but what spies may see, and welcome. If I was sure, therefore, that my *valet de place* was a spy, as he probably is, I think that I should not discharge him for that, if in other respects I liked him.' " [514]

"By Bancroft's own admission everything that took place between you and your fellow commissioners, all of your negotiations and agreements with the French, all of your correspondence with Congress, were reported to the chief of the British Secret Service, William Eden and his superiors. Worse still, the British admiralty learned about sailings, so their warships were able to intercept and capture shipments, dispatches, and men. Bancroft later claimed that when you and your two fellow commissioners, Lee and Deane, signed the Treaty of Alliance with France on February 6, he was able to get a copy of it to England within forty-two hours, and to report that you wore the same coat at the signing that you wore to the Cockpit the day Wedderburn abused you. He also used the intelligence information he learned through the American commission for personal gain by successfully speculating in stocks."[515]

Franklin watched as Petit refreshed his glass. "There is something about your accusation of Bancroft being a spy for the British government that doesn't fit," he said.

"What is that?"

"When Deane, Lee, and I learned that Stormont, the British minister to France, had in his possession original documents taken from Deane's lodging, we demanded that Bancroft return all our documents. Bancroft promptly sent us his resignation."[516]

"But you didn't accept his resignation," I said.

"We didn't, but if we had, his spying days for the British would have been over, and surely he knew that when he submitted his resignation."

"Bancroft took a terrific gamble. His letter was a bluff, but you didn't call it. Shortly afterward, he learned through the Lee brothers that he was accused of having divulged information to the Privy Council soon after meeting Deane in Paris. He tracked the rumor down, and when satisfied that there was nothing to it, he made new financial demands on the British Secret Service. These were nervous times for this master spy, but he managed to survive, and to come out with Deane and your confidence in him stronger than ever."[517]

"I remember Ralph Izard berating me for not sharing with him information about the treaty with France, saying that members of the British Parliament knew about it before it was signed."[518]

"Dr. Franklin," I said, "Izard's accusations were more specific than what you mention. To refresh your recollection, let me read what he wrote to you. 'How extraordinary will it appear to the public, if it can be proved, that notwithstanding your great kindness, and attention to me, speculations of various kinds to a very considerable amount have been constantly carried on by persons residing under your own roof; that one of the gentlemen engaged in these speculations was himself a commissioner; that you were informed of Lord North's having boasted of his lenity in not apprehending a friend of yours who was in London speculating in the funds for the benefit of the commissioners; and that after having been informed of this, you yourself communicated the treaty to that gentleman, at the very time when you refused to make such communication to Mr. William Lee and myself, in defiance of the express instructions of Congress.'" I looked up at Franklin and said, "He is, of course, referring to Silas Deane and Edward Bancroft."

Franklin nodded in the affirmative.

I continued reading, "'It will appear still more extraordinary if it can be proved, that a friend of yours was in the month of January made acquainted with the very day the Treaty was to be signed; that this information was transmitted to London, and in consequence of it, that insurances to a great amount were made; for whose benefit I will not take upon me to say. If these things can be proved, the world will judge by what motives you have been actuated. I have been confidently assured that they can be proved; and I beg that you will let me know if my information is true or false.'"[519]

Jefferson's eyes were on me as I read, and when I finished, he looked at Franklin in anticipation of his answer. Franklin stared at me but said nothing.

"Did you discuss with Ralph Izard the source of his information?" I asked.

"I did not because I did not believe him."

"But he flat-out accused Bancroft of providing the British authorities with secret information."

"And on what did Izard base his accusation?" Franklin asked.

"Musco Livingston, the Jamaican sea captain. Livingston came to Paris from London and told you that he had seen in London a letter written by Bancroft to John Wharton dated January 27, announcing that the treaty would be signed on February 5 or 6, and urging Wharton to speculate accordingly. In addition Livingston signed a statement to this effect. Surely Izard knew about Livingston's charge against Bancroft, probably from Arthur Lee."[520]

"Soon after I heard of Livingston's statement, I spoke with Bancroft, and he assured me the leak about the treaty, and his friend John Wharton's stock speculations, came from John Thornton, Arthur Lee's secretary. I asked Edward to put that in writing to the Commission, and he did. He wrote a letter blaming Thornton. Accordingly, given the choice between Bancroft and Thornton, I believed Bancroft. I should add that Bancroft's explanation also satisfied John Adams."[521]

"But that doesn't end the matter of Bancroft's being a spy, does it?" I said.

"No," Franklin said. "Early the next year, Arthur Lee wrote a letter to John Adams and me, objecting to our having appointed Bancroft to transact business for the Commission in England. His objections centered on his claims that Bancroft was a notorious stockjobber, lived with a woman to whom he was not married, and his enmity to Lee. Lee was also upset that we had not consulted him about Bancroft's appointment. Lee claimed that he had evidence that Bancroft was a criminal with regard to the United States, and that he would have him charged if he ever entered the jurisdiction of the United States."[522]

"Surely Lee's allegations were sufficient to alert you that Bancroft was a spy?"

"No, for the simple reason that I placed very little credence in anything Arthur Lee said. Again, given the choice between Lee and Bancroft, I chose to believe Bancroft, and he remained in my confidence throughout my time in France. I also think it is significant to note that John Adams did not consider Lee's charge of treason of sufficient worth to do anything about it."[523]

"I think Bancroft's influence as a British spy may have saved England from being invaded," I said.

"How?"

"At one point during the war, the French foreign minister, Vergennes, was considering a plan of raising a rebellion among Irish Presbyterians as a diversion for a planned Franco-Spanish invasion of England. Lafayette and you recommended Bancroft for the mission. Naturally, Bancroft, a British spy, in his report to Vergennes discouraged any hope of a rebellion, and the invasion never took place."[524]

I sipped my wine and formed the next question. "You and Arthur Lee served together as commissioners for over two years, but because of the enmity you felt for one another, I wonder how you were able to work together?"

"We didn't. Lee constantly complained that Deane and I failed to consult him about decisions we made. He resented being left out. [525] His incessant backbiting and mean temper provoked the angriest letter I ever wrote. It summarizes what I thought of him."

"Can we hear it?" I asked.

Franklin removed a paper from his jacket, and with wire-rimmed spectacles positioned low on his nose, he began to read. "It is true that I have omitted answering some of your letters. 'I do not like to answer angry letters. I hate disputes. I am old, cannot have long to live, have much to do and no time for altercation. If I have often received and borne your magisterial snubbings and rebukes without reply, ascribe it to the right causes: my concern for the honor and success of our mission which would be hurt by our quarrelling, my love of peace, my respect for your good qualities, and my pity of your sick mind, which is forever tormenting itself with its jealousies, suspicions, and fancies that others mean you ill, wrong you, or fail in respect for you. If you do not cure yourself of this temper it will end in insanity, of which it is a symptomatic forerunner, as I have seen in several in-stances. God preserve you from so terrible an evil; and for His sake pray suffer me to live in quiet.'" [526]

We all looked at one another in stunned silence. Finally, I said, "How did Lee react?"

A smile broke across Franklin's face. He took a sip of wine, looked from Jefferson to me, and said, "I did not send it. 'The next day I wrote a longer letter in which I answered his concerns point by point. I told myself I would not send that letter either, unless exceedingly pressed by Lee. [527] During this time, I had but two enemies, Lee and Izard. I deserved the enmity of Izard, because I might have avoided it by paying him a compliment, which I neglected. With Lee, I owe it to the people of France, who happened to respect me too much and him too little; which I could bear, and he could not.' I knew that Lee and Izard continued to talk against me in America." [528]

I turned to Jefferson, who turned the conversation back to Bancroft, the spy in our midst. "I too was completely taken in by Bancroft. When John Adams left as our minister to England in 1788, I wrote Dr. Bancroft, 'Since Mr. Adams's departure I have need of information from that country, and should rely much on yours. It will always therefore be acceptable.' [529]

"John and Lucy Ludwell Paradise, friends living in London, were having serious marital and financial problems and asked for my help. Dr. Bancroft was a constant source of assistance to me in this regard. The Paradises considered Edward 'a good and honest gentleman' and friend. [530] And when I thought that our country needed discreet and immediate help, I called on Bancroft."

"What were the circumstances?" I said.

"During my last winter in Paris, a Frenchman by the name of Foulloy stopped by my house and offered to sell me two volumes of Silas Deane's letter and account books. Foulloy said he had taken the books instead of money Deane owed him. He claimed Deane had six or eight additional volumes, and threatened to return to London, get them from Deane, and make us pay dearly for them. Concerned that the books might fall into hands that might make unf riendly use of them, I asked Bancroft to use his friendship and influence with Deane to buy the books on behalf of the United States. I suggested that Bancroft pay as much as fifty guineas, and I would reimburse him from public funds. I stressed that time was of the essence, because if Foulloy got there first, he would spoil the bargain."

"And as I recall," I said, "you asked Bancroft to do this as a patriotic act, or, as you put it, 'It is for our common country, and common interest.'" [531]

"Yes, that is exactly how I put it."

"Was Bancroft able to buy the books from Deane?"

"Bancroft reported that Deane had no other account or letter books. By way of explanation Bancroft said that two or three years earlier Deane had become very much attached to a prostitute, who over the years had fleeced him of all his money. As a result, Deane had become a drunk and lost his mental facilities, which 'produced a total loss of the powers of his body and mind, insomuch that he could not remember anything a single minute, nor use either his hands and feet. In this destitute, helpless situation, the woman became anxious to get him out of the house.' She told Bancroft that if Deane wasn't moved out, she and Foulloy, whom she represented to be her husband, would carry him out in the month of January, at midnight, and lay him down in the middle of the street and leave him there to his fate."

"My God," Franklin said, "I had heard that Silas was down on his luck, but I didn't realize that his life had plunged into the depths of hell. What did Bancroft do?"

"Bancroft moved Deane to other quarters along with some trunks that the woman said contained everything Deane owned. According to Bancroft, when he opened the trunks they contained nothing of value. Bancroft returned to the woman's house and questioned her. She said 'Foulloy was a villain and deserved to be hanged,' and that while Deane was still in the house, he had found the keys to the trunks, opened them, examined Deane's papers, removed everything of value, and left for France. The woman's 12-year-old daughter confirmed her story and described two large books of accounts and writings that Bancroft assumed were those that I bought from Foulloy." [532]

"What happened to Deane's other account and letter books? The ones you sent Bancroft to purchase." Franklin said.

"Bancroft said that Deane did not have other account or letter books, because when Deane's mental condition improved, he never complained about the loss of other books, nor were there any books or papers of importance in his possession."

"If Deane's mental condition improved, did his physical condition also improve? And if it did, to what degree did his mental and physical conditions get better?" Franklin asked.

"Bancroft said that contrary to all expectations, Deane recovered 'in some degree from the complicated disorders of dropsy, palsy and idiotism,' though he continued to subsist, as he had for a long time, on charitable subscription. Bancroft concluded his letter to me, 'And you may always be assured, that if in any matter,

174

in which you may honor me with your confidence, I should be unable to serve you, I will at least take care that no indiscretion of mine shall do any harm.'"

"And you believed him?"

"Yes. But now that I know he was a British spy, I think we can assume that if Deane had other books, as Foulloy represented, Bancroft turned them over to the British Secret Service."

"As a matter of curiosity," I said, "what eventually happened to Silas Deane?"

"About six months later I heard that Bancroft, who had undertaken the management of Deane and his affairs, raised enough money from friends in London to pay for his passage back to America. Deane was on board the *Boston Packet* in the Downs and scheduled to sail to Boston, when he suddenly died. This was reported to me by John Cutting, who said that he had seen Deane a few days before at John Trumbull's house and thought that he had never seen him look better. It was Dr. Bancroft's suspicion that Deane committed suicide." [533]

"Jack," Franklin said, "you can now add Edward Bancroft to my list of greatest disappointments."

"Turning to a more pleasant subject," I said, "I know from my reading of history that you both took several fascinating vacation trips, and I would love to hear you tell me about them." Franklin and Jefferson looked at one another. Jefferson waved his hand in deference to Franklin.

Franklin sat back in his chair and lifted his eyes to the ceiling as though organizing his thoughts. "In 1759 my son William and I took a trip to Scotland. We left London on the 8th of August. Before we left, William surprised me when he told me that he was to become a father. [534] On the way to Edinburgh we visited Birmingham, Derbyshire, Sheffield, Manchester, and Liverpool. Liverpool was a thriving seaport of thirty thousand, and twenty years later I would recommend Liverpool to Lafayette as one of the coastal seaports he should consider attacking. [535]

"At Lancaster, we took the western road to Edinburgh by way of Kendal, Carlisle, Hawick, and Selkirk. Travel conditions in Scotland were atrocious. Many of the roads were nothing more than narrow clay lanes, impassable after rain. The inn accommodations were wretched, with equally wretched food and wine. [536] The prospect of meeting highwaymen ready to waylay you on the lonely moors made our journey even more uncomfortable, but we arrived in Edinburgh without incident a month after setting out. [537] The sanitary conditions in Edinburgh were execrable. Until ten o'clock in the evening, stairways and passageways were blocked with 'luggies' containing household excrement. Then, at the appointed

*Milne Square,
Edinburgh*

hour, in accordance to a municipal ordinance, these luggies were emptied out the windows into the streets below to the warning cry of 'gary loo,' which has a translation of 'God have mercy on your soul.' [538] Because of the wretchedness of Edinburgh's inns, William and I took lodging at Mrs. Cowan's in Milne Square, one of the most respectable boarding houses in town. [539]

"Our first host in Scotland was Alexander Dick, a distinguished physician, whose medical career culminated in his election as President of the Edinburgh College of Physicians. Edinburgh was still enclosed by the battlements of its medieval period when William and I rode down High Street on our way to Dick's estate at Prestonfield. [540] Sir Dick's family consisted of himself, Lady Dick, and their two daughters. Sir Dick was a congenial host, and our five-day stay at Prestonfield was eventful and enjoyable. The week after our visit with the Dicks, we dined with Dr. William Robertson at his place in Cowgate. Dr. Robertson's successful *History of Scotland* had just been published, and he was only three years away from his appointment as principal of the University of Edinburgh. At dinner that evening was Alexander Carlyle, Adam Smith, David Hume, Dr. Wight and Dr. Cullen, and three or four others. [541]

"From Edinburgh we followed a muddy, winding road westward to Glasgow, a distance of only forty-six miles that took, on average, twelve hours to travel. Here we were met by Adam Smith, quaestor of the university, who was already working on his monumental work, *The Wealth of Nations*. Later, William and I joined Professor John Anderson of Glasgow University for a tour of the Perthshire Highlands by way of Dunkeld and Perth to St. Andrews. This route led through some of the most picturesque parts of the Highlands. I went to St. Andrews to express my appreciation for the doctor of laws degree conferred on me by the St. Andrews University faculty the previous February. I was shocked by the deplorable conditions of the town; it consisted of one street on both sides of which were the decaying remains of once stately mansions. The university had fared no better, with only twenty students shivering in shabby, fireless halls. [542]

"Nevertheless I was honored at two events: the ceremony on October 2 that elevated me as a guild brother of the town of St. Andrews, and my investiture as doctor of laws held at the university library and presided over by Rector Provost David Shaw. I recall that I was clad in the gown of doctor of laws, and over my shoulders was draped a hood of scarlet silk lined with white satin. I knelt on the graduation stool in front of the president of senatus who admitted me with the words:

Te ad gradum DOCTORIS LEGUM promoveo, cujus rei in symbolum super te hoc birretum impono.

With the words *hoc birretum* my head was covered for a moment with the historic 'graduation cap,' and when I rose from my kneeling position, I was no longer Mr. Franklin but Dr. Franklin. [543]

"From St. Andrews, we returned to Edinburgh for a round of sociability before heading back to London. On Friday evening we were invited to a meeting of the Speculative Society at the Advocates Library. Members debated such

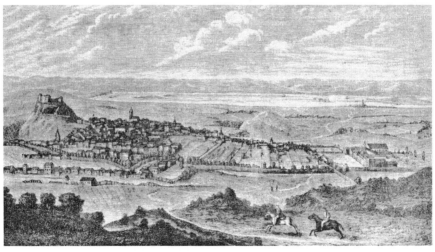

Edinburgh in Franklin's day.

177

topics as 'Was Brutus right in killing Julius Caesar?' After the debate, we joined the members in the custom of adjourning to the tavern of Luckey Boyd. [544] My stay in Edinburgh marks the beginning of my friendship with Henry Home, Lord Kames, judge of the Court of Session. It was a friendship that lasted until Lord Kames's death in 1782.

"On the return trip to London we stopped for a few days by invitation at Lord Kames's countryseat in Berwickshire, a fitting end to a memorable trip that, on the whole, marked 'six weeks of the densest happiness I ever met with in any part of my life.' " [545]

"You mentioned that when you and William set out on the trip to Scotland, William was about to become a father. I wasn't aware that William was married."

"He wasn't. The child, a son, was illegitimate."

"What happened to the child?"

"He was born in February 1760, three months after our return from Scotland. His mother was a woman of the streets, and William arranged for the child to be raised secretly by a foster family. He was named William Temple." [546]

"Did your son eventually get married?"

"Yes, but not to the mother of his son, nor did he acknowledge his son."

"Did William stay in London and practice law?"

"No. Through my influence and his own skillful lobbying, William was appointed by King George as royal governor of the Province of New Jersey. The pending appointment was announced in the newspapers the day I left for America. Less than two weeks later, William married Elizabeth Downes, an aristocratic young lady, and soon sailed to America to assume his new duties. [547]

"I remained in America just two years before again leaving for London in November 1764. Shortly thereafter, when William Temple was four, I brought him into my household at Craven Street, but Temple's paternity was kept a secret. Years later when the pretense was abandoned, and Temple was openly acknowledged as a Franklin, Polly Stevenson wrote me, 'We are all pleased with our old friend Temple changed into a young Franklin. We see a strong resemblance of you and indeed saw it when we did not think ourselves at liberty to say we did, as we pretended to be ignorant as you supposed we were or chose we should be.' " [548]

"I know, Mr. Jefferson, that you had several fascinating vacation trips, and I wonder if you would share them with Dr. Franklin and me."

"Yes, Thomas, I would love to hear about your journeys," Franklin said.

"I will be delighted, but you too, Benjamin, must tell Jack and me about some of your other interesting trips."

"Agreed," Franklin said.

"When you visited England in 1786, Mr. Jefferson, didn't you and John Adams spend some time together in the English countryside?" I said.

"Yes. On April 4, John and I set out on a six-day tour. During this trip, we visited magnificent landscaped gardens and battle sites, and shared thoughts, meals, and wines. Although we would both live another 40 years, never again would we experience such intimacy and friendship. Ten years later, we would be locked in political enmity, which Adams would win to become the second president of the United States, only to lose that office to me four years later.

"In the late eighteenth century, travel conditions in England were far more comfortable and better than in the United States. The roads between cities and towns were essentially well graded, and the stagecoach was a highly developed form of travel, with a 200-year tradition. The regular stagecoach was not the only choice: many of the inns served as posting-houses where the traveler could rent a chaise, a closed-body four-wheeled carriage, and horses for a few pence per mile. The horses were used for distances of about six to ten miles, and were left at another posting-house, where new horses were hired. Each inn branded its horses so they could be identified and returned. This was the method of travel employed by Adams and me. [549]

"Inn-keeping in England was more than a mere occupation or trade; as practiced by many innkeepers it was an honorable calling. Eighteenth-century inns often did not have common dining rooms. Adams and I usually dined in private rooms, while the common traveler took his meals in the kitchen. [550]

"The English landscape gardens that Adams and I visited were the antithesis of the earlier formal English gardens we were familiar with in colonial America, and the strictly defined gardens surrounding French palaces and châteaux. Pleasure gardening, as I called it, had emerged as the rave in 18th century England and was best associated with the gardens designed by William Kent and Lancelot 'Capability' Brown. William Kent was a fashionable architect of formal buildings in the Palladian style, but, paradoxically, he was the first important pioneer in the creation of the informal English garden. He was opposed to the stiff, regular English garden patterns of the seventeenth century, and he was one of the first to eliminate walls or boundaries. He replaced them with sunken fences or what became known as 'ha-has' to express surprise at finding a sudden and unnoticed barrier. Kent's guiding principle was 'nature abhors a straight line.' [551]

"The man who made the greatest impact on eighteenth century English landscape gardens was Lancelot 'Capability' Brown (1716–1783), whose nickname derived from his habit of saying of nearly every garden he was asked to improve that it 'had great capabilities.'" He worked at Stowe under Kent and made it one of the most talked-about gardens of that day. Brown was a fervent advocate that gardens should display their natural beauty and give the appearance of freedom, and he too employed the use of 'ha-has' as a method of disguising boundaries. [552]

"Our first day took us through Twickenham and then to Woburn, where we visited Woburn Farm, a pleasure garden of about thirty-five acres that was merely a highly ornamented walk through and around the divisions of the farm and kitchen garden. From Woburn, we traveled to Caversham, where we inspected Major Marsac's garden and park of 431 acres, the work of Capability Brown. The English countryside from Caversham to Reading was a prelude to the scenic beauty that would surround us for the next six days. In Reading we lodged at the Bear Inn on Bridge Street. We dined on chicken, potatoes, tarts, and custards, accompanied by punch, porter and sherry wine. [553]

"In the morning we rented horses and traveled the turnpike road to Wallingford, Thame, and Wooton. In the late seventeenth century, tolls were established for bridges, causeways, and the heaviest traveled roads. At first these toll roads were not barred or obstructed, but because some travelers would dash past the toll collector without paying, laws were enacted giving local authorities the power to block the roadway with a turnpike. The turnpike consisted of metal pikes fastened to a metal frame, which formed a barrier when placed across the road. After the traveler paid the toll, the frame was turned on a pivot, clearing the way. Since turnpikes were used on the most heavily traveled roads, the term 'turnpike' became synonymous with 'the main road.'" [554]

"Main roads are often still called turnpikes," I said, "though the actual pikes replaced with ordinary tollgates that we are faced with today in one form or the other."

"The owner of the Wooton gardens employed only two workers to keep the more than 300 acres in order, and we found the gardens much neglected. We lodged in Buckingham and paid almost twice as much for the beer and wine as we did for our dinners of veal chops and mutton steaks. [555]

"Early the next morning, we traveled to the pleasure gardens at Stowe. We approached the Stowe gardens along a magnificent avenue of elms with the mansion and a Corinthian arch in the distance. Because the arch was not a part of the house and had no independent destination, I thought it broke up a pleasing prospect and created an ill effect. The Stowe gardens, with the imprint of both Kent and Brown on them, were probably the best-known gardens in England at the time. Adams and I climbed to the top of the 115-foot Lord Cobham's Pillar for the view. [556]

"On the way to Banbury, we stopped at Edgehill, where the first great battle of their Civil War (1642–1651) was fought between the forces of King Charles I and Parliament. The battlefield is now covered with trees. In Banbury we stayed at the William Pratt Inn and had beer and wine with our dinner. After dinner we changed our chaise and horses and traveled to Shakespeare's birthplace, Stratford-upon-Avon. [557]

"My inn receipt does not reveal the name of the inn where we stayed for the evening, but Adams identified it as being 'three doors' from Shakespeare's birthplace, and the White Lion Inn, operated by John Payton on Henley Street was located three doors from Shakespeare's birthplace. We had dined earlier, so when we arrived at the White Lion Inn, we ordered only lemonade and tea before retiring. [558]

"I paid one shilling each to see Shakespeare's birthplace and gravesite. I owned all of Shakespeare's works, and considered Shakespeare and Alexander Pope two of the greatest English poets. Adams thought Stratford-upon-Avon interesting, as it was 'the scene of the birth, death, and sepulcher of Shakespeare.

White Lion Inn

Three doors from the inn was the house where he was born, as small and mean as you can conceive. They showed us an old wooden chair in the chimney corner where he sat. We cut off a chip according to custom. A mulberry tree that he planted had been cut down and carefully preserved for sale. The house where he died had been taken down, and the spot was only a yard or garden. The curse upon him, who should remove his bones, which is written on his gravestone, alludes to a pile of some thousands of human bones which lie exposed in that church. There is nothing preserved of this great genius which is worth knowing; nothing, which might inform us what education, what company, what accident, turned his mind to letters and the drama. His name is not even on his gravestone. An ill-sculptured head is set up by his wife, by the side of his grave in the church. But paintings and sculpture would be thrown away on his fame. His wit, fancy, his tastes and judgment, his knowledge of nature, of life and character, are immortal.' [559]

"In the morning we rented a chaise and horses, and visited Birmingham and viewed a manufactory of paintings on wallpaper. After dinner at the Swan Tavern, we set out for the gardens at Leasowes, situated between Birmingham and Stourbridge. Leasowes consisted of a 150-acre grazing farm encircled by a walk that looked like a common field path. After the opulence of Stowe, I was disappointed in the plainness of the gardens. Eleven years earlier, Leasowes had been described as abounding in attractive winding walks, 'serpentnizing' paths, and a variety of romantic scenes, but at the time of our visit its grandeur was a thing of the past. [560]

"Our next stop was Stourbridge, where we stayed at John Wiley's Talbot Inn on High Street. The inn's origins date back to the sixteenth century, and it was Stourbridge's most famous coaching inn during the eighteenth century. [561]

"On the morning of April 8, we rented a chaise and horses to Bromsgrove and visited the 1,000 acre garden and park at Hagley, located between the Clent and Witchbury hills. The estate house was in a hollow between the hills. The Witchbury hills rose in three swells, the summits of which provided striking views of the countryside, the Hagley estate-house, the town of Stourbridge, and the ruins of Dudley castle. [562]

"In Worcester, we visited battle sites, which Adams recorded as 'curious and interesting to us, as scenes where free men had fought for their rights.' Adams became annoyed, even indignant, because the people in the neighborhood appeared to be ignorant of the fact that Worcester was the scene of Oliver Cromwell's final victory in 1651 over the king's forces during England's bloody Civil

Shakespeare's birthplace.

War. Provoked, he asked, 'And do Englishmen so soon forget the ground where liberty was fought for? Tell your neighbors and your children that this is holy ground, much holier than that on which your churches stand. All England should come and pilgrimage to this hill once a year.'[563]

"Worcester's well-paved streets, public walks, and cathedral showed its affluence from flourishing trades in gloves, carpets, and china. We dined at Worcester's most expensive and popular inn, the Hop-Pole. It was located on Foregate Street on the road from Holyhead to Bath and Bristol.[564]

"Leaving Worcester, we rode through the hamlets of Moreton and Lynston and lodged at Woodstock, a neat little town that served as a convenient stop for a visit to the gardens at Blenheim Palace which we saw the next morning. Blenheim Palace had been built by the British nation for the Duke of Marlboro in commemoration of his defeating the French at Blenheim in 1704. Capability Brown had revised the gardens in the 1760s. I noted that the grounds consisted of 225 acres with gardens, lakes, and a park stocked with deer and sheep. I found the lakes very beautiful and very grand, but overall I was disappointed, complaining of too many temples and fountains and too few seats, and trees scattered thinly over the grounds.[565]

"In Oxford we visited several of the colleges, and then went on to High Wycombe, where we dined at the Antelope Inn on mutton chops accompanied by beer and wine. After dinner we traveled as far as Uxbridge, lodging at the White Hart Inn before returning to London the next day.[566]

"During our tour of the English landscaped gardens, I carried a copy of

Thomas Whateley's *Observations on Modern Gardening*, whose descriptions of the gardens I thought models of perfect elegance and classical correctness and remarkable for their exactness. My main inquiries were directed chiefly to such practical things as might enable me to estimate the expense of making and maintaining a garden in that style at Monticello." [567]

Jefferson had finished his account and I looked over to Dr. Franklin. "I suppose it is my turn," he said. I nodded.

"When I lived in London, I usually took summer health vacations away from the city. In 1766 my friend John Pringle, physician to the Queen, wanted to drink the waters at Bad Pyemont, a German spa, and that trip took us through Germany and on to the Netherlands. But the vacation I especially enjoyed was the next year, when Pringle and I went to France. We left London in late August for Paris. My principal health problems were rashes and boils on my back and a sour temper. The journey to Dover did nothing to alleviate my sour temper because the post chaises we rode in had canopies that obstructed our views of the countryside, and the drivers, for a variety of inane reasons, refused to change the riggings. In addition, along the way, I was engaged in perpetual disputes with innkeepers, hostlers, and postillions. We embarked for Calais with a number of passengers who had never been before at sea. Many of them ate a hearty breakfast in case the wind should fail, and we might not get over till suppertime. But they had scarce been out half an hour before the sea laid claim to it, and they were obliged to deliver it up. So it seems there are uncertainties even beyond those between the cup and the lip. Between the English and French boatmen and porters, it was a close call as to which were the most rapacious, but the French had, with their knavery, the most politeness.

"The roads from Calais to Paris were as good as those in England, paved in many places with smooth stones and lined with rows of trees. But then the poor peasants complained to us grievously that they were obliged to work upon the roads a full two months in the year without being paid for their labor. Whether this is truth, or whether, like Englishmen, they grumble cause or no cause, I was not able to determine.

"To my surprise, in France I was feted as a celebrity, and Pringle and I were invited to Versailles to attend a grand couvert, an event where King Louis XV and Queen Marie dined in public. I thought serenity, complacence, and beauty characterized the queen, and the king spoke to both of us very graciously and cheerfully. He was a handsome man, had a very lively look, and appeared younger than his fifty-seven years.

"Versailles was worth the trip. The range of buildings was immense; the garden front most magnificent, all of hewn stone; the number of statues, figures, urns, etc., in marble and bronze of exquisite workmanship was beyond conception. I estimated the cost at £80 million. Yet, despite Versailles's magnificence, the maintenance was poor. The waterworks were out of repair, and so was a great part of the front next to the town, looking with its shabby half brick walls and broken windows not much better than the houses in Durham Yard. There was, in short, both at Versailles and Paris, a prodigious mixture of magnificence and negligence, with every kind of elegance except that of cleanliness and what we call tidiness.

"Two things struck my fancy about Paris. The first had to do with the water supply, which was as pure as that of the best spring by filtering it through cisterns filled with sand. The second was streets, which by constant sweeping were fit to walk in though there were no paved foot paths.

"The French people were the politest I had ever met. Strangers were treated with respect and were shown the same deference here by being a stranger as in England by being a lady. At a customs house near Paris the officers were about to seize two dozen bottles of Bordeaux wine given to Pringle and me at Boulogne, but as soon as they found we were strangers, it was immediately remitted on that account. At the cathedral of Notre-Dame, where an immense crowd had gathered to see an exhibit dedicated to the recently deceased dauphiness, we initially despaired of getting in. But the officer, being told that we were strangers from England, immediately admitted us and accompanied and showed us everything.

"I concluded that traveling is one way of lengthening life, at least in appearance. It had been but a fortnight since we left London, but the variety of scenes we had gone through made it seem equal to six months living in one place. Perhaps I suffered a greater change, too, in my own person than I could have done in six years at home. I bought some stylish tailored clothes and a little bag wig that made me look twenty years younger. Although I had not felt well when I left London, I returned the first week in October in high spirits. The effects of exercise and change of air on this trip so invigorated me that I was once very near to making love to my friend's wife." [568]

Jefferson and I laughed. I noticed that my glasses were empty and both decanters half full. "With two such magnificent wines before us, it would be a shame not to drink them," I said, nodding in the direction of the decanters.

Franklin smiled, pushed his glasses forward, and said, "I quite agree."

Jefferson poured our glasses, took a sip of both wines, and said, "What do you think, gentlemen, are the wines getting better?"

We drank the wines in silence. Finally, Franklin said, "The Haut Brion has come around. It is softer than when first decanted, and is now smooth on the palate."

"I agree. Two wonderful wines to enjoy as Mr. Jefferson tells us about his fascinating three-and-a-half-month trip through southern France."

"It was probably my most interesting trip, and, incidentally, I first drank these two wines on my visit to Bordeaux. Traveling alone in my own carriage drawn by three horses, I left Paris on February 28, 1787, and did not return to Paris until June 10. My journey took me through southern France and over the Alps into Italy. I remember writing to a friend on my return that I 'never passed three months and a half more delightfully.' [569]

"When traveling the roads in France back then, the traveler was required to use post houses. These were franchises of the king and were way-stations along the roads. They provided horses, drivers, postillions, guides, meals, and, usually, overnight lodgings. The distance between post houses was about ten miles, and the average speed about seven and a half miles per hour. The safety of the roads was overseen by mounted troops engaged by the king for this purpose.

"As I traveled southeast toward Burgundy through Fontainebleau, Sens, Auxerre, and Vermenton, I found the people poorly clothed. I observed the women and children carrying heavy burdens, and laboring with the hoe, an unequivocal indication of extreme poverty. [570] Approaching Dijon, I observed the people as being well-fed and well-clothed, but noted that it was Sunday. I spent three days in Dijon. I traveled incognito throughout the rest of the trip. To ensure my anonymity, I intended taking on a new valet at every principal city. But the man I engaged in Dijon, Petit Jean, was so adept that I kept him on throughout the trip, engaging an additional local valet whenever I stayed more than a day. [571]

VUE DE DIJON

"Dijon was the former capital of the Duchy of Burgundy with a population of about 20,000. It was a handsome city with wide, well-paved streets and charming old houses centered around the Place Royal on which is situated the palace of the former dukes of Burgundy. Several miles south of Dijon I entered the heart of Burgundy, the Côte d'Or, a series of low hills that serve as home to its best vineyards. I described the côte as a solid rock overlaid with about a foot of soil and small stone in equal quantities, the soil red and of middling quality. The plains were in corn, the côte in vines. Of the vineyards nestled along the hillsides, Chambertin was the first in view, followed by 'Vougeot, Romanée, Vosne, Nuits, Beaune, Pommard, Volnay, Meursault and end at Montrachet.' I mounted a pony, put a peasant on another, and rambled through their most celebrated vineyards. [572]

"My stay in Burgundy lasted only a few days, but what I learned about the region's wines would last me a lifetime. I thought Chambertin the best of the reds, followed by Vougeot and Vosne because they were the strongest, and would bear transportation."

"Chambertin, a *Grand Cru*, still sells for astonishing prices," I said, "but its entitlement to the cachet as the best red wine of Burgundy is in serious question. This thirty-two acre vineyard is now owned by more than twenty proprietors, resulting in what has been called 'wines of enormous differences in quality,' with some wines of insipid quality bearing the Chambertin name. There are, of course, a few proprietors who can and do

Burgundy wine bottles.

produce in great vintages Chambertins that, when mature, justify its reputation and perhaps its extraordinary prices."

Jefferson nodded to indicate that he understood what I'd said, and then continued his account of his trip. "When I visited Clos de Vougeot, it was still owned by the monks. Its annual production was about 50,000 bottles and the wines had a reputation for excellence. The tiny village of Vougeot is named after the stream-like river Vouge that runs behind it. In the twelfth century, land was given to the monks of Citeaux, and by 1336, the monks owned all 124 acres of vineyards, which they surrounded with a stone wall. Over the years the monks built a large Renaissance château and its wall-enclosed vineyards, cellars, and twelfth century wine presses made it one of the principal attractions of the Côte de Nuits. Working with their primitive wine-presses, the monks made both red and white wines and became such skilled winemakers that for centuries the wines of Clos de Vougeot were considered the best of all Burgundies." [573]

"I'm sure you heard, Mr. Jefferson, that during the French Revolution, and just a year after you left France, Clos de Vougeot was sold at public auction, and an almost immediate loss of quality was reported after its divestiture," I said. "French inheritance laws have created today's chaotic web of eighty-six (the last count) different and independent owners producing wines from the original 124 acres. With such diverse ownership, there is no one standard for what modernday Clos de Vougeot should taste like. Therefore, bottles of Clos de Vougeot of the same vintage from different producers will vary in character and quality. Clos de Vougeot, however, with its ancient beauty and old presses remains an interesting place to visit. Also, Mr. Jefferson, in recognizing the wines of Vosne for their quality, you did not delineate their order of rank, but such an order did exist. About thirty-five years after your visit to Burgundy, an English writer by the name of Alexander Henderson singled out Romanée-Conti, Richebourg, La Tâche and Romanée St-Vivant for 'their beautiful color and exquisite flavor and aroma, combining qualities of lightness and delicacy with richness and fullness of body,' a remarkably accurate description of those wines today." [574]

Jefferson nodded his agreement with my comment and continued. "These vineyards are in the northern section of the Côte d'Or called the Côte de Nuits and were the wines of Burgundy that live longer and improve with age, and in so doing reach a degree of perfection that most other red burgundies fail to achieve. [575]

Clos de Vougeot

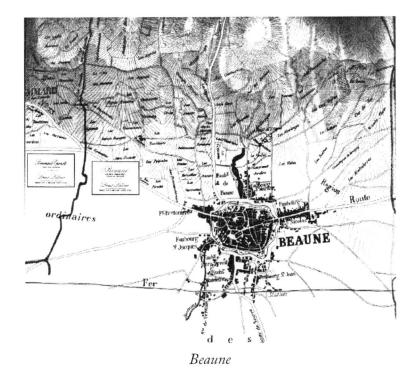

Beaune

"Arriving in the ancient town of Beaune on March 8, I lodged at Chez Dion à l'Écu de France and promptly hired Etienne Parent, a cooper and wine merchant, as a guide to the vineyards of Pommard, Volnay, Montrachet and Meursault. As I mentioned earlier, Parent and I became friends, and he became my Burgundian wine counselor. [576] Parent took me to the vineyard of Monsieur de la Tour, and it was here that I was introduced to the most expensive dry white wine of France—Montrachet, which Parent called the best white wine of Burgundy. My tasting confirmed Parent's opinion, and I ordered 125 bottles of 1782 Montrachet. Montrachet belonged to only two proprietors, Monsieur Clermont, who leased his portion to some wine merchants, and the Marquis Sarsnet from Dijon, whose part was farmed by Monsieur de la Tour. It sold for the same price as Chambertin and the four first growths of Bordeaux, three livres per bottle." [577]

"If I may interrupt, Mr. Jefferson, those are distinctions that Le Montrachet still retains—the best and the most expensive dry white wine in the world."

"As I said earlier," Franklin said, "some things never change."

"Although Montrachet has retained its charismatic taste over the past two hundred years," I said, "there is a difference in its size and production. Your

189

notes, Mr. Jefferson, record that the vineyard produced 30,000 bottles annually from about fifty acres. Today there are only 19.76 acres of Le Montrachet producing a scant 15,000 bottles yearly and owned by at least seventeen different persons or organizations." [578]

"Why would that be?" Franklin asked. "Since it's one of the most expensive wines in the world, why wouldn't the owners increase the size, not decrease it."

"The only explanation I can think of," I said, "is that Mr. Jefferson's guide did not distinguish between the three vineyards entitled at that time to use the suffix 'Montrachet' in their names, that is, Montrachet, now known as Le Montrachet, Chevalier-Montrachet (18.1 acres) and Batard-Montrachet (29.3 acres). [579] Two other vineyards have since been allowed to use the suffix Montrachet: Bienvenues-Bâtard-Montrachet (9.11 acres) and Criots-Bâtard-Montrachet (3.87 acres). [580]

"I'm sure you know, Mr. Jefferson, that other remarkably fine dry white wines are made in the vineyards surrounding the towns of Chassagne-Montrachet and Puligny-Montrachet. Of special note are the sixteen *Premiers Crus* vineyards of Chassagne-Montrachet and the fourteen *Premiers Crus* vineyards of Puligny-Montrachet that produce wines of elegance and finesse that are often equal in bouquet and taste to their *Grands Crus* neighbors. In fact, white Burgundies that carry the names Chassagne-Montrachet and Puligny-Montrachet, without a vineyard designation, are usually wines of breed and quality."

"That doesn't surprise me," Jefferson said. "After our visit to the de la Tour Montrachet vineyard, Parent took me to the quaint hamlet of Meursault completely surrounded by stone walls. The best wine of Meursault, I thought, came from the vineyard of Goutte d'Or (drop of gold), owned by the Bachet family. As you know, it became my favorite dry white Burgundy during my remaining two and a half years in France." Jefferson took a sip of wine.

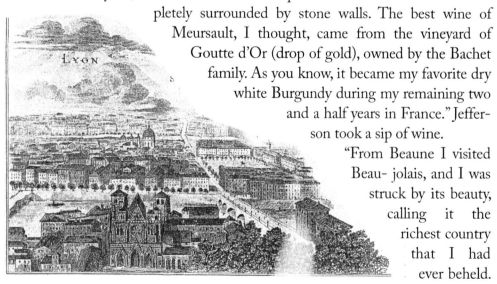

"From Beaune I visited Beau- jolais, and I was struck by its beauty, calling it the richest country that I had ever beheld.

Here I stayed four days with Monsieur and Madame de Laye-Epinaye at their Château de Laye, an estate of about 15,000 acres in vines, corn, pastures, and woods—'a rich and beautiful scene.'

"From Beaujolais I traveled to Lyon, where I wrote to Parent ordering 125 bottles of 1782 Montrachet and a price list for the best wines and vintages of Burgundy. With the hope of making my own wine, I asked Parent to send me a dozen vines from the vineyards of Montrachet, Vougeot, and Chambertin.

"Leaving Lyon, I headed down the Rhône with visits to the vineyards of Côte-Rôtie, and Hermitage. The wines of Côte-Rôtie (roasted slopes) date back at least to Roman times. Although the vineyards had ancient origins, their popularity developed a little later than those of Burgundy, Bordeaux, and Hermitage. At the time of my visit, Côte-Rôties were prized for their color, strength, bouquet, taste, and ability to age, but they were not yet of such high 'estimation as to be produced commonly at the good tables of Paris.'[581]

"I thought 'nature never formed a country of more savage aspect than that on both sides of the Rhône. A huge torrent, rushing like an arrow between high precipices often of massive rock, at other times of loose stone with but little earth. On the whole, it assumed a romantic, picturesque and pleasing air.'[582] I stopped at Tains, located between the river and its 'justly celebrated' terraced vineyards. I lodged at the post house and suffered a miserable night, because the master of the place was an 'unconscionable rascal.' But I was captivated by the wines, especially the white wine. I noted, 'The wine called Hermitage is made on the hills impending over the village of Tains; on one of which is the hermitage which gives its name to the hills for about two miles, and to the wine made on them. There are but three of those hills that produce wine of the first quality, and of these the middle regions only.'[583] I climbed to the top of the hill for the 'sake of the sublime' view from there. I enjoyed the red wines, but the white Hermitage from the House of Jourdan, I thought 'the first wine in the world without a single exception.'"[584]

"What did it taste like?" Franklin asked.

"It was not entirely dry. It was what I call silky, and when I use the term silky 'I do not mean sweet, but sweetish in the smallest degree only.'[585]

"From Tains south to Montélimar, the mountains of the Dauphine and Languedoc were covered with snow, and the plains planted in corn, clover, almonds, mulberries, and walnuts. In this part of the Rhône Valley, the people lived mostly in villages and their houses were made of mud or round stone and mud. Laborers made between sixteen to eighteen sous per day and were required to feed themselves. Women were paid only half that and often for the same work."

"In American money, how much did one sou equal?" I asked.

"One sou was slightly less than one cent American." [586]

Jefferson apparently read the astonishment on my face, because he added, "Yes, eighteen cents a day was poverty wages, and it helped bring on a revolution. A family rarely ate meat. A single hog salted was the year's stock for a family. [587]

"Although the woods abounded with wild game, the peasant population was not allowed to kill the game for their daily meat because of a law known as *Capitaineries*—the authority granted by the king to the nobility that gave a particular nobleman all rights to game within a certain locality, even on lands not belonging to him. Ordinary people had no rights to kill game for their meals on pain of going to prison and, for second offenders, often death." [588]

There was a pause in the conversation as we sipped our wines, and I thought for a moment about how birth dictates the destinies of most humans.

Jefferson continued. "Arriving at Orange on March 18, I saw at the entrance to the city a sublime triumphal arch erected in about 25 A.D. during the period of Marcus Aurelius. I lodged at the Royal Palace Hotel and went to the Roman Theater that dates from the second century A.D. I was outraged to find that at that moment people were pulling down the circular wall of these superb remains to pave a road." [589]

"On a recent visit to Orange," I said, "I attended a concert at the Roman theater, and I can assure you, Mr. Jefferson, that the desecration stopped, because the theater still stands in most of its glory. It is used today as a national theater for varied activities such as local school plays to professional performances."[590]

"I am delighted to hear that, Jack," Jefferson said. "The next day I left for Nîmes, and along the way I detoured to Remoulins to see the Pont du Gard, the magnificent Roman aqueduct built towards the end of the first century B.C. to carry fresh water from the town of Uzés to Nîmes. It was well preserved, and I thought it a sublime antiquity."

"I too have visited the Pont du Gard," I said, "and it remains in superb condition. Its huge blocks of uncemented stone look as if laid yesterday. An interesting time to visit it is early in the morning between six and seven. The sunrise casts a pink glow across the bridge, and its reflection shimmers in the river."

"I am pleased to hear that it still stands. After studying it, I went on to Nîmes, first settled as a Roman colony about 50 B.C. You will find there more monuments of Roman antiquity than any other city in France, which attests to its importance within the Roman Empire. I wasted no time investigating these treasures. I visited the Maison Carrée, one of the great Roman temples built in the time of Augustus. It is an oblong building with a portico and fluted Corinthian pillars that was part of the forum complex of ancient Nîmes. Admired through the ages, its architectural proportions and symmetry were later used by me in designing the state capitol in Richmond, Virginia."

"Some years later," I added, "during Napoleon's reign, the Maison Carrée was the model for the Church de la Madeleine in Paris."

Pont du Gard

"I'm glad to learn that Napoleon did something constructive. 591 Next, I went to see the Roman amphitheater built in the early first century A.D. Arles has a similar arena built about the same time. I visited both, and thought the arena in Nîmes the best preserved, calling it a superb remains. It was in amphitheatres like these throughout the Roman Empire that crowds delighted in seeing all types of

193

Maison Carrée de Nîmes

spectacles including gladiators fighting gladiators, gladiators fighting lions, domesticated panthers pulling chariots, bulls battling rhinoceroses, and chariot races. I also visited the Jardin de la Fontaine and the Temple of Diana and the Roman baths. The fountain flows from beneath the rocks of Mt. Cavalier into a series of basins constructed in about 1740 together with a series of walks and canals. The Temple of Diana survives only as ruins, and is to the left of the fountain gardens and in front of the Roman baths. Above the fountain gardens at the top of Mt. Cavalier is the Tour Magne. The original function of the Tour Magne is not known but it may have served as a watchtower."

"Two years ago, Mr. Jefferson, I spent three weeks following your travels through southern France, and I can tell you that from the fountain gardens the Tour Magne is now reached by walking up a series of paths that twist through a beautifully landscaped park. The visitor today can reach the top of Tour Magne by climbing its 140 steps and will be rewarded with a spectacular view of the Rhône Valley. I recall that from Nîmes you went on to Arles," I said.

"Yes, another Roman colony founded in 46 B.C. At one time, Arles competed as an important port with Marseilles. It is here that the Rhône River divides into two branches before emptying into the Mediterranean to the south. I stayed at a detestable tavern located on one of Arles's narrow, winding, cobblestoned streets. I visited three Roman antiquities, the Alyscamps, the GrecoRoman theater remains, and the amphitheater that I previously mentioned. In the suburbs of Arles, at the Church of Saint Honorat, I viewed hundreds of ancient stone coffins along the roadside. The ground is called *les champs élysées*. These are the Alyscamps or

Elysian Fields, the renowned Roman and early Christian burial grounds of Arles. In the Middle Ages, Alyscamps was considered sacred, and it became a pilgrimage shrine of the dead. At the request of the dying, friends would place their bodies, after death, in caskets and float them down the Rhône River to Arles. The bodies were then buried in the Elysian Fields in elaborately sculpted limestone coffins and tombs. When I visited Alyscamps, most of the elaborate sarcophagi had been removed, sold, or destroyed." [592]

"When I was there," I said, "all of the decorative sarcophagi were missing."

"What a shame. Did you see the Greco-Roman theater remains? In my time they consisted of 'two Corinthian columns, and the pediment with which they were crowned, very rich, having belonged to the ancient capitol of the place.' This theater seated 16,000, and the amphitheatre seated over 20,000. [593]

"The country from Arles to Aix-en-Provence waved in vines. As I vibrated along in my carriage, I amused himself with thoughts far removed from wine, architecture, sculpture, paintings, agriculture, politics, or Newton's laws of planetary motion. Instead, I focused on 'physical researches' such as why postillions wore such enormous boots encased like an Egyptian mummy, and concluded that it was 'because a Frenchman's heels are so light that, without this ballast, he would turn keel up.' [594] Before reaching Aix-en-Provence, I stayed the night in St-Rémy and lodged at the Cheval Blanc, where I found the tavern keeper an intelligent man."

Greco-Roman Theatre

"Mr. Jefferson, it might interest you to know that the Cheval Blanc continues as a hotel, and the room where you stayed the evening of March 25 still exists. It is located on the first floor, just to the left of the hotel's entrance. It appears remarkably well preserved with a ribbed vault ceiling, a large fireplace, and windows that look out to the town's church and its fourteenth century Gothic belfry."

"How do you know that, Jack?"

"It is not based on historical documents but on the spontaneous utterances of an elderly woman who was serving as the hotel concierge an early morning in May 2002, when I visited there. Although she spoke only French, I was able to convey to her my interest in the age of the hotel. She told me that the section of the hotel where we were standing was eighteenth century. She beckoned me to follow her into a room located just to the left of the entrance to the old section of the hotel. After I had looked around, she said in French: 'Your president slept here.' As she struggled to recall the name, I suggested 'Thomas Jefferson.' Excitedly, she said 'Yes, that is the name.' She told me that no hotel records remained of your visit, so obviously her knowledge of your stay was based on word-of-mouth, handed-down for more than two hundred years."[595]

Jefferson looked at Franklin, and said, "The French built buildings to last. The next morning I visited 'some fine ruins' about a half a mile south of the town, a mausoleum and the oldest triumphal arch outside of Italy. It is believed the arch was erected on orders from Julius Caesar to commemorate the Roman capture of the port of Marseilles. The date and purpose of the mausoleum, called the Tomb of the Julis, are less clear. I owned a 1777 print of these antiquities."[596]

"What you could not have seen, Mr. Jefferson, because it was not excavated until 1921, is the remains of the Roman town of Glanum. Just a stones throw from the two Roman monuments, these remains reveal outlines of a forum, baths, temples, and the only Greek dwelling unearthed in France.[597] When you were inspecting those two Roman antiquities, you may have noticed nearby the SaintPaul-de-Mausole Asylum, a converted twelfth century Augustinian monastery, which still operates as a mental hospital. The Saint-Paul-de-Mausole Asylum is where Vincent Van Gogh, a famous nineteenth century French artist, confined himself for a year, from May 1889 to May 1890, after the self-amputation of his right ear. It was in this setting that Van Gogh created many of his most vivid and powerful paintings. A visit to these Roman ruins today can be combined with a walking tour of seven metal placards holding color reproductions of landscapes that Van Gogh painted while confined to the asylum."

"Very interesting," Franklin said. After a pause his eyes and mine traveled back to Jefferson, who continued his account.

"From St-Rémy my journey took me to Aix-en-Provence. As I approached Aix, the valley rich and beautiful spread out towards the mouth of the Rhône and the Mediterranean. I arrived in Aix-en-Provence on March 26 and stayed four days at the Hotel St-Jacques. Aix-en-Provence was the raison d'être for my trip. In a letter to my daughter Martha I repeated what I had told several friends before leaving Paris, 'My journey hitherto has been a very pleasing one. It was undertaken with the hope that the mineral waters of this place might restore strength to my wrist.'"

"What happened to your wrist?" Franklin asked.

"How the right hand became disabled would be long story for the left to tell. It was by one of those follies from which good cannot come but ill may."

Directing my comment to Dr. Franklin, I said, "That is the same enigmatic answer Mr. Jefferson gave when John Adams inquired how he injured his wrist, which, of course, sheds no light on how it happened."

"Do you know how he injured his wrist, Jack?" Franklin asked.

"The romanticized version, Dr. Franklin, is that he fell while attempting to jump over a fence in the cour-la-Reine while walking with Maria Cosway. Mr. Jefferson's daughter Martha said it occurred while on a 'ramble' with a male friend, and Philip Mazzei said it happened when he fell from a horse." [598]

Jefferson smiled and continued his discourse. "Of course there were other considerations for the trip, such as 'instruction, amusement and abstraction from business, of which I had had too much at Paris.' [599] The mineral waters of Aix had been famous since Roman times for their healing powers. Over the centuries the baths were destroyed and the source of the water lost until accidentally rediscovered in 1704. The baths were reported to help the gout, the gravel, scurvy, dropsy, palsy, indigestion, asthma, and consumption." [600]

"Thomas, this is a trip we should have taken before I left France in July, 1785," Franklin said enthusiastically. "You will recall that I was suffering severely from gout and kidney stones. I was so incapacitated that I had to leave Paris on a stretcher. Your trip sounds fascinating in its own right, but given a chance to cure my gout and the stones, I would have accompanied you."

"I'm not at all sure, Benjamin, you would have derived any benefit from the baths. I took '40 douches, without any sensible benefit, and I thought it useless to continue them.' [601] But the Provence sun did for my spirits what the waters did not do for my wrist. I was in the land of corn, wine, oil, and sunshine.

'What more can man ask of heaven?' As I told William Short, 'If I should happen to die at Paris, I will beg of you to send me here, and have me exposed to the sun. I am sure it will bring me to life again.'

"Aix's streets, straight and from 20 to 100 feet wide, were as clean as a parlor floor. Rows of elms, 100 to 150 years old, made for delicious walks along the cours Mirabeau, the main street, lined with seventeenth and eighteenth century mansions. These handsome elms provided shade to the rich in their carriage rides and walks." [602]

"I'm sorry to report, Mr. Jefferson, but those beautiful trees died of elm blight, and were replaced by plane trees." [603]

"That's a shame," Jefferson said, shaking his head. "My second evening in Aix was spent at the Municipal Theater located about a hundred yards east of the cours. Troubadours, musicians and actors traveling north from Italy, Spain, Portugal, and Af rica, and traveling south from England, Scandinavia, Paris, and Lyons, routinely performed operas, ballets, tragedies, and comedies at the theater. 'I was treated with Alexis and Justine, and Mazet, in which the most celebrated actress from Marseilles came to bear a part for the advantage of her friend whose benefit night it was. She was in the style of Mne. Dugazon and had ear, voice, taste, and action. She was moreover young and handsome and had an advantage over Mne. Dugazon and some other of the celebrated ones of Paris, in being clear of that dreadful wheeze or rather whistle in respiration which resembles the agonizing struggles for breath in a dying person.' [604] I enjoyed Aix. It was a neat town with bread 'the equal to any in the world,' and the best olive oil.

"On March 29, I set out for Marseilles, a distance of about twenty miles. The country was hilly and intersected by chains of mountains of rock with vines, corn, mulberries, almonds, and willows growing among rows of olive and fig trees. The vineyards around Marseilles produced wines of good color, body, spirit and flavor. My journey to this point had been a continual feast of new objects and ideas. In order to make the most of the time available, 'I avoided good dinners and good company and courted the society of gardeners, vignerons, coopers, farmers, etc., and devoted almost every moment of every day to the business of enquiry.'

"I saw Marseilles as an amphitheater surrounded by mountains of rock and, within that amphitheater, a mixture of naturally rich valleys and plains that stretched to the mountain bases six to nine miles distant. I thought it a charming place, all life and activity, like London and Philadelphia, with an extensive society and an animated commerce. [605] I spent a week there staying at the Hôtel de la Princesse from March 30 to April 6.

"My stay in Marseilles was busy with excursions to the Château Borely and a boat ride to the Island Château d'If, and an evening at the theater. As usual, I took to the high ground and visited the château Notre Dame de la Gard on a hill

Marseilles

with a magnificent view of the city and the Mediterranean that included vine-clad hills, gardens, country houses, and clusters of islands, including the isle d'If, the place of Mirabeau's imprisonment.

"I looked up Mazzei's friend Soria and found him not only alive but also one of the most successful merchants in Marseilles. Soria's wealth, however, had been somewhat diminished a few days before my arrival as a result of his son having eloped with jewels and money to the value of 40,000 livres. [606]

"Through a letter of introduction from the Marquis de Chastellux, I made the acquaintance of Henri Bergasse, one of France's great wine merchants. Bergasse had Stephen Cathalan, our consul in Marseilles, and me to dinner, introduced me to friends, provided me with information, and took me to his wine cellars, where I saw in casks the equivalent of more than 1,500,000 bottles of wine. The temperature of Bergasse's wine cellar was a constant fifty-four degrees. I also learned that the best method of packing wine when bottled was to lay the bottles on their sides and cover them with sand. [607]

"As I traveled, I was always looking for products to transplant to America. In Marseilles I found several interesting articles of culture: 'the best figs, the best grape for drying, a smaller one for the same purpose without a seed, olives, capers, pistachio nuts, almonds. And I thought that all these articles may succeed on, or southward of the Chesapeake.' [608] From Marseilles, it was my intention to continue west through southern France, but I decided instead to detour over the Alps into northern Italy."

"Why?" I asked.

"Marseilles was a great emporium for Italian rice, and it was here that I hoped to find out whether it was the use of a different machine for cleaning rice that brought European rice to market less broken than ours. But despite inquiries, no one could explain to me the nature of the machine. Consequently, I decided to detour into the Piedmont area of Italy to find out if the Italians had a better rice machine."

"Did they have a better machine?" I asked.

"No! The machine was absolutely the same as ours, and I later learned that their rice was considered inferior in quality. [609]

"Leaving Marseilles, I headed east toward Italy leaving on April 7. My route took me northeast to Aubagne and Cuges through countryside laid up in terraces of vines, olives, and corn. From Cuges to Toulon, the mountains became higher, and as my carriage descended through narrow mountain passes, I could see the Mediterranean in the distance. Near Toulon, the mountains narrowed as I entered the high-walled north gorge of the village of Ollioules, an enclave that had become the haunt of outlaws. [610]

"From Toulon, I set out for Nice and my trip across the Alps into Italy. Approaching the village of Hyères, which has a population of about 5,000, I entered a plain three miles in diameter bound by the sea to my right and mountains on my left. Hyères's streets were about eight feet wide and twisted and turned up a steep hillside. Since the streets were so narrow, carriages could not enter the town, and the wealthier inhabitants were carried about in chaises. Here I visited a botanical garden established by King Louis XVI. [611]

"From Hyères, the road led through valleys and across mountain ranges with stretches of natural beauty, fishing hamlets, and medieval hillside villages. After spending the night of April 9 at Fréjus, I continued my journey through the Esterel Mountains to the Mediterranean seatown of Napoule." [612]

"Hidden among the beauty of these mountains were dangers of which you seemed unaware," I said.

"What dangers?"

"I have read that if there was a spot in France more dangerous for the traveler than the Ollioules mountain pass, it was the rugged Esterels, where highwaymen, many of whom had escaped from the prison in Toulon, had taken sanctuary in its gorges and ravines. But, since it was the only land route to Italy, it had to be crossed. A famous Swiss geologist, physicist, and botanist, HoraceBenedict de Saussure, explored the Esterels on foot the same year as your trip, Mr. Jefferson, and his captivation with its natural beauty was tempered by uneasiness for his safety. He reported 'The main road is entirely exposed, and is dominated by salient rocks, on which the brigands plant their sentinels. They suffer travelers to advance to some open space between these points of vantage. Then, from their ambushes in the woods, they swoop down on them and plunder them, whilst the sentinels keep a good lookout, lest the guards should come and surprise them. In the event of any of these appearing, a whistle suffices to warn the robbers, and they dive out of sight into the forest. It is impossible to reach them. Not only is the undergrowth very dense, but it is encumbered with huge blocks of stone. There are neither by-roads nor paths; and unless one knows the intricacies of the woods as well as do the brigands themselves, no one can penetrate into them except very slowly. The forest extends to the sea, and the whole district, entirely uncultivated, is a place of refuge for the convicts who have escaped from the galleys of Toulon, the nursery of all the robbers of the country.' " [613]

Franklin looked at Jefferson who shrugged, smiled, and continued. "In the middle of the mountain, I dined and changed horses at the post house. As my carriage descended the mountain, I could see glimpses of the Mediterranean between the mountain divisions. From Napoule, I traveled to Antibes along a road that passed near the Mediterranean and over hills and strings of valleys surrounded by the snow-capped mountains of the Alps.

"Reaching Nice on April 10, I found it a flourishing city with new houses and new streets being built in a section of the city called the New Borough. I lodged at the Hotel York. [614] The English so heavily populated Nice that I referred to it as an English colony. I found it a handsome city with good accommodations, a gay and dissipated society, and a superb climate. It had a magnificent sea view that was appreciated from a terrace that opened onto the sea and was formed from the roofs of a row of low houses on one side of the street, about a quarter of a mile long, covered with a stucco floor. [615]

"Through my Parisian friend, Abbé Arnoux, I was introduced to a local wine merchant, André Sasserno. At Sasserno's house, I sampled the wines of Bellet, white, red and rosé, which came from vineyards a few miles northeast of Nice. I thought the wines good though not of the first quality, but later changed my opinion and called them remarkably good, excellent and delicious."

"Were the wines from Sasserno's vineyards white or red?" I said.

"It was Sasserno's red wine that I esteemed. [616]

"From Nice, I counseled Lafayette to take a similar trip, and that to do it most effectively, he must be absolutely incognito. He must ferret the people out of their hovels as I had done, look into their kettles, eat their bread, loll on their beds under pretense of resting, but, in fact, to find if they are soft. I told him he would feel a sublime pleasure in the course of this investigation, and a sublimer one hereafter when he would be able to apply his knowledge to the softening of their beds, or the throwing of a morsel of meat into the kettle of vegetables. In this regard, I observed that laborers breakfasted on a piece of bread with an anchovy or an onion, and for dinner, bread, soup and vegetables. Their supper the same. But, overall, I was pleased to find among the peasants less physical misery than I had expected to find. They were generally well clothed with plenty of food, not animal indeed, but vegetables, which is as wholesome. [617]

"Because no highway existed along the Mediterranean coast from Nice to Genoa, my trip into Italy from Nice required me to cross the Maritime Alps, a distance of 93 miles, before reaching the town of Coni. The road was probably the greatest work of this kind ever executed in either ancient or modern times, and it did not cost as much as one year's war. The road was a series of twists and turns up and down the mountains, and in good weather wide enough for carriages to pass, but a problem developed when winter snows made the road impassable. Because the snows prevented carriages from passing, I put my carriage in storage, rented mules, and on April 13, my forty-forth birthday, started across the Alps on the back of a mule. [618]

"That night I stayed at the village of Tende, surrounded by precipitous walls of rock, in an inn, all black, dirty, stinking, and no glass windows. [619]

"Early the next morning I set out to cross the col de Tende, the mountain range that separates the Maritime from the Ligurian Alps. This was the most dangerous part of the trip. Col de Tende was the highest mountain I had to cross. It was still covered with ice and snow, with high winds or storms within the mountain passes often creating avalanches. Since the wind was 'most quiet' in the early morning hours, I left Tende at dark in order to cross col de Tende as soon after the break of day as possible. [620] Halfway up were quarters for a detachment of soldiers posted to prevent smuggling and an inn called La Ca (The House). It was here that I hired several men to assist me and my valet in ascending and descending the mountain. These men, called 'coulants,' used a hoe-like device to break the ice and made steps for the mules. Near the top, I had to get off my mule and climb on foot because, although the mountain mules were sure-footed and frost-shod, the ice was so hard and slippery that the mules often stumbled and fell. Although the climb to the top was arduous and dangerous, the way down was the envy of anyone who has ever enjoyed a sleigh ride. I descended the mountain in a wooden sleigh called a Lèze. One of the coulants sat in the front of the sleigh, I was in the middle, and another coulant stood in the rear. The front coulant used his feet to regulate the speed of the sleigh's descent, which was so rapid that the village of Limone was reached in about an hour. [621] Limone, at the base of col de Tende, was headquarters for the muleteers. Here I abandoned my mules, and rented post-horses and a carriage for the rest of the trip in Italy until I reached Genoa.

"I traveled to Turin through the towns of Coni, Centale, Savigliano and Racconigi and along the way I saw vines planted in a manner I had not seen before. On reaching the Po River, I crossed on what was called a swinging batteaux, two boats placed side by side with a common platform onto which the horses and carriage were driven.

"Arriving in Turin on April 17, I stayed two days at the Hotel d'Angleterre, the best hotel. It was here that I first tasted a wine called Nebiule. 'It was a singular wine, melding three contradictory characteristics. It was about as sweet as the silky Madeira, as astringent on the palate as Bordeaux, and as brisk as Champagne. It was a pleasing wine.'" [622]

"The Nebiule wine you drank, Mr. Jefferson, was the precursor of today's Nebbiolo grape, which makes some of northern Italy's best wines. But your comments as to the taste are out of character with the big, full-bodied, dry, tannic Barolos and Barbarescos that are made today in Piedmont from the Nebbiolo grape. Wines made today from the Nebbiolo grape are not sweet nor do they effer vesce, because the style of making these red wines has changed radically. Throughout the eighteenth century, and well into the nineteenth century, fermentation was never allowed to finish, leaving the wines sweet and often unstable. Cyrus Redding talks of these red wines being 'fermented but a short period and the best being vin de liqueur or sweet.' It was not until the 1840s that the big, dry wines we know today as Barolos and Barbarescos emerged. The incomplete fermentation also left them *frizzante*, which probably explains your 'brisk as Champagne' comment." [623]

"That's very interesting," Jefferson said. "In Turin I did more than enjoy the wine. I also did some sightseeing, took an excursion to the Village of Moncaglieri and visited the fifteenth century royal castle. The castle, on a hill above the village, had a view of the Po and the plains, which spread to a ridge of mountains that formed the dutchy of Montferrat.

"The next day I rented horses and traveled to Superga, the burial place of the Sardinian kings, situated on a hill east of Turin. From the dome of the Basilica of Superga, I looked out on the Alps and Apennines, the valley of the Po, and the vine-clad hills of Montferrat. Next, I traveled to Stupinigi and saw the royal hunting lodge. It was in Turin that I learned that the exportation of rice in the husk from Piedmont was prohibited and punishable by death. I had come a long way to determine the superiority of Piedmont rice, and I was not to be deterred by a death threat. I filled my coat pockets with rice and possibly risked the life of a muleteer by the name of Poggio to smuggle a bagful to Genoa. I succeeded in getting the rice out of Italy and sent it to the South Carolina Society for Promoting Agriculture. Responding on behalf of the society, Ralph Izard found the rice inferior to the South Carolina variety and, fearing that the commingling of the rice could lead to an undesirable hybrid, asked me to send no more. [624]

"From Turin to Vercelli the plains were cultivated in corn, pasture, vines, mulberries, walnuts, and some willows and poplars. The people were poorly clothed compared to the people of France, and the women worked at heavy laboring jobs. Stopping overnight in Vercelli, I lodged at the Hotel of the Three Kings. It was here that I drank 'a wine called Gatina made in the neighborhood of Vercelli, both red and white.' I thought the white Gatina resembled a Carcavelos, a sweet wine from Portugal. I also drank an 'esteemed' light red wine from Salussola." [625]

"I suspect, Mr. Jefferson, the red Gatina wine you drank is known today as Gattinara and made from the Nebbiolo grape."

Jefferson nodded knowingly. "From Vercelli to Novaro, the fields were in rice and mostly under water. Milan was so surrounded with vines, corn, pasture, and gardens that I could hardly see it until I was in its streets. I spent one day, from sunrise to sunset, in the town of Rozzano at a dairy, learning the intricacies of Parmesan cheese and examining the local ice houses and the methods of storing snow. I journeyed north to Lake Como, went to a casino, examined another rice-beating machine, visited Villa Simonetta, famous for its echo, and enjoyed an evening at the theater. [627]

"On the twenty-fourth, I headed south to Genoa, staying in Pavia at the Croce Bianco Inn. I visited the University of Pavia and saw a botanical garden laid out in the Linnaean system. [628]

"Genoa rose above the Mediterranean and was laid out in a semicircle. During my three days in Genoa, I stayed at Le Cerf, an inn more in the French style, with its back windows looking onto the Mediterranean. I made garden tours to some of the country seats of the Genoese nobility at Sestri, Pegli, and Nervi. Prince Lomellino's gardens at Sestri were the finest I had seen outside of England. [629]

"From Genoa, I decided to return to Nice by boat because there were no roads, just paths suitable only for mules and walking that led through the mountains and along the coast. I arranged passage on a felucca, an open boat propelled by one sail and a crew of twelve sailors: a master, ten rowers, and a boy who called commands. It was a well-built vessel with a wood railing around it over which could be thrown canvas to protect the passengers from rain or the sun. However, because of contrary winds and my own 'mortal sea-sickness,' I abandoned the sea voyage after two days and set in at the fishing village of Noli. [630]

"Noli had narrow streets, medieval towers, the ruins of a castle, and, hanging over the sea, precipices covered with aloes, vineyards, and olive groves—everything except a decent inn. I spent the night in a 'miserable tavern' and dined on sardines, fresh anchovies, ortolans, and strawberries, accompanied by an 'indifferent' white wine. [631]

Felucca

"The next morning I hired a guide and three mules and for the next two days clambered across the precipices of the Apennines. Once across, the change of scener y was as abrupt as it was exhilarating. To the horizon extended the blue Mediterranean, white sand beaches, orange and lemon groves, and the silver green of olive trees gilded by the sun. Descending to the coast, [632] I walked along the shore from Louano to Albenga, spending another unpleasant night in 'the most detestable *gite*, called a tavern that I ever saw in any part of the earth, and the dearest too.' [633] But despite physical discomforts, I was taken by Albenga's natural beauty: a rich plain opening from between two ridges of mountains triangularly to the sea and abounding in olives, figs, mulberries, and wine. [634] I stopped at the seaside towns of Oneglia and Port Maurice, a mile apart, considerable places, and in a rich country surrounded by vines and olive groves. [635]

"I spent the night in San Remo. The old section of town, with its narrow streets, flights of steps, archways, and crowded houses, occupied a steep hill that sat between two valleys, planted with orange and lemon groves. My room at the Auberge de la Postea looked into a handsome garden with palm trees under the windows. I also had available a very good *vin ordinaire* that was made in the environs. [636]

"The following morning I continued along the coastline to Nice. From Menton to Monaco, I was surrounded by groves of oranges and lemons, and I mused along the way that a superb road might be made along the margin of the sea from Laspeze to Nice, by which travelers could enter Italy without crossing the Alps." [637]

"Your idea of a coastal highway took almost a century to come about. The first road that followed the coast line and opened travel between Italy and France was built by Napoleon along the mountaintops from Nice to Menton," I said. "Begun in 1805 and completed seven years later, it became known as the Grande Corniche."

"How much easier such a road would have made my journey. As it was I was exhausted, but stayed only one night in Nice before retrieving my carriage, renting post horses and heading back through southern France by way of Antibes, Napoules, through the Esterel Mountains, and along the lower slopes of the Maures Mountains. Arriving in Aix on May 4, I returned to the Hotel StJacques and the next morning set out for Marseilles for three days of rest and recuperation. Rested and ready for the final leg of my trip, I left Marseilles for

Avignon

206

Avignon, stopping the night in the town of Argon on the Durance River. [638]

"Shortly after arriving in Avignon, I 'rented horses and made an excursion to the Fountain of Vaucluse, about twenty miles east of Avignon. I arrived at the fountain somewhat fatigued, and sat down by the fountain to repose myself. It gushes, of the size of a river, from a secluded valley of the mountain. To add to the enchantment of the scene, every tree and bush was filled with nightingales in full song.' [639] While at Avignon I came across a white wine I thought the equal of Montrachet and Sauternes, vin blanc de Rochegude, and I ordered a quantity for my Paris residence."

"As I recall, Mr. Jefferson, two years later you shared your discovery with President Washington and John Jay, describing it as one of the best white wines of France," I said.

"That's right. I thought it resembled a dry Lisbon, or perhaps Madeira."

"Of course, I wasn't around then, but the wine writers who came shortly after you report that Lisbon wines were fortified, having had their fermentation stopped by the addition of brandy, and even the dry Lisbons were sweet to some degree."

"I agree that so-called dry Lisbon wines had some degree of sweetness," Jefferson said. "Is the Rochegude wine still available, Jack?"

"It's my understanding that production ceased after the marquis's death in

Fountain of Vaucluse

207

1825, but I believe that there is a wine from that part of France still produced in the style of vin blanc de Rochegude," I said. "With only one exception, the wines produced today in these same vineyard areas are made from red grapes. The exception is a sweet, lightly fortified white wine made from the muscat grape that is grown in the vicinity of the valley town of Beaumes-de-Venise, lying between Rochegude and Avignon. It is unknown when the muscat grape was first planted there, although it is an ancient Greek variety thought to have been introduced to France by the Romans, and it is the only place in the southern Côtes du Rhône where it is planted, strong evidence that the marquis' vin blanc de Rochegude was the ancestor of today's Beaumes-de-Venise, a very nice wine when served as an aperitif or with dessert." [640]

Jefferson took a sip of wine, and at my request continued. "On May 10 I left Avignon and returned to Nîmes, and again visited the Roman amphitheater and Maison Carrée. [641] The next day I headed south to ancient Languedoc. This part of my trip would take me to Lunel, Montpelier, Frontignan, Sète, Agde, and from there along the Canal-du-Midi to Toulouse, where the canal ends. In Lunel, I discovered a fine sweet white muscat wine. A small amount of red muscat was also made, but the best wines were white.

"On the way to Sète I stopped at the small Mediterranean town of Frontignan, where I met a likable vintner by the name of Lambert who was also a physician. At the time of my visit, the white wine of Frontignan had already earned a reputation as a high-quality, sweet dessert wine made from the white muscat grape. That evening at dinner with Lambert, I learned that his vineyards produced ten percent of the finest quality Frontignan wines. [642] I immediately

Vintage in the South of France

ordered 250 bottles of his best. When the wine arrived, I was delighted to find that Lambert had added thirty-three bottles of his red muscat from a little barrel that I had seen in his cellar and expressed a desire of having."

"Is Frontignan similar to the Lunel white wine you liked?" Franklin asked.

"Yes. I compared the sweet fortified white wines of Lunel and Frontignan, and although similar in taste, Lunel I thought was not quite so rich. [643] The best grapes of both wines come from old vines with the sweetness achieved by allowing the grapes to remain on the vines until they have become shriveled, even raisin-like, and then stopping the fermentation after half a day by adding brandy." [644]

"If I may interrupt," I said, "the sweet muscat wines of Frontignan and Lunel were enjoying their greatest popularity at the time of your visit, Mr. Jefferson, and this popularity extended into the early part of the nineteenth century. Their popularity faded in the nineteenth century and by 1872 the vineyards of Frontignan were reduced to about 570 acres and those of Lunel to about 125 acres. This loss of popularity was directly attributable to cheap imitations that were concocted in the Sète laboratories and shipped throughout the world, and which bore little resemblance to the genuine wines of Frontignan and Lunel."

"That's a shame," Jefferson said, "because they were excellent wines. Anyhow, after leaving Lambert, I set off to Sète, the principal seaport for the Canal-duMidi and a city of growing commerce, principally related to wine. From Sète, I took passage on a boat through the Étang de Thau to the town of Agde. From Agde, I continued my trip along the Canal-du-Midi to Toulouse. The normal passage on the Canal-du-Midi from Agde to Toulouse by post boats was four days. I decided, however, to hire a boat, a horse, and a driver, and travel at my leisure. My passage took nine days. I always lodged at the town where I tied up for the night. [645] It was on this trip that I became acquainted with the wines of Roussillon, Rivesaltes and Limoux that I later imported and drank with friends at Monticello and the President's House. [646]

"The next two weeks were a special part of my travels. I recall telling a young friend that there was nothing in France so well worth seeing as the Canal-duMidi and Languedoc, and the wine country of Bordeaux. [647] As I traveled the Canal-du-Midi, I examined everything. I made from twenty to thirty-five miles a day, according to circumstance, always sleeping ashore. Of all the methods of traveling I had ever tried, this was the pleasantest. I walked the greater part of the day along the banks of the canal, level and lined with double rows of trees,

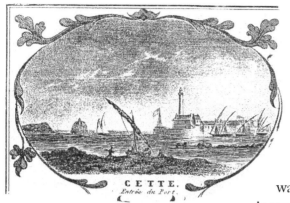

CETTE.
Entrée du Port.

which furnished shade. When fatigued I sat in my carriage on the barge where, as much at ease as if in my study, I read, wrote, or observed. My carriage, being glass on all sides, allowed a full view of all the varying scenes. [648]

"Approaching Carcassonne by way of the canal, I discovered that it was two distinct towns: the ancient fortress and the lower part. My arrival at Carcassonne on May 18 brought me into the lower part, but I could see from my boat the crenellated walled medieval section of Le Cité high on a hill to my left. I stayed the night in Carcassonne and walked the ramparts of the old fortress town that commanded the main road to Spain with magnificent views of Languedoc in every direction. [649]

"Le Cité is a medieval city with two walls at different heights, surmounted by fifty-four towers surrounding the town. The walls enclose centuries of history, beginning with the Romans and followed by a succession of conquerors including the Franks, Visigoths, Moors, viscounts of Bezier and, finally, the kings of France.

"From Carcassonne I went on to Castelnaudary. Here I rented horses and went into the Noire Mountains to visit the source of the canal's water. [650] At Toulouse, the Canal-du-Midi ended. I could have gone on by boat along the Garonne River but decided to travel to Bordeaux using the post roads, a journey of five days.

"At Langon I entered a different world—Bordeaux country. Crossing the Garonne River at Langon by ferry, I passed by the villages of Sauternes, Preignac and Barsac, where the best white wines of Bordeaux are made. In Bordeaux, I resided four days at the Hôtel de Richelieu. I visited Château Haut Brion and walked through its vineyards, describing the soil as sand mixed with round gravel or

Carcassonne

210

small stone and very little loam. Although Haut Brion is located in the Graves region at Pessac, southwest of Bordeaux, and not in the Médoc, I observed that this is the general soil of the Médoc." [651]

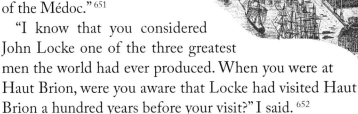

"I know that you considered John Locke one of the three greatest men the world had ever produced. When you were at Haut Brion, were you aware that Locke had visited Haut Brion a hundred years before your visit?" I said. [652]

"No." Jefferson said, shaking his head.

"Two of the world's great political thinkers enjoyed wine and, in this case, the same wine," Franklin said.

Franklin and Jefferson smiled when I added, "In fact, Locke lived in France for several years after his retirement at the age of forty-three, and became so interested in wine that he wrote a book about it, olives, and the production of silk. John Locke's book is titled *Observations upon the Growth and Culture of Vines and Olives, the Production of Silk and Preservation of Fruits.*"

"The same three items that brought Philip Mazzei to America," Jefferson said, and added, "am I boring you with this account?"

"No, no," Franklin said. "I traveled through France, and in Germany I visited Frankfurt, but I didn't have the good judgment to visit the vineyards. By all means, Thomas, continue." I could see from the look on Jefferson's face that Franklin's comment pleased him.

"Well, following my visit to Haut Brion, I sent my brother-in-law, Francis Eppes, six dozen bottles of Haut Brion, describing it as a specimen of what is the best Bordeaux wine, one of the four

Chateau Haut-Brion

established as the very best, and of the vintage of 1784, the only very fine one since the year 1779. [653]

"At the time of my visit, Bordeaux was a big, rich city with about one-third of its export business in wine. The Gironde was crowded with ships and the city had an air of opulence. Many of the foreign wine merchants were of English, Irish, German, or Dutch heritage. Many of these merchants had become wealthy and turned the Quai des Chartrons into one of the most exciting commercial and fashionable residential areas in the world, their mansions bordering the wide curving quays lined with elm trees. I visited the various wine merchant houses, and from Ferger, Gramont and Cie I ordered 252 bottles of Château Margaux: fifteen dozen for myself and six dozen for my brother-in-law, Francis Eppes. [654]

"While there, I saw a comedy at the new Grand Theater designed by Victor Lewis. It was among the finest in France. The front portico consisted of twelve Corinthian columns above a balustrade with twelve statues of the Muses and Graces. Above the huge vestibule was a concert hall with a staircase ascending two flights to a circular auditorium."

"And it is still there, Mr. Jefferson, in all its glory," I said.

"I had been told, and proved to my own satisfaction by drinking the wines, that the four vineyards of first quality were Châteaux Margaux, Latour, Lafite, and Haut Brion. I also included in my travel notes twelve other wines

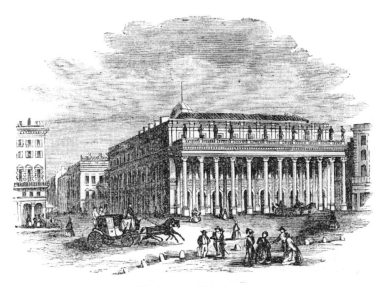

Theatre at Bordeaux

of particular quality behind the four First Growths: 'Rozan, Dabbadie ou Lionville, la Rose, Quirouen, Durfort, followed by a third class of wines consisting of Calons, Mouton, Gassies, Arboete, Pontette, de Terme and Candale. After these they are reckoned common wines.'"

"Although your visit to the Bordeaux wine country was sixty-eight years before the 1855 classification of the vineyards," I said, "your selection of Bordeaux's best Médocs and Sauternes was an extremely accurate projection of their later official rankings. In 1855 the vineyards of the Médoc were classified as First, Second, Third, Fourth and Fifth Growths, and the same four vineyards you designated of first quality were named as the only First Growths. Of the more than 1000 vineyards considered, only one outside the Médoc, Château Haut Brion, was chosen to join the sixty other elite Médoc vineyards given this distinction. The other twelve wines you singled out for merit were all listed in the classification. 'Rozan' or Rauzan is now known as Château Rauzan-Ségla, a Second Growth from Margaux; 'Larose' is Château Gruaud-Larose, a Second Growth from St-Julien; 'Durfort' is Château Durfort-Vivens, a Second Growth from Margaux; 'Calons' is Château Calon-Segur, a Third Growth from Saint Estephe; 'Mouton' is Château Mouton Rothschild, now a First Growth from Pauillac; 'Gassies' is Château Rauzan-Gassies, a Second Growth from Margaux; 'Pontette' is Château Pontet-Canet, a Fifth Growth from Pauillac; 'De Terme' is Château Marquis-de-Terme, a Fourth Growth from Cantenac.[655]

Château Latour

"Henri Martin, the late proprietor of Château Gloria, researched the names mentioned by you and concluded 'Dabbadie ou Léoville in St-Julien-Beychevelle, then belonged only to Monsieur d'Abadie.' Léoville has since been divided into three châteaux: Léoville-Las-Cases, Léoville-Poyferre, and Léoville-Barton, all of which are now Second Growths from St-Julien. 'Quirouen is the phonetic translation of Kirwan, a Third Growth which still exists at Cantenac. Arboete, or Château La Grange, is a Third Growth in St-Julien-Beychevelle, and Candale is Château d'Issan, a Third Growth at Cantenac.' [656] Incidentally, the wines were chosen and ranked not by taste, but by the prices they had brought over many years."

"For you it has been 150 years since the classification you speak of. What changes have been made to the rankings during that time?" Franklin asked.

"So unyielding and sacrosanct is the 1855 classification that only one change to the original list has occurred in the past 150 years," I said. "Mouton, now Mouton Rothschild, was elevated in 1973 from Second Growth to First Growth status by order of the French government."

"It seems to have become so complicated," Jefferson said. "Forget whether it is a First or Fifth Growth, and just enjoy the wine for what it is."

"The pedigree of the wine is only one of the factors that determine a wine's value. As you have noted, Mr. Jefferson, the vintage is important, and, of course, the age of the wine. How long did you keep your Bordeaux wines before drinking them, Mr. Jefferson?"

"It was my opinion that Châteaux Latour, Margaux, and Haut Brion were ready to drink after four years, and Lafite, because it was a lighter wine, after three years. I also thought that 'all red wines declined after a certain age, losing color, flavor and body. Those of Bordeaux began to decline after seven years.' "[657]

"I must say, Mr. Jefferson, your early drinking of quality Bordeaux wines is puzzling since present-day vinification methods are designed to bring more rapid maturation than earlier, primitive systems."

"Are you suggesting that I was drinking the great clarets too soon?"

"With all due respect to your palate, Mr. Jefferson, most wine connoisseurs of my time would say that you were drinking your Bordeaux wines too soon. To drink classified Bordeaux of outstanding vintages in less than seven years would be considered infanticide today, and ten and even more years of bottle age would be preferable. The late Elie de Rothschild (owner and former managing director of Château Lafite-Rothschild) thinks you were, and doubts the propriety of drinking the *Grands Crus* after only three or four years. 'From my experience and tasting and hearsay, I think that on the contrary the 1787 vinification methods were much cruder and the wine much harder. They often left the wine on the grapes for two or three months and that is one of the reasons I have drunk 1811 Lafite that was not dead." [658]

Chateau Lafitte

Jefferson, his eyes fixed on mine, said, "Have women's fashions changed in the past 200 years?"

"Yes, of course," I said.

"Then does it surprise you that our tastes in wine have changed too."

I thought for a moment. "No, I suppose not."

"Then perhaps that's the answer to your query. Anyhow, I enjoyed my stay in Bordeaux immensely, but on May 29, I left Bordeaux by boat from the Quai de Chartron. [659] Sailing up the Gironde, I passed on my left many of Médoc's famous vineyards. On my right, the hilly countryside was planted chiefly in vines. At Lamarque my ferry crossed to the east side of the Gironde and docked at the town of Blaye. My journey now took me north over hilly and barren terrain. Four days later I arrived in Nantes, near the mouth of the Loire. I enjoyed the comforts of Nantes, including its majestic theater, and took side trips to Lorient and Rennes. On June 7, I left Nantes for Paris and followed the Loire River through a countryside dotted with steeples, windmills, châteaux, and hillsides covered with vines, arriving back in Paris on June 10."

"What a fascinating trip," Franklin said, raising his glass in tribute to the story.

"Did you ever revisit Scotland, Dr. Franklin?

"Yes. It took twelve years, but when I did, I combined it with a visit to Ireland. But before leaving on that trip, I returned for a stay with my friend Jonathan Shipley and his family at their Tudor manor in Twyford, near Winchester. [660] It was here that I began my autobiography. I wrote by day, and in the evenings I read portions to the Shipleys. In less than three weeks I finished the first of four installments covering my younger years." [661]

"Dr. Franklin, I think it will please you to know that your autobiography has gone through more than a thousand editions, and been published in virtually every language," I said. "It is the world's most popular autobiography, [662] and it has served as an inspiration for millions of young Americans."

"I, for one, am not surprised at the enduring popularity of my friend's autobiography," Jefferson said. "I remember traveling through a dreadful snow storm before reaching Philadelphia in March 1790. [663] I was on my way from Monticello to New York, to take up my new post as Washington's secretary of state. At Philadelphia I called on Dr. Franklin, and we shared stories of friends in France, with me supplying the latest intelligence as to how they were surviving the revolution there. When I told Benjamin how pleased I was that he had finished so much of his autobiography, because the world would greatly benefit from reading it, he said, 'I cannot say much of that, but I will give you a sample of what I shall leave.'

He instructed his grandson William Bache to hand me the account he had written aboard ship on the way back from London in 1775 regarding the failed negotiations with Lord Howe. I said I would read it and return it. Benjamin insisted I keep it. Not certain of what he meant, I folded it for my pocket, and said again I would certainly return it. 'No,' said he, 'keep it.' I put it in my pocket, and shortly after took leave of him.' " [664]

Franklin smiled. "When I left the Shipleys, I returned to London for a week, and then left with Richard Jackson, Pennsylvania's other agent in England, for a three-month trip to Ireland and Scotland."

Thomas Jefferson. Copy of painting by Rembrandt Peale, circa 1805.

"Who was Richard Jackson?" I asked.

"Richard Jackson was from a wealthy English merchant family. He studied at Cambridge, and after a term at the Lincoln Inn became a barrister in 1744. Early in his career he showed an interest in American affairs. Jackson was appointed co-agent for Pennsylvania in London and shared equal authority with me. He was elected to Parliament in 1763. We became friends and I referred to him as 'my old friend and fellow-traveler.' In Birmingham we had a choice of two routes to Dublin. We decided to cross the Welsh mountains to Holyhead and take the Irish packet to Ireland. [665]

"We remained a day or two at Holyhead before leaving. The Irish packets were small, primitive, and highly dependent on the weather. One traveler complained that 'I never knew men make such poor lame excuses for not sailing as

217

these Holyhead captains do.' Another expressed his delay in more poetic terms:

There are unless my memory fails

Five causes why we should not sail:

The fog is thick; the wind is high;

It rains; or may rain by and by;

Or—any other reason why. [666]

"The discomforts of crossing the Irish Sea from Holyhead to Dublin in the eighteenth century," I said, "are well expressed by a character in Charles Shadwell's Irish play *The Intriguing Squire*: 'All that I know of the vessel was that she stunk confoundedly of pitch and tar. We were a representation of Noah's Ark. The captain himself was a brute beast, and we poor passengers wallowed in the mire we made.'"

"Nevertheless we crossed the Irish Sea and made it to the little port of Dunleary on the east coast, four miles from Dublin, and described by a contemporary as 'a horrible sink of filth inhabited by the dregs of creation.' [667] I distinctly remember that Irish cooking did not agree with my normally strong digestive powers. 'I was, after a plentiful dinner of fish the first day of my arrival, seized with a violent vomiting and looseness. The latter continued, no more moderate, as long as I stayed in this kingdom which was four or five weeks.'" [668]

"What did you and Mr. Jackson do in Dublin the five weeks you were there?"

"We took walks about the city, combed book shops, visited Trinity College on several occasions and socialized with members of the faculty. We attended several receptions at Dublin Castle, and met there the viceroy, George Townsend, and the Lord chancellor, Baron Liffey, and the speaker of the commons, Edmund Sexton Pery, and other notables. [669] In fact, 'we saw and were entertained by both parties, the Courtiers and the Patriots.' The Patriots favored an independent Parliament and were friends of America. A particular member of the Patriot faction whose house we visited was Dennis Daly, a bibliophile, who was almost as well known for his wine cellar as his splendid library. [670] The gathering spot for the Dublin literati while I was there was the bookshop of George Faulker, a fat, little one-legged man who told stories about Jonathan Swift and served his guests with plenty of claret. [671]

"The opening of the Irish Parliament on October 8 was saluted by the ringing of church bells and the booming of the guns of the castle. The procession of the members, led by Lord Townsend in his ceremonial robes and trailed by Jackson and me, marched across the green and entered the great portal of the

Parliament House. Two days later we again attended. Jackson, as a member of the British Parliament, was accorded the right to sit in the chamber, and I supposed that I had go to the gallery, 'when the speaker stood up, acquainted the house that he understood there was in town an American gentleman of distinguished character and merit' who represented American assemblies and proposed that I be extended the same privilege. 'On the question, the whole house gave a loud, unanimous Aye.' I esteemed it a mark of respect for our country. [672]

This act of courtesy, however, was short-lived. Four years later when news of the battle of Lexington reached these same legislators, they went on record expressing 'abhorrence and indignation at the unnatural rebellion.' "

"I thought you said they were friends of America?" I said.

"A few were, but on the whole the Irish Parliament was a British-controlled convocation of professionals and rich landowners representing but a small portion of the disenfranchised seven million people who populated Ireland. The extreme poverty among the lower people was amazing. They lived from hand-to-mouth in wretched hovels of mud and straw, clothed in rags, and subsisted chiefly on potatoes. Our New England farmers of the poorest sort, in regard to the enjoyments of all the comforts of life, were princes when compared to them." [673]

The Irish House of Commons in Franklin's day.

"When you left Ireland where did you go?"

"We traveled northward to Scotland through Drogheda and Belfast to the little port of Donaghadee, with a visit along the way to Lord Hillsborough's estate. [674] We made the crossing to Port Patrick between two storms, and I arrived in Edinburgh twelve years after my original visit. There were changes to the city, but the same stench assailed my nostrils. Fortunately, my old literary circle was much the same. Dr. William Robertson had become the principal of the college, Adam Smith was putting on the finishing touches to his *Wealth of Nations*, and James Boswell, a student at the university when I was first there, was now a popular man around town.

"I was rescued from the 'miserable' inn where I was staying by an invitation to stay for a fortnight with my old friend David Hume at his new house on St. David Street. [675] Hume, prided himself on his culinary talents, and the skills of his cook, Peggy Irvine. He planned on making his new residence not only the intellectual, but the gastronomic center of Edinburgh. Hume and I had many friends and interests in common, and the next two weeks were pleasantly spent in conversation with David and friends at elegant dinners. [676]

"Speaking of wine," I said, "Mr. Hume wrote a famous essay titled 'Of the Standard of Taste,' and I thought it interesting that one of the examples he used to illustrate a point is a passage from Don Quixote about wine."

"Hume often used that passage to prove that the delicacy of judgment was indeed an integral ingredient in applying a standard of taste."

"Do you remember the passage?"

"Yes. Sancho says 'I pretend to have a great judgment about wine. This is a quality hereditary in our family. Two of my kinsmen were called to give their opinion of a hogshead of wine, which was supposed to be excellent, being old and of a good vintage. One of them tastes it; considers it; and, after mature reflection, pronounces the wine to be good, were it not for a small taste of leather, which he perceived in it. The other, after using the same precautions, gives also his verdict in favor of the wine, but with a reserve of a taste of iron, which he could easily distinguish. You cannot imagine how much they were both ridiculed for their judgment. But who laughed in the end? On emptying the hogshead there was found at the bottom an old key with a leather thong tied to it.'"

Franklin took a sip of wine, looked up, and said, "Fresh and delicious with not a trace of either leather or iron." He smiled and continued, "From Edinburgh I traveled to Glasgow, and along the way stopped to visit my friend Lord Kames at his new estate Blair Drummond, inherited by Lady Kames in 1766. The morning after our arrival, Henry Marchant, a young lawyer from Rhode Island, and my traveling companion on this leg of my journey, and I went for a nine or ten-mile hike through the snow with views upon a winding river and the ruined battlements of Doune Castle. We returned with good appetites to an elegant dinner, wine, and conversation. [677]

"We spent five days with the Kames family, and then went on to Glasgow, where we dined with three of Marchant's young American friends. The next three days were spent sightseeing, and in the company of my old friends at the university whose acquaintance I had made on my first visit there twelve years earlier. On the way back to Edinburgh, we stopped overnight at Carron, and the next morning visited the Carron Iron Works, manufacturers of cannons. In Edinburgh I again stayed with David Hume, who gave a large dinner party in my honor that included Lord Kames and a number of old friends from the university. The following day, Hume and I dined with Lord Kames, and the next day, my last in Edinburgh, I dined with Dr. Robert Ferguson." [678]

"I understand that it was on this trip that you got to meet for the first time your son-in-law, Richard Bache."

A big smile broke across Franklin's face. "That's correct, and a very pleasant experience it was. In Edinburgh I received word from my daughter's husband, Richard Bache, saying that, having missed me in London, he had gone to Preston to visit his family. Three days later, I arrived in Preston and was warmly received by the Bache family, headed by Richard's mother, Mary Bache, a stately lady of sixty-eight, who had borne twenty children. She and I stayed up one night to midnight talking." [679]

"I have read that your daughter Sally was fearful of how Richard and you would get along."

"She had nothing to fear. I was immediately impressed by his worth and stability, and charmed by his mother and two sisters, Nancy and Martha." [680]

"How long did you stay in Preston?"

"Two days, but during that time, I got to know Richard and his family and heard all the news about my family in Philadelphia. I became friendly with James Cowburn, the mayor of Preston, and made the acquaintance of an interesting army officer by the name of John Burgoyne."

"Not the same John Burgoyne who surrendered to General Gates at Saratoga, and brought France into the war on our side?" I asked incredulously.

"Yes. He was then a colonel, had campaigned in France and Portugal, and was one of two Preston representatives in the British Parliament." [681]

"Was Preston Burgoyne's birthplace?"

"I don't know, but twenty-five years earlier he had eloped with Charlotte Stanley, the daughter of the Earl of Derby. The Stanley family accepted this dashing dragoon officer who had a flair for writing plays, and groomed him for one of the two Preston seats in Parliament." [682]

"Burgoyne wrote plays?" Jefferson said.

"Yes, and sometimes acted in them. The local tradition had it that he took part in one of his productions, *The Maid of the Oaks*, that was playing at the theatre in Woodcock Court during my visit. [683]

"From Preston, Richard and I returned to London, and Richard stayed with me for a while at Craven Street." [684]

"Although you experienced some hardships, your journey seems to have been pleasant and enjoyable," I said.

"Despite the comfortable accommodations afforded me by my wealthy hosts, the poverty I saw was astonishing and reinforced my belief that we in America had a better way of life. During my tour of Scotland and Ireland, I became acutely aware that 'in those countries a small part of society are landlords, great noblemen, and gentlemen, extremely opulent, living in the highest affluence and magnificence; the bulk of the people are tenants, living in the most sordid wretchedness in dirty hovels of mud and straw and clothed only in rags. I thought often of the happiness of New England, where every man is a freeholder, has a vote in public affairs, lives in a tidy, warm house, has plenty of good food and fuel, with whole clothes from head to foot.' " [685]

"I hope," Jefferson said, "that our discussion did not dull our appreciation of the beef."

"No, No," Franklin exclaimed. "It was as good a piece of beef as I've had and perfect with the wines."

"The meat was tender and succulent and the sauce added extra dimensions to its taste," I said. "I agree with Dr. Franklin; the food and wines were a perfect match."

"Another vacation I enjoyed started out as business and evolved into an interesting pleasure trip," Jefferson said. "I received a note from Abigail Adams explaining that John had left London for Amsterdam to tie up any loose ends that existed in financial arrangements between Holland and the United States. She said that John would be delighted to meet me there. I had had no experience in our financial dealings with the Dutch, and with the Adamses about to return to America, I realized that I might be called on to conduct future financial negotiations. I found the prospect of such a get-together exciting." [686]

"And when was this?" I asked.

"Just about a year after my trip through southern France. I left Paris on March 4 and met Adams at The Hague. From there we went on to Amsterdam. [687] At the time of our arrival in Amsterdam there were more than 250,000 residents, and it was the most important financial and commercial city in Europe. Its busy harbor was filled with ships; its streets, traversed with canals and quays, were crowded with merchants, sailors, and beautifully appointed shops and inns. [688]

"Adams and I lodged at the *Het Wapen van Amsterdam* (The Amsterdam Arms) where I stayed until March 30. I participated with Adams in negotiations with the Dutch bankers. The results of our negotiations led to the execution of bonds that, when later ratified by Congress, assured adequate financing for the United States for the next two years. [689]

"Adams left Amsterdam on March 11 for London, but I stayed on. My three weeks in Amsterdam were filled with sightseeing, attending concerts, interesting dinners, and the study of Dutch architecture. On March 20, I made a tenmile excursion to Haarlem, whose chief attractions were its world-renowned organ in the Church of St. Bavon and its tulips and hyacinths. Its old houses of hewn stone and brick caught my architectural eye. I visited the house of the Amsterdam banker Henry Hope, built by Jean-Baptiste DuBois, a famous Flemish architect. [690] Two days later I visited Zaandam, famous for its hundreds of windmills, and as the place where Peter the Great of Russia learned shipbuilding in 1696.

"Leaving Amsterdam on March 30, I decided to travel down the Rhine as far as Strasbourg 'in order to see what I have not yet seen.' [691] Before leaving, I wrote to my old friend Baron de Geismar, whom I had befriended when Geismar was an interned Hessian prisoner in the Charlottesville area in 1779. I asked Geismar to meet me, if possible, in Frankfurt at the Rothen House tavern where I would be staying, and he did. [692] I traveled by boat to Utrecht and along the way saw nothing but plains covered with grass, a few farms, and canals lined with country houses. I lodged in Utrecht at Aubelette's, 'the best tavern,' and had a bottle of Rhine wine with my dinner. [693]

"From Utrecht to Nijmegen, my carriage followed the post roads, and the hills of the Rhine served as the backdrop to windmills, hedgerows, canals, boats, cornfields and farmhouses built of brick and covered with tile or thatch, but I saw only a few châteaux. I crossed the Waal River, known as the Rhine in Germany, into ancient Nijmegen. The streets were wide and clean and the ramparts laid out as gardens. From a hill near the Chez un Anglois Inn on Place Royale, where I stayed the night, I took in a view up and down the Waal. I was told that the nearby Château of Valkhof (Falcon's Castle) had lodged Julius Caesar, which I thought apocryphal." [694]

"Actually," I said, "Charlemagne resided there for a time and later his son, Louis the Pious, so perhaps your guide simply confused the two emperors."

"Perhaps," Jefferson said with a nod. "Early the next morning, I left the Netherlands and entered Germany on a vibrating boat—a ferry large enough to hold carriages and horses. No sooner had I crossed into Germany than I noted a transition from ease and opulence to extreme poverty. The soil and climate were the same. The governments alone differed. [695] The bleakness of the village of Kleve, where I spent the night of April 1 at the post house, seemed to epitomize Germany's general poverty, with no shops or other signs of commerce or wealth. [696]

"At Duisberg, a walled village, I wanted to locate the remains of the encampment of Varus, in which he and his legions fell by the arms of Arminius, but there was not a single person to be found in Duisberg who could understand either English, French, Italian, or Latin. So I could make no inquiry. [697] My journey continued southeast through Germany, and the bumpy, dusty road to Düsseldorf led over hills and through the plains of the Rhine planted almost entirely in corn. Arriving in Dusseldorf on April 2, I stayed at Chez Zimmerman, the best tavern I saw in my whole journey. I visited the gallery of paintings in the Palace of the Palatinate elector. I thought the collection sublime and equal in merit to anything in the world, not because of the old faded red things of Rubens, but because of the room devoted to the paintings of Adriaen Vanderwerff. [698] That evening I dined alone and drank an old bottle of Rhine wine. [699]

"Following the post roads along the valley of the Rhine from Dusseldorf to Cologne, I stopped to see Schlossbernath, the elector's summer palace built by Nicolas de Pigage. I crossed the Rhine at Cologne on a pendulum boat. [700] Cologne, the birthplace of Rubens, was a sovereign city of about 60,000 inhabitants with more than one hundred churches.

"On April 5, I reached Coblenz at the confluence of the Moselle and the Rhine and an important wine trade center. I lodged at the Wild Man—au l'Homme Sauvage—a very good tavern. The Wild Man introduced me to a gentleman well acquainted with the vineyards and wines of the Moselle. I did not visit the Moselle, and it was through this acquaintance that I acquired much of my information about the relative merits of that area's wines.

"I learned that the best Moselle wines were made in a mountainous country about forty-five miles away. I thought the first quality, without any comparison, was that made on the mountain of 'Brownberg' adjoining the village of Dusmond." [701]

"Dusmond," I said, "can no longer be found on a map because in 1920 it took the name of its famous wine, Brauneberg, the Brown Hill."

"My classifying Brauneberg as the best Moselle was based on drinking a 1783 Brauneberg and comparing it with a Graach of the same year. The Brauneberg was 'quite clear of acid, stronger, and very sensibly the best.'[702]

"Brauneberg was followed in quality by Wehlen, Graach and Piesport, then Zelting and Bernkastel. After this there is a graduation of qualities. I was told that these ratings were based on the prices at which the wines sold per foudre, a foudre being the equivalent of 1100 bottles."[703]

"The vineyards of Bernkastel, Brauneberg, Graach, Piesport, Wehlen, and Zelting still produce wines of remarkable quality," I said. "Mr. Jefferson, you cautioned that these wines must be five or six years old before they are quite ripe for drinking. Today, with the exception of Ausleses, Beerenausleses, and Trockenbeerenausleses, most Moselle's can and should be drunk sooner." I paused, wondering if my comments were irritating my hosts. "I hope you will forgive my interruptions, but wine is a subject I enjoy talking about almost as much as history."

"We are very interested in your comments, Jack, so please continue them," Franklin said.

"I quite agree," said Jefferson. "After my afternoon wine tasting of the Moselle's best wines, I chose for my evening meal what was probably the Wild Man's house wine, a half pot of wine with soup, and a half pot of wine with dinner.[704]

"At Coblenz, I crossed the Rhine and journeyed over hills planted in corn, some vines, and forests of beach and oak. At Nassau, crowned by a ruined castle, the road to Schwelbach climbed over steep mountains that reminded me of my passage over the Alps. I decided that if I were to travel this route again, I would eliminate the mountain passage by following the Rhine as far as possible and travel by barge until the road resumed, a distance of only six to twelve miles. I was told that along this river route are the most picturesque scenes in the world."

"I have traveled this part of the Rhine by boat, and I can assure you that it is a most beautiful passage, and you would have enjoyed it," I said.

"I arrived in Frankfurt on April 6 and stayed four days at the Rothen House or The Great Red House owned by John Adam Dick and Son. Dick, a great wine merchant, had between three and four hundred tuns of wine in his cellar, the equivalent of 375,000 to 500,000 bottles.[705]

"You could taste at their tavern genuine hock, and the oldest. Dick's son had lived in London and spoke both English and French. Here I met Arnaud, a 'sensible, active, and obliging' valet de place, who became my guide to the vineyards of Hochheim, Johannisberg and Rüdesheim, where I found that wines of the very first quality were made. Dick's wine list included vintages from 1726 to 1783 of Hochheim, Rüdesheim, Johannisberg, Marcobrunn, Nierstein, Laubenheim, and Bodenheim. Johannisberg was the most expensive, with Hochheim and Rüdesheim selling for the same prices. Nierstein, Laubenheim, and Bodenheim were the least expensive and equal in price. [706] At dinner one night at the Rothen House tavern I drank a 1726 bottle of Hochheim, and later at supper with my old Albemarle friend, Baron de Geismar, we shared a bottle of 62-year-old Hochheim. [707]

"After supper we attended the theatre and saw a comedy, and the next day Geismar took me to his army garrison in Hanau, ten miles from Frankfurt. Here I met with many of the officers who had been stationed near Charlottesville while in captivity. The next day we visited the vineyards of Rüdesheim and Johannisberg, where the most celebrated wines were made. Geismar and I had dinner at the Red House tavern, and shared two bottles, a 1781 Johannisberg and a Rudesheim.

"In the morning I paid my bill at the Red House Tavern, rented horses and traveled with Geismar to Hochheim. 'The vineyards were on a gentle slope of about one-quarter of a mile wide, extending a half mile toward Mainz. I was told the vines begin to yield a little at three years old, and continue to one hundred years, unless sooner killed by a cold winter.' [708] The best vineyard owners kept their wines fifteen years before selling them. Before leaving Hochheim, I purchased a hundred vines for my Paris garden. From Hochheim, Geismar and I traveled to Mainz on the left bank of the Rhine. Riding through its narrow, crooked streets, I stopped at the Hotel Mainz where I found the accommodations good and reasonable. Geismar and I shared a bottle of Rudesheim with our dinner. [709]

"Up early and accompanied by my valet, Arnaud, I traveled down the Rhine in a small batteau, with two hands rowing with a large paddle and a square sail but scarcely a breath of wind. Traveling at only five miles an hour, it took three and a half hours to reach Rüdesheim. I noted that the vineyards at Rüdesheim were terraced up the hillsides and the soil consisted of slate, rotten stone, and clay. As for the wines, they were not at all acid, and to my taste much preferable to Hochheim, and at the same price. [710] The best Rüdesheim vineyards, I thought, were located a mile from the village and faced south along terraced hillsides. [711]

"Leaving Rüdesheim, I traveled back toward Mainz, stopping to taste the wines of Schloss Johannisberg. I thought them the best made on the Rhine without comparison and about double the price of the oldest Hock. I was particularly impressed with a thirteen-year-old bottle of 1775 Johannisberg." Looking at me, Jefferson said, "How does Schloss Johannisberg rate today?"

"Schloss Johannisberg remains the most famous vineyard in Germany. It is known for its bouquet and flavor, rather than strength, and its name epitomizes quality." I said.

Jefferson nodded, seemingly pleased, and continued. "Farther up the Rhine my little boat stopped at the vineyard of Marcobrunn on the water's edge between Hattenheim and Erbach. To my taste, Marcobrunn was slightly inferior to the wines of Rüdesheim, Johannisberg, and Hochheim. I recorded that Marcobrunn's mulatto and stone hillside yields wine of the second quality. And I should add, if price were the sole criterion, it deserved this rating because it sold for substantially less than its more famous neighbors. [712]

"I bought four bottles of wine and fifty Rüdesheim vine shoots that I planted in my Paris garden. I planned on transplanting them to my vineyard at Monticello. I wrote Geismar that the vines that I took from Hochheim and Rüdesheim were growing luxuriously in my garden here, and would cross the Atlantic next winter, and that if he ever revisited Monticello, I would be able to give him a glass of hock or Rüdesheim of my own making. [713]

"At Marcobrunn I abandoned the batteau and returned by carriage to Mainz. That evening at dinner I drank a bottle of Johannisberg Riesling. [714]

"Early the next morning I was on the road to Oppenheim, traveling through the cantons of Laubenheim, Bodenheim, and Nierstein, esteemed for producing high-quality wines just below that of the vineyards of Rüdesheim. I remembered that they had been prominently displayed on John Dick's wine list. [715] The wines of Laudenheim, a village about six miles from Mainz, were produced from grapes that grew on a steep hillside facing southeasterly into the sun. The vineyards between Laubenheim and Nierstein were planted on hillsides so steep that they were almost perpendicular to the Rhine. These are the only cantons on the south side of the river that yield good wine, the hills on this side being generally exposed to the cold winds, and turned from the sun." [716]

Jefferson looked to me as if expecting my comment. "Today," I said, "vineyards on these same hillsides continue to produce the best-quality wines of the Rheinhessen, with Nierstein being singled out for making some of the very best."

"Approaching Oppenheim, which is situated on a hill above the river and dominated by the Church of St. Catharine, I saw the commencement of the bergstrasse, mountains that separate the plains of the Rhine and Maine. [717] Late that evening, my carriage arrived at the cour du Palatin, a 'good tavern' in Mannheim. In the morning I purchased a guidebook and spent the day, my forty-fifth birthday, 'seeing things.' I visited the Elector's Palace, and in the evening, I went to the theater. From Mannheim, I took several side trips. I visited Kaeferthall and saw a herd of wild boar and a field of rhubarb. On an excursion to Dossenheim, I saw Angora goats, and at Schwetzinger, I thought the gardens behind the Elector's Castle among the best in Germany though not to be compared to the English gardens.

"At Heidelberg I made the long, steep ascent to the castle and thought it the most noble ruin I had ever seen. Among the ruins was a round tower and the remains of a chapel with statues of saints and warriors looking down from niches along massive walls covered with ivy. These ruins were the handiwork of man and nature. A hundred years before my visit, the Heidelberg Castle had been ravaged by wars, but the final insult was delivered by nature in the form of a series of lightning strikes in 1764 that reduced the castle to the ruinous condition that I found it in. I made precise measurements of the Great Tun of Heidelberg, which had been built in 1751 to replace an older vat. Although the tun was empty, I calculated that it was capable of holding 283,000 bottles. Looking from the edge of a precipice down on the Neckar River and across a green valley to the Black Forest, I was reminded of the view from Petrarch's château at Vaucluse, and thought it would stand well in majesty alongside the pyramids of Egypt. [718]

"The road from Heidelberg to Karlsruhe was one of the best of my journey, with the hills above the Neckar on one side and the plains sloping down to the Rhine on the other.

"In Strasbourg, I stayed at the Hôtel l'Esprit for three days. I visited Amand Koenig's bookstore, the best shop for classical books I ever saw. [719]

"I visited the cathedral and went to the top of its spire, 465 feet, highest in the world, and the handsomest. But it was not an easy climb, and a year later I advised two young American friends traveling through Europe to let it be the last operation of the day, because they would need a long rest after climbing it. [720]

Heidelberg

"It was here that I came across a curious type of wine, *vin de paille* or straw wine. 'Its name came from the circumstance of spreading the grapes on straw where they are preserved till spring, and then made into wine. The little juice then remaining in them makes a rich sweet wine, but the dearest in the world without being the best by any means. It is the caprice of wealth alone which continues so losing an operation. This wine is sought because dear, while the better wine of Frontignan was rarely seen at a good table because it was cheap.'[721]

"From Strasbourg my route led across France. Before returning to Paris, I traveled to Champagne staying in Épernay at the Aubergiste de l'hôtel de Rohan. Monsieur Cousin, the owner and a vintner, was my guide to the Champagne vineyards. Of all the Champagnes I tasted during this visit, I found Dorsay's the best. The Benedictine monks at Hautvilliers produced first quality Champagnes that supplied the King's table, but on tasting them I did not think their white as good as Dorsay's. I bought all Monsieur Dorsay's remaining supply of nonsparkling Champagne of the year 1783. I observed that the best winemakers bought most of their grapes from small proprietors who could have made first quality wines if they had been able to cull their grapes, but being poor they could not afford this luxury. Consequently, small vineyard owners entered into contracts with established proprietors, who bought only their best grapes."

"The practice of large Champagne houses buying most of their grapes under contracts from small vineyard owners continues to this day, and most of the

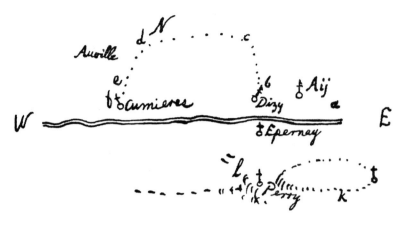

Jefferson's sketch of towns of Champagne.

grapes crushed and made into Champagne are not from vineyards owned by a particular Champagne house," I said.

"As Dr. Franklin said, Jack, some things never change." He took a sip of wine and continued. "After two days of tasting the wines from the vineyards of Épernay and the surrounding villages I left, convinced that I had learned just enough to know that there was more to learn about the intricacies and nuances of Champagne.

"Jack," Jefferson said, "I'm tired of talking and would like to listen for a while."

"Dr. Franklin, what other memorable trips did you take?"

"As postmaster I traveled all over the Colonies and into the English countryside, but no journey stands out like the trip I took with John Pringle to France and my travels to Ireland and Scotland."

"What about the trip you took with the attractive, vibrant, twenty-three year old Catharine Ray? You and Catharine were together for more than two weeks from the time you left Boston on December 30, 1754, until you saw her off to her parents' house on Block Island."

"Yes, that was a most delightful time in my life."

"How did you first meet Catharine?"

"My duties as deputy postmaster general of the colonies took me away from home for long periods, and in August 1754, I set out on an extensive inspection tour. At Christmas time, I was staying at my brother John's house in Boston. Catharine 'Caty' Ray, whose sister Judith was married to John's stepson, was also staying at John's house. Caty and I met during this time, and when Caty decided to return home to Block Island, where she lived with her elderly parents, I volunteered to accompany her. Traveling by carriage, we left Boston on December 30 for Newport, Rhode Island, a distance of about seventy miles. When we reached an icy hill, our improperly shod horses kept falling, 'no more able to stand than if they had been shod on skates. Despite the deplorable road conditions, a wintery journey, a wrong road and a soaking shower, we talked away the hours.' The weather conditions, and the fact that our carriage traveled at less than seven miles an hour, required us to spend overnight at a tavern. [722] In Newport, Caty stayed with her relatives the Wards, and I with my brother Peter, or my sister-in-law Anne. At this time, I don't remember which. When we left Newport, we traveled to Caty's sister's farm near Westerly. From there, Caty returned to her parents' house on Block Island." [723]

"How long was it from the time you and Caty left Boston until she returned to Block Island?"

"As I recall, a little less than three weeks."

"Years later Caty said that much of her life's happiness was due to the lessons you had given her on that trip." [724]

"Our friendship began on that trip and lasted the rest of our lives."

"The barrage of letters that you and Caty exchanged after this trip has caused some historians to believe that a romantic relationship developed. From my reading of the letters, it seems clear that Caty fell in love with you, and you in turn were smitten with her charms."

Franklin's eyebrows arched and he looked surprised. "What specifically have you read that has left you with that impression?"

I removed some papers from my jacket. "If I may, I would like to read a sample of your sentiments expressed in your first letter to her." Franklin, smiling, nodded his approval. " 'I thought too much was hazarded, when I saw you put off to sea in that very little skiff, tossed by every wave. But the call was strong and just, a sick parent. I stood on the shore and looked after you, till I could no longer distinguish you, even with my glass. I left New England slowly, and with great reluctance. With short day's journeys and loitering visits on the road, I almost forgot I had a home, till I was more than half way towards it. Persons subject to the hyp complain of the northeast wind, as increasing their malady. [725] But since you promised to send me kisses in that wind, and I find you as good as your word, it is to me the gayest wind that blows, and gives me the best spirits.' " [726]

"In a letter to you, Caty said it had caused her distress, or as she put it 'a vast deal of uneasiness and occasioned many tears,' that she had not received 'one line from you in answer to three of my last letters in which I said a thousand things that nothing should have tempted me to have said to anybody else for I knew they would be safe with you. I'll only beg the favor of one line and love me one thousandth part so well as I do you.' In a postscript she wrote, 'Pray take care of your health and accept the Sugar Plums. They are every one Sweetn'd as you used to like.' " [727]

I looked over at Jefferson. He was grinning broadly. "Caty's concerns were probably relieved when she received your letter of September 11. 'I have now before me, my dear girl, three of your favors, viz. of March the 3d March, the 30th & May 1st.' Unfortunately, we can only guess what love mots Caty's letters contained because they have never been found. [728] Dr. Franklin, did you destroy them?"

Franklin smiled but said nothing. I waited for a response, but he remained silent, so I continued. "And you wrote to Caty, 'I should write to you by every post: For the pleasure I receive from one of yours, is more than you can have from two of mine. I long to hear whether you have continued ever since in that monastery [729]; or have broke into the world again, doing petty mischief, and what the state of your heart is at this instant?—but what, perhaps I ought not to know; and therefore I will not conjure, as you sometimes say I do.' [730]

"In an earlier letter to you," I said, "Caty had enclosed a love letter from a Spanish suitor. You translated it and added, 'I honor that honest Spaniard for loving you: It showed the goodness of his taste and judgment. But you must forget him and bless some worthy young Englishman.' But then you teasingly added, 'You have spun a long thread 5022 yards! It will reach almost from Block Island hither. I wish I had hold of one end of it, to pull you to me. You would break it rather than come.' " [731]

Franklin looked sternly at me. "I think the sentiments of those letters speak for themselves. I was married, twice her age, and in every letter I wrote to her I mentioned my wife. I decided that it was time to call a halt to our budding epistolary romance. So I told her: 'Let me give you some fatherly advice. Kill no more pigeons than you can eat. Be a good girl, and don't forget your catechise. Go constantly to meeting—or church—till you get a good husband; then stay at home, and nurse the children, and live like a Christian.' And Caty took my advice, because the next time I met her she was Mrs. William

Greene, wife of the future governor of Rhode Island, and mother of the first two of their six children." [732]

Jefferson was beaming, clear evidence that he had enjoyed Franklin's account of his journey with Caty Ray. I turned to Mr. Jefferson, "The trip that you and James Madison made to New England, will you tell us about it?"

"Of course, but it does not have the romantic panache of Benjamin's tale. Still, we had a fine time together. On May 17, 1791, I left Philadelphia and joined Madison in New York City. Our itinerary was to tour upstate New York and parts of New England for the purpose, as Madison said, of 'health, recreation and curiosity.' Because of the length of the trip and our mutual enjoyment of wine, I brought along bottles of wine and a corkscrew. [733] I also took along some Madeira and Sherry. These wines were carried in a portable wooden case that contained ten compartments for holding eight large and two small mold-blown bottles with spherical stoppers. [734]

"We spent four weeks walking over battlefields, fishing, killing rattlesnakes, shooting squirrels, studying botanical curiosities, and visiting friends. [735] Not everyone, however, saw our trip in the same light. One of Hamilton's supporters reported to him that we 'scouted silently through the country, shunning the gentry and quarreling with the eatables; nothing good enough for them.' [736]

"Madison and I departed New York on May 21. James Hemings, who had accompanied me to France, was along and took my phaeton and horses on to Poughkeepsie while we traveled up the Hudson by boat. From Poughkeepsie, we headed north and were in Albany on May 26. The following day we visited Cohoes Falls on the Mohawk River near its confluence with the Hudson River. At Bemis Heights (formerly Stillwater) we explored the battlegrounds, which were the principal scenes of Burgoyne's defeat and which cost so much blood to both sides.

"Three miles north of Bemis Heights we stopped at the home of Dr. Elias Willard (1756–1827) to discuss the Hessian fly. After breakfast at Ezekiel Ensign's tavern, we traveled eleven miles north to Schylerville (formerly Saratoga) where we viewed the encampments and ground where the British piled their arms."

"Today," I said, "a monument commemorates the place where General John Burgoyne surrendered his army of British and Hessian troops to General Horatio Gates on October 17, 1777."

Both Franklin and Jefferson smiled at that, and Jefferson nodded as well before continuing his account. "After dining at Archibald McNeil's tavern, we traveled to the French and Indian War outposts at Fort Edward. The following day we reached Lake George, and after visiting Fort George and Fort William Henry, we sailed the lake's entire length. 'I thought Lake George, without comparison, the most beautiful water I ever saw. It is formed by a contour of mountains into a basin thirty-five miles long, and from two to four miles broad, finely interspersed with islands, its water limpid as crystal, and the mountainsides covered with rich groves of thuja, silver fir, white pine, aspen, and paper birch down to the water-edge; here and there precipices of rock to checker the scene and save it from monotony. An abundance of speckled trout, salmon trout, bass and other fish, with which it is stored, added, to our other amusements, the sport of taking them.' [737]

"Our thirteen-mile journey from Lake George to Fort Ticonderoga was through a verdant valley enclosed by the Adirondack Mountains. Built by the French as Fort Carillon in 1755, Fort Ticonderoga's strategic location on the southern tip of Lake Champlain had been considered important from the time of the French and Indian Wars. [738]

"After dinner at Ticonderoga 'we sailed fifteen miles up Lake Champlain to Crown Point, which had seen scenes of blood from a very early part of our war history.' [739] We lodged at Chimney Point in Vermont, directly across the lake from Crown Point. [740] On May 31, we sailed halfway to Split Rock, but, because of rough water and headwinds, our voyage was cut short. I found Lake Champlain much larger but far less pleasant than Lake George.

"Retracing our steps, we visited on June 2 two very remarkable cataracts on the Hudson River, Wing's Falls and Sandy Hill Falls, [741] and later we crossed the Hudson at Saratoga. We lodged at Colvin's tavern in the town of Cambridge near the Vermont border and headed the next day for Bennington, Vermont, through mountains covered with sugar maple, white oak, and beech.

"Before reaching Bennington, we visited the Bennington battle sites in Hoosick Falls, New York. Standing on top of the hill where Colonel Baum and his Hessian troops had camped before being routed, we were told how it came about. As General Burgoyne's army pursued the American army, following its retreat from forts Ticonderoga and Mt. Independence, the British learned that an American cache of food and ammunition was stored at Bennington. Burgoyne ordered a detachment of Hessian troops under Colonel Baum to seize it. What the British didn't know was that a tough New Hampshire Indian fighter, John Stark, had assembled a colonial force of New

Hampshire, Vermont, and Massachusetts volunteers to defend Bennington. On August 16, the fighting, which Stark described as 'one continuous clap of thunder,' began. Within two hours Baum and more than two hundred of his troops had been killed and the rest captured. Later that evening Stark's troops, with the help of Colonel Seth Warner and the Green Mountain Boys, engaged and defeated a British reinforcement detachment led by a Colonel Breymann. What started out as a routine foray turned into a stunning defeat for Burgoyne's invading army and laid the groundwork for his surrender at Saratoga two months later. [742]

"Arriving in Bennington on June 4, Madison and I lodged at Captain Elijah Dewey's tavern. Dewey, an active revolutionary, served as a captain in the battles at Bennington and Saratoga and hosted many revolutionary meetings at his inn. Saturday evening was spent with a political ally and friend, Moses Robinson, the former governor and the newly elected Senator from Vermont. [743]

"Early on Monday morning we continued our journey southwest across Connecticut, breakfasting at Killock's in Williamstown, [744] and stayed at Sarah Williams Marsh's public house in Dalton. The following day we dined at Smith's Inn in Worthington and lodged at Pomeroy's in North Hampton. On June 8, although with cavalry in part disabled, [745] we arrived in Hartford, where we stayed for two days at the town's most prominent tavern, Frederick Bull's, at the sign of the bunch of grapes on Main Street, opposite the court house. A few days later we reached Guilford on Long Island Sound, had dinner at Medab Stone's tavern, and sailed for Long Island. We were on the sound all night. Landing on the northeastern tip of Long Island at Oyster Pond Point, [746] we breakfasted at Tupple's Inn.

"On June 13, we dined at Griffin's in Riverhead and lodged at Downs in Morichies. In the morning we breakfasted with my old friend and fellow Congressional delegate, William Floyd at his home on the Forge River in Brookhaven Township and visited the Unquachog Indians, a tribe of about twenty souls. I had had a lifelong interest in Indian languages, and I compiled a vocabulary of Unquachog words. [747] We then traveled to Flushing, Long Island, where we stopped at the Prince Nursery, the most famous nursery in America. The man from whom I attempted to buy the nursery's entire stock of sugar maple trees, William Prince, was the third proprietor. On returning to Philadelphia, I ordered from the Prince catalogue thirty-one additional items, including a variety of roses. [748] When Prince filled the order he sent me sixty sugar maple trees, six cranberry trees, and ten different kinds of roses. We spent that night in Jamaica.

"The following day, June 16, we returned to the mainland via the Brooklyn ferry and ended our trip in New York City. Our journey of more than 700 miles had been, in the words of Madison, 'a very agreeable one, and carried us through an interesting country new to us both.'[749] I rated the inns and taverns where we stayed by assigning * for good, + for middling, and — for bad. Of the twenty-eight inns rated, five were noted bad, twelve middling, and eleven good. Dewey's in Bennington and Fred Bull's Tavern in Hartford got top ratings.[750] I arrived in Philadelphia tired but pleased with our journey and with only $8.60 cash in hand."[751]

Petit had removed our dinner plates, and entered carrying a tray with three wine glasses and a decanter of white wine. Jefferson, as he had for most of evening, poured the wine and passed a glass to each of us. He lifted his glass and said, "As you requested, Jack, 1784 Yquem. This particular wine proved most excellent 'and hit the palate of the Americans more than any wine I had ever seen in France.' The 1784 vintage, as you know, was a great one."[752]

Our attention immediately turned to the wine. It was lightly golden with a bouquet of figs, apricots, and perhaps a touch of vanilla. On the palate it was rich, full-bodied, honeyed, with a crisp acidity and balanced sweetness.

Jefferson looked at me. "Well, Jack, do you agree with the assessment of my American colleagues?"

"Yes. This is a remarkable wine," I said, as I spooned into the ice cream covered in the puff pastry. "It goes very well with the dessert, but it could be enjoyed equally as well as an aperitif."

"Have you drunk Yquem before, Jack?" Franklin asked.

"Yes. I have had the privilege of drinking several of the great Yquem vintages, including 1967, 1971, 1975, 1976, and 1983."

"How does this wine compare with the Yquem you have had?" Franklin said.

I took another sip and let the wine cover my palate before I swallowed. "It compares very well, but there is a difference; it is less sweet." I looked over at Dr. Franklin who was obviously enjoying the Yquem and the dessert. "Dr. Franklin, we have talked about some of your travails in London, but who were your close friends, and what were your social activities while there?"

"Over the years I had carried on extensive correspondence with Peter Collinson, a merchant and member of the Royal Society, about my observations on electricity, and William Strahan, printer of Samuel Johnson's dictionary,

Hume's history, and later the works of Adam Smith, Gibbon, Robertson, and Blackstone. So, when I arrived in London in 1757, I had instant friendships with these two prominent Londoners. [753]

"On my arrival, I took lodgings at 7 Craven Street with Margaret Stevenson, a widow living with her daughter Polly—of whom we have already spoken at length—and entered my son, William, in the Middle Temple Inn to study law. [754]

"Within a few years I had become quite comfortable in England. I eventually became the agent for three colonies besides Pennsylvania: Georgia, New Jersey, and Massachusetts. [755] I had become friends with most of the men of science and literature throughout England, Scotland, and Ireland. My company was so desired that I seldom dined at home in winter, and I could have spent the whole summer in the country houses of friends, if I chose it. Almost all the learned and ingenious foreigners who came to England made a point of visiting me, and I heard too that the king had spoken of me with great regard. I was also flattered to learn that I had been chosen a foreign member in the French Royal Academy, one of only eight such members among the most distinguished names of science." [756]

"During your years there, you were a member of a number of clubs. What were some of your favorites?"

"The Royal Society was scientific and serious in nature, but its activities were not entirely confined to science. One member offered a paper on repeal of the Stamp Act, and another criticized the ministry's American policies. [757] But for camaraderie, friendship, and entertainment, there were meetings with friends at the Dog tavern, and more regular meetings at the George and Vulture. My favorite, however, was the Honest W higs, which met ever y other Thursday evening at a coffee house in St-Paul's churchyard. Club membership was eclectic: clergymen, teachers, editors, writers, dramatists, composers, physicians, librarians, and other assorted intellectuals. There were no rules of attendance, some members attended regularly, and others came when they pleased. I was a regular." [758]

"What was a typical club evening like?"

"One of our members was James Boswell, [759] and he left this account of a typical Honest Whigs evening: 'We have wine and punch on the table. Some of us smoke a pipe, conversation goes on pretty formally, sometimes sensibly, and sometimes furiously. At nine there is a sideboard with Welsh rabbits, apple puffs, porter, and beer. Our reckoning is about 18d. a head. Much was said this night against Parliament. I said that, as it seemed to be agreed that all members of Parliament become corrupt, it was better to choose men already bad and so save good men.' " [760]

"Speaking of smoking, we have learned that smoking causes many serious illnesses, and death. Did either of you smoke?"

"I never smoked," Franklin said. "In fact, I never took suff, chewed or smoked tobacco." [761]

St. Paul's Cathedral

"I cultivated and sold tobacco, but I did not smoke it," Jefferson said. [762]

"Please continue, Dr. Franklin."

"When I left England in 1762, I realized that I loved my life in England: my surrogate family of Margaret Stevenson and her daughter Polly, my friends, and the respect and acclaim that was accorded me. I was torn on leaving; the attraction of reason was to return home, but my inclination was to stay in England. As I wrote Strahan before sailing, 'You know which usually prevails. I shall probably make but this one vibration and settle here forever. Nothing will prevent it if I can, as I hope, prevail with Mrs. F. to accompany me, especially if we have peace.' [763] I planned a short visit when I returned two years later, but immediately settled back into the life I loved and stayed for eleven years."

"Mr. Jefferson, you have told us about your fascinating six days with Mr. Adams in the English countryside visiting the great landscape gardens, but you were in England a total of forty-eight days. How did you spend the rest of your time?"

"Most of that time was spent in London shopping its establishments, visiting its historic sites, meeting new friends such as John and Lucy Paradise and the American artists John Trumbull and Mather Brown, visiting publishers and bookshops, buying books, sitting for my portrait, and visiting the British Museum and Windsor Castle. My evenings included the theatre, the opera and concerts, a ball at the French embassy, dinners at the homes of the Adamses and their friends, a visit to one of London's pleasure haunts, the Ranelagh, and a late evening at Dolly's Chop House." [764]

"You spent five years in Paris. Who were your French friends?"

"My social acceptance into Paris society came about mainly through introductions by Dr. Franklin, the Marquis de Lafayette, and the Marquis de Chastellux. Among the French friends I dined and socialized with were Lafayette and his wife Louis-Alexandre; the Duc de Rochefoucauld, his beautiful young wife, Rosalie, and his wealthy mother, the Duchesse d'Anville; Chastellux and his wife; the mathematician and permanent secretary of the French Academy, the Marquis de Condorcet; the scientist Lavoisier; Comtesse d'Houdetot; Comtesse de Tesse; Madame Helvétius; Madame de Corny; and the Abbés Mably, Chalut, and Arnoux. Other distinguished men I got to know were Baron Grimm; Beaumarchais; Marmontel; Comte de Buffon; the great sculptor Jean Antoine Houdon; the king's finance minister, Jacques Necker; Mirabeau; Malesherbes; the painter Jacques-Louis David; and the king's foreign ministers, counts Vergennes and Montmorin."

"How did you spend your non-working time?"

"I explored Paris, combing the bookstalls along the Left Bank for bargains that would become part of my wide-ranging book collection, eventually the nucleus of the Library of Congress. I wandered the streets of Paris absorbing its architecture. I took daily walks through the Bois de Boulogne, usually for two hours at a time. I sampled the pleasures of the Palais Royal. I attended dinner parties at the homes of my French friends, and during my first year in Paris, at the homes of Dr. Franklin and Abigail and John Adams. I attended concerts, plays, and operas. I shopped the elegant stores that lined rue Saint-Honoré; and I made almost daily visits to the Tuileries Gardens, which stretched toward place Louis XV and faced the Seine. Here, surrounded by the beauty of its gravel walks, beds of flowers, raised terraces, marble statues, rows of trees, and water basin, I viewed the construction of a mansion whose architectural beauty had 'violently smitten' me. Known as the Hôtel de Salm, [765] it was going up directly across the Seine from the Tuileries Gardens. The Château des Tuileries [766] and its gardens were the settings for Sunday and holiday evening *Concerts Spirituels* performed by many of the best musicians of the day. Six livres got me the best seat in the house where an orchestra of fifty-eight performed Hayden symphonies and shorter selections." [767]

"You mentioned the Palais Royal. Would you describe what it was like in your day?"

"The Palais Royal was the center of the city's social life and the most interesting place for entertainment and shopping in all Europe. It was enclosed on three sides by elegant apartment houses, and along the lower levels were arcaded galleries extending from below to above ground level, that housed cafes, restaurants, coffee houses, all kinds of shops, art galleries, theatres, gamblinghouses, and other facilities for every vice. The most popular theatre was the *Variétés Amusantes*, and as its name indicates, it featured a variety of plays and other performances. The Duc de Chartes's personal art gallery was open to the public and it contained many masterpieces by Raphael, Rubens, Rembrandt, and other famous artists. One of Paris' historians, Sebastien Mercier, said of the Palais Royal that 'there is no spot in the world comparable to it. Visit London, Amsterdam, Madrid, Vienna, you will see nothing like it; a prisoner could live here free from care for years with no thought of escape.' Walking in the garden during daylight hours was a fashionable Parisian pastime. It was the place to hear the latest gossip, observe women's fashions, and to see and be seen. At night, it was a different scene with courtesans available to satisfy one's evening pleasure. [768]

"In January 1789, Gouverneur Morris, whose pen, according to Madison, had 'styled' the Constitution, arrived in Paris on private business and immediately contacted me. Though we were political opposites, Morris and I held an intellectual respect for one another that transcended our political differences, and, during the eight months that I remained in Paris, we were social companions. Morris was a frequent dinner guest at the Hôtel de Langeac."

"Morris obviously enjoyed himself at your dinner table," I said, "because he wrote in his diary, 'Mr. Jefferson lives well, keeps a good table and excellent wines which he distributes freely, and by his hospitality to his countrymen here possesses very much their good will.'"

"It was with Gouverneur Morris that I witnessed from the balcony of my place on the Champs-Elysées the annual Parisian rite of spring known as the Promenade à Longchamps. I had been away from Paris in 1786, 1787, and 1788 during the Easter holidays, so this was the first time I had seen the fête. [769] Each year on Wednesday, Thursday, and Friday in the week before Easter, Parisians paraded along the Champs-Elysées and across the Bois de Boulogne to the little church at Longchamps. The origin of this rite had been to enjoy the music of the Tenebrae services at the Abbaye de Longchamps church, but over time it evolved into a parade featuring Parisians from every walk of life dressed in their Sunday best, most on foot, but many riding in ornate carriages.

"John Adams, who witnessed the fete on a number of occasions, said that 'Everybody that has got a splendid carriage, a fine set of horses, or an elegant mistress, sends them out on these days to make a show at Longchamps.' [770] According to Adams its popularity evolved from boredom, and he told an anecdote about a beautiful prostitute whose carriage was so superior to any other that it brought on the wrath of Marie Antoinette. According to Adams she had sold her charms for such profit that she appeared in the most costly and splendid equipage of all, six of the finest horses in the kingdom, the most costly coach that could be built, more numerous servants, and richer liveries than any of the nobility. Her show was so audacious an insult

Gouverneur Morris

to all modest women and to the national morality and religion that the queen sent her a message warning that if she ever appeared again, anywhere, in that equipage, she would find herself in the Bastille in the morning."[771]

I wondered how much of this tale was true, but decided to direct my curiosity in a different direction, and to Jefferson I said, "Did you ever feel that you wanted to escape Paris' social swirl and just be alone?"

"Yes. Despite the social and intellectual stimuli of Paris, I sometimes felt a compelling need to be alone, and when I did, I usually headed to what I called 'my Hermitage.' The Hermitage was a communal retreat of a group of lay brothers known as the 'Hermites.' To reach the Hermitage, I rode through the Bois de Boulogne to Longchamps, took the ferry across the river to the village of Suresnes, and then climbed to the top of Mont Valerien, known also as Mont Calvaire, where the monastery stood. The Hermitage was an idyllic retreat. [772] Housed in a stately old monastery on top of Mont Valerien, it provided a sweeping view of the countryside: the villages of Suresnes, Puteaux, Longchamps, the Bois de Boulogne, Paris, Sevres, Saint-Cloud, and Bellevue, all connected by the winding Seine. With silence enjoined, except at dinner, I could relax and use my time for working, reading, walking, thinking or simply resting. At dinner, conversation among the guests, who usually knew one another, was allowed, and the meals were accompanied by wine from their vineyards known as *vin de Suresnes*. [773] The food was good if the Hermites knew you were expected, but as one habitué warned, 'If you plan to go to Hermit brothers tomorrow, please pay my respects to the gentlemen of our table and tell good Brother Joseph to tell the cook to have something good for you. If they're not forewarned, the cuisine lacks variety and is very lean.' [774]

"The Hermites supported themselves by providing accommodations to paying guests like me, by selling wood, honey and silk stockings from their manufactory, and wine from their vineyards. The vineyards were located on the lower slopes of Mont Valerien and faced southeast toward Paris. Vineyards had flourished on these hillsides for over 900 years and the wine had the reputation of a good quality *vin ordinaire*. It was popular with Parisians who by leaving the city could eat and drink for only a fraction of what it cost in Paris because of taxes levied on everything entering the city." [775]

"And Thomas," Franklin said, "another available retreat was in the comfort of a warm bath aboard one of the boats that plied the Seine for this purpose. I remember John Adams telling me about boarding such a boat near the Pont Royal and taking a bath in a little room, which had a large window looking out over the river into the Tuileries. There was a table, a glass and two chairs, and you were furnished with hot linens, towels, etc. There was a bell which you rang when you wanted anything." [776]

"Yes, France offered pleasures that were not available in our country. I wrote my friend Charles Bellini, professor of modern languages at William & Mary College, some of my impressions on the vaunted scene of Europe! I had to admit that I wanted words to describe how much I enjoyed their architecture, sculpture, painting, and music. And in the pleasures of the table, they were far before us, because with good taste they united temperance.' [777] As to French food, there was but one opinion, for every man in Europe who could afford a great table, he either kept a French cook, or one influenced in the same manner. There is no better beef in the world. The variety given by their cooks was astonishing. They dressed a hundred dishes in a hundred different ways, most of them excellent, and all sorts of vegetables." [778]

"As we have experienced here this evening," Franklin said.

Jefferson nodded his agreement and continued. "I felt, however, that the great mass of people suffered under physical and moral oppression and that among my aristocratic friends, conjugal love had no existence, and domestic happiness was utterly unknown. To friends in America I expanded on how the benefits of freedom enriched the lives of Americans as compared to the wretched existence of the vast majority of the French people."

"What did you tell them?"

"I urged my friend James Monroe to come to France. I assured him that such a visit would make him better appreciate his 'own country, its soil, its climate, its equality, liberty, laws, people, and manners. My God!' I admitted, 'how little do my countrymen know what precious blessings they are in possession of, and which no other people on earth enjoy. I confess I had no idea of it myself. While we shall see multiplied instances of Europeans going to live in America, I will venture to say no man now living will ever see an instance of an American removing to settle in Europe and continuing there.' [779]

"I told another friend. 'I am much pleased with the people of this country, The roughnesses of the human mind are so thoroughly rubbed off with them that it seems as if one might glide through a whole life among them without a jostle. Perhaps, too, their manners may be the best calculated for happiness to a people in their situation, but I am convinced they fall far short of effecting a happiness so temperate, so uniform, and so lasting, as is generally enjoyed with us. The domestic bonds here are absolutely done away. And where can their compensation be found? Perhaps they may catch some moments of transport above the level of the ordinary tranquil joy we experience, but they are separated by long intervals, during which all the passions are at sea without rudder or compass. Yet, fallacious as the pursuits of happiness are, they seemed on the whole to furnish the most effectual abstraction from a contemplation of the hardness of their government. Indeed, it is difficult to conceive how so good a people, with so good a king, so well-disposed rulers in general, so genial a climate, so fertile a soil, should be rendered so ineffectual for producing human happiness by one single curse, that of a bad form of government. But it is a fact. In spite of the mildness of their governors, the people are ground to powder by the vices of the form of government. Of twenty millions of people supposed to be in France, I am of opinion there are nineteen millions more wretched, more accursed in every circumstance of human existence, than the most conspicuously wretched individual of the whole United States.' " [780]

"We have talked about you wife, Mr. Jefferson, the wonderful relationship you had with her, and the emotional devastation her death caused you. But before you married Martha Wales Skelton, what women were there in your life?"

"When I was nineteen I thought I was in love with a beautiful young woman by the name of Rebecca Burwell. A year later while dancing with her at the Raleigh Tavern, I tried to tell her of my love. 'But good God! The words came out in a few broken sentences, uttered in great disorder, and interrupted with pauses of uncommon length, visible marks of my strange confusion.'"[781]

"What was Miss Burwell's reaction?" Franklin asked.

"Though only seventeen, she was not impressed and turned her amorous attentions to a fellow classmate at William & Mary, Jacquelin Amber. They married shortly thereafter."[782]

"We have talked about some of the women in your life Dr. Franklin, including your marriage to Deborah. What about Margaret Stevenson, the woman you lived with for sixteen years in London?"

"I rented lodgings from her."

"Your friend Strahan seems to have thought there was something more to your relationship with her than lodger and landlady."

"Why do you say that?"

"The letter he wrote your wife in which he said, 'Now madam, as I know the ladies here consider him in exactly the same light I do, upon my word I think that you should come over with all convenient speed to look after your interest; not but that I think him as faithful to his Joan [783] as any man breathing, but who knows what repeated and strong temptation may in time, and while he at so great a distance from you, accomplish.' And if that were not enough to cause anxiety for your wife, Strahan added, 'I cannot take my leave of you without informing you that Mr. F. has the good fortune to lodge with a very discreet gentlewoman who is particularly careful of him, who attended him during a very severe cold with an assiduity, concern and tenderness which, perhaps, only yourself could equal; so that I don't think you could have a better substitute until you come over to take him under your own protection.'"[784]

"Strahan offered to lay me a considerable wager that his letter to Deborah would bring her immediately to London. I wrote Deborah and told her what Strahan said and added, 'I will not pick Strahan's pocket, for I am sure there is no inducement strong enough to prevail with you to cross the seas.'"[785]

"It seems to me," I said, "that you were in effect telling your wife 'I'm glad that you are not coming to London.'"

"Deborah was a good wife and a good mother, but she would have been out of place in the London in which I lived and she knew it. Besides, she had a mortal fear of the sea, so that, in itself, eliminated any chance that she would come to London."[786]

"Deborah's letter telling you that she would not be becoming over," I said, "obviously pleased you because you wrote her, 'Your answer to Mr. Strahan was just what it should be; I was very much pleased with it. He fancied his rhetoric and art would certainly bring you over.' [787]

"In the eyes of your mutual friends, there seems to have been no doubt that Margaret Stevenson was in love with you, and after your wife's death, hoped to marry you."

"Why do you say that?"

"When you returned home in 1762, she was planning on coming to Pennsylvania to see you, but was dissuaded from making the trip by her daughter Polly. You were considered a couple by your London friends, who often invited you together. Then there was the veiled suggestion of a romantic liaison with Mrs. Stevenson in Strahan's letter to your wife urging her to come to London in order to protect her marital turf. On your return to Philadelphia, your friend Priestly wrote you that 'Mrs. Stevenson is much as usual. She can talk about nothing but you.' [788] Mrs. Stevenson made it clear that she wanted to be with you. Her letters to you are full of anticipation of the 'hapey day' when you would see each other again. Your mutual friend, Dolly Blunt, after your wife's death and your return to America, wrote you that Mrs. Stevenson 'gives frequent proof of weak spirits, which I am sure will be still weaker if your letter whenever it comes does not contain the strongest assurances of your return; for I am firmly persuaded that without the animating hope of spending the remainder of life with you she would be very wretched indeed, for though many of your friends are also her friends, yet all of us are less to her than you.' [789] Shortly after you went to Paris, Emma Thompson reported that 'your good friend Mrs. Stevenson I think would have risked all tarring and feathering to have paid you a visit in Philadelphia.' [790]

Benjamin Franklin

"Am I being unfair, Dr. Franklin, if I suggest that your response was at best cold? You addressed Mrs. Stevenson as 'my dear, dear friend,' offered advice on her financial affairs, and sent tidbits of news about Temple, but gave no hint whatever that you missed her company any more than that you were grieving for your lost wife. You held out the unrealistic prospect of dancing with her at the marriage of your grandson Benny Bache to her granddaughter Elizabeth Hewson, six and not quite two at the time." [791]

Franklin gave me what I thought was the first unfriendly look of the evening. Jefferson broke the awkward silence. "Benjamin, tell Jack about the two French women who were recipients of your fervor and attention during your years in France."

"Anne-Louise de Harancourt, Brillon de Jouy, known as Madame Brillon, and Anne-Catherine Helvétius were the two main women in my life during my eight and a half years in France."

"How did you meet them?" I asked

"Through my circle of friends in Passy."

"This was a time in your life when, as John Adams said, at the age of seventyodd you had neither lost your love of beauty nor your taste for it." [792]

"I suppose so. A step-niece mentioned the kindness of the French ladies to me. Here is how I explained it to her. 'This is the civilest nation upon earth. Your first acquaintances endeavor to find out what you like, and they tell others. If 'tis understood that you like mutton, dine where you will, you find mutton. Somebody, it seems, gave it out that I loved ladies; and then everybody presented me their ladies (or the ladies presented themselves) to be embraced, that is have their necks kissed. For as to the kissing of lips or cheeks, it is not

Franklin and the ladies of Paris.

the mode here: the first is considered rude, and the other may rub off the paint.' " [793]

"But despite the fact that you liked women and women liked you, your attempts to match your children, grandchildren, and yourself with spouses were failures."

"You are correct, Jack. As a matchmaker, I was a failure. As I mentioned earlier, when I was a young man, my aim was to marry a woman with money. When that failed, I married Deborah. I wanted my son, William, to marry Polly Stevenson. He wasn't interested. Instead, he had an illegitimate son, William Temple, whom I raised. I wanted my daughter Sally to marry the son of my friend, William Strahan, but my wife wouldn't hear of it. My attempt to interest Madame Brillon in allowing her daughter, Cunégonde, to marry my grandson, Temple, met a firm rejection. [794] To top it off, Madame Helvétius rejected my proposal of marriage to her." [795]

"Tell me about Madame Brillon and Madame Helvétius," I said.

Franklin's eyes took on a nostalgic look. "I first met Madame Brillon soon after I arrived in Paris. We took an immediate fancy to one another. She was in her late thirties, and according to Abigail Adams, with whom I fully agree, she was 'one of the handsomest women in France,' [796] and married to a philandering husband twenty-four years her senior. Of course, our age difference was even greater, nearly forty years. Nevertheless, Madame Brillon and I became close friends, and she became particularly dependent on me when in the spring of 1779 she discovered her husband's affair with Mlle Jupin, the governess of their children. I usually visited her on Wednesday and Saturday when we enjoyed tea, chess, and music. She once told me that people had the audacity to criticize her pleasant habit of sitting on my knee, and mine of always asking her for what she always refused." [797]

"At seventy-odd years the amorous pursuit of a woman half your age is a rather ambitious undertaking," I said.

Jefferson smiled. "I will only repeat what our friend du Pont de Nemours said, 'All of Dr Franklin's proportions proclaim the vigor of Hercules, and at the age of 75 years he still has the suppleness and nimbleness of his character.' " [798]

"There was a dichotomy to our relationship," Franklin said, "the paternal and the sensual. Every time I saw Madame Brillon, I was guilty of breaking the Commandment that forbids coveting one's neighbor's wife. I told her that the best way to get rid of a certain temptation is to comply with and satisfy it. [799]

"Unfortunately, all my amorous advances were repulsed by her commitment to virtue. Here is how she put it, 'You are a man, and I am a woman, and while we might think along the same lines, we must speak and act differently. Perhaps there is no great harm in a man having desires and yielding to them; a woman 'The Sage and the Gout,' and suggested that my malady stemmed from having had too many mistresses. Not so, I told her, and sent her 'My Dialogue with the Gout' and a note that explained that when I was a young man and enjoyed more favors from the sex than at present, I never had the gout. 'If the ladies of Passy had more than Christian charity which I have so often recommended to you, in vain, I would not have the gout now.' [801] She told me there are many pains in life that must be borne with patience, and I agreed, pointing out, however, that there are also many pleasures, and that the name of sin has been given to several of them so that we might enjoy them more." [802]

"It seems that love and kisses ran all through your relationship with Madame Brillon," I said.

"Yes, but on a heavenly note she did relent. I pointed out that I would die forty years before her. When I asked her how we might manage our affairs in paradise, she gave me her word that she would become my wife in paradise, on condition, however, that I not make too many conquests among the heavenly maidens while I waited for her. She said, 'I want a faithful husband when I take one for eternity.'" [803]

"Your ability to have women love you, I think, was best expressed by Madame Brillon."

"What did she say?" Jefferson said.

"'To have been, to still be, forever, the friends of this amiable sage who knew how to be a great man without pomp, a learned man without ostentation, a philosopher without austerity, a sensitive human being without weakness, yes, my good Papa, your name will be engraved in the temple of memory, but each of our hearts is, for you, a temple of love.'" [804]

Pleased with the comment Franklin smiled broadly. "My other serious amour in France was with Madame Helvétius, a wealthy widow whose estate in Auteuil was within walking distance of my place in Passy. Although approaching sixty when I met her, she was still attractive and vivacious, and fifteen years my junior. She maintained the intellectual salon her late husband had established, and that is where I first met her. Statesmen, philosophers, historians, poets, and men of learning of all sorts were drawn around her. [805]

"A routine developed between us where I would visit her in Auteuil once a week and she would visit me once a week. On one occasion when I failed to show up and she complained, I told her, 'Madame, I am waiting till the nights are longer.'" [806]

"Are you aware that John Adams was a bit suspicious of Madame Helvétius's show of faithfulness to her late husband?"

"In what way?"

"He recorded in his diary, 'She might not be, however, entirely without the society of gentlemen, there were three or four handsome abbés who daily visited the house, and one at least resided there.' Adams added, 'The Ecclesiasticks I suppose have as much power to pardon sin as they have to commit one, or to assist in committing one. Oh mores! said I to myself.' " [807]

"Actually, two abbés, Morellet and de La Roche, resided with Madame Helvétius, , and a young medical student by the name of Cabanis" Franklin said. "And does it surprise me that Adams was suspicious of Madame Helvétius's morals? No! Adams was suspicious of my morals." [808]

"Is it true, Dr. Franklin, that you proposed marriage to Madame Helvétius and she rejected your proposal?"

A slight smile creased the doctor's lips. "Her response, Jack, was a bit more subtle than a blatant 'no,' but the effect was the same. She said that she had resolved to be faithful to the memory of her late husband, a former farmer-general and philosopher. Mortified I went home that night and dreamed that I was in the Elysian Fields where I met Monsieur Helvétius. He received me with much courtesy, having known me by reputation, he said, for some time. He asked me many things about the war and about the present state of religion, liberty, and government in France. 'You ask nothing then,' I said to him, 'about your dear friend Madame Helvétius; and yet she still loves you to excess. I was with her less than an hour ago.' 'Ah!' he said, 'you remind me of my former happiness. But we must forget if we are to be happy here. For several years at first, I thought of nothing but her. At last, I am consoled. I have taken another wife; the most likely I could find. She is not, it is true, altogether so beautiful, but she has so much good sense and plenty of wit, and she loves me infinitely. She studies continually to please me, and she has just now gone out to search for the best nectar and ambrosia to regale me with this evening. Stay with me and you will see her.' 'I perceive,' I said, 'that your former friend is more faithful than you; she has had several good offers and refused them all. I confess to you that I love her, to madness; but she was cruel to me and absolutely rejected me for love of you.' 'I pity you,' he said, 'in your misfortune; for she is indeed a good and beautiful woman, and very amiable.' Then the new Madame Helvétius came in with the nectar. Immediately I recognized her as Madame Franklin, my former wife. I claimed her again, but she said coldly: 'I was a good wife to you for forty-nine years and four months, almost half a century. Be content with that, I have formed a new connection here, which will last for an eternity.' Indignant at this refusal from my Eurydice, I at once resolved to quit these ungrateful shades, return to this good world, and see again the sun and

Madame Helvétius. And when I saw her, I told her of my dream and said, 'Here I am. Let us avenge ourselves.'" [809]

"Did her rejection affect your friendship?" I asked.

"No, we remained close friends until I left France four years later, and we carried on intimate correspondence for the rest of our lives. Realizing that we would never meet again in this world, she wrote that perhaps in the next world 'we shall meet again, with all those who love us, I a husband and you a wife— but I believe you have been a rogue and will find more than one'" [810]

"Dr. Franklin, two of your biographers, Claude-Anne Lopez and Eugenia Herbert, have studied your relationship with women outside your marriage— Catharine Ray, Margaret Stevenson, Polly Stevenson, Madame Brillon, Madame Helvétius—and concluded that they were all platonic relationships short of the grand passion," I said. [811]

Franklin took a reflective sip of wine and thought for a long moment. "If Lopez and Herbert are correct, it would mean that I was celibate for the last thirty-three years of my life," he said with a smile.

I didn't want to go there, so I turned to Jefferson and said, "Without trying to flatter you, you had all the qualities that attract women: wealth, good looks, intelligence, position, power, fame, and an incredible range of interests, and yet, after your wife's death, your life had lacked a romantic involvement. Did there come a time, when, like Dr. Franklin, that you were captivated by the charms of a French woman?"

"She was not French, but I was captivated by a young woman I met in Paris one day in August, 1786. She was the beautiful, blond, musically and artistically talented twenty-seven-year-old Maria Cosway. I met her through John Trumbull. She was married at the time to Richard Cosway, a famous painter of miniatures. My attention was riveted on Maria from the time we met beneath the dome of the Halle aux Bleds, the newly completed Parisian grain market. So that I could be with her, I changed my plans, including dinner with the Duchesse de la Rochefoucauld, by 'lying messengers,' and whisked away the Cosways and Trumbull for dinner at the Palais Royal and a ride to the royal park at Saint Cloud. On our return to Paris, we visited Ruggieri's, which featured elaborate displays of fireworks combined with pantomimes. 'The Forges of Vulcan beneath Mount Etna' and 'The Combat of Mars' were on the program that night, and afterwards, we attended a performance by the famous harpist Krumpholtz at the Tuileries Gardens. This first day was a prelude to many spent over the next three weeks on trips together, soon without her husband and Trumbull. I recall those days vividly. I asked Maria to 'paint me the day we went to St-Germain. How beautiful was every object! The Pont de Neuilly, the hills of the Seine, the rainbows of the machine of Marly, the terraces of St-Germain, the châteaux, the gardens, the statues of Marly, the pavilion of Lucienne. Recollect to Madrid, Bagatelle, the King's Garden, the Désert. The wheels of time moved on with a rapidity of which those of our carriage gave but a faint idea, and yet in the evening, when one took a retrospect of the day, what a mass of happiness we traveled over!' [812]

"Our journey of twelve miles to St-Germain-en-Laye took us up the ChampsElysées, past the Bois de Boulogne and across the Seine at the Pont de Neuilly. The Pont de Neuilly was a beautiful stone bridge that spanned the Seine at the Bois de Boulogne. I thought it the handsomest bridge in the world. [813] The road then turned west and followed the Seine on our left, and hills and valleys on the right, cultivated mainly in vines and wheat. [814]

"Our romantic outings ended when I fell and laid myself up with a dislocated wrist. [815] Although I knew Maria and her husband were leaving Paris for Antwerp on October 5, I sent a note to her that morning: 'I have passed the night in so much pain that I have not closed my eyes. It is with infinite regret therefore that I must relinquish your charming company for that of the surgeon whom I have sent for to examine into the cause of this change. I am in hopes it is only the having rattled a little too freely over the pavement yesterday. If you do not go today I shall still have the pleasure of seeing you again.' Maria replied by return messenger that she would be leaving that morning, and said that she was 'very, very sorry for having been the cause of your pains in the night.' [816]

Maria Cosway

"Despite my wrist pain, I accompanied the Cosways as far as St-Denis, and having performed the last sad office of handing Maria into her carriage at the pavilion de St-Denis, and seeing the wheels of her carriage get actually into motion, I turned on my heel and walked, more dead than alive, to the opposite door, where my own carriage was awaiting me. [817] Returning home, I sat by the fireside and wrote Maria, with my left hand, a long letter."

"Your letter has become known as 'A Dialogue between My Head and My Heart,' [818] and, in my opinion, it clearly shows that you had formed a strong romantic attachment to this beautiful married woman."

"Certainly my statement that 'I am indeed the most wretched of all earthly beings expresses how emotionally devastating Maria's departure for England was to me.'"

"Yes, but then you allow your head to admonish you for becoming emotionally attached to Maria, arguing that 'the art of life is the art of avoiding pain,' by retiring 'within ourselves.'"

"It is a polemic that allows in the end the heart to triumph by knowing that 'nobody will care for him that cares for nobody' and that 'hope is sweeter than despair.'" [819]

"With such an emotionally charged beginning, how did the relationship end?"

"The next few months saw letters back and forth between us, in English, in Italian, at first passionate, then scolding, and ultimately cooling."

"In your 'Head and Heart' letter you worried that you and Maria might not see one another again. Did you?"

"Yes. The next year in September she returned to Paris for a three-month visit, but we saw almost nothing of each other during that time."

"Why?"

"The reason I recall was that 'from the mere effect of chance, she happened to be from home several times when I called on her, and I, when she called on me.'" [820]

"Or perhaps," I said, "the spark of romance had died."

An enigmatic smile crossed Jefferson's face. "Actually I planned a 'great dinner' in Maria's honor in early December and left the selection of some of the guests to her. She attended the dinner but left early. She was leaving for London the next day, and I made plans to have breakfast with her and accompany her part of the way. When I showed up for breakfast, Maria was gone. She left a note that showed her annoyance with me. 'I cannot breakfast with you tomorrow; I bid you adieu. Once is sufficiently painful, for I leave you with very melancholy ideas. You have given, my dear sir, all of your commissions to Mr. Trumbull, and I have the reflection that I cannot be useful to you.' A few days later she wrote again saying that we had met so little because I did not want to share her company with other people." [821]

"Was that the situation?"

"Yes, but only unless it be a fault to love my friends so dearly as to wish to enjoy their company in the only way it yields enjoyment, that is, *en petit comité*. I told her, 'you make everybody love you. You are sought and surrounded therefore by all. Your mere domestic cortege was so numerous, *et si imposante*, that one could not approach you quite at their ease, nor could you so unpremeditatedly mount into the phaeton and hie away to the Bois de Boulogne, St-Cloud, Marly, St-Germain, etc. Add to this the distance at which you were placed from me.' I ended that letter saying, 'When you come again, you must be nearer, and more extempore.'" [822]

"Did you meet again?"

"No, but we remained friends and we corresponded for the rest of our lives."

"What happened to Maria?"

"When she learned that I was leaving France for America, she wrote and said she hoped I could stop in London to see her, but that was not possible. A year later I learned from Lucy Paradise that Maria was pregnant. [823] Several months later I received a letter from Maria reproaching me for not writing to her. [824] I wrote and congratulated her on her pregnancy. [825] I next heard that she had left her philandering husband and child and fled to Paris with Luigi Marchesi, a famous Italian singer. [826] About three years later I was told that she had entered a convent, but eventually returned to her husband and daughter in London. The death of her daughter at age six, and other circumstances, threw Maria into a deep depression, and she left for Paris in the hope of reviving her artistic career. It didn't work out, and she entered a convent in Lyon, but after a brief stay, she went to Lodi, Italy and founded a convent school for girls. 'Our letters had been rare but they let see that her gaiety was gone, and her mind entirely placed on a world to come.'" [827]

"One's spirits—high or low—often motivate behavior," Franklin said.

We paused for a moment to savor the rich, honey-like taste of the Yquem wine. "As I understand the situation, Dr. Franklin, you asked Congress to relieve you of you duties as minister to France. Why?" I said.

"I was approaching my eightieth birthday, my work in France was done, and although I hated to leave my French friends, I felt it time to go home. I sent Congress my resignation. On May 2, 1785, I sent a letter to Adams advising him that Paul Randolph Randall, a New York lawyer, had arrived in Paris with the commission papers appointing Adams minister to the Court of St. James's. Adams went to the Hôtel d'Orléans, where Randall was staying, and picked up his commission. He then went to Jefferson's place and found that Jefferson had received his commission as sole minister to France along with confirmation that my resignation had been accepted by Congress." [828]

"Were your French friends sad to see you leave them, Dr. Franklin?" With tears in his eyes, he nodded. "They did everything to persuade me to stay, but my work was done, and I thought 'tis time I should go home, and go to bed.' [829] At our final meeting Madame Brillon, a dear friend, said, 'If it ever pleases you to remember the woman who loved you most, think of me.' As I was boarding the boat I received a note from Madame Helvétius, 'Come back, my dear friend, come back to us.' I had traveled from Paris to the port of Le Havre in Queen Marie-Antoinette's personal enclosed litter borne by Spanish mules." [830]

Jefferson's diplomatic calling card.

"When Dr. Franklin left Passy for home, I came to see him off," Jefferson said. "It seemed as if the village had lost its patriarch. The Chaumonts, and his two favorite lady-friends, Madame Brillon and Madame Helvétius, begged him to stay and spend his remaining years with them. [831] The ladies smothered him with embraces, and when he introduced me as his successor, I told him I wished he would transfer those privileges to me. 'You are too young a man,' he said." [832]

"I know you were sorry to see Dr. Franklin leave, but did your appointment please you?" I said

"I was very pleased with my appointment and wrote to Monroe, 'I have received the appointment of Congress to succeed Dr. Franklin here. I give them my sincere thanks for this mark of their favor. I wish I were as able to render services which would justify their choice as I am zealous to do it.'" [833]

"Did the French ever ask why Congress appointed you to replace Dr. Franklin?" I said.

"Yes, and when asked whether I had replaced Dr. Franklin, I would reply, 'No one can replace him, sir, I am only his successor.'"

"How did it feel, Dr. Franklin, to be home after so many years away," I said.

"It felt good. During my years in England, I became the friend of David Hartley, a merchant, inventor, and member of Parliament, who had worked hard for peace between America and Great Britain both before and during the war. In fact, Lord Shelburne sent him to Paris to conduct the final peace negotiations, and he signed the Treaty of Paris with John Adams, John Jay and me on September 3, 1783. Before I left Passy for home I wrote to Hartley, 'I cannot quit the coasts of Europe without taking leave of my dear friend Mr. Hartley. We were long fellow-laborers in the best of works, the Work of Peace. I leave you still in the field; but having finished my day's task, I am going home *to go to bed*. Wish me a good night's rest, as I do you a pleasant evening. Adieu.'" [834]

"But the 'ease and rest' that you had looked forward to, was not to be, was it?" I said

"No. When my two grandsons and I arrived at Philadelphia's Market Street wharf, we were warmly greeted by a crowd that accompanied us to my door. I was in the 'bosom of my family' and found 'four new little paddlers who cling

Signatures to Treaty of Paris, 1783

about the knees of their Grandpapa and afford me great pleasure.' I resumed club meetings, played cribbage and cards with friends, did a little gardening, and gave up drinking wine." [835]

"Gave up drinking wine?" I said.

"Yes," Franklin said with a sad smile. "The pain from my gout and the stone had become quite severe, and as I thought that wine might be a contributing factor, I decided to give it up—at least temporarily. [836] But as you said, the 'ease and rest' was not to be. A few weeks after my arrival, I was elected to the executive council of Pennsylvania, and the council elected me their president or head of the Commonwealth of Pennsylvania, a position I held for three years. In March 1787, the Pennsylvania Assembly appointed me a delegate to the Constitutional Convention that met in Philadelphia in May." [837]

"When the Constitutional Convention met, did you have any doubts about its success, Dr. Franklin?"

"First, I thought the presence of George Washington essential to the success of the convention and told him so. [838] Fortunately, he was persuaded and came to Philadelphia and served as president. In a letter to Thomas, I expressed my hope that good would emerge from the meeting, fearing that 'If it does not do good it must do harm, as it will show that we have not wisdom enough among us to govern ourselves, and will strengthen the opinion that popular governments cannot long support themselves.' [839]

Franklin's return to Philadelphia in 1785.

"While the last delegates were signing the Constitution, I looked at the president's chair, on the back of which was painted a picture of the sun, and commented that 'I have often in the course of the session, and the vicissitudes of my hopes and fears as to its issue, looked at that behind the president without being able to tell whether it was rising or setting.

256

But now at length, I have the happiness to know that it is a rising and not a setting sun.'[840]

"After the new government, headed by Washington as president, had taken office, I wrote in the spring of 1789 to Charles Carroll, a senator from Maryland, and my colleague from the 1776 expedition to Canada that, 'Our grand machine has at length begun to work. If any form of government is capable of making a nation happy, ours I think bids fair now for producing that effect.' "[841]

"Mr. Jefferson, I know that you were in France when the Constitutional Convention met in Phila-

First page of the Constitution.

delphia and the Constitution was written, but I believe you were kept informed of how things progressed by your friend, James Madison."

"That's true. And after it had been drafted, I thought there was a great deal of good in it. There were two things, however, which I disliked strongly, and I expressed my thoughts at the time to Madison and George Washington. First, the want of a declaration of rights, and I expressed the hope that the opposition of Virginia would remedy this, and produce such a declaration. Second, the perpetual reeligibility of the president. This, I feared, would make that an office for life, first, and then hereditary. I promised on election to a second term to follow the example of President Washington of voluntary retirement after eight years."[842]

"Mr. Jefferson, you were witness to the unfolding of the French Revolution. Did the major events that set it off come suddenly or evolve over time?"

"For those perceptive enough to look, the signs and warnings were there to see before the actual fighting. Fourteen months before the storming of the Bastille, I noted that the times were sad and eventful. The gay and thoughtless Paris had become a furnace of politics. All the world was now political and mad. Men, women and children talked of nothing else, and they talked much, loud and warm. Society was spoilt by it, at least for those who, like myself, were but lookers on.[843]

"Six months before I left Paris for home, a peasant insurrection was spreading through-out France. The people began to hunt and kill game, tithes and other forms of taxation were ignored, and such feudal rights as *banalité du moulin* and *droit du four*, the obligation of the peasantry to have their corn ground in the seigneur's mills and their bread baked in the seigneur's ovens, were disregarded. This seething disobedience de-

The Bastille

veloped into attacks on the nobility and clergy and their property, especially their archives and feudal title-deeds. [844]

"A month before the storming of the Bastille, I told Madison that the third estate (the common people) requested the nobles and clergy to eliminate the distinction of orders and to do the business of the nation. This was on the tenth. On the fifteenth they moved to declare themselves the National Assembly. The commons had in their chamber almost all the talents of the nation; they were firm and bold, yet moderate. There were indeed among them a number of very hotheaded members; but those of most influence were cool, temperate, and sagacious. The *noblesse*, on the contrary, were absolutely out of their senses. They were so furious they could seldom debate at all. They had few men of moderate talents, and not one of great talent. Their proceedings were very injudicious. The clergy waited to profit of every incident to secure themselves and had no other object in view. Among the commons there was an entire unanimity on the great question of voting by persons. [845]

"On June 20, the representatives of the third estate were locked out of their meeting hall by order of the king. They promptly reassembled on the tennis court at Versailles, and they there bound themselves to each other by an oath never to separate of their own accord till they had settled a constitution for the nation on a solid basis, and if separated by force, that they would reassemble in some other place. [846]

"On the Fourth of July I held a large dinner party

that included, among others, the Marquis de Lafayette, Gouverneur Morris, Philip Mazzei, and John Paradise. After dinner, Morris, whose sentiments were clearly on the side of the nobles, urged Lafayette to preserve, if possible, some constitutional authority to the body of the nobles as the only means of preserving any liberty for the people. The current was setting so strongly against the *noblesse* that I apprehended their destruction. [847]

"Four days later, I advised the French foreign minister, Comte de Montmorin, that my residence had been robbed, for the third time, and I asked for police protection. I was concerned enough to have bars and bells put on the windows of my house. [848]

"The spark that set off the insurrection in Paris was the king's dismissal of his popular finance minister, Jacques Necker. News of Necker's exile to Geneva reached Paris at noon on July 12. Thousands of Parisians flooded the Palais Royal (whose owner, the Duc de Chartres, had joined the third estate), where orators gave the call to arms. That night and the next day, crowds swarmed throughout Paris looking for arms. I told Thomas Paine that, on the morning of July 14, the mobs immediately shut up all the playhouses. The king's foreign troops were advanced into the city. Engagements took place between some of them and the people. The first was at the place Louis XV, where, when a body of German cavalry being drawn up, the people posted themselves behind piles of stone collected there for the bridge, and attacked and drove off the cavalry with stones. Having won the first skirmish, a crowd of more than 7,000 crossed the river and moved on to the Invalides in search of arms and ammunition. [849] When they were refused, the people forced the place and got a large supply of arms. They then went to the Bastille and made the same demand. The governor, after hoisting a flag of truce and deploying a hundred or two within the outer drawbridge, fired on them. The people then charged the Bastille, captured it, beheaded the governor and lieutenant governor, and armed themselves. Gouverneur Morris, on seeing the governor of the Bastille's head paraded through the streets, called it 'the Liberty Pole of France.' "

"Were you actually at the Bastille when the people attacked it?"

"I was not an eyewitness to the siege of the Bastille, but I was privy to eyewitness accounts. The tumults in Paris which took place on the change of the ministry, the slaughter of the people in the assault of the Bastille, the beheading of the governor and lieutenant governor, and the provost des marchands, excited in the king so much concern that bursting from the shackles of his ministers and advisors, he went to the States-General with only his two brothers, opened his heart to them, asked them what he could do to restore peace and happiness to his people, and showed himself ready to do everything for that purpose, promising particularly to send away the troops. The king ordered away all the troops and came to Paris in procession, having in his coach the most popular characters, the States-General walking on foot in two ranks on each side of it, and the Marquis de Lafayette on horseback at their head. There were probably 60,000 or 80,000 armed bourgeois lining the streets through which he was to pass. This was the sum of this astonishing train of events.'[850] Sensing the tumult over, I felt I had seen in the course of fourteen years two such revolutions as were never before seen."[851]

"At some point didn't your involvement in the French Revolution change from spectator to participant?"

"Yes. At the request of Lafayette I allowed my home to become a secret meeting place for Lafayette and seven others attempting to forge a coalition 'to prevent a total dissolution and civil war.'"

"Do you remember what took place at that secret meeting?"

"As I recall the meeting, 'the cloth being removed, and wine set on the table, after the American manner, the marquis introduced the objects of the conference. The discussions began at the hour of four, and were continued till ten o'clock in the evening; during which time I was a silent witness to a coolness and candor of argument unusual in the conflicts of political opinion, to a logical reasoning and chaste eloquence disfigured by no gaudy tinsel of rhetoric or declamation, and truly worthy of being placed parallel with the finest dialogues of antiquity, as handed to us by Xenophon, by Plato and Cicero. The result was an agreement that the king should have a suspensive veto on the laws, that the legislature should be composed of a single body only, and that to be chosen by the people.'[852]

"On September 26, 1789, after five years in France, and with two years of my appointment as minister remaining, my two daughters, my slave-servants, Sally and James Hemings, and I left Paris for what I thought would be a six-month leave of absence. As it turned out, I never returned."

"I gather Dr. Franklin that when you left France in July 1785 you did not have a hint of the revolution to come." I said.

"I was not nearly as perceptive as Thomas that a revolution was on its way in France," Franklin said.

"Why?" I asked.

"I suppose because I lived a cloistered existence during my years in France.

My time was spent almost exclusively with the intelligentsia, the rich, and the privileged. I did not travel beyond Paris and its environs; I did not mingle with the peasantry, so I knew virtually nothing about their plight."

"But by your own admission you witnessed in your travels through England, Scotland, Ireland, and Germany the wretched conditions under which the vast majority of the people lived. Was there any reason to believe that living conditions were better in France?"

"I suppose my answer must be that the success of my mission to France depended on persuading the ruling class to support our war effort economically and militarily, and that took one hundred percent of my time. But I make no apologies for my time in Paris and the nine years 'of happiness I enjoyed there in the sweet society of a people whose conversation was instructive, whose manners were highly pleasing, and who, above all the nations of the world, had, in the greatest perfection, the art of making themselves beloved by strangers.' "[853]

"After you returned to America, Mr. Jefferson, did you stay in touch with your French friends as the cauldron of revolution boiled around them?"

"Yes. My friend Condorcet, a passionate revolutionary, was an influential member of the General Assembly. He chaired many commissions and committees of the revolutionary governments, and became a great champion of civil rights that included political freedom and religious tolerance. Two years after I left France I wrote to him and said, 'I am looking ardently to the completion of the glorious work in which your country is engaged. I view the general condition of Europe as hanging on the success or failure of France.' "[854]

"What happened to Condorcet?"

"His influence eroded with the rise to power of Robespierre and the Committee of Public Safety. On October 3, 1793, a warrant was issued for his arrest. He fled Paris, and for a time roamed the French countryside under a fictitious identity and the assumed name of Pierre Simon. Eventually, he went into hiding in a Paris garret and wrote while under the sentence of death 'A Sketch for a Historical Picture of the Progress of the Human Mind.'[855]

"He was arrested on March 27, 1794 and imprisoned in Bourg-Egalité. He died the next day, probably suicide by poison."[856]

"America was lucky to be spared the madness and bloodletting that cost revolutionary France so many of its best and brightest. Even Lafayette almost lost his life, didn't he?" I said.

"Yes, though at first he seemed invulnerable. Shortly after the fall of the

Bastille, Lafayette was appointed commandant of the Paris National Guard, and for the next two years he was the most powerful man in France. Disillusioned with the course the French Revolution was taking, he resigned as commandant of the guard, but a year later assumed command of the Army of the Center at Metz to meet the Austrian invasion of France. It was at this time that I wrote to him, 'Behold you, then, my dear friend, at the head of a great army, establishing the liberties of your country against a foreign enemy. May heaven favor your cause, and make you the channel through which it may pour its favors.'[857]

"Shortly thereafter, in August 1792, the Monarchy officially fell, and the Committee of Public Safety led by Danton and Robespierre immediately accused Lafayette of treason, and issued a warrant for his arrest. Knowing that arrest was tantamount to being guillotined, he attempted an escape to Belgium, but he was captured and imprisoned for five years at Wesel, Magdeberg, Neisse, and Olmutz."

"Did the United States try to get him freed?"

"Certainly, but we had virtually no influence with the Austrian emperor. Lafayette's release from prison was negotiated by Gouverneur Morris in 1797 through the influence of Napoleon. When he returned to France, he learned that his fortune had been wiped out in the revolution, and he retired to La-Grange, a place he owned near Paris and became a gentleman farmer."

"If you don't mind, I would like to change the subject to something more pleasant than the terrible losses that attended the French revolution."

Both Franklin and Jefferson nodded their enthusiastic approval, and I turned to Franklin. "Dr. Franklin, as a septuagenarian, you seemed to have found the fountain of youth."

"I did? Now that is something I would like to know about, Jack. Refresh my memory."

"You wrote a friend in Philadelphia, 'I do not find that I grow any older. Being arrived at seventy, and considering that by traveling further in the same road, I should probably be led to the grave, I stopped short, turned about, and walked back again, which having done these four years, you may now call me sixty-six. Advise those old friends of ours to follow my example; keep up your spirits, and that will keep up your bodies; you will no more stoop under the weight of age than if you had swallowed a handspike.' "[858]

"I may have talked of turning back my age, but at age seventy-four I had an attack of the gout that laid me up for six weeks and inspired my essay *Dialogue between Franklin and the Gout.* Two years later, in the midst of the peace negotiations, a bladder-stone attack suddenly disabled me, and never left me during the rest of my life."[859]

"We spoke earlier about Mr. Jefferson's three crowning achievements, writing the Declaration of Independence and the Virginia Statute of Religious Freedom, and founding the University of Virginia. It occurs to me, Dr. Franklin, that you are the only Founding Father who signed all four of the major documents that secured our independence and freedom: the Declaration of Independence in 1776; the Treaty of Alliance with France in 1778; the Treaty of Paris in 1783; and the Constitution of the United States in 1787."

"That's true, and I am proud to have been associated with all four of those great documents because of what they meant to our freedom."

I looked at our glasses; they were empty. I had asked all the questions I could think of. It was time to go. "Dr. Franklin, Mr. Jefferson, it has been a pleasure and an honor to have been with you, and I thank you for having me to dinner and answering my questions. It is an evening I will always remember."

We stood, and as we shook hands, I said, "Do you have any thoughts or messages you would like me to take back to your fellow Americans?"

"Yes," Jefferson said. "I would like to send back the same message I expressed in the last letter I ever wrote. Because of my health I had to decline an invitation to attend a celebration in Washington of the 50th Anniversary of American independence. With a knowledge of what freedom meant then, and a prescience of what it would mean to future generations, I said, 'May it be to the world, what I believe it will be (to some parts sooner, to others later, but finally to all), the signal of arousing men to burst the chains under which monkish ignorance and superstition had persuaded them to bind themselves, and to assume the blessings and security of self-government. All eyes are opened, or opening, to the rights of man. The general spread of the light of science has already laid open to every view the palpable truth, that the mass of mankind has not been born with saddles on their backs, nor a favored few booted and spurred, ready to ride them legitimately, by the grace of God. These are grounds of hope for others. For ourselves let the annual return of this day[860] forever refresh our recollections of these rights, and an undiminished devotion to them.' "[861]

I turned to Dr. Franklin. "I would hope, Jack, that all of my fellow Americans will always remember that the 'blessings and security of self-government' are embodied in the Constitution. I remember on leaving the final session of the Constitutional Convention a woman accosted me and demanded, 'after four months of secrecy, what have you produced?' I stopped dead in my tracks, looked her in the eye, and said, 'A republic, if you can keep it.'" [862]

Petit entered and showed me out to a waiting carriage. Only after he shut the carriage door did it occur to me that I had no idea where I was headed. Nevertheless, I was strangely content as the gentle rocking of the carriage began to lull me to sleep.

The rocking seemed to intensify, and I was surprised to find my fiancée shaking me awake. "I got back early and I wanted to surprise you," she said. Looking around, I saw that everything was as before. "Jack, are you all right?"

It must have been a dream. Yet it was so real, and I had learned so much!

Bibliography and Works Consulted

Adams, Charles Francis, ed. *Letters of Mrs. Adams, The Wife of John Adams*, Boston: 1848. [Hereafter cited as *Letters of Mrs. Adams*.]

Adams, Charles Francis, ed. *The Works of John Adams*, 10 vols., Boston: 1851. [Hereafter cited as *Works*.]

Adams, John Quincy. *Memoirs*, edited by Charles Francis Adams, 12 vols., Philadelphia: Lippincott & Co., 1874. [Hereafter cited as *Memoirs*.]

Aldridge, Alfred Owen. *Benjamin Franklin: Philosopher and Man*. Philadelphia: J. B. Lippencott, 1965. [Hereafter cited as Aldridge.]

Ambrose, Stephen E. *Undaunted Courage: Meriwether Lewis, Thomas Jefferson, and the Opening of the American West*, New York: Simon & Schuster, 1996. [Hereafter cited as Ambrose.]

Anderson, Burton. *The Wine Atlas of Italy*, New York: 1990. [Hereafter cited as Anderson.]

Andrews, C. Buryn, ed. *The Torrington Diaries, John Byng, 5th Viscount*, 4 vols., London: 1934–38. [Hereafter cited as Andrews.]

Bacon, Edmund. *Jefferson at Monticello*, edited by James A. Bear Jr., 1967. [Hereafter cited as Bacon.]

Bear, James A. Jr. and Lucia C. Stanton, eds. *Jefferson's Memorandum Books: Accounts, with Legal Records and Miscellany 1767–1826*, 2 vols., Princeton, NJ: Princeton University Press, 1997. [Hereafter cited as Bear & Stanton.]

Beirne, Francis F. *Shout Treason: The Trial of Aaron Burr*, New York: 1959. [Hereafter cited as Beirne.]

Beran, Michael Knox. *Jefferson's Demons: Portrait of a Restless Mind*, New York: Free Press, 2003. [Hereafter cited as Beran.]

Bernard, John. *Reflections of America, 1791–1811*, New York: 1887. [Hereafter cited as Bernard.]

Betts, Edwin Morris. *Thomas Jefferson's Garden Book*, Philadelphia, 1944. [Hereafter cited as Betts.]

Boswell, James. *Boswell on the Grand Tour: Italy, Corsica, and France, 1765–1766*, New York: McGraw Hill, 1955. [Hereafter cited as Boswell.]

Boyd, Julian P. "Silas Deane: Death by a Kindly Teacher of Treason?" *William & Mary Quarterly*, 3rd Ser., XVI (April and July), 165–187, 319–342. [Hereafter cited as Boyd.]

Boyd, Julian P., ed. *Papers of Thomas Jefferson*, Princeton, NJ: Princeton University Press, [Hereafter cited as PTJ.]

Bowers, Claude G. *The Young Jefferson: 1743–1789*, Boston: Houghton Mifflin, 1945. [Hereafter cited as Bowers.]

Brands, H.W. *The First American: The Life and Times of Benjamin Franklin*, New York: Doubleday, 2000. [Hereafter cited as Brands.]

Broadbent, Michael. *Michael Broadbent's Vintage Wine: Fifty Years of Tasting Three Centuries of Wines*, New York: Harcourt, 2000. [Hereafter cited as Broadbent.]

Brodie, Fawn M. *Thomas Jefferson: An Intimate History*, New York: W.W. Norton & Company, 1974. [Hereafter cited as Brodie.]

Brown, Everett Somerville, ed. *William Plumer's Memorandum of Proceedings in the United States Senate, 1803–1807*, New York: 1923. [Hereafter cited as Brown.]

Burke, Thomas. *Travel in England*, London: 1942. [Hereafter cited as Burke.]

Butterfield, L.H., ed. *Diary and Autobiography of John Adams*, 4 vols., Cambridge, MA: 1961. [Hereafter cited as Butterfield.]

Chastellux, Francois Jean, Marquis de. *Travels in North America in the Years 1780, 1781 and 1782*, 2 vols., Chapel Hill, NC: 1963. [Hereafter cited as Chastellux.]

Clark, Ronald W. *Benjamin Franklin: A Biography*, New York: Random House, 1983. [Hereafter cited as Clark.]

DeConde, Alexander. *This Affair Louisiana*, New York: Charles Scribner's Sons, 1976. [Hereafter cited as DeConde.]

Dion, Roger. *Histoire de la Vigne et du Vin en France*, Paris: 1959. [Hereafter cited as Dion.]

Dumbauld, Edward. *Thomas Jefferson: American Tourist*, Norman, OK: 1946. [Hereafter cited as Dumbauld.]

Eckenrode, H.J. *Separation of Church and State in Virginia*, Richmond, VA: 1910. [Hereafter cited as Eckenrode.]

Ferrand, Max, ed. *The Records of the Federal Convention of 1787*, 4 vols., New Haven, CT: Yale University Press, 1911. See: http://www.memory.loc.gov. [Hereafter cited as Ferrand.]

Fisher, M.F.K. *Map of Another Town*, Boston, MA: 1967. [Hereafter cited as Fisher.]

Fitch, Raymond E., ed. *Breaking with Burr: Harman Blennerhassett's Journal*, Athens, OH: Ohio University Press, 1988. [Hereafter cited as Fitch.]

Fitzpatrick, John C., ed. *The Writings of George Washington from the Original Manuscript Sources 1745–1799*, 24 vols., Washington, DC: U.S. Government Printing Office. [Hereafter cited as Fitzpatrick.]

Fleming, Candace. *Benjamin Franklin's Almanac: Being a True Account of the Good Gentleman's Life*, New York: Simon & Schuster, 2003. [Hereafter cited as Fleming.]

Franklin, Benjamin. *Autobiography*. [Hereafter cited as ABF.]

Franklin, Benjamin. *Franklin Papers*, American Philosophical Society, Philadelphia. [Hereafter cited as the *Franklin Papers*.]

Franklin, Benjamin. *The Papers of Benjamin Franklin*. See Labaree, Leonard.

Foner, Phillip S., ed. *Basic Writings of Thomas Jefferson*, New York: Willey Book Company, 1944. [Hereafter cited as Foner.]

Gabler, James M. *Passions: The Wines and Travels of Thomas Jefferson*, Baltimore, MD: Bacchus Press Ltd., 1995. [Hereafter cited as Gabler.]

Gabler, James M. *Wine into Words: A History and Bibliography of Wine Books in the English Language*, Baltimore, MD: Bacchus Press Ltd., 2004. [Hereafter cited as *Wine into Words*.]

Garlick, Richard Cecil, Jr. *Philip Mazzei, Friend of Jefferson: His Life and Letters*, Baltimore: The Johns Hopkins Press, 1933. [Hereafter cited as Garlick.]

Gibbon, Edward. *Private Letters, 1753–1794*, 2 vols., London: J. Murray, 1896. [Hereafter cited as Gibbon.]

Gordon, John Steele. *An Empire of Wealth: The Epic History of American Economic Power*, New York: HarperCollins, 2004. [Hereafter cited as Gordon.]

Halliday, E.M. *Understanding Thomas Jefferson*, New York: HarperCollins, 2001. [Hereafter cited as Halliday.]

Henderson, Alexander. *The History of Ancient and Modern Wines*, London: 1824. [Hereafter cited as Henderson.]

Idzerda, Stanley J., ed. *Lafayette in the Age of the American Revolution: Selected Letters and Papers, 1776–1790*, 2 vols., Ithaca, NY: Cornell University Press, 1977–1983. [Hereafter cited as Lafayette.]

Isaacson, Walter. *Benjamin Franklin: An American Life*. New York: Simon & Schuster, 2003. [Hereafter cited as Isaacson.]

Jefferson, Thomas. *Autobiography*. [Hereafter cited as ATJ.]

Jefferson, Thomas. *Notes on the State of Virginia*. [Hereafter cited as *Notes on Virginia*.]

Jefferson, Thomas. *The Papers of Thomas Jefferson*. See Boyd, Julian P.

Jefferson, Thomas. *Thomas Jefferson's Tavern Bills*, Charlottesville: University of Virginia. [Hereafter cited as TJ's tavern bills, UVA.]

Johnson, Hugh. *Vintage: The Story of Wine*, New York: Simon & Schuster, 1989. [Hereafter cited as *Vintage.*]

Johnson, Hugh. *The Atlas of German Wine*, New York, 1986. [Hereafter cited as Johnson.]

Johnson, Hugh. *The World Atlas of Wine*, 4th ed., London: 1994. [Hereafter cited as H. Johnson.]

Jullien, André. *The Topography of All Known Vineyards*, London: 1824. [Hereafter cited as Jullien.]

Kay, Bill and Cailean Maclean. *Knee Deep in Claret*, Edinburgh: Mainstream Publishing, 1983. [Hereafter cited as Kay.]

Labaree, Leonard, ed. *Papers of Benjamin Franklin*, New Haven, CT: Yale University Press, 1959. [Hereafter cited as PBF.]

Labaree, Leonard, and Bell, Whitefield J. Jr., ed. *Mr. Franklin: A Selection from His Personal Letters*, New Haven, CT: Yale University Press, 1956. [Hereafter cited as Labaree and Bell.]

Lavalle, M.J. *Histoire de la Vigne, et Statistique et des Grand Vins de la Côte d'Or*, Paris: 1855. [Hereafter cited as Lavalle.]

Latzko, Andreas. *Lafayette*, New York: 1936. [Hereafter cited as Latzko.]

Lemay, J.A. Leo. *Benjamin Franklin Writings*, New York: Library of America, 1987. [Hereafter cited as Lemay.]

Lewis, James E., Jr., *The Louisiana Purchase: Jefferson's Noble Bargain?* Charlottesville: Thomas Jefferson Foundation, 2003. [Hereafter cited as Lewis.]

Library of Congress. *Thomas Jefferson Papers*. [Hereafter cited as LCTJP, Reel number.]

Lopez, Claude-Anne. *Mon Cher Papa*, New Haven: Yale University Press, 1966. [Hereafter cited as Lopez.]

Lopez, Claude-Anne and Eugenia W. Herbert. *The Private Franklin: The Man and His Family*, New York: W.W. Norton, 1975. [Hereafter cited as Lopez & Herbert.]

MacNeil, Karen. *The Wine Bible*, New York: Workman Publishing, 2001. [Hereafter cited as MacNeil.]

Malone, Dumas. *Jefferson and His Times*, 6 vols., Boston: Little Brown and Company, 1948–1977. [Hereafter cited as Malone and volume title.]

Mazzei, Philip, translated by Howard R. Marraro. *Memoirs of the Life and*

Peregrinations of the Florentine Philip Mazzei, 1730–1816, New York, 1942. [Hereafter cited as Mazzei.]

McCullough, David. *John Adams*, New York: Simon & Schuster, 2001. [Hereafter cited as McCullough.]

Morgan, Edmund S. *Benjamin Franklin*. New Haven: Yale University Press, 2002. [Hereafter cited as Morgan.]

Nevins, Allan and Commager, Henry Steele. *The Pocket History of the United States*, New York:1951. [Hereafter cited as Nevins & Commager.]

Nolan, J. Bennett. *Benjamin Franklin in Scotland and Ireland 1759 and 1771*, Philadelphia: University of Pennsylvania Press, 1938. [Hereafter cited as Nolan.]

Padover, Saul K. *A Jefferson Profile: As Revealed in His Letters*, New York: John Day Company, 1956. [Hereafter cited as Padover.]

Parton, James. *Life and Times of Benjamin Franklin*, 2 vols., New York: Mason Brothers, 1864. [Hereafter cited as Parton.]

Parker, Robert M. Jr. *Burgundy*, New York: Simon & Schuster, 1990. [Hereafter cited as Parker.]

Peterson, Merrill. D. *Thomas Jefferson and the New Nation*, New York: Oxford University Press, 1970. [Hereafter cited as Peterson.]

Pope-Hennessy, James. *Aspects of Provence*, London: 1952. [Hereafter cited as Pope.]

Rafalko, Frank J., ed. *A Counterintelligence Reader. American Revolution to World War II*, Vol. 1, Chapter 1: "The American Revolution and the Post Revolutionary Era: A Historical Legacy," www.fas.org. [Hereafter cited as Rafalko.]

Randall, Willard Sterne. *Thomas Jefferson: A Life*, New York: Henry Holt, 1993. [Hereafter cited as Randall.]

Redding, Cyrus. *A History and Description of Modern Wines*, London: 1833. [Hereafter cited as Redding.]

Rice, Howard C., Jr. *Thomas Jefferson's Paris*, Princeton, NJ: 1976. [Hereafter cited as Rice.]

Robinson, Jancis, ed. *The Oxford Companion to Wine*, Oxford: Oxford University Press, 1994. [Hereafter cited as Robinson.]

Roosevelt, Theodore. *Gouverneur Morris, American Statesman Series*, vol. III, Boston: 1899. [Hereafter cited as Roosevelt.]

Saussure, Horace-Benedict de. *Voyages dan les Alpes*, 4 vols., 1779–90. [Hereafter cited as Saussure.]

Seale, William. *The President's House*, Washington, D.C.: 1986. [Hereafter cited as Seale.]

Seward, Desmond. *Monks and Wine*, London: Mitchell Beazley, 1979. [Hereafter cited as Seward.]

Shaw, Thomas George. *Wine, the Vine, and the Cellar*, 2nd edition, London: Longman, Green, Longman, Roberts & Green, 1864. [Hereafter cited as Shaw.]

Simon, André L. *Bottlescrew Days*, London: Duckworth, 1926. [Hereafter cited as Simon.]

Simon, André L. *The Star Dinner Accounts*, London: The Wine & Food Society, 1959. [Hereafter cited as A. Simon.]

Smyth, Albert Henry, ed. *The Writings of Benjamin Franklin*, New York: 1905–07. [Hereafter cited as *Writings*.]

Sparks, Jared. *Memoirs of the Life and Travels of John Ledyard*, New York: 1828. [Hereafter cited as Ledyard.]

Sparks, Jared, ed. *The Works of Thomas Jefferson*, Boston: 1840. [Hereafter cited as Sparks.]

Srodes, James. *Franklin: The Essential Founding Father*, Washington, D.C.: Regency Publishing, Inc., 2002. [Hereafter cited as Srodes.]

Stanton, Lucia C. "Wine and Food at the White House, The Presidential Table," from *Jefferson and Wine*, edited by Treville Lawrence Sr., The Plains, VA: 1976. [Hereafter cited as Stanton.]

Stein, Susan. *The Worlds of Thomas Jefferson*, New York: Harry N. Abrams, Inc., 1993. [Hereafter cited as Stein.]

Stinchcomb, William. *The American Revolution and The French Alliance*, Syracuse, NY: 1969. [Hereafter cited as Stinchcomb.]

Stone, Geoffrey R. *Perilous Times: Free Speech in Wartime From the Sedition Act of 1798 to the War on Terrorism*, New York: W.W. Norton, 2004. [Hereafter cited as Stone.]

Taylor, Robert J., ed. *Diary of John Quincy Adams*, 2 vols., Cambridge, MA: 1981. [Hereafter cited as Taylor.]

Thomas, Evan. *John Paul Jones: Sailor, Hero, Father of the American Navy*, New York: Simon & Schuster, 2003. [Hereafter cited as Thomas.]

Smollett, Tobias. *Travels Through France and Italy from the Miscellaneous Works of Tobias Smollett*, London: 1856. [Hereafter cited as Smollett.]

Tise, Larry E., ed. *Benjamin Franklin and Women*, University Park: The Pennsylvania State University Press, 2000. [Hereafter cited as Tise.]

Trumbull, John. *The Autobiography of Colonel John Trumbull, 1756–1843*, New Haven, CT: 1953. [Hereafter cited as Trumbull.]

Turner, W.J. *The Englishmen's Country*, London: 1935. [Hereafter cited as Turner.]

Van Doren, Carl. *Benjamin Franklin*, New York: Viking Press, 1938. [Hereafter cited as Van Doren.]

Van Doren, Carl. *The Secret History of the American Revolution*, New York: Viking Press, 1941. [Hereafter cited as *Secret History*.]

Wandell, Samuel H. and Minnigerode, Meade. *Aaron Burr*, New York: G.P. Putnam's Sons, vol. 1, 1927. [Hereafter cited as Wandell.]

Weld, Isaac, Jr. *Travels through the States of North America and the Provinces of Upper and Lower Canada during the years 1795, 1796 and 1797*, 2nd ed., London: 1799. [Hereafter cited as Weld.]

Weymouth, Lally, ed. *Thomas Jefferson: The Man The World His Influence*, New York: G.P. Putnam's Sons, 1973. [Hereafter cited as Weymouth.]

Wheelan, Joseph. *Jefferson's War: First War on Terror 1801–1805*, New York: Carroll & Graf, 2003. [Hereafter cited as Wheelan.]

Whipple, A.B.C. *To the Shores of Tripoli: The Birth of the U.S. Navy and Marines*, Annapolis, MD: Naval Institute Press, 2001. [Hereafter cited as Whipple.]

Wood, Gordon S. *The Americanization of Benjamin Franklin*, New York: The Penguin Press, 2004. [Hereafter cited as Wood.]

Wright, Esmond. *Franklin of Philadelphia*, Cambridge: Harvard University Press, 1986. [Hereafter cited as Wright.]

Young, Arthur. *Travels During the Years* 1787, 1788 and 1789, London: 1792. [Hereafter cited as Young.]

Ziff, Larzer. *Return Passages: Great American Travel Writing 1780–1910*, Hew Haven: Yale University Press, 2000. [Hereafter cited as Ziff.]

Source Notes

1. Tobias Smollett, (1721–1771) a Scottish physician and novelist, traveled many of the same routes as Jefferson and describes the dangers encountered on such a crossing.
2. TJ to Benjamin Rush, January 15, 1811; Gabler, 115, 189; *Wine into Words*, 231.
3. Hôtel de Langeac was demolished in 1842, and is now represented by a plaque on a commercial building located half way up the Champs-Elysées on the right. The house was located just inside the city limits on the Champs-Elysées and the rue de Berri. Jean F.T. Chalgrin, a popular architect of that time, designed it in 1768. Jefferson rented it for 7,500 livres a year. Stein, 22–23
4. The artist was Jean-Simon Berthelemy.
5. Jefferson's description is a composite from various sources including David McCullough, Daniel Webster, Edmund Bacon, a Monticello overseer, and portrait paintings.
6. TJ to Ferdnand Grand, 20 April 1790, PTJ, XVI: 369.
7. Wood, 51.
8. Van Doren, 637.
9. Clark, 309–10; Gabler, 204.
10. Gabler.
11. TJ to John Bannister, 19 June 1787, PTJ, XI: 477.
12. Jefferson's "Notes on Macaroni," PTJ, XIV: 544.
13. PTJ, XIII: 30; Gabler, 153.
14. TJ to Nicholas Lewis, 17 September 1787, PTJ, XII: 135; TJ to Baron Geismar, 13 July 1788; Bear & Stanton; Gabler, 31, 71, 147.
15. BF to John Lathrop, 31 May 1788.
16. BF to Barbeu DuBourg, Late April 1773, PBF, 20:189–90, an English translation can be found in Smyth, *Writings*, VI: 42–44.
17. Meriwether Lewis was President Jefferson's first secretary.
18. Gordon, xiii–xiv.
19. The American-Israeli Cooperative Enterprise. Sources: Chronology of Terrorist Incidents 1961–2001, State Department 'Patterns of Terrorism' reports 1995–2000; State

Department Institute for Counter-Terrorism database.

20. The words of President George W. Bush.

21. TJ to James Monroe, 11 November 1784, PTJ, VII: 511–12. Tripoli is today's Libya.

22. American commissioners Thomas Jefferson and John Adams to John Jay, 28 March 1786, PTJ, IX: 358; TJ to William Carmichael, 5 May 1786; TJ to James Monroe, 10 May 1786.

23. TJ to John Adams, 11 July 1786, PTJ, X: 123–25; ATJ.

24. Malone, Dumas, *Jefferson the President: Second Term 1805–1809*, 37–38; Peterson, 799.

25. Wheelan, 190–94, 214–15.

26. Wheelan, 203–07; Whipple, 177–240. Before starting his march across the desert, Eaton gave himself the rank of general.

27. TJ to John Jay, 23 Aug. 1785, PTJ, VIII: 427.

28. BF to William Strahan, 5 July 1775, PBF, 22: 85.

29. Isaacson, 421–22; Van Doren, 702.

30. Stone, 539–40, 552–54.

31. Nevins & Commager, 143.

32. Stone, 36–38.

33. TJ to Abigail Adams, 22 July 1804, TJ to Abigail Adams, 11 September 1804, Foner, 668–671; McCullough 577.

34. The initial U.S. Army investigation was titled *Investigation of Intelligence Activities at Abu Ghraib*, conducted by General Taguba. Taguba's report found widespread abuse of Iraqi prisoners and detainees by Military Police and Military Intelligence. Two other high profile reports substantiated the Abu Ghraib tortures: *Final Report of the Independent Panel to Review DoD Detention Operations* (The Schlesinger Report), and the *AR 15–6 Investigation of the Abu Ghraib Detention Facility and 205th Military Intelligence Brigade* (The Fay Report). It was reported in *The New York Times* that "Thousands of pages of military reports and documents released under the Freedom of Information Act to the American Civil Liberties Union have demonstrated that abuse like that at Abu Ghraib involved multiple branches of the service in Afghanistan, Iraq, and Guantánamo Bay and lasted much longer than initially indicated." *The New York Times*, Thursday, January 6, 2005. For other comment on torture see *The New York Times*, Thursday, February 10, 2005; Saturday, March 12; and Friday, March 18, 2005.

35. BF to John Paul Jones, 28 April 1779, PBF, 29: 386–87.

36. John Paul Jones to BF, 1 May 1779, PBF, 29: 405–06.

37. TJ to Patrick Henry, 27 March 1779, PTJ, II: 242.

38. Malone, *Jefferson the Virginian*, 293.

39. Malone, *Jefferson the Virginian*, 293–97; Gabler, 141, 146–47. Hessian troops were a part of the English army fighting in America because of a contract King George, III, had made through the Duke of Brunswich to furnish 4,200 soldiers for service in America. Riedesel's troops were a major part of General Burgoyne's army.

40. Van Doren, 577.

41. Van Doren, 588.

42. Silas Deane served as a commissioner along with Franklin and Arthur Lee at the court of France.

43. Brands, 543–44; Isaacson, 345–46; Van Doren, 590–593; Wood, 190–91; *Secret History*, 59–61.

44. Paul Wentworth to William Eden, 7 January 1778, PBF, 25: 436–38; Isaacson, 345–46; Van Doren, 590–593, Wood, 190–91. The day after Wentworth arrived in Paris, the French foreign minister, Vergennes, wrote to the French minister in Madrid, "The power which first recognizes the independence of the Americans will be the one to gather all the fruits of this war." *Secret History*, 61.

45. Brands, 583–84.

46. Edmund Burke was a member of Parliament, agent for New York, and a friend of Franklin's and the Colonies.

47. Edmund Burke to BF, 15 August 1781; Van Doren, 627–28; Brands, 611.

48. Henry Laurens (1724–1792) was a South Carolina business man who was elected a delegate to the Continental Congress, and succeeded John Hancock as that body's president (November1, 1777 to December 9, 1778.) In 1780 he was sent by Congress to Holland to secure a loan, but he was captured at sea by a British warship and imprisoned in the Tower of London on the charge of high treason. Laurens was released from the Tower after fourteen months, and immediately appointed by Congress a peace commissioner to help negotiate the peace with Great Britain. He participated to some degree with Franklin, Adams and Jay in the peace negotiations, but returned home before the final signing because of ill health.

49. BF to Edmund Burke, 15 October 1781, *Works*, 9: 84–85; Brands, 611–12.

50. Captain Lippincott's court-martial proceedings show that William Franklin was primarily responsible for Huddy's execution. Fitzpatrick, vol. 25: 40, note.

51. Fitzpatrick, vol. 24: 305–306. General Moses Hazen advised General Washington on May 27, 1782, that when the lots were drawn, in the presence of Major Gordon and all the British captains, "the unfortunate lot had fallen on the Honorable Captain Charles Asgill, of the Guards; a young gentleman seventeen [*sic*] years of

age; a most amiable character; the only son of Sir Charles Asgill; Baronet; heir to an extensive fortune; an honorable title; and of course he has great interest in the British court and armies. The British officers are highly enraged at the conduct of Sir Henry Clinton; they have solicited my leave to send an officer to New York on this occasion, or that I would intercede with the minister of war to grant it."

52. The Earl of Shelburne had served as secretary of state for the colonies and had been a close friend and admirer of Franklin's during his years in England.

53. Samuel Cooper to BF, 15 July 1782; Robert Livingston to BF, 23 June 1782; BF to Richard Oswald, 26 July 1782; Isaacson, 413.

54. Isaacson, 413.

55. GW to Brigadier General Elias Dayton, 4 June 1782, Fitzpatrick, vol. 24: 306–07. See also George Washington's letter to John Dickinson 19 June 1782. Despite doubts expressed by Dickinson regarding the legality of retaliation on Asgill, Washington held fast in his determination to carry it out. Washington mentions that Asgill had made application to general Sir Guy Carlton, the new British commander in chief, "begging his interposition to avert his fate." General Washington received a letter from Sir Guy Carleton stating that he was prepared to disclose the results of the court-martial trial of Captain Lippincott for the murder of Captain Huddy 'with other documents and explanations which he *says he has no doubt will give full satisfaction.*' GW to Major General William Heath, 3 August 1782.

56. Instructions to Major General William Heath, 3 August 1782, GW to Heath, 3 August 1782, Fitzpatrick, vol. 24: 456–59.

57. GW to the Secretary at War, 10 June 1782, Fitzpatrick, vol. 25: 40–41.

58. GW to the President of Congress, 25 October 1782.

59. GW to Comte de Vergennes, 21 November 1782.

60. Brands, 189–90.

61. Advice to a Young Tradesman, 1748.

62. ABF.

63. Virtually all of the above, and much of what follows about Franklin's personal life, comes from the *Autobiography of Benjamin Franklin*.

64. Isaacson, 367; Van Doren, 91–92.

65. It is not entirely clear that Franklin's reference in his autobiography to his association with "low women" relates also to his time in London. But given his youth, his "hard-to-be-governed passions," the fact that he was working every day but still broke when he decided to return to Philadelphia, the probabilities are strong that it does relate to this period too.

66. Isaacson, 74–75.

67. It is not clear who William's mother was or when he was born, although a letter from Benjamin to his mother in 1750 seems to place William's birth in 1731. Isaacson, 75–76; Lopez & Herbert, 22–23. Some Franklin biographers have speculated that Deborah was the mother, but this is unlikely for several reasons. First, there are no birth records relating William Franklin to Deborah. Second, Deborah, who had a "turbulent temper," made it known that she did not like William. Daniel Fisher, who boarded with the family while working as a clerk at Franklin's print shop, wrote in his diary that Deborah on seeing William one day, remarked, "Mr. Fisher, there goes the greatest villain on earth." *Pennsylvania Magazine of Historical Biography*, 1893, 276–77; Brands, 24; Isaacson, 75–78; Lopez & Herbert, 60; *Diary of Daniel Fisher*, 28 July 1755, C.R. Howard, ed. Third, Franklin's friend George Roberts said, "'Tis generally known here his birth is illegitimate and his mother not in good circumstances." Brands, 111.

68. Wood, 52.

69. ABF.

70. ABF.

71. ABF; Wood, 52.

72. ABF; Wood, 53–54.

73. Lopez & Herbert, 36–40.

74. Now the University of Pennsylvania.

75. Isaacson, 103–06; Lopez & Herbert, 52–3.

76. Van Doren, 182–83.

77. ABF, Van Doren, 182–86.

78. ABF; Van Doren, 186–87.

79. ABF; Isaacson, 140–43; Lopez & Herbert, 44–9.

80. Isaacson, 148–50.

81. BF to John Sargent, 27 June 1775, BF to Jonathan Shipley, 7 July 1775, PBF, 22: 72, 95; Clark, 45; Wood, 54.

82. ABF; Brands, 167.

83. "Positions to be Examined, Concerning National Wealth," 4 April 1769, *Writings*, 5: 202; Van Doren, 372.

84. Brands, 277; Isaacson, 100; Van Doren, 109, 267–68; Wood, 83–84.

85. PBF, ??: 115–128.

86. Malone, *Jefferson the Virginian*, 31–33. Randall, 111–12.

87. Bear and Stanton; Betts, 12–16; Gabler, 1–2.

88. TJ to Marquis de Chastellux, 26 November 1782.

89. Halliday, 35–37.

90. TJ to Marquis de Chastellux, 26 November 1782; Malone, *Jefferson the Virginian*, 396–97; Randall, 348–49; TJ to Elizabeth Eppes, 3 October 1782; PTJ, 6: 198, 203.

91. Brands 110, 358; Isaacson, 75–76.

92. Brands, 243–44; Isaacson, 153–57.

93. Brands, 328; Isaacson, 203.

94. Isaacson, 204.

95. William Franklin to BF, 3 July 1774, PBF, 21:238; BF to William Franklin, 7 September, PBF, 21: 287; Isaacson, 204, 282.

96. BF to William Franklin, 16 August 1784; Isaacson, 256.

97. PBF 22: 521–22; Brands, 425–26; Lopez & Herbert, 210–11.

98. Elizabeth Franklin to BF, 6 August 1776. Elizabeth ended her letter, "I am now pleading the cause of your son, and my beloved husband."

99. PBF, 22: 552.

100. Isaacson, 413.

101. Lopez & Herbert, 279–81, 305.

102. ATJ.

103. PTJ, IX: 399; Gabler, 36. John Adams's grandson and biographer, Charles F. Adams, reported that the king and queen turned their backs on Jefferson and Adams. *Works*, I: 420.

104. The reigning English monarch appointed the king's Privy Council. Originally the council advised the king on matters of state and made the laws for the kingdom. Over time, some of the lords of the Privy Council, including the Lord Chancellor and the Archbishop of Canterbury, met as a court for judicial purposes in a large apartment adjacent to the old Palace of Westminster in London. The room they met in was ornamented on the ceiling with gold stars applied over a blue background, and the court came to be known as the Court of the Star Chamber. These "Lords of the Star Chamber were a law unto themselves; there was no appeal allowed and no hope left when sentence had been passed by them." Since their procedures did not follow the English common law, great abuses of judicial power occurred. The lords dispatched summary and erratic "justice," which could and did involve torture and humiliation. Their regard for women (unless one was a countess) was abysmal. Yet, their judicial barbarity did not prevent the court from drinking and dining superlatively well. Finally, their zeal in suppressing the opponents of Charles I led to the abolition of the Star Chamber by the Long Parliament in 1644. *Wine into Words*, 340.

105. Brands, 452–54.

106. BF to Joseph Galloway, 18 February 1774, PBF, 21: 95, note 7, 109. Thomas Cushing (1725–1788) was a Massachusetts politician and patriot.

107. BF to Joseph Galloway, 18 February 1774; Brands, 452–54, 459–60, 466, 469; Isaacson, 271–76; Van Doren, 458–59.

108. Brands, 465.

109. PBF, 21: 75–77, 152, BF to Massachusetts House Committee of Correspondence, 2 February 1774, BF to Thomas Cushing, 22 March 1774.

110. Van Doren, 483–85.

111. William Pitt, the Earl of Chatham, was a friend of Franklin's and politically favorable to America.

112. BF to Charles Thomson, 5 February 1775; *Writings*, VI: 306, 371; Van Doren, 511–13.

113. Van Doren, 518.

114. Isaacson, 276.

115. Alexander Wedderburn's speech to the Privy Council, 29 January 1774, PBF, Vol. 21: 37–41; Brands, 471–475; Isaacson, 276–78; Srodes, 248.

116. Isaacson, 278; Van Doren, 473–74.

117. Brands, 475; Isaacson, 278; Van Doren, 476.

118. BF to Cushing, 15 February 1774.

119. BF to Jane Mecom, 17 February 1774, PBF, 21:103.

120. BF to John Foxcroft, 18 February 1774, PBF, 21:106; Isaacson, 277–78.

121. Brands, 481; Srodes, 250–52. In a letter to a Dutch friend, Jan Ingenhousz, Franklin denied that the Cockpit incident had lost him friendships stating, "I do not find that I have lost a single friend on the occasion." But as Carl Van Doren points out, Franklin knew that the letter might be opened and read, and "he may have written it as much for some inquiring secretary as for Ingenhousz." BF to Jan Ingenhousz, 18 March 1774, *Writings*, VI: 219; Van Doren, 477.

122. Srodes, 247.

123. Van Doren, 594.

124. Gibbon and Franklin had two British mutual friends, David Hume and William Strahan. This story is perhaps apocryphal, but Edward Gibbon (1737–1794) is reported to have retold what he called "an anecdote of some point, and not too improbable for belief." Van Doren, 577–78. Gibbon and Franklin met again in Paris "by accident." Gibbon, vol. 1: 313.

125. PBF, 21: 550; Van Doren, 495.

126. PBF, 21: 552; Isaacson, 283–85.

127. PBF, 21: 408, 565.

128. PBF, 21: 409, 437, 448, 499–500, 514–15, 573; Isaacson, 284–86; Morgan, 231.

129. Srodes, 254.

130. BF to William Strahan, 19 August 1784, *Writings*, IX: 261; Van Doren, 519, 523.

131. Malone, *Jefferson the Virginian*, 349; Randall, 329–33.

132. TJ to James Madison, 20 May 1782; Randall, 333–36; Malone, *Jefferson the Virginian*, 349.

133. Gabler, 9.

134. Gabler, 9, 10.

135. Brodie, 135–36; Randall, 334.

136. Malone, *Jefferson the Virginian*, 308–12; Brodie, 135.

137. *Writings* 8: 220–22; Van Doren, 623–26.

138. Brands, 599.

139. Van Doren, 526–27.

140. Brands, 600.

141. Brands, 600–07, 616.

142. Van Doren, 437, 669.

143. Brands, 479.

144. Van Doren, 667–68.

145. Brands, 601, 602.

146. Van Doren, 680.

147. Butterfield, 3: 38, 82; Isaacson, 399–407.

148. Brands, 635.

149. TJ to George Washington, 2 May 1788; TJ to James Madison, 29 December 1787; TJ to David Humphreys, 18 March, 1789; TJ to John Taylor, 6 January 1805. Taylor (1753–1824), a friend of Jefferson's, was a political writer and three time U.S. senator.

150. TJ to John Langdon, 5 March 1810.

151. TJ to Walter Jones, 2 January 1814.

152. Gabler, 12. The Congressional committee did not quibble over Mann's bill of $644, calling "the entertainment … exceedingly plentiful, the provisions and liquors good in their kind."

153. Malone, *Jefferson the Virginian*, 406–07.

154. The actual room where Washington resigned his commission has been preserved and is located in the Maryland State House in Annapolis, Maryland. It is open to the public.

155. BF to GW, 5 March 1780.

156. GW to BF, 16 and 23 September 1789, *Writings*, 10: 41–42.

157. TJ to Benjamin Rush, 16 January 1811.

158. TJ to Thomas Paine, 19 June 1792.

159. TJ to Benjamin Rush, 16 January 1811.

160. Brands, 618, 638.

161. McCullough, 420.

162. Butterfield, 2: 363, 369.

163. Gabriel de Sartine was the French minister of marine.

164. BF to John Adams, 24 April 1779, Butterfield, 2: 363, note 3.

165. Donatien Le Ray de Chaumont was Franklin's friend and landlord at Passy.

166. Butterfield, 2: 369; Isaacson, 382–84.

167. Butterfield, 3:38; Brands, 618–19.

168. *Works*, I: 660–63, extract from *The Boston Patriot*, 15 May 1811.

169. *Works*, I: 660–63.

170. BF to Robert Morris, 7 March 1783.

171. BF to Henry Laurens, 29 April 1784; Brands, 638.

172. TJ to James Madison, 30 January 1787; PTJ, XI: 94–95.

173. TJ to Abigail Adams, 13 June 1804.

174. Butterfield, 25 June 1774, 2: 97.

175. *Memoirs*, 314–15; Wandell, 306–09.

176. Malone, *Jefferson the President: Second Term, 1805–1809*, 247–51.

177. Beran, 171–72.

178. Beran, 172–73; TJ used the expression "crooked gun" in a letter to William Branch Giles, 20 April 1807.

179. Malone, *Jefferson the President: First Term, 1801–1805*, 397–98.

180. Malone, *Jefferson the President: First Term, 1801–1805*, 405–06; 427.

181. Beran, 172–73.

182. Beran, 173–75.

183. Malone, *Jefferson the President: Second Term, 1805–1809*, 329.

184. Marshall instructed the jury to the effect that the overt act set out in the indictment could not be proved. Beirne, 233–44; Fitch, xxxvii–viii, xli, 69–70, 86–89; U.S. Constitution, Article III, Section 3; Malone, *Jefferson the President: Second Term, 1805–1809*, 338–39.

185. Beran, 181.

186. Stein, 23.

187. Stein, 337.

188. Jefferson's interest in serving wine in crystal decanters had early organs as is evi-

denced from the engraved cartouche and grapevine motifs that festooned an English decanter recovered from the drywell at Monticello and dating from the 1760s. Stein, 340.

189. The Bachet family traces its Burgundian roots to the 16th century and, at the time of Jefferson's visit, Goutte d'Or was operated by Jean Joseph Bachet (1757–1839). PTJ, XI: 417. Letter to the author from Jacques d'Angervville, 30 December 1990. The total vineyard area of Goutte d'Or was just over 13 acres, about the size it is today. By 1855, records show that it had become the property of a number of families, one of which remained Bachet. Lavalle, 152.

190. Jullien, 78. André Jullien (1766–1832) was a wholesale wine merchant in Paris who regularly visited the principal wine-producing districts of France. According to André Simon, "he obtained a vast amount of practical knowledge about the vineyards he visited, the different species of vines he saw, and the different wines he tasted, and he made it a practice to write down everything that interested him. Later on in life, he undertook to visit most of the vine-growing districts of Europe, and even passed into Asia. In 1816, he published in Paris a book entitled *Topographic de tous les Vignobles Connus*, which is of the highest interest because of the information it contains is absolutely original."

191. Gabler, 65.

192. In the northern region of Burgundy called Chablis, there are seven vineyards that carry the imprimatur of *Grands Crus*.

193. MacNeil, 193.

194. Gabler, 298.

195. Gabler, 72–73.

196. Gabler, 76–77.

197. TJ to Stephen Cathalan, 1 February 1816.

198. Gabler, 75–76.

199. Lambert was a vintner and physician whom Jefferson met when he stopped in Frontignan.

200. Gabler, 97.

201. Steven Spurrier was the wine merchant who organized the tasting.

202. *Wine into Words*, 352, 412. George Taber wrote the *Time* article.

203. Gabler, 182.

204. TJ to Abigail Adams, 25 September 1785, PTJ, VIII: 547.

205. On March14, 1788, at the *Het Wapen van Amsterdam* in Amsterdam, Jefferson dined alone and drank a half bottle of Graves wine and ate fifty oysters! The next night, he and a dinner companion consumed another 50 oysters and one and a

half bottles of wine. TJ's tavern bills, UVA; Gabler, 140.

206. Garlick, 26.

207. Garlick, 40–41.

208. TJ to John Dorti, 1 October 1811; Gabler, 4.

209. Mazzei, 192–93.

210. Garlick, 26–29; Gabler, 5–6.

211. TJ to Albert Gallatin, 25 January 1793; LCTJP, Reel 49.

212. Weld, 206–09.

213. TJ to John Dorti, 1 October 1811.

214. Isaacson, 291, 293–94; Van Doren, 527–28.

215. Van Doren, 532.

216. Van Doren, 537–39; Wood 169.

217. *Writings*, VI: 450; Van Doren, 541–47.

218. PTJ, I: 225–33, 405 note.

219. TJ to William P. Gardner, 19 February 1813.

220. John Adams to Timothy Pickering, 22 August 1822; McCullough, 119.

221. McCullough, 119.

222. Isaacson, 313.

223. TJ to Robert Walsh, 4 December 1818, PTJ, XVIII: 169; Isaacson, 313; Van Doren, 550–51.

224. Brodie, 122–2.

225. Brodie, 121.

226. ATJ; Brodie, 121.

227. Van Doren, 549–50.

228. Sparks, 1: 408; Van Doren, 551–52. A number of historians believe this exchange between Hancock and Franklin is apocryphal.

229. Weymouth, "The Declaration of Independence," by Henry Steele Commager, 182–83.

230. Jefferson did not literally speak these words; they are an interpretation by historian Henry Steele Commager of what Jefferson meant by "created equal." Weymouth, "The Declaration of Independence," by Henry Steele Commager, 186.

231. Malone, *Jefferson the Virginian*, 242–43.

232. *Works*, III: 75–76; Van Doren, 559.

233. PBF, 22: 630–32, "Sketch of Propositions for a Peace."

234. Wood, 169–70.

235. Malone, *Jefferson the Virginian*, 245. Jefferson had asked to be replaced in Congress. It is not known what health problem provoked his near-hysterical plea to

Richard Henry Lee to come and replace him, but his wife, Patty, suffered bouts of depression. On July 29, 1776, he wrote Richard Henry Lee: "For God's sake, for your country's sake, for my sake, come. I receive by every post such accounts of the state of Mrs. Jefferson's health that it will be impossible for me to disappoint her expectation of seeing me at the time I have promised ... I pray you to come. I am under a sacred obligation to go home." TJ to R.H. Lee, 29 July 1776, PTJ, I: 472; Randall, 281–82.

236. TJ to John Adams, 27 May 1813. Elbridge Gerry (1744–1814) represented Massachusetts, Charles Carroll (1737–1832) represented Maryland, Robert Treat Paine (1731–1814) was a signer from Massachusetts, and William Floyd (1734–1821) represented New York.

237. Van Doren, 147, 260.

238. Thomas O'Gorman to BF, 4 January 1773.

239. Thomas Livezey to BF, 16 November 1767, PBF, 14: 309.

240. BF to Livezey, 20 February 1768, PBF, 15: 54.

241. Thomas O'Gorman to BF, 10 March 1778, PBF, 26: 87–88.

242. John Bondfield to BF, 3 October 1778; Saussett & Masson to BF, 31 October 1778, PBF, 27: 669.

243. V. & P. French to William Temple Franklin, 27 December 1783, unpublished. See Franklin Papers, American Philosophical Society, 41u 60. "Invoice of eight cases of choice claret, sixty bottles each, shipped on board the *Nestor* of Bordeaux, Charles Noel, master, bound to Rouen, there addressed to Messes. Robert & Anthony Garvey, to be forwarded to his Excellency Benjamin Franklin, Esquire, being by his orders and for his account and risk transmitted to us by Mr. Jonathan Williams of Nantes."

244. PBF, 28: 455–56.

245. Gabler, 298.

246. *Etat du vin au* 1 September 1782, *Franklin Papers*, American Philosophical Society, 38u 1. William Temple Franklin recorded the daily consumption of wine and beer at Franklin's residence for the month of September 1782: forty-two bottles of *vin ordinaire*, nine bottles of Madeira, eleven bottles of red Bordeaux, and twenty-four bottles of beer. William Temple Franklin: Record of Wine Use in September, *Franklin Papers*, American Philosophical Society, 38u 2.

247. Jonathan Williams, Franklin's grandnephew, lived for a time in Nantes where he oversaw shipments to America, and on occasions he supplied his uncle with wine. In a letter to Temple, Jonathan said he was sending Franklin a half pipe of Madeira that "has the true nut flavor," a quality in Madeira that Jefferson also liked. Jonathan

Williams, Jr. to William Temple Franklin, 26 December 1781, *Franklin Papers*, American Philosophical Society, 36u 322. Williams later attracted the attention of Jefferson who appointed him the first superintendent of West Point. Van Doren, 576, 600–01.

248. BF to William Strahan, 2 February 1784, *Franklin Papers*, American Philosophical Society, 41u 348. Later that year Franklin reported to Strahan that because he was suffering from the gout and the stone, "I have drank no Madeira these ten months." BF to Strahan, 19 August 1784, *Franklin Papers*, American Philosophical Society, 42u 137.

249. ca 1745.

250. The phrase "bear the bell," answers to the French expression, "obtain the prize." ABF.

251. To Mary Stevenson: Verses on Her Birthday; To Miss Stevenson, on her Birthday, June 15, 1767. *Franklin Papers*, American Philosophical Society; PBF, 14: 187–88.

252. Kay, 93–94; Nolan, 201. Franklin's fondest for claret is perhaps best exemplified by the three bottles of claret that he and Lord Clare drank one evening. BF to William Franklin, 2 July 1768, PBF, 15: 163.

253. Kay, 71.

254. Kay, 59.

255. Kay, 59–60.

256. Kay, 9.

257. Kay, 99–101.

258. Kay, 63, 149–51.

259. Butterfield, vol. 2: 370–71; Gabler, 124.

260. Butterfield, 2: 292–94. The "mountain wine" referred to by Adams is known today as Malaga. It was called mountain wine in the eighteenth century because the grapes were grown in the mountainous regions surrounding the Spanish town of Malaga. It was a sweet wine made principally from the Pedro Ximenes grape. Henderson, 193.

261. John Adams to TJ, 27 May 1785.

262. John Adams to TJ, 7 June 1785.

263. TJ to John Adams, 2 June 1785; TJ to Anthony Garvey, 2 June 1785, PTJ, VIII: 175; Anthony Garvey to TJ, 5 June 1785.

264. TJ to Abigail Adams, 21 June and 7 July 1785; John Adams to TJ, 7 August 1785; TJ to Abigail Adams, 25 September 1785; Abigail Adams to TJ, 24 November 1785, PTJ, IX: 25.

265. PTJ, VIII: 175; Anthony Garvey to TJ, 5 June 1785; John Adams to TJ, 7 June 1785; TJ to Abigail Adams, 21 June 1785; John Adams to TJ, 16 July 1785.

266. Thomas Appleton was the American Consul in Leghorn. Appleton was a good judge of Tuscan wines, and he usually selected Jefferson's Montepulciano from "a particular very best crop of it known to him," which Jefferson described as being light in body with a taste equal to the best Burgundy. The Montipulciano wines that Appleton purchased for Jefferson were "produced on the grounds formerly belonging to the order of Jesuits and sold for the benefit of the government in 1793." Jefferson instructed that his Montepulciano be shipped to Monticello "in black bottles, well corked and cemented, and in strong boxes." TJ to Thomas Appleton, 14 January 1816.

267. TJ to James Monroe, 8 April 1817; TJ to S. Cathalan, 6 June 1817.

268. Gabler, 170–73.

269. *Wine into Words*, 160.

270. ABF, Brands 17–18.

271. BF to B. Rush, 14 July 1773.

272. Brands, 75; Isaacson, 48; Van Doren, 55.

273. Brands 70; Van Doren, 53–54.

274. BF to William Franklin, 19 August 1772, PBF, 19: 256–57.

275. PTJ, XI: 484.

276. TJ to Thomas Mann Randolph, 27 August 1786.

277. TJ to Marquis de Chastellux, October 1786, undated, PTJ, X: 498.

278. Malone, *Jefferson and His Time: the Sage of Monticello*, 16.

279. TJ to Peter Carr, 19 August 1785.

280. "The Speech of Miss Polly Baker," PBF 3:123–25.

281. Isaacson, 121.

282. PBF, 3: 123–25.

283. PBF, 3: 120–23; Van Doren, 721–22; Reynal's getting it wrong with regard to Polly Baker certainly did not surprise Jefferson who thought that much of the abbé's information contained "a great deal of falsehood." See TJ to John Adams, 27 August 1786, PTJ, X: 302.

284. Tise, 23–25; PBF, 3: 24–28.

285. Wood, 110.

286. Wood, 106–07.

287. Brands, 360–64.

288. Brands, 365–67; Wood, 110–11.

289. Wood, 117–120.

290. DF to BF, 3 July 1767; PBF, 14: 207; Wood, 132.

291. Wood, 131.

292. BF to William Franklin, 5 October 1768; PBF, 15: 224–27.

293. Benjamin Franklin did not actually speak these words, but given the physical and emotional neglect of his wife during this time, he could not have honestly said less. Deborah wrote Franklin her last letter on October 29, 1773. She suffered another stroke on December 14, 1774, and died a few days later. Not a single surviving letter of Franklin's mentions his wife after her death. Equally surprising is the fact that no one wrote a note of condolence. It was as though Deborah had never lived. PBF, 21: 402–04; Isaacson, 300–01; Lopez and Herbert, 201. Deborah's correspondence with her pleas of "cum home" paints a vivid picture (but not a pretty picture) of her desperate hope that he will soon return. She tells him that she has become "father and mother" to their daughter Sally, who has become interested in a young man; DF to BF, 20–25 April 1767. In another letter she confesses that she is in the "darke" as to when he might return, and her "life of old age is one contineuwd state of suspens. I muste endever to be contente;" DF to BF, 3 July 1767. Finally, when she has about given up hope, she says, "I shall only say that I find my selfe growing verey febel verey faste;" BF to BF, 30 June 1772.

294. Isaacson, 151; Van Doren, 129; Wood, 226.

295. Fleming, 101.

296. Brands, 278; Isaacson, 176, 190–91, 269; Van Doren 197–98.

297. Brands, 246–47.

298. BF to John Waring, 17 December 1763; Isaacson, 152–53.

299. BF to Benjamin Rush, 14 July 1773, PBF, 20: 314.

300. Lemay, 1154–55; Brands 703–04.

301. *Federal Gazette*, 23 March, 1790; Isaacson, 466.

302. *Notes on the State of Virginia.*

303. Halliday, 143; Malone, *The Sage of Monticello*, 330–31; *Notes on the Sate of Virginia.*

304. Malone, *Jefferson the Virginian*, 266.

305. Malone, *Jefferson the Virginian*, 264–65.

306. ATJ; Malone, *Jefferson the Virginian*, 121–22, 141, note 49.

307. Malone, *Jefferson the Virginian*, 264; Randall, 301–03, 354.

308. Malone, *"Jefferson the Virginian,"* 412–14.

309. The actions by Jefferson to abolish slavery beginning with the words "In 1769, while a member of " and ending "did I consent to its publication" come from an interesting article titled " 'Words Fitly Spoken': Thomas Jefferson, Slavery, and

Sally Hemings," by David G. Post, professor of law at Temple University Law School in Philadelphia. It can be found on the Internet.

310. Abraham Lincoln to Henry L. Pierce and others, 6 April 1859.

311. This is a quote from Professor Post's article "Words Fitly Spoken" and the position he sets out.

312. TJ to Thomas Jefferson Randolph, 24 November 1808.

313. TJ to Victor Aldolphus Sasserno, 26 May 1819.

314. TJ to Stephen Cathalan, 26 May 1819. Eighteenth-century wine glasses were much smaller than what we use today. The six wine glasses that remain at Monticello (all of which descended through the Jefferson family) when filled to three-eighths of an inch" from the top vary in capacity from about two ounces (55 ml) to three ounces (85 ml). Assuming that Jefferson drank from the larger glass (a reasonable assumption given his love of wine), his daily wine consumption was in the range of a third to half of a bottle of wine—less than during his days in Europe. The volume measurements were not taken with scientifically precise equipment and should be considered approximate. Gabler, 282, note, 53.

315. *The New York Times*, 27 September, 2004.

316. PB 11: 158, 195, note, 318; Brands 357–58; Isaacson, 216–17; Morgan, 128–140; Wood, 97–101.

317. McCullough, 537. Eleven years later Adams remarked, "If I am to judge by the newspapers and pamphlets that have been printed in America for twenty years past, I should think that both parties believe me to be the meanest villain in the world." John Adams to Benjamin Rush, 28 August 1811.

318. Malone, *Jefferson and the Ordeal of Liberty*, 470–73.

319. Abigail Adams to TJ, 1 July 1804; McCullough, 582–83.

320. TJ to Abigail Adams, 22 July 1804; TJ to Benjamin Rush, 16 January 1811.

321. McCullough, 543–44; Peterson, 637–39.

322. TJ to Uriah McGregory, 13 August 1800.

323. Benjamin Rush to John Adams, 16 December 1811.

324. John Adams to Benjamin Rush, 25 December 1811.

325. John Adams to TJ, 1 January 1812; McCullough, 602–03; Peterson, 953.

326. TJ to John Adams, 21 January 1812.

327. TJ to John Adams, 28 October 1813.

328. TJ to Elbridge Gerry, 26 January 1799; TJ to Philip Mazzei, 18 July 1804.

329. TJ to John Tyler, 28 June 1804.

330. Malone, *Jefferson the President, First Term, 1801–1805*, 207.

331. Malone, *Jefferson the President, First Term, 1801–1805*, 495–498.

332. Brodie, 74–79; Randall, 116–17. The *New York Evening Post*, a flamboyant Federalist paper, reported that Jefferson "stole to the chamber of his absent friend at dead of night and attempted to violate his bed—and had not the shrieks of the outraged female awakened an attendant who slept in the room, which obliged him to slink away, probably the crime of Tarquin had here been perpetrated." Reported in Brodie, 78.

333. Randall, 558–59. For a detailed account of the Jefferson/Walker affair, see Malone, *Jefferson the Virginian*, Appendix III, 447–51.

334. For a more detailed account of the material examined by the Thomas Jefferson Foundation committee, visit the official Thomas Jefferson Web site: www.Monticello.org. For the complete 500 page scholars' committee report visit the Thomas Jefferson Heritage Society site: www.tjheritage.org and click on Scholars Commission.

335. TJ to Martha Jefferson, 28 November 1783, PTJ, VI: 359–60; Chastellux to TJ, 24 August1784, PTJ, VII: 410, note. Martha was 13.

336. Tise, *xx*, 44–45.

337. Isaacson, 118–19.

338. BF to Collinson, 28 March 1747; Tise, 13, 43.

339. Tise, 46–49.

340. PBF, 8: 122, note; Brands, 318; Isaacson, 177–78; Tise 57, 72–74; Van Doren, 294–96; Wood, 132.

341. BF to Polly Stevenson, 13 September 1760; PBF, 9: 212–17; Tise, 57.

342. Isaacson, 177.

343. PBF, 10: 142–43.

344. Polly Stevenson to BF, 1 September 1769, PBF, 16:191; BF to Polly Stevenson, 2 September 1769, PBF, 16: 193; Isaacson, 240–41; Van Doren, 406. William Hewson (1739–1774) was also a distinguished anatomist, physiologist, writer and teacher of medicine.

345. PBF, 9: 327, note 1; Tise, *xvii*.

346. PBF, 17: 220–24; Isaacson, 241–43.

347. PBF, 16: 191, note 6; Tise, 58–59; Van Doren, 412.

348. BF to Polly Stevenson, 11 June 1760, PBF, 11: 121.

349. TJ to Martha Jefferson, 11 December 1783; PTJ, VI: 380–81.

350. TJ to John Banister, 15 October 1785. Banister (1734–88) was a member of the Virginia House of Burgesses and a friend.

351. TJ to Benjamin Rush, 3 January 1808.

352. TJ to Martha Jefferson, 22 December 1783.

353. TJ to Martha Jefferson, 7 April 1787.

354. TJ to Martha Jefferson, 8 May 1790.

355. TJ to Maria Jefferson, 7 January 1798.

356. TJ to Thomas Jefferson Randolph (1792–1875), 24 November 1808.

357. For a detailed account of the historical machinations surrounding the hiding of this essay from the public, see PBF, 3: 27–29, and Tise, 2–10.

358. BF to My Dear Friend, 25 June, 1745, PBF, 3: 30–31.

359. zFacts.com.

360. TJ to Elbridge Gerry, 26 January 1799.

361. Malone, *Jefferson the Sage of Monticello*, 473–82.

362. Ibid, 512.

363. BF to Benjamin Vaughan, 26 July 1784; Brands, 624; Isaacson, 424.

364. It is not entirely clear that Jefferson drank Lafite, although he probably did. We know that he met Lafite's owner, Pichard, when he visited Bordeaux in May 1787; he called Lafite an "excellent" wine; he attempted to order it for himself and secured 240 bottles of Lafite for President Washington as a substitute for Latour. TJ to President Pichard, 22 February 1788; Gabler, 136–37; TJ to Joseph Fenwick, 6 September 1790; TJ to Comte de Miromenil, 6 September 1790; Comte de Miromenil to TJ, 18 January 1791; Joseph Fenwick to TJ, 10 February 1791; Joseph Fenwick to TJ, 10 February 1791; PTJ, XVIII: 630. In addition, Lafite was served at the dinner tables of Jefferson's aristocratic French friends, particularly at the home of Comte de Moustier, the cousin of Mne de Pichard, wife of Lafite's owner. The probability that Jefferson drank Latour is even stronger. Jefferson visited the vineyards of Latour and told the owner that "[I] know that it is one of the best crus." And, of course, Latour (better known then as vin de Segur) was frequently severed at fashionable Paris tables.

365. The wine descriptions are not Jefferson's but those of Alexander Henderson, an English physician, who wrote *The History of Ancient and Modern Wines*, London: 1824, 167. Henderson devotes fourteen chapters and 228 pages to modern wines, and many of his observations are as valid now as then.

366. Robinson, "Tannins," 947.

367. Christie's Catalog, December 5, 1985.

368. TJ to Alexander Donald, 15 February 1788; Bear & Stanton, vol. 1: 679, note. The quote from the Christie's Catalogue, "Finest and Rarest Wines Thursday 5 December 1985" mentions only one bottle being from the 1784 vintage, i.e., Yquem. Michael Broadbent in his recent book at page 11, however, describes opening a half bottle engraved "1784 Ch Margau Th.J." There is nothing in Jefferson's records to substantiate that he ever purchased half bottles of Bordeaux wines.

368a. See Appendix A, at page 314 paragraph 1.

369. TJ to Francis Eppes, 26 May 1787. The parcel contained six dozen bottles of Haut Brion to be delivered by Captain Gregory.

370. Ferger, Gramont & Cie to TJ, 2 June 1787, TJ to Ferger, Gramont & Cie, 19 June 1787; R. & A. Garvey to TJ, 24 August 1787, Bear & Stanton, vol. 1: 679; TJ to Alexander Donald, 15 February 1788; Gabler, 117.

371. TJ to M. d'Yquem, 18 December, 1787; TJ to John Bondfield, 18 December 1787; Bondfield to TJ, 15 January 1788; Lur-Saluce to TJ, 7 January 1788.

372. TJ to Pichard, 22 February 1788; TJ to John Bondfield, 22 February 1788.

373. John Bondfield to TJ, 7 March 1788.

374. John Bondfield to TJ, 19 April 1788; PTJ, XIII: 96.

375. TJ to John Bondfield, 3 November, 1788.

376. Bondfield to TJ, 6 September 1788.

377. TJ to John Bondfield, 14 December 1788.

378. Broadbent, 11.

379. Vin de Segur was also known as Chateau Latour.

380. TJ to Joseph Fenwick, 6 September 1790.

381. Not Th.J. as engraved on the Rodenstock bottles.

382. George Washington.

383. TJ to Comte de Lur Saluce, 6 September 1790.

384. TJ to M. Lambert, 6 September 1790.

385. TJ to Comte de Miromenil. 6 September 1790.

386. Broadbent, 171.

386a. TJ to John Jay, September 17, 1789.

386b. William Koch vs. Eric Greenberg, Case Number: 1:07-cv-09600-JPO-DCF, Judge: J. Paul Oetken, United States District Court for the Southern District of New York.

387. Broadbent, 11.

388. Brands, 153–54; Isaacson, 87.

389. ABF; Isaacson, 89–90.

390. Ezra Stiles to BF, 28 January 1790.

391. BF to E. Stiles, 9 March 1790.

392. Malone, *Jefferson the Virginian*, 274.

393. Bowers, 216.

394. Bowers, 194–96; Eckenrode, 9–1; *Notes on Virginia*.

395. Bowers, 210–16.

396. TJ to Samuel Miller, 23 January 1808.

397. TJ to Elbridge Gerry, 26 January 1799.

398. Bowers, 199–201.

399. Malone, *Jefferson the Virginian*, 275.

400. TJ to Benjamin Rush, 23 September 1800.

401. Weymouth, 189–94.

402. Weymouth, 194, 209.

403. PTJ, XVIII: 169; TJ to John B. Colvin, 20 September 1810; Malone, *Jefferson the Virginian*, 292–93.

404. TJ to John Wythe, 19 May 1809; Peterson, 50–56, 712–13, 956–61.

405. TJ to William Canby, 18 September 1813.

406. BF to Peter Collinson, 9 May 1753; Isaacson, 148–49, 268.

407. Roosevelt, 287; Gabler, 195.

408. Gabler. 197, 277, note 11.

409. John Adams to Benjamin Rush, 25 December 1811.

410. Gabler, 197.

411. Stanton, 202–12.

412. Bacon.

413. Brown, 168.

414. Seale, 86, 102.

415. Brown. No Jefferson dinner menus have survived.

416. Seale, 104–05, 108.

417. Gabler, 199.

418. Gabler, 200.

419. "I cannot live without books." TJ to Thomas Jefferson Smith, 21 February 1825.

420. "Music is the favorite passion of my soul." TJ to Giovanni Fabbroni, 8 June 1778.

421. "Wine is a necessary of life."

422. Bernard, 235–36.

423. Bernard, 235; Gabler, 199.

424. TJ to Stephen Cathalan, 6 June 1817; Gabler, 203, 212.

425. Stephen Cathalan to TJ, 4 June 1816; Gabler, 203, 278, note 34.

426. *Memoirs*, vol, 1: 317.

427. TJ to Pierre Samuel Dupont de Nemours, 2 March 1809. Dupont de Nemours (1739–1817) was a French economist who came to the U.S. in 1799 and was employed by Jefferson on a diplomatic mission to France. Jefferson's term of office expired on March 4, two days after this letter was written.

428. TJ to Benjamin Rush, 22 September 1809.

429. TJ to William Wirt, 10 January 1808. Wirt (1772–1834), a Virginia lawyer, was U.S. attorney-general under presidents Monroe and John Quincy Adams.

430. TJ to John Adams, 12 October 1823.

431. TJ to B. Peyton, 21 November 1824.

432. Isaacson, 146–48.

433. Lewis, 15.

434. TJ to Thomas Mann Randolph, 5 July 1803.

435. James Madison to James Monroe, 25 June 1803; Lewis, 13–15.

436. DeConde, 136–37, 184.

437. Lewis, 57–59.

438. Chastellux, II: 390–91. François-Jean, Marquis de Chastellux (1734–1788) was a major general and the third ranking officer with the French Expeditionary Forces in America.

439. Chastellux, II: 292–94.

440. Chastellux, II, 294.

441. Visit the Thomas Jefferson Foundation Web site, www.Monticello.org, for a detailed account of the facts surrounding the preservation of Monticello.

442. *Journal of Mrs. Adams*, 61.

443. Wright, 263.

444. PBF, 27: 455; Stinchcomb, 7–11; Wright, 265.

445. See TJ's Summary Journal of Letters, 20 May, 1785.

446. TJ to Alexander Donald, 17 September 1787.

447. Donald to TJ, 15 December 1787.

448. TJ to John Jay, 17 September 1789; Gabler, 132–33.

449. Butterfield, III: 171; Gabler, 18–19.

450. Thomas Barclay (1728–1793), as American Consul General and a commissioner, had full power to settle the financial accounts of the United States in Europe.

451. *Letters of Mrs. Adams*, 240–41.

452. Dumbauld, 62–63. Located in what is presently the vicinity of the Opera. The house no longer exists. PTJ, VII: *xxviii*, 452; Rice, 37–42.

453. Thomas Barclay to TJ, 17 November 1784.

454. Gabler, 19.

455. GW to TJ, 2 June 1784. David Humphreys (1753–1818) was born in Derby, Connecticut and graduated from Yale in 1771. He joined the Continental Army, and in 1778 was an aide-de-camp to General Putnam, and two years later an aidede-camp to George Washington. He became a close friend of George Washington and lived with the Washingtons at Mt. Vernon after his return from

France. In 1790 President Washington appointed him minister to Portugal. Four years later he was appointed minister plenipotentiary to Spain, and in 1797, he married John Bulkeley's daughter in Lisbon. One of the first acts that Jefferson performed as president was to recall Humphreys and replace him because of his Federalist leanings. His literary accomplishments included poetry and the biography of General Putnam.

456. Gabler, 20.

457. TJ to William Short, 15 November 1807; Gabler, 176, 204, 272, note 41. The President's residence was not known as the White House until later. During Jefferson's time it was called the President's House.

458. John Adams to TJ, 22 January 1825.

459. ATJ.

460. Ledyard, 212, 227.

461. John Ledyard to TJ, 16 August 1786, PTJ, X: 259–61; TJ to Charles Thomson, 20 September 1787, PTJ, XII: 159–60; TJ to William Carmichael, 4 March 1789, PTJ, XIV: 616; ATJ.

462. ATJ; Ziff, 50.

463. Ledyard to TJ, 16 August 1786; TJ to John Ledyard, 16 August 1786, PTJ, IX: 259–60; XI: 217; ATJ; Trumbull, 103–04.

464. Ziff, 39–40.

465. Ziff, 42–43.

466. May 1788.

467. Ziff, 49–50.

468. TJ to William Short, 28 February 1789, PTJ, XIV: 180–83, 597.

469. John Ledyard to TJ, 15 November 1787, PTJ, XIV: 180–83; Ziff, 53.

470. Ambrose, 68.

471. Ambrose, 69–71. The subscription list is the only document known to contain the signatures of each of the first four presidents of the United States: George Washington, John Adams, Thomas Jefferson and James Madison. Other Founding Fathers who subscribed to Michaux's expedition included Secretary of the Treasury Alexander Hamilton, Secretary of War Henry Knox, and Robert Morris, "financier of the American Revolution." "Treasures of the American Philosophical Society," 1–2.

472. Ambrose, 70–71.

473. PTJ, XXV, 79–80. For a detailed account of "Jefferson and André Michaux's proposed Western Expedition," see PTJ, XXV, 75–81; "American Philosophical Society's Subscription Agreement for André Michaux's Western Expedition," see

PTJ, XXV, 82–84; "American Philosophical Society's Instructions to André Michaux," see PTJ, XXV, 624–25.

474. BF to John Paul Jones, 14 March 1779; Thomas, 153.

475. John Paul Jones to BF, 6 March 1779; Thomas, 154.

476. Thomas, 158; LP, Vol. 2, 244.

477. Lafayette to Comte d'Estaing, 21 September 1778; Brands, 576; Latzko, 81. Jean-Baptiste-Charles-Henri-Hector, Comte d'Estaing, 1723–1794, was a distinguished French admiral who commanded a fleet of warships and assisted the Colonies against Great Britain. During the French Revolution he was charged with being a reactionary and sent to the guillotine, April 28, 1794.

478. BF to Lafayette, 22 March 1779, PBF, 29: 185–87.

479. Lafayette to BF, 31 March 1779, PBF, 29: 239–40, 382.

480. BF to John Paul Jones, 27 April 1779, PBF, 29: 383–84.

481. John Paul Jones to BF, 1 May 1779, PBF, 29: 405–06.

482. Lafayette to JPJ, 27 April 1779.

483. BF instructions to John Paul Jones, 28 April 1779.

484. John Paul Jones to BF, 1 May 1779.

485. John Paul Jones to BF, 26 May 1779, PBF, 29: 549, note; BF to John Paul Jones, 2 June 1779, PBF, 561–62, 563, note 9.

486. Thomas, 183.

487. Thomas, 188–89.

488. Jones probably did not shout these immortal words. He said he answered "in the most determined negative," which he undoubtedly did. It was not until forty-five years later that one of Jones's lieutenants (Captain Richard Dale, USN Ret.) told a biographer that Jones defiantly shouted, "I have not yet begun to fight," Thomas, 192. Brands, 580.

489. Thomas, 194–95; Brands, 580.

490. John Paul Jones to BF, 3 October 1779.

491. JPJ to BF, 3 October 1779, PBF 29: 444–62; Thomas, 195–98.

492. Butterfield, 2: 370–71.

493. *Letters of Mrs. Adams*, 208.

494. Lafayette, vol. 1: *xxii*, 223–24.

495. Lafayette, vol. 1: 223–24.

496. TJ to John Adams, 6 August 1785; John Adams to TJ, 18 August 1785, PTJ, VIII: 347, 400.

497. John Adams to TJ, 18 August 1785; John Paul Jones to TJ, 8 October 1785; TJ to JPJ, 8 October 1785; PTJ, VIII: 400, 597; BF to Edward Bancroft, 31 May 1779.

498. TJ to Edward Bancroft, 26 February 1786.

499. TJ to James Madison, 9 February 1786; Lucy Paradise to TJ, 5 May 1786; James Madison to TJ, 12 May 1786; Edward Bancroft to TJ, 27 March 1787; TJ to Edward Bancroft. 6 May 1787; Paradises to TJ, 22 June 1787. Lucy Paradise was a thirty-five-year-old scatterbrained Virginia heiress who had lived in London since the age of nine. She is reputed to have been beautiful but with a temper so violent that she was frequently out of control. At the age of eighteen she married John Paradise, an intellectual whose world revolved around scholars, professionals and artists. He and Jefferson became friends. The Paradises often called upon Jefferson for help: financial, political, marital, and, in Lucy's case, emotional.

500. BF to James Lind, 25 October 1769; PBF, 16: 224, note 4. This is Franklin's first mention of Bancroft.

501. PBF, 16: 224–25, note; Butterfield, 4: 71–74; Brands, 608–09; Rafalka, Chapter 1, "Dr. Edward Bancroft."

502. Adams was obviously annoyed with Bancroft's review of the first volume of his work *Defence of the Constitution of Government of the United States of America*, and that of his son's book on his travels in Silesia, and Adams entered in his diary, "in both which the spirit of Franklin, Deane and Bancroft is to me very discernible." Bancroft's review of Adams's book begins, "We have not met with a greater disappointment, in our literary labors, than we have experienced with respect to the work now before us."

503. Butterfield, 4:74. Adams said, however, that Bancroft did not drink "a great deal."

504. Butterfield, 4: 74.

505. BF and the Committee of Secret Correspondence to Silas Deane, 2 March 1776, PBF, 22: 372–74.

506. Rafalka, Chapter 1, "Dr. Edward Bancroft."

507. John Adams in a letter to William Whittle, 11 September 1779, refers to Bancroft as Franklin's "confidential friend." Elbridge Gerry to John Adams, 12 October 1779; John Adams to Elbridge Gerry, 25 October 1779.

508. Brands, 609.

509. John Jay was also taken in by Bancroft. In the autumn of 1789, President Washington was considering appointing an agent in London to advise on the attitude of the British Ministry on questions of commerce and treaty obligations, and Jay recommended Bancroft for the position of agent calling him 'a man in whom entire confidence might be placed.'"

510. The remarks are those of Julian P. Boyd, professor of history at Princeton University, and the first editor of the *Papers of Thomas Jefferson*.

511. Brands, 610.

512. Edward Bancroft to the Most Honorable Marquis of Carmarthen, 17 September 1784.

513. Brands, 609–10; Isaacson, 334–35; Van Doren, 580–81; Wood, 186.

514. Juliana Ritchie to BF, 12 January 1777; BF to Juliana Ritchie, 19 January 1777; Isaacson, 336; Van Doren, 569.

515. Lord North was convinced that all three American commissioners, Deane, Lee, and Franklin, were involved in stockjobbing through Bancroft, but probably only Deane was guilty. PBF, 25: 22–25, 417, note; Isaacson, 347; Van Doren, 582, 594.

516. Edward Bancroft to Silas Deane, Arthur Lee and BF, 3 October 1777, PBF, 25: 22, 25.

517. PBF, 25: 22.

518. Izard, a friend of Arthur Lee's and a wealthy South Carolina planter, had come to Europe as envoy to Tuscany. When he was not received there, he ended up staying in Paris. Isaacson, 333.

519. Ralph Izard to BF, 17 June 1778, PBF, 26: 640–53.

520. Musco Livingston to American Commissioners, 8 April 1778; Ralph Izard to BF, 17 June 1778, PBF, 26: 256, note, 640–53; PBF, 27: 229.

521. Edward Bancroft to Commission, before 7 August 1778, PBF 27: 229–33; 28: 479, note 9.

522. Arthur Lee to BF and John Adams, 7 February 1779; PBF, 28: 479–80. John Adams in his diary makes mention of Bancroft living with a woman in France to whom he was not married. According to Adams, the French called her "la femme de Monsieur Bancroft." Apparently Bancroft did not take her out socially, because even though his friendship with Franklin brought him daily to his house where he often dined with Adams and Franklin, Adams said, "she never made her appearance." Butterfield, 4: 71–74.

523. Butterfield, 4: 72, note.

524. BF to Edward Bancroft, 31 May 1779, PBF, 29: 580.

525. Van Doren, 597–99.

526. BF to Arthur Lee (unsent), 3 April 1778; *Writings*, 7: 132; Van Doren, 598.

527. Van Doren, 598.

528. *Writings* 8: 220–22; Van Doren, 624–25.

529. TJ to Edward Bancroft, 26 January 1789, PTJ, XIV: 494.

530. Lucy Paradise to TJ, 22 June 1787, PTJ, XI: 501; Edward Bancroft to TJ, 20 February 1789, 10 March 1789; TJ to Edward Bancroft, 15 March 1789, PTJ, XIV: 578–80, 629–30.

531. TJ to Edward Bancroft, 2 March 1789, PTJ, 14: 605–06.

532. Edward Bancroft to TJ, 10 March 1789, PTJ, XIV: 630–32.

533. John Brown Cutting to TJ, 30 September 1789 and note. Deane died on September 22, 1789. Cutting told Jefferson that there was reason to believe that Deane deliberately took a lethal dose of laudanum. Historian Julian Boyd offers the hypothesis that Deane was murdered by Bancroft while they drank wine. See *William & Mary Quarterly*, 3rd Ser., XVI (April and July) 165–187, 319–342. Jefferson considered Deane's career "a wretched monument of the consequence of a departure from right." TJ to James Madison, 28 August 1789, PTJ, XV: 368.

534. The child's mother has never been identified, but she is believed to have been a street woman. Nolan, 28.

535. Nolan, 35.

536. Nolan, 41.

537. Nolan, 43.

538. Nolan, 45–46, 214, note 5.

539. BF to William Strahan, 6 September 1759; Nolan, 44.

540. Nolan, 56.

541. Nolan, 62–64. The editors of the *Papers of Benjamin Franklin* have Strahan and others having Franklin to dinner on September 11 and not visiting the Dicks at Prestonfield until October 6. PBF, 8: 430–32, 440, note 2.

542. Nolan, 74–77.

543. Nolan, 78–79. The official details of Dr. Franklin's investiture are sketchy, and the ceremony described is a reconstruction of the historic scene by a distinguished scholar who held the post of principal of St. Andrews in 1938. The graduation cap belonged traditionally to John Knox, and its adoption as the symbol of admission to the fellowship of the university began at the time of the Reformation. Franklin was in London when St. Andrews conferred the doctor of laws degree on him *in absentia* on February 12, 1759. The circumstances surrounding who proposed the honor and how Franklin received it are unknown. PBF, 8: 277–80. One of the students who witnessed Benjamin Franklin's investiture that October day in 1759 was James Wilson, a future signer of the Declaration of Independence, and the first associate Justice of the Supreme Court of the United States.

544. The minutes of the social clubs of Edinburgh for the period of Franklin's visit have been lost, and this account is reconstructed. Nolan, 85–86.

545. BF to Lord Kames, 3 January 1760; Van Doren, 282; Nolan, 93.

546. Isaacson, 199.

547. Isaacson, 203–04; Nolan, 103.

548. Isaacson, 221; Nolan, 105–06.

549. Gabler, 39.

550. Turner, 258–60.

551. Gabler, 39.

552. Turner, 238–42. At age 35, Brown was appointed royal gardener at Hampton Court.

553. PTJ, IX: 370; TJ's tavern bills, UVA.

554. *Jefferson Memorandum Books*; Burke, 56–89.

555. PTJ, IX: 370–71; TJ's tavern bills, UVA. Although Jefferson's travel receipts do not identify the specific wines they drank with their dinners, they were expensive, usually costing twice as much as their meals. There are two explanations: the quantity and the quality of the wines. The English imposed exorbitant duties on French wines during the entire eighteenth century, and these taxes caused French wines to cost more than wines from Germany, Portugal, and Spain. Jefferson and Adams, both lovers of French wines, when given the choice, would probably have selected claret, burgundy, or champagne. Simon, 144–98.

556. PTJ, IX: 371–75. Jefferson did not actually record climbing the pillar, but given his penchant for viewing things from the highest point, he probably did.

557. TJ's tavern bills, UVA; *Jefferson's Memorandum Books*.

558. Letter to the author from Robert Bearman, senior archivist, Shakespeare Birthplace Trust, 31 March 1992; *Torrington Diaries*, 2: 224; TJ's tavern bills, UVA.

559. Butterfield, 3: 185; PTJ, IX: 374–75.

560. *Jefferson's Memorandum Books*; PTJ, IX: 371–73; Butterfield, 3: 185.

561. It still operates as a hotel, now the Talbot Hotel, and though such modern amenities as televisions, telephones, radios and hair dryers are standard in all the rooms, much of its seventeenth and eighteenth century character remains. *A Gentleman at the Talbot Stourbridge*, H.E. Palfrey, 1927 and Mark Moody, 1952.

562. *Jefferson's Memorandum Books*; TJ's tavern bills, UVA.

563. PTJ, IX: 374–75; Butterfield, 3: 185.

564. *Jefferson's Memorandum Books*; TJ's tavern bills, UVA. Letter to the author from Mary Butt, 7 April 1992; *Worcester Evening News*, 6 July 1976.

565. PTJ, IX: 374–75.

566. *Jefferson's Memorandum Books*; TJ's tavern bills, UVA.

567. PTJ, IX: 444–46. John Adams carried his own copy of Whateley's book.

568. BF to Polly Stevenson, 28 August and 14 September 1767; Isaacson, 238.

569. TJ to John Bannister, 19 June 1787.

570. PTJ, XI: 415.

571. TJ to William Short, 15 March, TJ to William Short, 27 March 1787, PTJ, XI: 415–16.

572. TJ to Short, 15 March 1787, PTJ, XI: 416–18, 484.

573. Seward, 55–69.

574. Henderson, 163–64.

575. PTJ, XI: 417.

576. TJ to William Short, 15 March 1787; Gabler, 64–65.

577. PTJ, XI: 418; Gabler, 64–67.

578. Parker, 558–60.

579. Henderson, 167–68; Jullien, 77.

580. For vineyard sizes see Parker, 558–62.

581. TJ to William Short, 15 March 1787; TJ to William Short, 27 March 1787, PTJ, XI: 415–16; Henderson, 168; Jullien, 62–64.

582. PTJ, XI: 421.

583. PTJ, XI: 421–22, XIII: 273.

584. LCTJP, Reel 3.

585. TJ to Stephen Cathalan, 1 February 1816.

586. Gabler, 295.

587. PTJ, XI: 421–22.

588. Young, 535; Gabler, 77.

589. TJ to Mme de Tessé, 20 March, 1787, PTJ, XI, 423.

590. Gabler, 78.

591. Jefferson was no fan of Napoleon's. During his first term as president, and before the acquisition of Louisiana, Jefferson believed America's future was most endangered by Imperial France. Malone, *Jefferson the President: Second Term*, 458–59.

592. Gabler, 82–85.

593. PTJ, XI: 424–25.

594. TJ to Mme de Tott, 5 April 1787.

595. See Gabler, 85, 253–54, note 15.

596. PTJ, XIII: 274.

597. Pope-Hennessy, 43–45.

598. Gabler, 246, note 22.

599. TJ to Martha Jefferson, 28 March 1787.

600. See Smollett, or Gabler, 86, for an account of what the baths looked like and how they worked.

601. TJ to William Short, 7 April 1787.

602. Gabler, 87. The cours was developed in 1651 after Marie de Medici brought to

France from Italy the aristocratic custom of "taking the air in public," either in carriages or on foot or in sedan chairs instead of walking in one's own garden. It was described by some as the most beautiful street in Europe.

603. Fisher, 22, 258–60.

604. TJ to William Short, 29 March 1787.

605. TJ to William Short, 9 April 1787.

606. TJ to Mazzei, 4 April 1787.

607. Stephen Cathalan to TJ, 5 June 1816, PTJ, XI: 427–28. Jefferson's notes give the cellar temperature at 91/2 degrees Réaumur, a scale developed in 1730 by French scientist René-Antoine Ferchault de Réaumur. Réaumur's temperature scale was widely used in the eighteenth century but has now practically disappeared. See O.T. Zimmerman and Irvin Lavin, *Industrial Research Services Conversion Factors and Tables*, Dover, N.H., 1961, 539.

608. TJ to Philip Mazzei, 4 April 1787.

609. TJ to John Jay, 4 May 1787.

610. PTJ, XI: 429.

611. PTJ, XI: 430–31; XIII: 274.

612. PTJ, XI 439–31; Young, 185–87.

613. Saussure.

614. PTJ, XIII: 27, *Jefferson's Memorandum Books*. The Hotel York no longer exists and its exact location cannot be established from the Nice City Archives because the archives of this period were destroyed in the French revolution. It was located, however, on the sea front in a section of Nice now called Croix de Marbre. Croix de Marbre is an area of Nice loosely bordered by the sea to the south, Boulevard Gambetta to the west, Boulevard Victor Hugo to the north, and Rue Dalpozzo Royale to the east. Letter to the author from M. de Bodman, Nice Tourist Office, 25 October 1990.

615. PTJ, XI: 287; Young, 188. Although today the famous promenade des Anglais is longer and extends along the sea between the beach and the roadway, the rooftop promenade still exists. It is found on the roofs of the houses and shops in the old-town section that face the sea and adjacent to the château ruins. Jefferson did not make note of it, but he certainly would have climbed to the top of the château ruins for a view of Nice, the Mediterranean, the Alps, and the countryside. Today, from the château ruins, the visitor can follow a walkway through a landscaped park that leads to a point above the château that provides an even more spectacular view.

616. Jullien confirms that the only wine of repute produced from the Bellet vineyards was a red wine described as "delicate and agreeable."

617. TJ to Lafayette, 11 April 1787.

618. TJ to Short, 12 April 1787; Gabler, 92–93.

619. PTJ, XI: 442–43; Young, 191–92. Jefferson did not record where he stayed in Tende and this information is from Young's account of his stay in Tende two years after Jefferson's visit. Because travelers had few, if any, options as to where they could lodge in small villages, it is probable that Jefferson stayed in the same or a similar place.

620. Young, 192.

621. Jefferson did not describe his assent and descent of col de Tende. This account is by Tobias Smollett, who did. Smollett, 706–08; Gabler, 96. Today col de Tende is the dividing point between France and Italy and is crossed by driving through a tunnel; sleigh rides down its mountain slopes are a thing of the past.

622. PTJ, XI: 435; Young, 194, 254–55.

623. Redding, 246; *Vintage*, 419; Jullien, 189. Cyrus Redding (1785–1870) wrote the first book in English that deals exclusively with modern wines, *A History and Description of Modern Wines*, London, 1833.

624. PTJ, XI: 436; TJ to John Jay, 4 May 1787; TJ to Edward Rutledge, 14 July 1787; Ralph Izard to TJ, 10 November 1787; Leon Drayton to TJ, 25 November 1787.

625. PTJ, XI: 435, XIII: 272.

626. This observation is from Arthur Young's account.

627. PTJ, XI: 437–40; XIII: 272; TJ to J. Skinner, 24 February 1820. James Boswell visited Simonetta twenty-two years before Jefferson and fired a pistol "from the window of an upper story opposite to a wall" and counted the sound repeat fiftyeight times. Boswell, 43.

628. PTJ, XIII: 272.

629. PTJ, XI: 441; XIII: 270.

630. *Jefferson's Memorandum Books*; Smollett, 203–04. James Boswell also left Genoa aboard a felucca and because of contrary winds had to put ashore. The description of the felucca and crew is Boswell's. See Boswell, 225. TJ to William Short, May 1, 1787; TJ to Martha Jefferson, May 5, 1787; TJ to Philip Mazzei, 6 May 1787, PTJ, XI: 441.

631. PTJ, XI: 441; XIII: 271. Jefferson called the Noli tavern "miserable" but does not tell us why. Smollett stayed in Noli and reported having "after a very odd kind of supper, which I cannot pretend to describe, we retired to our repose; but I had not been in bed five minutes, when I felt something crawling on different parts of my body, and, taking a light to examine, perceived above a dozen of large bugs." Smollett, 748.

632. Now known as the Italian Riviera.

633. PTJ, XI: 442; TJ to Martha Jefferson, 5 May 1787; TJ to William Short, 1 May 1787. A "gite" is a French term to designate a certain type of accommodation: villa, apartment, room, tavern.

634. PTJ, XI: 441–42; Albenga, like so many of its coastal neighbors, has become a seaside resort but without any evidence of its past. There are a few vineyards in the plains, but the best wine is made from the Pigato grape that grows on the coastal hills around Albenga. It makes a white wine that is "rich and velvety with a sunny yellow color, a hint of wild fennel in its ample aroma." Anderson, 75.

635. PTJ, XI: 442. Boswell noted that the commerce of Port Maurice was supported by olive oil and that the figs were the best that he had ever eaten. He drank a wine there that he called "a little inferior to Madeira." Boswell, 233.

636. PTJ, XI: 442; XIII: 271; Jullien, 190.

637. PTJ, XI: 442–43; XIII: 271.

638. PTJ, XI: 443; XIII: 273–74.

639. TJ to Martha Jefferson, 21 May 1787.

640. Letters from Robert Bailey to the author, July 12 and 27, 1974; Jullien, 133; Gabler, 105–06.

641. PTJ, XIII: 274.

642. PTJ, XI: 444–45; XIII: 274; Shaw, 355.

643. PTJ, XI: 443–44; LCTJP, Reel 3; *Jefferson Memorandum Books*.

644. Henderson, 176–77.

645. PTJ, XI: 446.

646. Now the White House.

647. TJ to John Rutledge, Jr., 25 March 1789.

648. TJ to Martha Jefferson, 21 May 1787, PTJ, XI: 446–47.

649. Jefferson did not say he visited Le Cité, but given his penchant for seeing the sights from the highest point and its architecture, he surely walked the ramparts of the ancient fortress town.

650. PTJ, XI: 447–48; XIII: 275.

651. PTJ, XI: 454–55, 457.

652. *Wine into Words*, 230–32.

653. TJ to Francis Eppes, 26 May 1787.

654. Gabler, 115–117.

655. Gabler, 118.

656. Letter to the author from Henri Martin, 3 July 1974; Gabler, 120.

657. Gabler, 118.

658. Letter to the author from Elie de Rothschild, 23 January 1974.

659. TJ to John Rutledge, Jr., 25 March 1788.

660. Jonathan Shipley, 1717–1788, was the Anglican bishop of St-Asaph, Wales, and a close friend of Franklin's.

661. Isaacson, 254–57.

662. Isaacson, 257; Van Doren, 415.

663. TJ to Thomas Mann Randolph, Jr., 28 March 1790, PTJ, XVI: 277–78.

664. ATJ.

665. Nolan, 132–37.

666. Nolan, 139–40.

667. Nolan, 141.

668. Franklin's Journal of His Health, 4 October 1778–16 January 1780, PBF, 27: 496; Nolan, 143, 220, note 5. Franklin states in his Journal that he was in Ireland in 1773 which is incorrect. He visited Ireland only in the fall of 1771. Unfortunately, Franklin did not keep an account of his stay in Ireland, and a letter he wrote his wife Deborah from Dublin has been lost. Therefore, we do not know where he stayed or his precise itinerary. Sites that he would have seen, however, include the Royal Exchange on Cork Street, Trinity College, the new Parliament House, Merrion Square, and the mansions of the Irish nobility, some of whom he visited. Nolan, 141–53.

669. BF to William Franklin, 30 January 1772; Nolan, 144–46.

670. BF to Samuel Cooper, 13 January 1772; BF to James Bowdoin, 13 January 1772; Nolan, 148–49.

671. Nolan, 153.

672. BF to Thomas Cushing, 13 January 1772; Nolan, 154–57.

673. BF to Thomas Cushing, 13 January 1772.

674. Hillsborough served as secretary of state for colonial affairs, but he was neither a friend of the Colonies nor Franklin's.

675. David Hume (1711–1776) was a Scottish historian and philosopher, and one of the great intellects of his time.

676. Nolan, 70–73.

677. The hike is described in Henry Marchant's diary, 1771–1772.

678. Nolan, 200–01.

679. Nolan, 202–03, Isaacson, 261–62.

680. BF to Mary (Polly) Hewson, 29 November 1771; BF to Deborah Franklin, 28 January 1772; Nolan, 202–03.

681. Nolan, 38, 203–04. Nolan states that Franklin and Burgoyne met during Franklin's stay in Preston, but he cites no authority.

682. Nolan, 38, 203.

683. Nolan, 203–04.

684. Isaacson, 262.

685. BF to Joshua Babcock, 13 January 1772; BF to Joseph Galloway, 6 February 1772, PBF, 19: 71; Van Doren, 392–93.

686. TJ to John Adams, 2 March 1788.

687. TJ to William Short, 10 March 1788.

688. Gabler, 140.

689. Dumbauld, 110–15, has a more detailed account of their negotiations.

690. PTJ, XIII: 11–12.

691. TJ to John Trumbull, 27 March 1788.

692. TJ to Baron de Geismar, 18 March 1788; Baron de Geismar to TJ, 26 March 1788.

693. PTJ, XIII: 264; TJ's tavern bills, UVA.

694. PTJ, XIII: 12; Lambert, 139.

695. PTJ, XIII: 13.

696. PTJ, XIII: 264.

697. PTJ, XIII: 13.

698. Adriaen Van Der Werff, Dutch painter, 1659–1722.

699. TJ's tavern bills, UVA.

700. PTJ, XIII: 14, 265.

701. PTJ, XIII: 15–16, 265.

702. Brauneberg is still a wine of great distinction. "Brauneberg has more spiciness and richness than any other Moselle," writes wine expert, Hugh Johnson. "It is the most hocklike wine of the river, and perhaps, for this reason, used to be considered easily the best in the last century … 100 years ago it was reckoned the greatest wine of the Mosel, perfectly satisfying the taste for wine that was full-bodied and golden." H. Johnson, 150.

703. PTJ, XIII: 15–16, 265.

704. TJ's tavern bills, UVA. It is not clear how many ounces a pot contained, but it probably was the equivalent of about a liter, i.e., 33.8 ounces.

705. PTJ, XIII: 20, 266. This calculation assumes that Jefferson used the American wine measure, i.e., one tun being equal to 252 gallons and the bottle capacity about the same as today's bottle, i.e., 750 ml.

706. PTJ, XIII: 16. See wine list of John Dick & Son, XIII: 20–21.

707. TJ's tavern bills, UVA. The student of wine will immediately perceive that the Rheingau wines that Jefferson drank, made from the Riesling grape, were far different from today's generally sweet German wines. Eighteenth century German vintners aged their wines for long periods, often keeping their wines ten to fifteen

years before releasing them for sale. Dr. Hans Ambrosi, a leading German oenologist, points out that the eighteenth century practice of drinking German wines old was based on necessity. Their high acid content could only be reduced to an acceptable taste by years of storage. High acid content in a young wine today can be prevented or corrected in a variety of ways. Gabler, 148, 267, note 64.

708. PTJ, XIII: 16–20, 266.

709. TJ's tavern bills, UVA.

710. PTJ, XIII: 18–21. Actually, Jefferson's notes show that the wines of Rüdesheim of the same year (1783) sold for a little more than those of Hochheim.

711. Today the word "Berg" appears before the names of these vineyards, i.e., Rottland, Roseneck and Schlossberg to distinguish them from the parish vineyards. The Berg vineyards still produce outstanding wines, but as Hugh Johnson said, "not always in the hottest years." H. Johnson, 156.

712. PTJ, XIII: 21.

713. TJ to Baron de Geismar, 13 July 1788. The vines probably were still growing in his Paris garden when he left France in September 1789 to return to America for a six-month leave of absence, a 'temporary stay' that became permanent with history's turn of events. There is no evidence that he took them with him or that they were ever planted at Monticello.

714. TJ's tavern bills, UVA. His tavern bills do not reveal what he ate, but it appears that he drank wine with his meal, not after the meal as was the American custom.

715. PTJ, XIII: 21.

716. PTJ, XIII: 21. Johnson, 92; H. Johnson, 163.

717. PTJ, XIII: 22–25, 266–67.

718. PTJ, XIII: 22–24, 267.

719. PTJ, XIII: 267. The building was destroyed in 1944 by aerial bombing.

720. PTJ, XIII: 267.

721. PTJ, XIII: 26.

722. There is no written evidence that Franklin and Caty Ray spent overnight on the road, but given the deplorable weather and road conditions, and the slow rate of carriage travel under the best of conditions, there is a strong probability that they did. Abigail Adams on a similar journey was required to stay overnight.

723. PBF, 5: 502, note; Brands, 258–60; Isaacson, 162. Catharine Ray Greene and Franklin's friendship lasted until Franklin's death.

724. Tise, 52–55.

725. hyp, i.e., hypochondria.

726. BF to Catharine Ray, 4 March 1754, PBF, 5: 502–04.

727. Catharine Ray to BF, 28 June 1754, PBF, 6: 96–97.

728. PBF, 5: 536, note.

729. Block Island.

730. BF to Catharine Ray, 11 September 1755, PBF, 6: 182–85; Van Doren, 237–38.

731. BF to Catharine Ray, 11 September 1755.

732. BF to Catharine Ray, 16 October 1755, PBF, 6: 225; Tise, 55.

733. *Jefferson's Memorandum Books* record the purchase of several corkscrews. Jefferson also carried a multipurpose knife that included a corkscrew.

734. Jefferson owned such a portable chest and bottles, and it was used for carrying wines and other beverages. Stein, 344–45. Although there is no recorded evidence that Jefferson brought wine on this trip, given the fact that he drank wine on a daily basis, had a supply of wine in his Philadelphia residence, carried a corkscrew in his travel case, owned a portable wooden chest for carrying non-bottled wine and other beverages, and his travel companion was known to enjoy wine, there is a strong probability that wine accompanied them on the trip.

735. James Madison to TJ, 12 May 1791.

736. N. Hazard to Alexander Hamilton, 25 November 1791.

737. TJ to Martha Jefferson Randolph, 31 May 1791.

738. As Jefferson walked the fort's ramparts and looked out on Lake Champlain and the distant Green Mountains, he must have had mixed emotions, realizing that the fort's contribution to winning the war had been made possible in part by the heroism of America's most infamous traitor, Benedict Arnold, who had embarrassed Jefferson with his surprise attack on Richmond ten years earlier, causing Jefferson and the Virginia Assembly to flee.

739. TJ to Thomas Mann Randolph, 5 June 1791.

740. Crown Point, at Lake Champlain's narrowest point, is now a historical national park displaying the ruins of the old English and French forts, a view of Lake Champlain and a display of excavated wine glasses, wine bottles, and other seventeenth and eighteenth century artifacts.

741. TJ to TMR, 5 June 1791.

742. The battle sites are now within a historic state park located two miles beyond the Vermont border just off Route 67 in New York State. At the top of the hill where Baum and his troops were routed, the visitor has a sweeping view of the surrounding hillsides. A bronze memorial depicting the battle sites and three large placards facing north, south, and east with photographs are displayed and outline the countryside with descriptions of how the troops maneuvered before and during the battles. In Bennington, an obelisk marks the site of the American storehouses that Baum had expected to capture.

743. Gabler, 181–82.

744. Now the site of Williams College and the Clark Museum.

745. TJ to George Washington, 5 June 1791.

746. Now Orient Point.

747. PTJ, XX: 467–70.

748. Joseph Frey to TJ, 9 August 1791; TJ to William Prince, 6 July 1791; TJ to James Brown, 28 November 1791; Betts, 166–69.

749. James Madison to James Madison, Sr., 2 July 1791.

750. Gabler, 178–83.

751. *Jefferson's Memorandum Books*.

752. TJ to John Bondfield, 14 December 1788.

753. Isaacson, 104, 176; Van Doren, 272; Sparks, VII: 157–8.

754. Van Doren, 272.

755. Van Doren, 359.

756. BF to William Franklin, 19 August 1772, PBF, 19: 257–60.

757. Van Doren, 420.

758. Van Doren, 420–22.

759. Scottish lawyer and writer, James Boswell, 1740–1795, was the biographer of Samuel Johnson.

760. Van Doren, 402.

761. Van Doren, 770; Wood, 29.

762. TJ to Thomas Jefferson Randolph, 24 November 1808.

763. PBF, 10: 149; Isaacson, 202; Van Doren, 301.

764. Gabler, 36–38, 44–47.

765. Now the Palais de la Légion d'Honneur.

766. Torn down in 1841.

767. Gabler, 23–24.

768. Gabler, 24–25.

769. Gouverneur Morris in his diary under date of April 8, 1789 records, "Dine early with Jefferson to see the Procession to Longchamps."

770. Butterfield, vol. 1: 239.

771. Butterfield, vol. 4: 62–63.

772. Jefferson usually, but not always, went to the Hermitage on Fridays or Saturdays and his account book entries indicate that he made several visits to the retreat between September 5 and October 12, 1787. PTJ, XII: 199, 214.

773. Both Jefferson and Roger Dion fail to tell us whether *vin de Suresnes* was red or white, but given the Paris climate, I suspect it was a white wine.

774. Fremyne de Fontenille to TJ, 23 October 1787; TJ to Fremyne de Fontenille, 24 October 1787.

775. Dion, 215, 659, 673; Gabler, 133–35. The vineyards gave way to military fortifications in 1840, and after World War I, it became a cemetery for Americans killed in the war.

776. Butterfield, II: 293–94. This story comes from Adams' Diary, and although he may have shared this experience with Franklin, there is no recorded evidence that he did.

777. TJ to Charles Bellini, 30 September 1785.

778. Young, 276–77. These comments are not those of Jefferson, but of a contemporary, Arthur Young, an Englishman. Arthur Young (1741–1820) was a prolific writer in the field of agriculture. He wrote nine volumes on his three agricultural tours of England in 1768 to 1771. In 1784, he began a periodical, *Annals of Agriculture*, which appeared until 1809 and ran to 45 volumes. In 1787, 1788 and 1789, Young traveled throughout France and published his notes in 1792, titled *Travels During the Years 1787, 1788, and 1789*. He carried on a wide correspondence with many famous people including George Washington and the Marquis de Lafayette. Although Jefferson and Young were traveling through France at the same time, there is no evidence that they met, then or later. Jefferson's *Farm Book* reveals that he became aware of Arthur Young's agricultural interests and activities through George Washington.

779. TJ to James Monroe, 17 June 1785. Monroe (1758–1831), a lifelong friend, became the fifth president of the United States.

780. TJ to Elizabeth Trist, August 18, 1785. Mrs. Trist was a Philadelphia friend with whom Jefferson lodged his daughter Martha.

781. TJ to John Page, 7 October 1762, PTJ, I: 12.

782. Halliday, 19.

783. Franklin's nickname for Deborah.

784. William Strahan to Deborah Franklin, 13 December 1757, PBF, 7: 297.

785. BF to Deborah Franklin, 14 January 1758, PBF, 7: 359.

786. Isaacson, 178–81; Brands, 341; Van Doren, 125. Deborah Franklin was virtually illiterate and her lack of education was reflected in her speech as well as her writing.

787. See BF to Deborah Franklin 14 January, 19 February, 10 June 1758, PBF, 8:93; Brands, 179; Clark 142–43. Deborah's reply to Strahan has not been found, but he wrote David Hall, June 10, 1758, "I received Mrs. Franklin's letter … I am sorry that she dreads the sea … There are many ladies here that would make no objection to sailing twice as far after him, but there is no overcoming prejudices of that kind." PBF, 8: 93, note 6; BF to Deborah Franklin, 14 January 1758; Brands, 179.

788. Tise, 56. Joseph Priestly (1733–1804) was one of Franklin's close English friend's

and, by profession, a Presbyterian minister. He was also a historian (especially on electricity) and an expert in ancient and modern languages.

789. Dorothea Blunt to BF, 19 April 1775.

790. Emma Thompson to BF, 6 February 1777, PBF, 23: 292; Isaacson, 301.

791. Lopez & Herbert, 201.

792. *Works*, III: 134.

793. BF to Elizabeth Partridge, 11 October 1779, PBF, 30: 514; Van Doren, 639.

794. Van Doren, 290–92, 300.

795. Isaacson, 363–65; Lopez, 95; Van Doren, 651.

796. Aldridge, 281.

797. *Writings*, X: 431; Isaacson, 359; Van Doren, 641.

798. Aldridge, 282.

799. BF to M. Brillon, 10 March ca1778, *Writings*, X: 437–38; Aldridge, 282–83; Isaacson, 358.

800. Tise, 75; Lopez, 40–41.

801. *Writings*, X: 414–15; Aldridge, 284.

802. *Writings*, X: 436; Van Doren, 643–44.

803. Van Doren, 643.

804. Lopez, 314.

805. Isaacson, 363–64; Van Doren, 646; Wood, 208. For a more complete account of Franklin's relationships with Madame Brillon and Madame Helvétius see Lopez, particularly 29–121, 243–301.

806. Van Doren, 647.

807. Butterfield, 4:58–9.

808. Butterfield, 4: 69.

809. Isaacson, 366–67; Van Doren, 651–52.

810. Madame Helvétius to BF, July, no date, 1787, *Writings*, X: 442–44; Van Doren, 652.

811. This is the argument put forth by Claude-Anne Lopez and Eugenia Herbert in *The Private Franklin*. See also Tise, 67–82.

812. TJ to Maria Cosway, 12 October 1786, "My Head and My Heart." See Diane Ketcham's book *Le Désert de Retz* for an account of Jefferson and Maria Cosway's visit to the Désert, near Chambourcy, about ten miles west of Paris, now restored and open to the public.

813. Rice, 107–08.

814. The Château de Madrid bordered the Bois de Boulogne, as did the Bagatelle, a Neoclassic pavilion built in 1777. It is now the property of the City of Paris and open to visitors. The rainbows of Marly were created by the famous hydraulic ma-

chine constructed a hundred years earlier in the reign of Louis XIV to carry water from the Seine to the gardens of Versailles and Marly. From the terrace of the royal château at St-Germain, Jefferson and Maria could see Mont Calvaire and Paris. The "Dessert" that they visited on September 16, was Le Désert de Retz, the country estate of a Farmer-General, M. de Monville, and located four miles from St-Germain on the edge of the forest of Marly. The grounds included a garden, an obelisk, a pyramid, and a huge column house. Rice 111–12.

815. The precise cause of Jefferson's dislocated wrist is not known. Attempting to jump over a fence in the cours-la-Reine is the romanticized version. For a more detailed account of how it might have happened, see *William & Mary Quarterly*, January 1948, "Jefferson's Earliest Note to Maria Cosway with Some New facts and Conjectures on His Broken Wrist," by L.H. Butterfield and Howard C. Rice Jr.

816. TJ to Maria Cosway, 5 October 1786; Maria Cosway to TJ, 5 October 1786.

817. TJ to Maria Cosway, 12 October 1786.

818. TJ to Maria Cosway, 12 October 1786.

819. TJ to Maria Cosway, 12 October 1786.

820. TJ to John Trumbull, 13 November 1787.

821. Maria Cosway to TJ, 10 December 1787; Gabler, 135.

822. TJ to Maria Cosway, 14 January 1788.

823. Lucy Paradise to TJ, 2 March 1790; PTJ, XVI: 198.

824. Maria Cosway to TJ, 11 June 1790.

825. TJ to Maria Cosway, 23 June 1790, PTJ, XXVI: 550–51.

826. Randall, 517–18.

827. TJ to Angela Church, January 11, 1789, PTJ, 30: 23. Her work with the school was recognized by the emperor of Austria who made her the Countess Maria of Lodi. See also Maria Cosway to TJ, Nov13 and 24, 1794.

828. Elbridge Gerry to TJ, 25 February 1785; Gabler, 2–27, 235, note 51.

829. BF to Jane Mecom, 13 July 1785.

830. Isaacson, 433.

831. PTJ, VIII: 129; Van Doren, 723.

832. Brodie, 425.

833. TJ to James Monroe, 11 May 1785.

834. BF to David Hartley, 5 July 1785; Labaree and Bell, 60–61.

835. BF to John and Sarah Jay, 27 September 1785; Isaacson, 437–40.

836. Franklin's sacrifice of wine was probably unnecessary because recent studies indicate that although men who drink alcohol increase the risk of gout "only if they drink beer or spirits; wine drinkers had no greater incidence of gout than non-

drinkers." See *The New York Times*, Monday, June 20, 2005, "Like Champagne, You've Got Gout," by Timothy Gower.

837. Wood, 214–16.

838. BF to GW, 3 April 1787.

839. BF to TJ, 19 April 1787, PTJ, XI: 302.

840. Farrand's Records of Convention, II, 648, see www.memory.loc.gov/ammem/amlaw/lwfr.html; Van Doren, 754–55.

841. BF to Charles Carroll, 25 May 1789.

842. TJ to James Madison, PTJ, XV: 367–68; Malone, *Jefferson and the Rights of Man*, 169–72.

843. TJ to Mrs. William Bingham, 11 May 1788. She was the wife of a Philadelphia banker and senator whose house was a gathering place of the public figures of the day.

844. Gabler, 162.

845. TJ to James Madison, 18 June 1789.

846. TJ to John Jay, 24 June 1789.

847. Lafayette to TJ, 25 August 1789, PTJ, XV: 240–41, 354–55.

848. TJ to Montmorin, 8 July 1789; TJ to John Trumbull, 5 August 1789, PTJ, XV: 260–61.

849. TJ to Thomas Paine, 13 July 1789.

850. TJ to John Bondfield, 16 July 1789; TJ to John Mason, 16 July 1789; TJ to Thomas Paine, 17 July 1789; TJ to Richard Price, 17 July 1789.

851. TJ to C.W.F. Dumas, 27 July 1789; TJ to Maria Cosway, 25 July 1789.

852. Lafayette to TJ, 25 August 1789, PTJ, XV: 354–55 and note.

853. Van Doren, 760.

854. TJ to Condorcet, 30 August 1791.

855. Angelica Church to TJ, 19 August 1793, PTJ, XXVI: 722–23.

856. Marie-Jean-Antoine-Nicolas de Condorcet (1743–1794) was a brilliant mathematician, philosopher, historian, politician, reformer, economist, and educator. For an informative essay on Condorcet's life by David Williams visit the Web site www.LitEncyc.com.

857. TJ to Lafayette, 16 June 1792.

858. BF to Thomas Bond, 6 March 1780.

859. Van Doren, 632–34.

860. The Fourth of July.

861. TJ to Roger Weightman, 24 June 1826.

862. Brands, 716.

Appendix A

Thomas Jefferson's Wines—Available Today

Thomas Jefferson was the most knowledgeable wine connoisseur of his age, and his favorite wines continue to be favorites of wine enthusiasts today.

FRANCE

Red Burgundies

Chambertin – Jefferson rated Chambertin the best of Burgundy's red wines. He imported 100 bottles of Chambertin during the third year of his presidency.

Clos de Vougeot – When Jefferson visited Clos de Vougeot in 1787 it was still owned by the monks of Citeaux. Its annual production was 50,000 bottles and the wines had a reputation for excellence. Jefferson rated it second in quality behind Chambertin. During the French Revolution the monks were evicted and the vineyards and chateau were sold at public auction. A loss of quality was soon reported following the divestiture. The reason for the loss of quality is clear. The monks knew that the quality of Clos de Vougeot's wines varied depending on the part of the vineyard from which the grapes came, and they priced their wines accordingly. "The wines made from those in the middle selling for one-third more than that made in the upper part, and three time as much as that made from those at the lower end." The new owner of Cos de Vougeot did not follow the monks' practice but blended the wines together.

Vosne-Romanée – Jefferson did not designate the order of rank but one did exist. Alexander Henderson writing during Jefferson's time singled out Romanée-Conti, La Tache, Richebourg, and Romanée St. Vivant for "their beautiful color and exquisite flavor and aroma, combining . . . qualities of lightness and delicacy with richness and fullness of body," a remarkably accurate description of these wines today.

Volnay – Jefferson considered Volnay the equal in flavor to Chambertin but relegated it to fourth place because it was lighter in body, lacked longevity, and did not bear transportation as well. However, it had two advantages over the wines of Chambertin and Clos de Vougeot; it cost only one-quarter as much and was ready to drink after one year. Jefferson never identified a particular vineyard from which he purchased his Volnay wines but vineyards of special recognition then were Cailleret and Champans.

Pommard – Clos de la Commaraine. This wine was sent to Jefferson in fulfillment of an order for Volnay. He was not told that it was from neighboring Pommard, and not a Volnay, just that it was of the "best element."

White Burgundies

Montrachet – Jefferson was first introduced to Montrachet when he traveled to Burgundy in March 1787. He called it the best white wine of Burgundy, a distinction it still retains. It sold then at a price that was equal to the best Bordeaux, i.e., Lafite, Haut-Brion, Latour and Margaux.

Meursault – Jefferson thought the best wine of Meursault came from the vineyard of Goutte d'Or (Drop of Gold). Other Meursaults of equal reputation at the time were Les Perrières, Les Combettes, Les Charmes, and Les Genevrières. These five vineyards continue to make outstanding dry white Burgundies and along with ten other Meursault vineyards enjoy Premiers Crus classification. The main exporters of Goutte d'Or today are Arnaud Ente, Bouchard, Buisson-Charles, Comtes Lafon, Francoise Gaunoux, Louis Jadot, Louis Latour, René Emanuel, Vincent Bouzereau.

Rhone Valley

Côte Rôtie – Although the red wines of Côte Rôtie were recognized for their color, strength, bouquet, taste and ability to age, Jefferson made the comment that they were not yet of such high "estimation to be produced commonly at the good tables of Paris." Eighteenth century winemakers recognized their merit, however, often blending them with Bordeaux and Burgundy wines to add strength and character.

Chateau Grillet – Jefferson called Grillet the best white wine of the northern Rhone, a distinction that is in dispute today.

Red Hermitage – Although Jefferson did not single out the red wines of Hermitage for special praise, he did acknowledge their high quality. He listed the owners of the best vineyards, and the great red Hermitages of today come from those same vineyards.

White Hermitage – Jefferson so esteemed white Hermitage "marked with a touch of sweetness" that he called it the "first wine in the world without exception." During his presidency he purchased 550 bottles of white Hermitage from the House of Jourdan. The Jourdan vineyards were eventually inherited by the Monier family who, because of their ancestry, revived the name Chastaing de le Sizeranne. The Jourdan vineyards presently belong to M. Chapoutier who calls his red Hermitage La Sizeranne. Chapoutier produces two white Hermitage wines, Chante-Alouette (Lark's Song) and the more expensive Ermitage de l'Orée. A sweet white Hermitage was also made during Jefferson's time.

Provence and Languedoc

Bellet (near Nice) – Jefferson was first introduced to these wines before starting over the Alps on the back of a mule on his 44th birthday. He found Bellet wines good "though not of the first quality." He later called them "remarkably good." Robert M. Parker, Jr. describes the wines of Bellet as "Nice's best-kept secret." Red, rosé and white wines are made in this small appellation, but the whites are the wines that excel today. The best white wines are made from a grape called the Rolle. Most of the wines of Bellet are consumed at restaurants along the French Riviera but some are exported and can be found in major wine markets.

Frontignan – a fortified sweet white dessert wine made from the white Muscat grape. Jefferson first tasted this wine on the spot over dinner at the home of Monsieur Lambert, a physician and vintner. Jefferson remarked, "It is potable the April after it is made, is best that year . . . It is not permitted to ferment more than half a day, because it would not be so liquorish [sweet]. The best color, and its natural one, is amber." The sweet Muscat wines of Frontignan were enjoying their greatest popularity at the time of Jefferson's visit to this small Mediterranean town. Although still available, there aren't many Monsieur Lamberts making Muscat de Frontignan today. Its production is now dominated by cooperatives.

Nimes – In Nimes Jefferson drank an "excellent" red vin ordinaire from nearby vineyards called Ledenon, and according to Jefferson "served pure at tables of the finest rank in France." Known for its agreeable bouquet, it was considered the equal in quality and taste to the wines of Chateauneuf-du-Pape. It was one of his favorite wines in retirement. The wines from this region are known today as Costieres de Nimes and are reasonably priced and readily available.

Vin Blanc de Rochegude – A sweet fortified white wine, probably the ancestor of today's Beaumes-de-Venise. Jefferson thought highly of this wine and sent it as a gift to President George Washington.

Muscat de Rivesaltes – A variety of wines were produced (and still are) in Roussillon, but those Jefferson liked best were the sweet wines of Muscat de Rivesaltes. They were considered "lighter on the stomach than Frontignan." In his seminal wine treatise (1816), André Jullien ranked Muscat de Rivesaltes "first" of all Vins de Liqueur. Jefferson first drank this wine when he traveled on the Canal du Midi in May 1787. Its taste lingered on his palate because he continued to import it until the last year of his life.

Blanquette de Limoux – from vineyards around the town of Limoux near the medieval city of Carcassonne. Jefferson spent a night in Carcassonne and it was probably here that he became acquainted with the wines of Limoux that he imported in retirement. Blanquette de Limoux, made from the mauzac grape, was sweet and sparkling, the same as it is today.

Red Bordeaux

Chateaux Haut-Brion, Lafite, Latour, Margaux – Jefferson drank all four of these wines and referred to them as "first growths." He also mentioned for special recognition Rozan (Rauzan-Segla), Larose (Gruard-Larose), Dabbadie, ou Lionville (now three chateaux: Leoville-Las-Cases, Leoville-Poyferre, Leoville-Barton and then owned by Monsieur d'Abadie), Quirouen (Kirwan), Durfort (Durfort-Vivens), followed by a "third class" of wines consisting of Calons (Calon-Segur), Mouton (Mouton-Rothschild), Gassie (Rauzan-Gassies), Arboete (LaGrange), Pontette (Pontet-Canet) de Terme (Marquis-de-Terme) and Candale (d'Issan). From this group Madame Rauzan's was his favorite. He wrote Madame Rauzan, "I had the opportunity on a tour I made during my stay in Paris of visiting the canton of the best Bordeaux wines, among which was de Rozan, your cru, of excellent quality." In a letter of wine advice to a friend he said, "Rozan-Margaux which is made by Madame de Rozan. This is what I import for myself, and consider it equal to any of the four crops [growths]."

White Bordeaux

Carbonnieux – Several other white wines that Jefferson mentioned no longer exist having been lost to urban development.

Sauternes

Chateau d'Yquem – Jefferson praised Yquem as the best. On his return to Paris he ordered 250 bottles of Yquem. While secretary of state he ordered it for himself and 360 bottles for President Washington. When he became president he served Yquem at White House dinners. Two other Sauternes he mentioned were President du Roy's vineyards, now known as Chateau Suduiraut, and President Pichard's, now Lafaurie Peyraguey and Haut-Peyraguey. While president he shared 150 bottles of Filhot with dinner guests.

Champagne

Monsieur Dorsay's in Ay – Jefferson preferred non-sparkling Champagne. There is evidence that Monsieur Dorsay's vineyard in Ay is now owned by Champagne Bollinger.

GERMANY

Mosel

Brauneberg – followed in order by Wehlen, Grach, Piesport, Zelting, Bernkastel.

Rheingau

Schloss Johannisberg – He also singled out for praise the wines of Rudesheim and Hochheim. To a German friend who accompanied him on this part of his German vineyard trip he wrote, "I take the first moment to inform you that my journey was prosperous: that the vines which I took from Hochheim and Rudesheim are now growing luxuriously in my garden here, and will cross the Atlantic next winter, and that probably, if you ever revisit Monticello, I shall be able to give you a glass of Hock or Rudesheim of my own making." There is no evidence that Jefferson took these vines with him when he left France in September 1789 to return to America.

ITALY

Piedmont

"Nebiule" – Jefferson's phonetic spelling of the Nebbiolo grape which makes many of Italy's best wines, Barolo, Barbaresco, Gattinara and Ghemme. He found the "Nebiule" wine singular, melding three contradictory characteristics. "It is about as sweet as the silky Madeira, as astringent on the palate as Bordeaux, and as brisk as Champagne. It is a pleasing wine." The full-bodied, dry, tannic Barolos and Barbarescos of today are not sweet and do not effervesce because the style the wines has changed. Throughout the 18th century, and well into the 19th century, in the Piedmont region of Italy, the fermentation was not allowed to finish, leaving the wines sweet. The incomplete fermentation also left them frizzanti, which probably explains Jefferson's "brisk as Champagne" comment.

Tuscany

Montepulciano – also Chianti, Carmignano, Artimino and Pomino. Jefferson's "very favorite" Tuscan wine, which he sometimes referred to as a Florence wine, was Montepulciano. He described Montepulciano as a high-flavored, light bodied wine "equal to the best Burgundy."

SPAIN

Dry Sherry – Saying "that if I should fail in the means of getting it, it will be a privation which I shall feel sensibly once a day." Jefferson's taste in Spanish wines ran from Malaga and Pedro Ximenes, both sweet, to pale and dry sherry and dry and sweet Paxarete. Paxarete (also spelled Pacharetti) was made from the Pedro Ximenes grape at an ancient monastery about fifteen miles from Jerez. Pedro Ximenes made sweet and dry wines that resembled sherry in taste. Its name comes from a grape said to have been imported from the Rhine by a man named Pedro Simon (corrupted to Ximenes). Jefferson also drank a red, sweet wine made from the muscadine grape called Tinto di Rota, which was known in England as Tent, and was made near the village of Rota north of

Cadiz. Jefferson imported substantial amounts of these Spanish wines during his eight years as president.

PORTUGAL

Madeira – Like most of the Founding Fathers, Jefferson was a Madeira enthusiast. While in Paris Jefferson and Marquis de Lafayette agreed to share a pipe (110 gallons) of Madeira "of the nut quality and of the very best."

Appendix B

Thomas Jefferson's Favorite Foods

Jefferson's tastes in food were eclectic. In his garden at Monticello he grew a wide variety of vegetables and a variety of the same vegetable. For example, he grew over 30 kinds of peas, and at least 25 kinds of beans.

VEGETABLES: artichokes, asparagus, green beans, lima beans, snap sugar beans, red and white beets, broccoli, Brussels sprouts, cabbage, capers, carrots, cauliflower, celery, collards, corn, cress, cucumbers, endives, fennel, kale, leeks, lentils, lettuce, mushrooms, okra, olives, onions, parsley, parsnips, peas, peppers, potatoes, sweet potatoes, radishes, salsifis, savory, shallots, sorrel, spinach, sprouts, squashes, tomatoes, turnips.

MEATS: bacon, beef, chicken, duck, game, geese, guinea fowl, ham (fresh and smoked), lamb, mutton, pork, turkey, veal.

SEAFOOD: anchovies, clams, crabs, fish (fresh and salted): bass, carp, chub, eels, herring, shad, speckled trout, salmon trout, lobsters, mussels, oysters, shrimp. He loved oysters. One evening in Amsterdam he dined alone and ate 50 oysters before dinner.

DAIRY: butter, cheeses, eggs, ice cream.

FRUITS: apples, apricots, blackberries, blueberries, cantaloupes, cherries, cranberries, currants, figs, gooseberries, grapes, lemons, melons, mulberries, nectarines, peaches, pears, pineapples, plumbs, pomegranates, prunes, pumpkins, quinces, raisins, raspberries, strawberries, watermelons.

NUTS: almonds, chestnuts, chinquapins, hazelnuts, pecans, peanuts, pistachios, walnuts.

HERBS: balm, chicory, marjoram, mint, lavender, rosemary, sage, tarragon, thyme.

SPICES: cayenne, horseradish, mustard, garlic, pepper, salt, sugar, vinegar.

GRAINS: barley, bread, buckwheat, cornmeal, flour, pasta, rice, oats, rye, wheat.

BEVERAGES: beer, brandy, cider, coffee, milk, porter, tea, water, wine.

Index

Bacon, Francis 48, 53

Bainbridge, William 12

Balloon(s) 13, 14

Bancroft, Edward 164–75

Bank, Sir Joseph 156

Barbaresco wine 64–5, 203

Barbary Pirates & States 9, 11, 13, 101, 164

Barclay, Thomas 152–53

Barolo 64–5, 203

Bastille 241, 257–59, 262

Baum, Colonel 234–35

Beaujolais 190–91

Beaumes-de-Venise 208

Beaune 187, 189–90

Beef à la mode 6, 124

Beerenausleses wine 225

Bellet, wines of 64, 88, 104–05, 201

Bellini, Charles 242

Bemis Heights 233

Benedictine monks 6, 229

Bennington, Vermont 234–36

Bergasse, Henry 142, 199

Bernkastel wine 64, 225

Berri, rue de 2

Blaye 86, 216

Blenheim Palace 183

Blount, Dorothea 115–16

Bois de Boulogne 4, 91,152, 239–41, 251, 253

Bondfield, John 80–1, 127–28, 150, 152

Bonhomme Richard 160–62

Bordeaux 2, 64, 81, 85–6, 127, 151, 186, 210, 212, 216

Bordeaux wines 62–6, 80–1, 85–7, 125–28, 141, 150–51, 185, 189, 203,

209–16

Boston Packet 175

Boston Tea Party 37–8

Boswell, James 220, 237

Brandy 153, 207, 209

Branne Mouton 125

Brauneberg wine 225

Brillon de Jouy, Madame 91, 246–48, 250, 254

British army 13, 38

British Ministry 17, 19, 35–8, 40, 43, 46, 58, 98, 116, 168, 237, 259

Broadbent, Michael 125, 128, 130

Brodie, Fawn 112

Brown, Lancelot "Capability" 180, 183

Burgoyne, General John 16–7, 19, 221, 233–35

Burgundy 61–2, 186–88

Burgundy wines 8, 59–62, 68–9, 72, 81, 85, 141, 150, 165, 188–91

Burke, Edmund 19

Burr, Aaron 57–9

Burwell, Rebecca 243–44

Bush, George W. 10, 13, 105

Caesar, Julius 53, 177, 196, 223

Cahusac wine 87

Calcavallo 104

California 66–7

Callender, James 106–08, 110–13

Calon-Ségur 213

Canada 8, 17, 73, 257

Canal-du-Midi 63, 209–10

Capitaineries 192

Capitol building, Washington, D.C. 10, 137

Capitol, Richmond 193